D1070950

Great
Dynasties

Great Dynasties

Capets• Hohenstaufens• Plantagenets
Hapsburgs• Valois• Stuarts• Tudor
Bourbons of France• Romanovs
Braganzas• Bourbons of Spain
Hohenzollerns• House of Savoy
House of Hanover-Windsor
Bourbons of Naples• Bonapartes

MAYFLOWER BOOKS
NEW YORK

GREAT DYNASTIES

Translations of French, German, Italian, Portuguese and
Spanish texts by Carol Appleyard, Caroline Bidwell,
Antonio Carvalho, Judith Elphick, Nicholas Fry,
Paul Knopinski, Susanna McMahon, Olive Ordish,
Hugh Young.

Translation copyright © 1979 by Arnoldo Mondadori
Editore, S.p.A., Milano

Originally published in Italian in 1976 by Arnoldo
Mondadori Editore, S.p.A., Milano under the title *Grandi
Dinastie*
Copyright © 1976 by Arnoldo Mondadori Editore, S.p.A.,
Milano

Library of Congress Catalog Card Number 79–5333

ISBN: 0 8317 3966 5

Printed and bound in Italy by Officine Grafiche di Arnoldo
Mondadori Editore, S.p.A., Verona

First American Edition

Contents

The authors

Régine Pernoud
French, archivist, docteur-ès-lettres; curator of Rheims Museum and the Museum of French History in the National Archives in Paris. Winner of prizes for history: Femina, Ville de Paris, Ville de Bordeaux. Author of various historical works, dealing with the Middle Ages, among which are *Vie et Mort de Jeanne d'Arc*; *Histoire de la Bourgeoisie en France, des Origines aux Temps Modernes*; *Alienor d'Aquitaine*; *Héloïse et Abélard*; *La Reine Blanche*; *Les Templiers*; *Pour en Finir avec le Moyen Age*.

Carl Ernst Köhne
German, Doctor of Philosophy, former university lecturer in the history of civilization. Political and scientific writer. Author of: *5000 Jahre Europa*; *Glanz des Abendlandes*; *Michel und Marianne*; *Testament des Augustus*; *Sie trugen die Krone*.

Timothy Baker
English, editor of the Victoria County History of Middlesex, member of the Royal Historical Society. Author of works on English history, among which *The Island Race*; *The Normans*; *Medieval London*.

Janko von Musulin
Austrian, former director of Fischer Verlag, vice-president of Sigmund Freud Gesellschaft. Historical and political essayist: *Degen und Waage*; *Prinz Eugen von Savoyen*; *Proklamationen der Freiheit*; *Der Frende Bruder*; *Die Kranke Welmacht*; *Niedergang und Wiederaufstieg der Amerikanischen Gesellschaft*.

René de La Croix Duc de Castries
French, man of letters, president of the Société d'Histoire Diplomatique, member of the Académie Française. Author of numerous historical works, among which *Mirabeau*; *Maurice de Saxe*; *De Louis XVIII à Louis Philippe*; *La Vie Quotidienne des Emigrés, Madame Récamier*; *Figaro ou la vie de Beaumarchais*; *La France et l'Indépendance Américaine*; *Chateaubriand ou la Puissance du Songe*; *Histoire de France des Origines à 1976*; *La Vieille Dame du Quai Conti*.

John Philipps Kenyon
English, former Fellow of Christ's College, Cambridge, professor of modern history at the University of Hull. Author of various works on English history, among which: *Robert Spencer, Earl of Sunderland*; *The Stuarts*; *The Stuart Constitution*; *The Popish Plot*; *Stuart England*. Now working on a life of Charles I.

Alasdair Hawkyard
English, research assistant with the History of Parliament Trust. Specialist in English late-medieval architecture, he has published several articles on houses and castles in learned journals.

Daria Olivier
Born in Russia, French by naturalization. Prolific translator of Russian classic and modern literature and of English-speaking authors. Her historical works include: *Elizabeth de Russie*; *L'Incendie de Moscou*; *Les Grandes Heures des Villes Russes*; *Catherine la Grande*; *Les Romanov*; *Alexandre Ier, Prince des Illusions*. She has also written historical fiction: *Les Neiges de Décembre*; *L'Anneau de Fer*.

Luíz de Bivar Guerra
Portuguese, general Secretary of the Academia Portuguesa da História and Chancellor of the Instituto Português de Heráldica. Former librarian of the Arquivo Geral do Tribunal de Contas, now engaged as researcher into the history of Portuguese art at the Fundação Calouste Gulbenkian.

Manuel Espadas Burgos
Spanish, professor of contemporary history, researcher and member of the Executive Council at the Consejo Superior de Investigaciones Científicas. His works include: *Alfonso XII y los Orígenes de la Restauración*; *Historia de Madrid*; and about a hundred essays and articles on contemporary history.

Walter Görlitz
German, writer, head of the editorial department dealing with contemporary history of *Die Welt*. He has written a number of biographies as well as books on the history of the Second World War including *Der Deutsche Generalstab*. Trustee of the journals and papers of Field-Marshals Paulus, Keitel and Model and of Admiral von Müller.

Ugoberto Alfassio Grimaldi
Italian, high-school teacher of history and philosophy, journalist, editor of *Critica Sociale*. Author of a study of Umberto I of Savoy. He is both author and co-author of writings on politics and contemporary history.

Theo Aronson
English. Having worked in advertising he now writes biographies on the Royal Families of Europe, which have been translated into several languages. His books include: *Queen Victoria and the Bonapartes*; *Grandmama of Europe*; *Royal Ambassadors*; *A Family of Kings*; *Victoria and Disraeli*.

Ruggero Moscati
Italian, professor of modern history at the University of Rome and president of the Commissione per la Pubblicazione dei Documenti Diplomatici Italiani. His studies on foreign policy and the problems of the south include: *Il Mezzogiorno nel Risorgimento*; *Ferdinando II*; *I Borboni d'Italia*; *Una Famiglia Borghese*.

Jean Thiry
French, former advocate at the Court of Appeal in Paris, historian, life secretary of the Académie de Stalislas and member of several other academies. Author of numerous works, some of which have won Académie Française awards, on the Napoleonic era, including *Collection Napoléon Bonaparte* in twenty-eight volumes.

6

Preface

'Therefore choose as your leader the duke who recommends himself to you by his deeds, his noble rank and his troops; choose the duke as your leader and in him you will find a protector not only of public affairs but also of your private interests. . . .' So, according to the chronicler Richer, Adalbero, Archbishop of Rheims spoke to the assembly of magnates that elected Hugh Capet as king in 987. It is a record of kingship, of the institution of monarchy, at its moment of inception.

The political address itself is clear and direct: the restricted electorate (the great, who were possessors of land and men and therefore powerful) is reflected in the opposition of 'public affairs' and 'your private interests', the interests of the limited electoral body. The candidate's suitability for the office is presented in simple terms: an individual element, his personal capacities (his deeds); an objective element, that of force, power (his troops); and an intangible cultural element, his noble rank. This representative case of the creation of a king is characterized by the need for these three qualifications and also for a fourth, consisting in his election by a body of his peers, in a kind of contract or demonstration of consent.

It is clear that what is missing is just that element which later became characteristic and on which this book is based – heredity, dynastic continuity. We also read in Richer that one of the primary concerns of the new King, Hugh Capet, was to have his son crowned as well. Adalbero finally agreed to this, although reluctantly, objecting at first that two kings could not be crowned in one year.

For it to be generally accepted that the Crown could be handed down by inheritance, just as the magnates – who created the kings – handed down lands, castles, stables, jewels and servants, another element was needed: the belief in a privileged relationship between the king (and his descendants) and God, in short, divine right. The sovereign 'by the grace of God' would no longer need Adalbero's election addresses.

Another significant text is the phrase found in Otto of Freising, from a letter written by Frederick Barbarossa, King and Emperor (this is therefore a special case, but significant in the context of medieval ideas about the 'two swords', the Papacy and the Empire): 'Thanks to the choice of the princes we rule the kingdom and the empire only through God. . . .'

Nevertheless, as we know, it was a long process. Of the three political elements in Adalbero's address for Hugh Capet, personal qualities, effective power and noble rank, the first is wholly and the second at least partly rendered superfluous by 'the grace of God'. There were unsuitable kings and also kings who were devoid of ability, who serenely held the Crown until their deaths.

We now come to the 'deeds' that Adalbero spoke of. Not many decades later, William of Poitiers, praising a king, William the Conqueror, who had won his Crown with the sword even though he had some right to the Crown, or rather pretended to have, wrote: 'In their iniquity, kings hide their greed under the pretence of punishing crimes and condemn the innocent to suffer so as to take possession of the property of the condemned. But he [William] never condemned anyone whom he could with justice have let go free, since he kept himself above greed, as above the other passions. He had understood that regal majesty should show itself in ostentatious generosity and not gain anything at the expense of justice.' About eight hundred years later, the last great Hapsburg, Francis Joseph, considered himself and acted as the servant of the State ('independent official', as he once described himself on a form, perhaps with some irony but with conviction).

There is a link between these two chronological extremes: the persistence of a conception of power rendered acceptable by its spirit of service. Whether this has contributed more or less than, or as much as, the concept of 'the grace of God' to the duration of the institution and of the dynasties which embodied it in Europe, is a question that cannot be answered, but that arouses our interest as we read through the internal history of the dynasties brought together in this book.

Although limited in number, these dynasties – presented here in the chronological order in which they came to their thrones – cover almost all of Europe, from Britain to Italy and from Portugal to Russia, and they span about a thousand years of European history. The history of Europe is made up, in part, of their fortunes.

Opposite: *The Crown of the Holy Roman Empire. The goldsmith's work shows strong Sicilian-Byzantine influence and was produced at the abbey workshop of Reichenau, probably in the tenth century. (Vienna, Schatzkammer, Kunsthistorischesmuseum).*

Great Dynasties

When this miniature was painted, the rule of the Capetians had been over for more than a century and they had been replaced by their younger Valois branch. However, in representing the fervour of Gothic church-building in the 'sweet land of France', the miniature illustration suggests the atmosphere of the time of St Louis, and the construction of the cathedrals.

The Capets

For over three hundred years a wise dynasty
cultivates that 'square field of land' where
'bread, wine and merriment' are to be found

One of the most striking features of the Capetian dynasty is that it reigned, uninterrupted, for more than three hundred years.

Hugh Capet came to power in 987, and his last direct descendant died in 1328. Between these two dates a period of three hundred and forty-one years elapsed.

For contemporaries, however, the election at Senlis was the fourth of its kind and Hugh Capet was the fourth of his line to wear the Crown. A further hundred years, then, should be added to the previous total in order to take account of the full duration of the Capetian dynasty. The Capets also have a prehistory.

The name of the defender of Paris against the Normans was not quickly to be forgotten. He was of illustrious ancestry, son of Robert the Strong who, some twenty years previously, had faced the Northmen at the Battle of Brissarthe. For, at that time, the realm of France was caught between two invaders. In the south were the Arabs, the famous 'Saracens', who imposed a reign of terror until their last stronghold in Provence was destroyed at La Garde-Freinet in 972; in the north were the Normans.

Eudes was Count of Paris, just as Robert had been Count of Anjou. Eudes was elected on 13 January 888, and by June of the same year he was renewing the exploits that had made his father famous in Anjou, against the Normans at Montfaucon-en-Argonne.

But the shadow of Charlemagne was not so quickly to be eclipsed; the Emperor, who had held all of Europe in his powerful hands, had a great-grandson, Charles, known as the Simple, and his presence was enough to rally a legitimist party. When he came of age, he was crowned at St-Rémi by Fulk, Archbishop of Rheims, on 28 January 893. There was some contention, but when Eudes died on 1 January 898,

Charles the Simple came to power. The interregnum had lasted ten years.

The descendants of Robert the Strong, however, were not to release their grip on the throne. While the Carolingian had more or less established his capital at Laon and was pursuing a far-sighted policy (it was he who settled the Normans in Normandy, which was certainly an intelligent way of tackling the problem), the nobles of the Ile de France were watching for the slightest sign of weakness. Eudes had a brother, Robert, who was only waiting for the right moment to rally support for a succession to the throne which had been denied him by the coronation of the Carolingian. Robert himself had a son-in-law, Raoul, Duke of Burgundy, husband of his daughter Emma, who was no less ambitious. A pretext was eventually provided by intrigues at the Court. Charles the Simple took refuge at his capital in Laon, where he was defeated and forced to take flight. Then followed an obscure period during which, in the interval between two battles, first Robert, then Raoul, had themselves 'elected' king. For Robert, royalty was short-lived (22 June 922 – 15 June 923); for Raoul, who was crowned at St-Médard de Soissons on 13 July 923, it was more stable and he held power right up until his death in January 936. Meanwhile, Charles the Simple remained a prisoner in the tower of Péronne, where he died on 7 October 929.

The year 936, then, marked a break in the pattern which had seen royal power alternate between the descendants of Charlemagne and those of Robert the Strong. The new king could well have been the son of the previous Robert, known to history as Hugh the Great. Hugh, however, took the unexpected step of recalling Louis IV, son of Charles the Simple, to

11

France. Louis had previously taken refuge in England and for this reason was known as the Exile. He was crowned at Rheims on 19 June 936 under the aegis of his powerful vassal, the 'Duke of Francia'. On his death, in 954, Louis was succeeded by his son, Lothaire; but two years later, in the duchy of Francia, Hugh the Great was succeeded by a new Hugh, who was to be known to history as Hugh Capet.

It was at Senlis where kings used to stop on their way back from their coronation at Rheims that the dramatic events which led up to the birth of the Capetian dynasty took place.

The principal feudatories of the realm had assembled here in 977, but if they had responded to the appeal made to them several weeks earlier, it was in order to form a Court rather than an electoral assembly. King Lothaire, who died at an early age, was succeeded, on 2 March 986, by his son Louis v. The latter, like his father before him, had a grievance against the Archbishop of Rheims, Adalbero. He suspected him and his secretary, Gerbert of Aurillac,

of plotting against him together with the Emperor, or rather the Empress his mother, Theophano, a Greek, who was related to the Court of Byzantium. Louis saw fit to convoke an assembly intended to pass judgement on the offenders, Adalbero and Gerbert, once he had exposed their schemes. The prelate and his accomplice, as they probably realized, were in an awkward situation, for they had had the castles belonging to the king in their diocese burned to the ground. They had been brought to Compiègne and their trial was about to begin when an unexpected accident occurred. The young Louis (he was twenty at the time) suffered a fall while hunting in the forest between Compiègne and Senlis, and a few days later, on 22 May 987, he died. The assembled barons seemed to have gathered only to attend the funeral of the last of the Carolingians.

The Archbishop managed to get himself acquitted and hence it was an electoral assembly, then, which transferred to Senlis a few days later. By this time, however, Adalbero, the accused of a short time ago, had assumed control of the proceedings. The realm

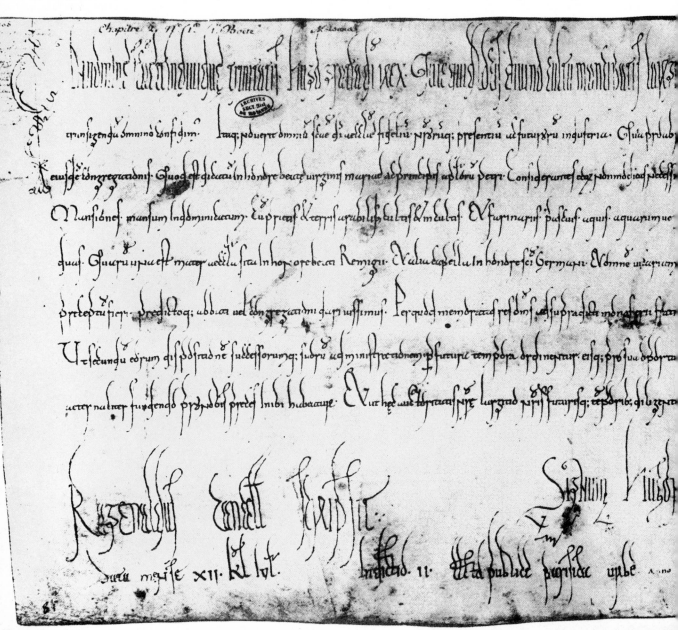

needed a king, but who was it to be? Louis v had neither brothers and sisters nor children. His only relative was an uncle, Charles, who was Duke of Lower Lorraine and thus a vassal of the German Emperor. The Archbishop of Rheims had made up his mind: 'Take Hugh, the Duke of Francia, for your leader.'

Hugh was crowned at Noyon on 3 July of the same year. Born in 941, Hugh was now forty-six and a man in the prime of life. Why was the great-grandson of Robert the Strong called Capet? There is no written indication of this, but it is thought to derive from a detail of clothing, the chaperon, which was an old form of Celtic head-gear, or the cope, an ecclesiastical garment of similar design, which Hugh might well have worn as a result of his connections with various abbeys. At the time, it was current practice to give nicknames; apart from Capet there was a Duke known as *Courtmantel* (the short mantle), or again, another known as *Grisegonnelle* (the grey-robed).

Many historians have treated the Capets as 'parvenus' and, indeed, this is how they might seem by comparison with the Carolingians, whose ranks included that most famous name of all, Charlemagne. Yet for all that, Charlemagne, or rather his immediate ancestors, had also seemed parvenus two centuries earlier, when the Merovingian dynasty came to a close. The speech made by Adalbero of Rheims contained propositions that our own age would not disown. 'The throne,' he said at Senlis, 'should not be acquired by hereditary right; at the head of the realm, we should only place a man who stands out not only for the nobility of his bearing, but also for the qualities of his mind; a man who is recommended both by his honour and his magnanimity.' Adalbero and Gerbert, and Hugh Capet, were representatives of a new and rising order.

The Capetian dynasty corresponded exactly with the progression of the feudal order which, with the accession of the Capets, became a reality. From a political point of view, Europe took on a new outline. While the Byzantine Empire, in the Near East, was conserving the features it had inherited from the

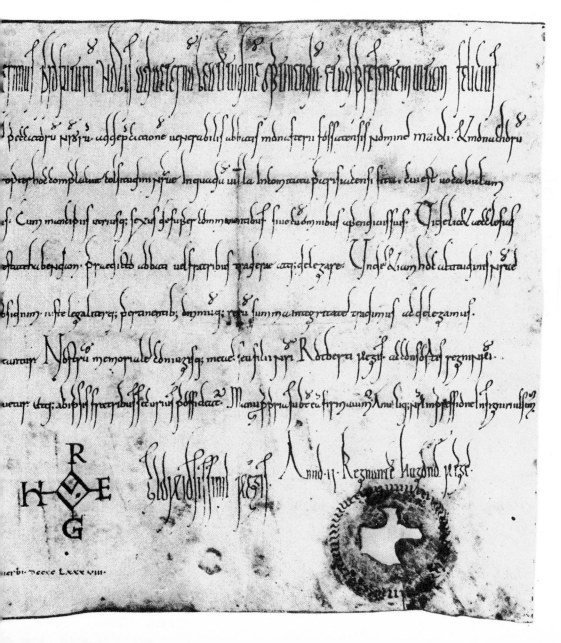

Ancient World, the Western Empire was reviving in the Germanic regions, where it was attempting to restore Carolingian traditions. It eventually succeeded in this when Otto I, the Great, in a position of strength after his victory over the invading Hungarians at Lechfeld in 955, received the Imperial Crown from the hands of Pope John XII, in Rome on 2 February 962.

Western Europe, however, remained beyond his reach, particularly the realm in which the man who called himself the 'Duke of the Franks' had become King 'by the grace of God'.

The kingdom of the Duke of the Franks, where, as a lord amongst other lords, he was owed homage, and where he attempted to gain respect for his power as arbiter and provider of justice, was, in the main, the same kingdom that Charlemagne had entrusted to his youngest son, Charles the Bald, stretching from Flanders to Gascony. His actual domain, however, was very restricted. It included two rather spread-out groups of land – on the one hand, the counties of Orléans and Etampes, on the other, the county of Senlis, enlarged by three 'castellanies', Béthisy, Verberie and Compiègne; three other seigniories, Montreuil-sur-Mer, Attigny and Poissy, formed, as it were, small detached islands. To this could be added rights, by no means negligible, over certain dioceses.

Hugh Capet married Adelaide, daughter of the Duke of Aquitaine, and it was certainly not without significance for Hugh's career that of his two sisters, one, Beatrice, had married Frederick, Duke of Upper Lorraine, and the other, Emma, had married the Duke of Normandy, Richard I, a man from a powerful family background. Hugh's only brother, Eudes-Henry, had inherited Burgundy, and had it not been for these various alliances, the outcome of the assembly at Senlis could well have been quite different.

Hugh Capet died in 996, at the age of about fifty-five, probably from an eruptive disease such as smallpox, and was buried at St-Denis.

His son Robert, who was to be known as 'the Pious', succeeded him – a succession made all the easier by the fact that Robert had already been crowned by his father's own hand as long ago as 987. Modern historians have seen this action, associating the son with the father on the throne, as a wise precaution taken by a dynasty well aware of the fragile nature of its position in those, its early days. This sentiment may not have been far from their minds, but it must be pointed out that in 978, Lothaire, the Carolingian, had associated his son Louis (the future Louis V, who was thirteen at the time) with the throne in the same way. In fact, this action should be seen as much more than a mere insurance of the future, it was a custom of the day.

Robert, then, became King in 996; at the time he was aged about twenty-four and there was ample oppor-

tunity for him to prove himself in action – not least because of the prevailing situation between the Capets and the Carolingians. Indeed, the anxieties caused by the last descendants of the Carolingian dynasty had cast a shadow over the later years of Hugh Capet's reign. In 988, Charles, Duke of Lower Lorraine, had seized Laon with the aid of a bastard son of King Lothaire. The siege had dragged on for a long time, punctuated by various warlike incidents and a number of cases of treachery amongst King Hugh's vassals, notably that of Charles the Pretender, who was eventually captured in 991 and who died two or three years later in prison at Orléans where his rival had had him confined.

The struggle with the Carolingians was over, but Robert still had to reckon with the German Empire, which, implicitly at least, claimed superior authority over the whole of Western Christendom.

One potential source of strife between France and the Empire existed, and that was Lorraine, the strip of territory separating Germany from France, which had been called Lotharingia after its first possessor, King Lothaire. The Treaty of Verdun, signed a century earlier in 843, had given Lorraine to the Emperor. Much later, the disputes as to which of the two countries was to control Lorraine resulted in wars, but the wars which eventually took place in the seventeenth century could as well have broken out at the beginning of the Capetian dynasty. This is illustrated by the events which took place on the banks of the Meuse in 1023.

Two armies faced each other across the river. On the right bank, at Ivoy, was the Imperial army, led by Emperor Henry II, who had hopes of occupying a position in secular Europe similar to that held by the Pope in Christendom; on the left bank, at Mouzon, was King Robert, with all the vassals he had been able to muster. On 6 August, a confrontation began which was to be one of the great dramas of our history. The suspense lasted for four days until, on 10 August, the Emperor decided to cross the river with a small retinue and to pay a peaceful visit to the French King. The latter returned the visit on the following day.

On the night following the interview between the two sovereigns, Henry offered the realm of Italy to King Robert the Pious, either for himself, or for his eldest son, who had been associated with him on the throne since 1017. Robert refused, and in doing so showed a sound common sense which his indirect successors in the sixteenth century would have done well to imitate.

Almost exactly one hundred years later another dangerous situation developed, but again, as before, nothing was to come of it. In 1124, Emperor Henry V was threatening to invade Champagne. The King of France, Louis VI, went to St-Denis and brought forth the royal oriflamme (*auri-flamma*, the red, gold-fringed standard), an action which rallied his vassals to his side to such good effect that the Emperor, in the face of the solidarity shown by this young kingdom, was obliged to retreat. The wars against the German Empire were thus reserved for a later date.

Robert the Pious was something of a scholar and is known to have written liturgical hymns. He was thus well-suited to an era which saw vigorous reforms within the Church, prompted, in particular, by the monks of Cluny. Nevertheless, he remained excommunicated for a considerable part of his life – a consequence of his involvement with women. Robert had first of all married Rozalle-Suzanne, widow of the Count of Flanders; she was a good deal older than the King and was unable to provide him with any offspring. Robert repudiated her, and did so all the more readily because he had by now fallen madly in love with Bertha, wife of Count Eudes of Chartres, who very conveniently died. Robert married Bertha, but they were related as cousins within a degree forbidden by canon law. Robert was excommunicated, but held out against the wrath of the Church for five years before eventually submitting. He then married Constance, daughter of William, Count of Arles. Constance, however, according to contemporary reports, proved to be such an ill-tempered wife that Robert made a journey to Rome in order to ask the Pope to annul his marriage to her and, at the same time, to validate his marriage to Bertha. Neither request was granted. He may well have acquired his reputation for saintliness as a result of his unhappy married life, which he eventually came to accept. Yet the fact remains that, even after the death of her husband in 1031, Queen Constance justified her reputation by setting two of her children against each other. She preferred Robert to his elder brother, Henry, and tried in vain to put him on the throne. The two brothers were eventually reconciled, Henry became King of France and Robert, by parage, received Burgundy, where his descendants were to reign for a period equal in length to the duration of the royal dynasty. In fact, Burgundy passed from one heir to the next in direct succession right up until 1361.

To return to Henry, the first of that name, little is known of his life, although one rather surprising fact does stand out. This King of a small dynasty in the most westerly realm of Europe, married a Russian Princess, Anna, daughter of the Duke of Kiev, Yaroslav I.

The son of Henry I and Anna of Russia was given an ambitious forename at his christening – that of Philip, calling to mind the Byzantine dynasty and the conquering kings of Macedonia. Philip, the first of that name, was also the first King of whose coronation we have details, notably the text of the oath he gave on the gospel, in the presence of the Archbishop of Rheims, before receiving unction. The anointing was a re-enactment of the coronation of David. Henceforth, the coronation ceremony was held at Rheims, preceded by the royal oath and the consent of the people. In other words, the idea of an election was still strong in people's minds: it was to be custom, the most powerful force of the age, which was to establish the Crown as a hereditary right, inseparable from the dynasty, to be handed down from father to son for centuries.

Philip I was also the first King of the Capetian dynasty to be portrayed surrounded by his Court. The picture is in a miniature on a manuscript kept in the British Museum. It is an accurate representation of the royal Court with the King seen in the company of his counsellors, both lay and clergy, whose presence is by no means merely symbolic. The King never made decisions without the aid of his counsellors, and when serious matters involving the peace of the realm were to be discussed, he was obliged to convoke all his barons – indeed, without their support, he was unable to act effectively. He was an elected arbiter amongst them whose task it was to see that justice and peace were maintained.

In reality, to judge from the various accounts that have preserved his memory for us, Philip I was a man ill-equipped to occupy such an exalted position. He was a glutton and a sensualist. Not only that, but his behaviour was scandalous. He repudiated his wife, Bertha of Frisia, and abducted the wife of one of his vassals, Bertrada of Montfort, with whom he had fallen passionately in love. Bertrada was the wife of the Count of Anjou, Fulk Réchin (the Quarrelsome). The King managed to find a bishop to bless their marriage, but the Pope saw the matter otherwise. Philip and Bertrada were excommunicated and their excommunication was later renewed on two occasions. In the chronicle, we see the royal couple leaving a town and hearing the bells ring in the distance after their departure: 'Hark, hear how they drive us out!' Where they lived, in fact, the bells no longer rang and masses were no longer celebrated.

Louis VI, who succeeded Philip, inherited his father's obesity (he was known as 'the Fat'), but not his other interests. He was an emotive man, fond of food and drink and yet astonishingly active. He was decisive, quick-tempered, and, despite his size, he was a tireless horseman. In his youth, he was probably affected by the disorder which had reigned in his father's Court, for Bertrada had tried all she knew to have the son she gave the King, also called Philip, accede to the throne in place of Louis. The latter's moral conduct, however, was beyond reproach. It was during his reign that Pope Pascal II called France 'the eldest daughter of the Church'. In addition, Louis had a lifelong, faithful friend in Suger, who, though of humble origin, was

Philip I founding the abbey of Saint-Martin-des-Champs. The third successor of Hugh Capet, and the son of a Russian Princess, Philip was 'weighed down by his massive bulk and more interested in food and drink than in fighting'.

brought up alongside the King's son at the Abbey of St-Denis, where he was one day to become abbot.

Yet Louis, like his father, took no part in the 'crusades' (it should not be forgotten that this is a relatively modern term, dating from the eighteenth century at earliest) taking place during his reign; he restricted his ambitions to the 'square field of land' which was his domain. Here, justice was strictly enforced and no breaches of the law were tolerated.

There was no shortage of problems with the Duke of Normandy, the King of England. At one stage, the situation bordered on the disastrous, when Louis was defeated at Brémule in 1119. The tragedy of the *white ship*, however, in the following year, crushed any hopes that Henry Beauclerc, the King of England, might have placed in his own dynasty. His only legitimate son, William, was drowned at sea off the Channel coast, along with his half-brother, one of his sisters and all the *jeunesse dorée* of England.

By the end of his life, Louis VI had much to occupy his mind. Three great feudal Houses, Normandy, Anjou and Champagne, whose wealth by far eclipsed that of his own domain, had consolidated their positions. The only remaining daughter of the King of England, Matilda, who had been married at the age of nine to Henry V, Emperor of Germany, was, now that she was a widow, about to marry the young Geoffrey the Handsome, heir to the county of Anjou, also known as Geoffrey Plantagenet. At the same time, Anjou-Normandy-England was becoming a worrying power in the West.

A counter to this danger came in quite unexpected manner. The Duke of Aquitaine fell ill during a pilgrimage to St James of Compostella and, before his death, made his companions promise to offer his fifteen-year-old daughter and heir, Eleanor, in marriage to the son and heir of the King of France, Louis the Young. Louis VI must have welcomed this promise of an unexpected increase in his domain and lost no time in replying. Yet he was not himself to see the realization of this hope. By the time Louis and his wife had returned to the Ile-de-France, accompanied by a magnificent escort which included Suger, now Abbot of St-Denis, the King had died, on 1 August 1137.

Louis VII, who succeeded him, owed his Crown to a riding accident, which had cost his elder brother, Philip, his life. Brought up, like his father, at the abbey of St-Denis, it is more than likely that he would have preferred to remain there, had he not been sent in 1131, when he was eleven, to be associated with his father on the throne, in accordance with custom. Indeed, he subsequently returned to the abbey to complete his studies, which were to help make him a monarch of great learning. He had several brothers, one of whom, Henry, later became Archbishop of Rheims, and another, Philip, who became Dean of St-Martin de

Philip II Augustus. This tenacious and war-like King, although he did not achieve all his ambitions, at his death in 1223 he left his territories greatly extended.

Tours. But feudal custom held that primogeniture should decree the rightful heir, which was Louis. His brother, Robert, Count of Dreux, probably had ambitions to the throne and at one stage hatched a plot, to which Suger skilfully put paid.

The dowry which Eleanor of Aquitaine brought to her young husband suddenly made the King of France, in material terms, the equal of the richest of his vassals. The acquisitions that Louis VI had managed to make during his lifetime only amounted to a few acres of land: the county of Corbeil and a few castles in the Gâtinais and Orléans, notably the castle of Montlhéry, which for a long time had prevented the King from travelling in safety between Etampes and Orléans. Yet to this were now added the immense domains of the county of Poitiers and the dukedom of Aquitaine, stretching from the Loire to the Pyrenees.

It was the Queen who took the lead in political affairs. This had been the case in the reigns of both Robert the Pious and Philip I, and the same could be said for most of the great feudal dynasties. But if Bertrada had, for the most part, kept her husband in a state of inertia, the same could not be said of Eleanor. She was irresponsible and her excessive enthusiasm led her husband into situations of extreme complexity. She caused him to quarrel in turn with his mother, his devoted counsellor, Suger, and even with the Pope. She forced Louis to take harsh measures against the inhabitants of Poitiers, when they were intent on becoming a commune. Finally, she induced him to undertake an unwise expedition against the county of Toulouse, which William IX had formerly surrendered, and over which she intended to re-establish direct dominion. All these were minor affairs compared with the strife she was to cause with the House of Champagne, which, until that time, had been a faithful ally to the Capetian dynasty. What were her motives? To promote the marriage of her young sister, Péronelle, who had designs on a member of the Court. The man in question was married to the sister of the Count of Champagne, but she induced him to obtain a divorce. An expedition against Champagne ensued, in the course of which, the King's troops set fire to a church at Vitry, in which the local population had taken refuge, which was henceforth known as Vitry-le-Brûlé (the Burned). This horrible incident, however, did have a salutary effect upon Louis. He pulled himself together, recalled Suger to his side and, as the news from the Holy Land was bad – a report had arrived that the county of Edessa, which had been reconquered with such a struggle fifty years previously, had again fallen into the hands of the Saracens – the royal couple decided to go on the Crusade.

It was the first time that a king and a queen had left France to go to the Holy Land. Their presence, however, did not prove beneficial to the expedition. Their lack of discipline caused a real disaster during the crossing of Asia Minor, when the advanced guard which they were forming, under the leadership of Geoffrey de Rancon from Saintonge, unwisely cut themselves off from the rest of the expedition. The main section of the army, hindered by waggons and luggage, was literally cut to pieces and was only saved by the timely arrival of the King, who was in command of the rearguard. The Crusade almost ended there, on this 'execrable mountain' which figures so prominently in the history of the Latin Kingdom of the East.

But worse was to follow. At Antioch, which the army eventually reached after ten months of travel over land and sea, Eleanor met her handsome uncle, Raymond of Poitiers, who, being considerably younger than her father, had been one of her childhood companions. Raymond had become Prince of Antioch after a series of unlikely adventures (he had reached the Holy Land disguised as a merchant, to conceal his identity both from the Turks and from the dowager Princess Alix, whose daughter, the heiress to the principality, he contrived to marry). Was there, between Raymond and his niece, an affection other than that which they were legitimately entitled to feel for each other? The fact remains that Louis took umbrage and left Antioch after ten days, compelling his Queen to leave with him.

As a husband, his behaviour was understandable, as leader of an expedition, its consequence was the lamentable failure of that expedition.

When the royal couple returned to France, despite the reconciliation effected by the Pope himself during their homeward journey, a distance had grown between them. Abbot Suger strove to keep their relationship on good terms, but after the death of this prudent and energetic little man, who, by an extraordinary quirk of fate, had risen from a background of serfdom to become administrator of the realm in the absence of the King and Queen, their reconciliation did not last. A Council assembled at Beaugency on 21 March 1152, annulled the marriage which had been contracted fifteen years before. Eleanor, who, in accordance with the custom of the day, regained her personal estates, returned to Poitiers. Less than two months later, a startling piece of news reached the Court of France – Eleanor had married Henry Plantagenet, Count of Anjou and Duke of Normandy.

Eleanor in future had only an indirect bearing on the fortunes of the Capetian dynasty – through alliances, but mostly through the influence she exerted when her

The meeting between Philip II Augustus and Richard Cœur de Lion, before their departure on crusade. The English King was the vassal of the King of France for his lands across the Channel.

husband became King of England in 1154. For a period of fifteen years their fortunes continued to rise. The joint domains of Henry and Eleanor stretched from England to the Pyrenees, including all the western part of the realm of France. Of course, Louis VII remained Henry's suzerain for Normandy, Anjou, Britanny and the adjacent regions, and Eleanor's for Aquitaine, which extended across western France from the Loire to the Pyrenees. Indeed, he lost no opportunity in proving his suzerainty, sometimes with great success, as when answering an appeal for help from his vassal, the Count of Toulouse in 1159. Eleanor had never forgotten her former claims to the county of Toulouse and she persuaded Henry, as she had persuaded Louis before him, to undertake an expedition which only came to an end when Henry realized that his suzerain was present in the city. Not daring to break his feudal oath, he reluctantly withdrew. Yet his wealth, his life style, his conquests, indeed everything in the Plantagenets' kingdom far outshone the rival dynasty, including the five sons which Eleanor gave to Henry – she had only had two daughters by Louis, who were, of course, incapable of wielding a sword.

Louis, for his part, also remarried, this time to Constance, daughter of the King of Castile; he had two daughters by her, Margaret and Adelaide. On the death of his second wife, he married Alice of Champagne, thereby strengthening his ties with the only House capable of competing, albeit on far from equal terms, with the House of Anjou. With this marriage Louis complicated the task of future genealogists, for the eldest of his daughters, Marie, married Alice's brother, Henry, and his second daughter, Alice, married her other brother, Thibaut of Blois, thus making Louis the brother-in-law of his two sons-in-law. Small matter, the main thing, as far as he was concerned, was that Alice, in August 1165, eventually provided him with his long-awaited heir, Philip, who was later to be known as Philip Augustus.

A vast chess-game then began between the King of France and the King of England, who was his vassal for more than half of the realm. It is quite certain that Henry and Eleanor hoped to see the Crown of France on the head of their eldest son, the Young Henry. Their Chancellor, Thomas à Becket, a counsellor with great influence over the King, came himself as an ambassador to fetch the little girl on whom the ambition depended, Margaret, daughter of Louis VII and Constance of Castile. She was thus betrothed to the Young Henry, despite the fact that she was only a few months old and her future husband was three. This union was the basis for a settlement and peace was restored between the King of France and his overpowerful vassal.

The arrival of a male heir to the French Crown

crushed the hopes that Eleanor and her husband had cherished for their son, and, strangely enough, from this moment onwards, their fortunes began to decline. Henry II, dazzled by his successes, began to act like a despot, deceiving his wife and causing the murder of Thomas à Becket, whom he himself had made Archbishop of Canterbury. His tyrannical behaviour turned his sons, many of his vassals and Eleanor against him. By comparison, the Capetian King, full of humility, self-effacing, concerned with providing rights for his people, continued to grow in stature, with the result that on one occasion Eleanor attempted to return to her former husband. She was trying to reach the domains of the King of France, disguised as a man, when she was captured and imprisoned by men in the pay of Plantagenet. The latter lost no time in removing her from the kingdom of France, where the chess-game continued with advances and withdrawals, neither player able to put the other in checkmate.

Here in conflict, were two different concepts of power and of life in the persons of two Kings, or rather of two dynasties. While Louis' only concern was to strengthen his ties with his immediate vassals, Champagne and Blois, Henry and Eleanor, for their part, married one daughter, Matilda, to the Duke of Saxony, another, Joan, to the King of Sicily, and a third, called Eleanor after her mother, to the King of Castile. This meant that, at each of the cardinal points, there was a new branch of this prolific tree! Meanwhile the Capetian King, attracted as he was to the Holy Land, never lost sight of the 'square field of land'.

Louis VII died on 18 September 1180, almost a year

after he had associated his heir, Philip, with him on the throne, on 1 November 1179. Philip, whom his father had nicknamed 'the God-given', was only fourteen at the time. The major ambition of his reign was to seize Normandy and, if necessary, to stage a successful landing in England, similar to that made by William the Conqueror over a hundred years earlier. This was to form the crux of his policies. In his attempts to carry them out, he proved to be adept in turning circumstances to his own advantage. He was politically minded to a greater extent than any of his predecessors. Where they had been content to administrate, to consolidate and bring together their lands and to contract useful alliances, Philip's ambitions were to conquer and to rule.

During the early years of his reign, he found opponents who were worthy of him. Henry Plantagenet, and then his son, Richard Coeur de Lion, were formidable whether as friends or as enemies. Philip soon had occasion to realize this, and having measured his strength against both of them, did not take matters further. Nevertheless, on his return from an expedition to the Holy Land, undertaken at the same time as Richard, and during which his only achievement had been to contract a malignant fever, he thought he could take advantage of his opponent's absence to pillage the castles of Normandy. This proved to be a grave error; he had hoped to carry the venture through without difficulty by coming to an agreement with Richard's youngest brother, John, the famous John Lackland, but he found himself confronted by an unexpected adversary in the shape of Queen Eleanor. It was to her and not to John that Richard had entrusted the kingdom in his absence. Philip succeeded in gaining control of the coveted fortress of Gisors by bribing its chaplain, Gilbert Vascoeuil, but he failed at Rouen, where the Queen had lost no time in installing a seneschal who was devoted to her son's cause, and he had to fight every inch of the way to maintain his hold on several domains in Norman Vexin. Immediately on his return, Richard took up arms and the King of France suffered a defeat at Fréteval in 1194 which had far-reaching consequences. He was forced to abandon his treasure, his archives and even his personal seal on the field of battle. Philip soon had cause to regret his unwise manoeuvres. The Plantagenets were victorious on all fronts – Richard had brought his brother to his senses, one of Eleanor's grandsons, Otto of Brunswick, was in line to become German Emperor, and, in addition, the Queen herself had fulfilled a youthful ambition by marrying her daughter, Joan, widow of the King of Sicily, to Raymond VI, Count of Toulouse, which was an indirect way of recovering a county over which she had always claimed to have rights.

It was at this juncture that an unforeseen event completely altered the situation. Richard was struck by an arrow during a minor campaign against the Lord of Châlus, and died on 6 April 1199. Now, although Philip might have seemed better placed than most to benefit from the opportunities offered by this unexpected death, there was another, equally gifted in political ingenuity, who was ready to take full advantage of the situation. Once again it was Queen Eleanor, who, realizing that in the hands of her youngest son, John, the Plantagenet kingdom was doomed to certain ruin, decided at once to attempt to save as much of it as could be saved. At the age of eighty, she embarked upon an extraordinary tour of her personal estates, distributing charters of liberties in order to obtain in return military aid from her burgesses. In July, she came in person to pay Philip the homage which she owed him as her suzerain. This was an extremely clever manoeuvre, for it removed any pretext the King may have had for attempting to overcome Aquitaine. Yet this was only a beginning. She then resumed the ten-year-old negotiations between England and France, whose aim had been to guarantee peace between the two countries by means of a marriage alliance; she crossed the Pyrenees herself and brought back a bride of her own choice for Louis, the heir of the King of France. This was her granddaughter, Blanche of Castile, third daughter of Eleanor of Castile; Queen Eleanor had chosen her in preference to her elder sister, Urrace, whom she no doubt judged unsuitable. So it was, then, that on 23 May 1200, Blanche was married to Louis. Eleanor had been unable to put one of her sons on the French throne, but at least the Crown would now fall to a grand-daughter descended from her line.

In fact, it was the death of Eleanor, rather than that of Richard, which left Philip a free hand. The weakness of John Lackland, who, when he acted, did so with disastrous consequences, turning his barons against him and killing his nephew, Arthur of Brittany, left the way clear for the Capetian ruler to invade Normandy. For Philip, this was only the first step since he fully intended to complete his venture with the conquest of England. Yet, in his haste, he rather compromised his victory, for he now found himself confronted by a coalition which had been previously formed to oppose him. He was faced not only by John, but also by the Emperor Otto of Brunswick, and the Count of Flanders, with the result that the royal domain found itself attacked on all sides (Guienne had remained under the dominion of the Plantagenets). It needed the victory at Bouvines on 27 July 1214, as well as that won by Prince Louis over John at La Roche-aux-Moines on 2 July, to release this grip and prevent an invasion. Two years later, the planned invasion of England took place and Louis, the heir to the French throne, asserting the rights of his wife, Blanche, established himself in London, to the acclamation of people.

The coronation of Louis VIII and Blanche of Castile. The eighty-year-old Eleanor of Aquitaine had crossed the Pyrenees to bring Louis, then heir to the French throne, the bride she had chosen for him, her granddaughter Blanche.

Events then took a new dramatic turn. John Lackland, whose name was despised throughout the kingdom, had meanwhile died on 19 October 1216. It might have seemed that the Crown of England would now fall to the French heir, but this would be to reason from a French standpoint. True the English barons, who hated John, had given Louis a warm welcome; but once John was dead, they recognized the legitimate right of his son, little Henry III, nine years old, against whom they had no grievance. Opinion swung in his favour and when Louis was defeated at the siege of Lincoln Castle on 19 May 1217, the French Prince realized that he had no choice but to withdraw, which he did some months later.

King Philip died in 1223 without entirely fulfilling his ambitions; nevertheless, he had left his heir a much-enlarged kingdom, which now included not only Normandy, but a large part of the western estates, Maine, Anjou, Touraine and Poitou. Louis and Blanche were crowned King and Queen of France on 6 August 1223, the feast of the Transfiguration.

Louis VIII was the son of his father's first wife, the sweet and gentle Isabella of Hainault, who gave birth to him when she was sixteen and died when she was eighteen.

Some time after Isabella's death, Philip married Isambour, a Danish Princess, for whom he quickly developed a physical repugnance which is difficult to explain, since her contemporaries thought her both beautiful and gracious. This union caused Philip a number of difficulties. He was excommunicated for having repudiated her and, even more serious, for having immediately afterwards married Agnes of Meran; he had two children by Agnes including a son, Philip. Blanche and Louis had twelve children, of whom several died at an early age. The descendants of Isabella of Hainault had also inherited her fragile disposition. At the time of their coronation, however, the dynasty seemed in a strong position, for the royal couple had five sons: Louis, who became heir to the throne after the death of his elder brother Philip, Robert, John, Alphonse and another Philip, who was also known as Dagobert; they also had a daughter, Isabella, and their last child was a boy, Charles.

A bright future seemed to be in store for the dynasty. Louis VIII distinguished himself almost immediately in a successful campaign against the town of La Rochelle, which meant that the Capetians now had a sea-port under their control. Their only cause for concern was in the Languedoc region of the Midi, where the interminable Albigensian War was still being fought in the territory of the Count of Toulouse. The war had been started by Pope Innocent III against the Cathar heretics, who had swarmed into the country after the assassination of the papal legate, Pierre de Castelnau, in January 1208. King Philip, although he did not take part himself, had allowed those of his barons who had responded to the Pope's appeal to take action. Louis had only made a brief visit to the Midi in 1215, just before the affair with England which was occupying most of his attention at that time. But in 1226, the papal legate came to urge him to take up arms and, at the same time, the leader of the Crusade (the son of Simon de Montfort, its original leader), bequeathed him his rights over the southern fiefs. Louis decided to go. He made his will and set out for the Rhône valley, having taken his leave of his wife and children. He was never to see them again.

The Queen and her retinue met the returning royal army, but the King was dead. So violent was Blanche's grief that, for a while, there were fears for her life. However, she regained her self-control and used all the means at her disposal to have her son, the young Louis who was only twelve, crowned as soon as possible. The coronation took place on 29 November of that tragic year of 1226. It was during the reign of Louis IX that the Capetian dynasty reached its zenith.

This was also a period of peace and prosperity, for which the realm was indebted not only to the King who, in his own lifetime, was to be known by the people as 'the Holy King' but also to his mother, Blanche. She governed on behalf of her son until he was of an age to do so himself, and both by her actions and by her counsel she contributed to the smooth running of the kingdom. In fact, she became Regent again in 1248, when Louis IX, following in the footsteps of his ancestors, embarked with his wife for the Holy Land at Aigues-Mortes, the port he had created specially for that purpose. Blanche died in 1252, without seeing her son again; but at least she had left him a realm which was intact and in good order.

If the realm had remained intact, it was because, in line with the thinking of the times, little attempt had been made to enlarge its frontiers; efforts were rather directed towards the consolidation of existing ties, created by the feudal oath. Thus it was that, in 1234, after several years of refusing to do so, Brittany recognized the suzerainty of the King of France. For a hundred years or more, right up to the time of the Anglo-French wars, this suzerainty was never again called in question. Similarly Blanche, after the accession of her son, attempted to restore peace in the Midi, which had been the scene of so much bloodshed and of so many horrors. In 1229 a treaty was signed in Paris, in which Raymond of Toulouse formally recognized the suzerainty of the King of France and promised his only daughter, Joan, in marriage to one of the King's brothers, Alphonse, who was already Count of Poitou and Auvergne. Raymond VII was Blanche's German cousin, and when at a later date the latter allied himself with the King of England against his suzerain, in a coalition which was threatening to break the peace, he did not hesitate to invoke this connection in order to obtain a pardon when the coalition broke down.

It was also Blanche who took the initiative in arranging a marriage outside the realm for her son, Louis. Like her grandmother, she had European ambitions. Louis, then, married Margaret, eldest daughter of the Count of Provence, Raymond-Bérenger IV. Raymond's hopes of continuing the succession of his county, which had long been coveted by the Counts of Toulouse, were frustrated by the fact that his only offspring were girls.

However, the union of Beatrice and Charles of Anjou opened up new horizons in the valley of the Rhône, in those lands of the Barolingian Empire which, unlike the other Languedoc territories, had never belonged to the realm of France. It also provided the Capetian dynasty with another female personality of great ability. Young Margaret (she was thirteen in 1234 at the time of her marriage to Louis, who was then twenty) was at first kept out of public affairs by her mother-in-law, mistrustful of her capabilities; nevertheless she more than made up for this later on.

She certainly played a decisive part in bringing to an end the long-standing hostilities between England and France. Henry III, who had come to power in dramatic circumstances in England, had no intention of giving up permanently the provinces previously conquered by Philip Augustus (Poitou, Maine, Anjou and above all, the duchy of Normandy); he therefore refused to do homage for Guienne, which he hoped to use as a base for future expeditions to regain his lands. Intending to exploit the grievances of the southerners and, in particular, of Raymond Trencavel, who was claiming the viscounty of Carcassonne (he had not signed the 1229 peace treaty), Henry landed at Royan in 1242 with plans for large scale military manoeuvres, which were thwarted by the crushing victories won by Louis IX at Taillebourg and at Saintes on 21 and 22 July 1242. These were the only military operations that the King of France had to conduct on his own territory, apart from the capture of various castles in the Midi, such as Montségur in 1244 and Quéribus in 1255 – tasks which he entrusted to his seneschals.

Peace was to reign uninterrupted in the realm, once the uprisings in Brittany – begun by rebel barons, hoping to seize the Crown while it was in the hands of a woman and a child – had been quelled. Peace was finally made with England in 1258 by the Treaty of Paris, which was solemnly ratified by the King of England in the following year. The terms of the Treaty were original: Louis handed over to the King of England all the fiefs and domains held by him in the dioceses of Limoges, Cahors and Périgueux, with rights over a part of Saintonge, the Agenais and Quercy, which were held by Joan of Toulouse; in exchange, his suzerainty was to be recognized throughout Guienne. A situation was thus created, which had not been seen since the beginning of the century, whereby the King of England pledged fidelity to his suzerain for his Continental domains. This was to be the end of Anglo-French disputes over the provinces lost by John Lackland.

Margaret played a part in the negotiations which led up to this settlement. As a result of her close relationship with her sister, Eleanor, Henry III placed great confidence in her; later, when he felt threatened by rebel barons, he entrusted her with his personal treasure, which she kept in the safety of the Temple in Paris.

Louis was also the king who restored the use of gold currency in France. None had been minted for five centuries. It was on his return from the Holy Land in 1254 that Louis took this initiative; the gold crown, bearing the fleur de lys, became the strongest European currency, used not only in France, but throughout the Western world.

The University of Paris was a splendid example of the learning, referred to by Guillaume de Nangis. It was a 'fountain of knowledge' whose teachers included the greatest scholars of Europe, among them, Albertus Magnus, Thomas Aquinas and Roger Bacon. Students flocked to it from all parts. Following the treaty of 1229, another university was founded in the south, at Toulouse.

This was the period of the construction of the great cathedrals of the realm: Rheims, Sens, Amiens, Rouen and Chartres. In addition, many parish churches were built (there are twelve on the Ile de la Cité alone) with an architectural boldness made possible by the great innovations of the era, innovations such as intersecting ribs and flying buttresses which led to such achievements as the 'wall of windows' – which can still be admired at the St-Chapelle, built by the King in the Palais de la Cité.

To complete the picture, mention should also be made of the introduction of the Inquisition, although it must be stressed that it would be incorrect to attribute its introduction to the Capetians, as it was a Papal, and not a royal, institution. It operated in France from 1233 onwards, and if the King lent his support to the inquisitors, at least he was never guilty of the excesses committed by the Count of Toulouse, Raymond VII, who, in 1249, at Berlaigues, near Agen, sent to the stake eighty heretics whom the inquisitors themselves had not condemned.

The King, however, died with one ambition unfulfilled – he had wanted to recapture Jerusalem. For him, the Holy Land was more important than his own small square of land. He had devoted six years of his life from 1248 to 1254, to restoring not only the castles of Palestine but also order amongst the barons who had settled in the Near East after the failure of his expedition against Egypt. His second expedition in 1272, probably through the intervention of his brother, Charles of Anjou, was diverted to Tunis. There Louis died, not of the plague, as school books would have it, but of a dysentery epidemic, which took a cruel toll of his army. His remains were brought back to the abbey of Royaumont, which he had founded, and were later conveyed to St-Denis when, by popular consent, he was canonized on 6 August 1297. The fleur de lys was flowering, even on the altars of the Church.

Who could have foreseen, at the time of Louis' canonization, that the Capetian dynasty had only thirty years or so left to run? King Philip the Fair had been on the throne for twelve years and his father, Philip the Bold, had reaped the benefits of a vast legacy. His personal domain had been increased by the addition of that of Alphonse of Poitiers, brother of St Louis, and his wife, Joan of Toulouse, who had remained childless. He also benefited from the legacies of his uncles, Jean-Tristan, Count of Valois, and Peter, Count of Alençon and Perche and, by some far-sighted political manoeuvring, he had succeeded in annexing the Vivarais and the Lyonnais. He also had his heir apparent, Philip IV, married to Joan, sole heir to Navarre and Champagne. As a result, his realm was gradually becoming part of his personal domain.

Not only this, but the dynasty itself was showing no signs of faltering. Philip IV's nickname, the Fair, was also given to his youngest son Charles; his second son was known as *Le Long*, the tall; and his heir apparent Louis, must have been a vigorous character, for he was known as *Le Hutin*, meaning the turbulent or the quarrelsome.

The reign of Philip IV remains something of an enigma; indeed, the same could be said of his character. He gradually became so unpopular that when he died, at the age of forty-six, his son had to go to great lengths to get a mass celebrated in his memory.

The year 1289 saw the opening of the University of Montpellier, where Roman Law was to be taught. Later, in 1312, a School of Roman Law was founded in Orléans. Previously, Roman Law had only been taught in Italy, notably in Bologna, but also in Naples. These developments were significant because Philip the Fair, unlike his predecessors, employed administrators, known as 'legists', who were trained in Roman Law, which was fundamentally opposed to feudal law. Guillaume de Nogaret and Guillaume de Plaisians, who were for practical purposes in charge of the affairs of the realm, together with Pierre Dubois and Pierre Flote, were all fully versed in Roman Law. They dreamed of setting up a centralized and authoritarian State, based on the Roman model, and they supported their dream with formulae taken from the Digest and the Justinian Code: 'The King of France is Emperor in his own kingdom. . . . His will should be law . . .'. They even outlined a vision of a universal monarchy, a notion totally at odds with the customs and thinking of the feudal age. The numerous conflicts and struggles at home and abroad, in religious and administrative affairs, which made this one of the most turbulent reigns in French history, may well have had their origins here.

St Louis had made peace with England and had even acted as arbiter in the dispute between the King of England and his barons (the famous Mise of Amiens in 1264). Philip the Fair, however, embarked upon a war against England, for which no historian has ever been able to suggest a convincing explanation. He seized Guienne, on the pretext of intervening in disputes between sailors, which would normally have come under local jurisdiction. Five years later, he was forced to surrender and to hand over a territory for which the King of England had never intended to refuse him homage.

In Flanders, St Louis had formerly arbitrated in the family conflicts which had made the situation in this county so complicated (the Mise of Péronne, 1256). Philip the Fair, however, went to war, supporting the rich magnates of the textile industry against the common people; but, for the first time, the French cavalry was defeated, in extremely humiliating circumstances at Courtrai, in 1302. The weavers and fullers, the working people, oppressed by the powerful merchants whose side Philip had taken, won a totally unexpected victory, defending themselves with iron-shod Poles against the French cavalry charges. The

The death of St Louis, shown in a stained glass window of the Sainte-Chapelle at Champigny-sur-Veude. The King died in 1270 in Tunis, where his second crusade had been diverted by the dysentery epidemic that decimated the army.

A fourteenth-century miniature showing Louis X. He reigned for only two years from 1314 to 1316, and the Capetian dynasty was to die out twelve years later, after the reigns of his brothers Philip V and Charles IV.

Son bon
seigneur
loys fil
du roy de
france. par la grace de
dieu roy de nauare.
de champaigne et de bri
e conte palazin. Jehan
sur de romuille son se
neschal de champaigne.
salut et amour. et

lonneur. et son serui
se appareille. Chier sire
ie vous fait a sauoir
que ma dame la roy
ne nostre mere qui
moult mamoit a cui
dieu bone merci face:
me pria si a certes co
me elle pot que ie li fe
isse faire .i. liure des sai
tes paroles. et des bons

war with Flanders continued throughout almost the entire reign and a series of obscure episodes ended in the annexation of three castellanies, Lille, Douai and Orchies; scant spoils indeed – especially when it is remembered that, sixty years later, they were to become part of the empire of the powerful Duke of Burgundy. This exhausting war, waged in the mud of Flanders, created an incessant, almost obsessive need for funds. St Louis had established the strongest gold currency in Europe; Philip the Fair, however, by continual devaluations of this currency, utterly disrupted economic life.

In religious matters, St Louis had succeeded in taking a firm stand against Papal authority. Philip the Fair, however, made successive assaults on the Church and its representatives, sometimes with no foundation whatsoever. The King himself, together with his evil genius Nogaret, attacked Pope Boniface VIII with an unrelenting fierceness, which was to culminate in the incident at Anagni, where the Pope was held prisoner and actually struck by Sciarra Colonna, a companion of Nogaret. Even after the Pope's death, the campaign continued against his memory and against his corpse – a call was made for its exhumation, so that it might be burned and the ashes scattered to the wind. Philip would not rest until he had seen the enthronement of a Pope of his own choice, the southerner, Bertrand de Goth, who, as Clement V, was the first of the Avignon Popes.

This rather erratic Pope, whose only real concern was with ecclesiastical benefices, in spite of some resistance on his part, eventually became the King's instrument in the affair of the Templars. Philip discredited the Military Order of the Templars by bringing the most vile accusations against them, including blasphemy, sodomy and heresy. He had chosen his target well. The fall of St John of Acre, the last bastion of what had been the Latin kingdom of the Near East, had made unpopular the men who, despite their bravery, which even their enemies acknowledged, had been unable to prevent its downfall. The Templars were criticized for their wealth, their arrogance and their inefficiency. But against the accusations and the confessions – wrung from them by torture and retracted, for the most part, at a later date – stands the fact that only in France were the Templars persecuted in this way; elsewhere their innocence was recognized. Nevertheless, Philip the Fair had the Order suppressed in 1312, by a Pope who was now entirely at his disposal. When Jacques de Molay, Grand Master of the Templars, and Geoffroy de Charnay, one of his companions, were executed at the stake on 18th March 1314, they proclaimed the innocence and the purity of the Order. Both the Pope and the King, however, died shortly after the execution of the two Templars; the Pope two months later, and the King on 29 November.

During Philip's reign a crushing burden of taxes was placed on the people throughout the domain, which had now grown to almost the size of the realm. Administration, which was no longer itinerant, now had its seat in Paris and was thus less accessible to those wishing to appeal to the King's justice. Last but not least, there was the sombre drama which cast a blemish on the dynasty itself. In the last year of his life, Philip had his three daughters-in-law arrested. Margaret and Blanche of Burgundy were accused of committing adultery with two knights, Philippe and Gautier d'Aunay, and Joan was charged with being their accomplice. A critical part in this incident was played by a figure who has been rather neglected by history, Philip the Fair's daughter, Isabella, whom the English called the 'she-wolf of France'. Isabella was married to King Edward II of England and she later had her husband assassinated on 21 September 1327 with the aid of her lover, the famous Mortimer, in dreadful circumstances, after she had forced the King to abdicate. It was this same Isabella, whose appalling behaviour was to scandalize the whole of the Western world, who, together with her father, was the accuser of her three sisters-in-law in this instance.

On his death, Philip the Fair left an empty treasury, counsellors so unpopular that their leader, Enguerrand de Marigny, was later hanged, while most of the others were imprisoned and their goods confiscated. The King's three sons, one after the other, died childless, although the eldest, Louis X had a posthumous son, John I, who lived for only five days. Philip the Fair, by his last statute, in November 1314, had debarred women from succession to the throne. This was the origin of the notorious 'Salic Law', which was really a justification by the clerks of the University of Paris of Philip's interdiction, unprecedented in feudal times, debarring women from exercising power. The consequences of this measure were not only the complications of the Hundred Years War, but also the hostility shown by the sons of Philip the Fair towards Edward III of England, who was himself the son of the 'she-wolf of France'.

The Capetian dynasty, then, came to an end on 31 January 1328, when King Charles IV died at the age of thirty-four without leaving an heir. Nevertheless, this same sturdy stock was to produce not only the Valois dynasty, which succeeded the Capetians, but also, three hundred years later, the Bourbon dynasty, which came to the throne in the person of Henry IV, a descendant of St Louis' son, Robert of Clermont, who was Duke of Bourbon in his wife, Beatrice's, right.

Strangely, when the Bourbon dynasty was nearing its end, the name of Capet – an unexpected backward glance to a period whose history was not well-known at that time – was given to the last representative of the traditional monarchy, the ill-fated Louis XVI.

Conrad III, the first Hohenstaufen King, on the ill-fated Crusade of 1149. He died in Germany in 1152, while preparing to go to Rome for his coronation as Emperor.

The Hohenstaufens

Victims of the vicissitudes of fortune, in their dreams
of empire, the Hohenstaufens emerge a unique
and splendid anachronism

'Mother, mother – how they are hurting you. . . .!' The boyish voice sounded high and clear over the Mercato Vecchio in Naples. Then the executioner's men went to work, and the curly head of Conradin, last of the Hohenstaufens to wear the Crown, rolled in the sand of his lost kingdom in the South.

On the beflagged balcony above, Charles of Anjou, Count of Provence, brother of Louis IX, King of France, condottiere of His Holiness Clement IV, and already designated by him as Papal representative in the 'kingdom of the Two Sicilies', the Norman heir to the Hohenstaufens, looked down on the grisly last act of a struggle for power that had lasted for decades.

But the victorious Frenchman was no more than a pawn in the game of chess played by the gentlemen in Rome's Lateran Palace. Ever since the death of Charlemagne in 814 they had been striving to realize an age-old concept: to secure for the Pope, as heir to the Roman Caesars, a supranational ascendancy over all the princes of Europe.

After centuries of struggle over this Investiture, as it was called, the emperors of the House of Hohenstaufen had countered by reviving the idea, already rather old-fashioned, of a new Holy Roman Empire independent of the Pope, albeit cooperating with him. The whole of the Western world would be united within a great confederation of kings under the shelter of an Imperial role no less supranational.

The Roman Curia had never accepted this. What it wanted was the overall balance of powers, each holding the others in check, so that, as supreme authority, it could play the part of arbiter in their conflicts. Moreover, in its resistance to a centralized power of kings and emperor, it was able to count on the willing alliance of princes within Germany as well as of the city-republics of Italy, whose special protector the Bishop of Rome felt himself to be.

Thus the rise, the years of dominion and the dramatic downfall of the House of Hohenstaufen were all played out against a background of struggle with national, dynastic, regional and indeed local self-interests, often directly coordinated by Papal legates.

The Hohenstaufens began as petty military nobility, manorial lords who for generations lived a simple life on the poverty-stricken hills above the Remstal in Swabia, at the foot of the as yet unfortified Hohenstaufen. In the eleventh century, one of the Hohenstaufens managed to elevate himself into the local princely aristocracy: Frederick von Büren, knight, in about 1040 married Hildegard, daughter of Otto II, Duke of Swabia. Their son, given the same name (the eldest sons of the Hohenstaufens were always called Frederick), inherited the duchy in 1079 from his grandfather, who had no other children. His lands reached from the middle Neckar to Chiavenna, and from Lech, near Augsburg, to the Vosges mountains. This made him one of the great men of the Empire, and he married Agnes, the daughter of Emperor Henry IV. At the same time he built a splendid residence on the 2,400-foot-high summit of Hohenstaufen; from its turrets he could gaze far out across the heartland of his princedom. Henceforth his family took their name from this summit.

But soon the gaze extended beyond the borders of the princedom. The next Frederick married Judith, sister of Henry the Proud, Duke of Bavaria. Thereafter the two most powerful hereditary princes of Germany, the Hohenstaufens and the Guelphs, were related by marriage to one another – a link that in the next generation was to lead to a struggle for power between the two families, shaking the Empire to its foundations and involving the whole of European politics. This struggle was waged at the negotiating table and by means of political marriages – but it was also fought out on the battlefield.

The first summer lightning appeared in 1125, when the Salian-Frankish ruling House, established mainly on the middle Rhine, was extinguished with the death of the Emperor Henry v. The Emperor's brother-in-law Frederick of Swabia, who was also heir apparent to the ducal crown of Bavaria, automatically stood next in succession to the throne. Many of the Imperial and Church princes were appalled at the prospect of so much power in one family, and a majority of them elected Duke Lothair of Saxony to the throne.*

Lothair II tried in vain to overcome by force the powerful resistance offered particularly by the Imperial cities of south Germany. His opponents declared the election void and on 18th December 1127, when Frederick of Swabia refused to offer himself, they put up his brother Conrad as anti-King. As spring broke, Conrad crossed the Alps and at Monza, on 29 June 1128, the crown of the kingdom of Italy was placed on his head. There and then he summoned an Imperial Diet and began to rule as if King Lothair of the Saxons simply did not exist.

But farther away, in north Germany, Lothair played his trump card, the support of the princes of the Church. The great prince-bishoprics with their rich farmlands on the Rhine, the Meuse and the Main, the Weser and the Elbe, still made up more than one quarter of the State's domains. With their help, Lothair had the Swabian brothers excommunicated, which meant that their feudal knights, officers and camp followers were released from their oath of allegiance, while he himself was crowned Holy Roman Emperor by the Pope in 1133.

On 4 December 1137 Lothair, bearer of the Imperial title whom only the Church and his own country recognized, died. The struggle for power continued, but the prospects were now reversed. Lothair's only daughter Gertrude was married to Duke Henry the Proud of Bavaria. He should now have been heir apparent, for his father-in-law had assigned the duchy of Saxony to him on his deathbed. Such a duplication of family power would have made the Guelphs masters of half Germany. For the other German princes, that was reason enough to deny him the Crown. In his place they called on Conrad von Hohenstaufen, whom they had already elected in 1127 and who had been Duke of East Franconia since 1116, finally to assume the kingship.

* We refer here and in following passages to the ancestral lands of the old Germanic Saxons, reaching from the lower Rhine to the Elbe and from the Harz mountains to the North Sea. This is not the region now called Saxony on either side of the Elbe, colonized by the Saxons since the tenth century, but originally settled by Slavs.

Conrad's great adversary, the Guelph Duke Henry, had stayed away from his coronation in Aachen on 13 March 1138. Three months later, at an Imperial Diet in Bamberg, Conrad deprived him of the right of succession to the duchy of Saxony. At a second Diet, called at Würzburg on the nothern border of Bavaria, Conrad was accompanied by a large levy of troops. Here he declared Duke Henry an outlaw, and bestowed the duchy of Saxony on the Margrave Albert 'the Bear' of the House of Ascania, established in the northern Harz. These decisions brought about a struggle for the succession, and for power and prestige that lasted for decades, long after the death of both contestants.

Naturally enough, the Saxon nobility refused any further allegiance to their new ruler, the King's appointee, Margrave Albert. They demanded that the ducal crown be given to Henry's ten-year-old son, also called Henry, who one day was to wield great influence as 'the Lion'. The Bavarians, too, refused to recognize the regent set over them by Conrad, the Count Palatine Leopold IV of Austria – the King's half-brother through a second marriage contracted by his mother in 1106 with the Margrave Leopold III, The Bavarians were prepared to be 'good Guelphs', but, more important, they were afraid of losing their independence in a Danubian empire of the House of Babenberg, centred at Klosterneuburg, near Vienna.

Two years later the problem was solved: Bavaria went to Conrad's step-brother Henry, Count Palatine on the Rhine; the young Lion now received the duchy of Saxony, the County Palatine itself went to Hermann von Stahleck, husband of Conrad's sister Gertrude; the old Bavarian bishopric of Freising to the King's half-brother Otto; and the duchy of Lower Lorraine to Godfrey of Louvain, a Flemish brother-in-law of the Queen. This family system was completed by liaisons abroad: Conrad's half-sister became Queen of Bohemia; her son Henry, a minor, was betrothed to the daughter of King Bela of Hungary; Conrad's cousin Agnes was married to the Crown Prince Wladyslaw of Poland; and the Emperor Manuel of the Eastern Roman Empire married one of the King's sisters.

Notwithstanding all these activities, Conrad's political record remained a fiasco. An attempt to join the Poles to his empire by the enforced enthronement of Prince Wladyslaw, expelled by his brothers on account of his connexion with the German King, was a total failure. Even more dismal was the dispatch of a crusade for the liberation of northern Syria from the 'infidels' in September 1149, which sustained heavy losses and had to be broken off with nothing achieved.

When Conrad III returned to Germany, the young Duke Henry of Saxony made a vigorous demand for the return of his Bavarian patrimony. At the next

Frederick I Barbarossa, in a relief in Freising Cathedral. Blond, courteous and imposing, he obstinately pursued his Imperial designs, only to have them frustrated by the opposition of the Papacy and the Italian City States.

Imperial Diet, when the King put him off, the Lion suddenly marched with powerful forces from Brunswick to the Danube. Thereupon Conrad surprised and occupied Goslar, and captured Henry's residence in Brunswick. Then, just as quickly, Henry reappeared in the north and drove the Imperial troops out of his duchy.

A year later Conrad died. He would have liked to have made up for his German disaster with an even more spectacular happening: his coronation as Emperor in Rome, which he had been putting off since 1127. Once more he summoned the Imperial Diet to Bamberg. Ambassadors had already been sent out to Constantinople to invite the Byzantine Emperor, and to Rome to prepare a worthy reception for the German King. But, on 15 February 1152, in his castle above the Red Main, he succumbed to a disease from which he had been suffering for a long time.

He had just time to make what is perhaps the only fortunate decision of a reign overshadowed by failure: he recommended to the Imperial princes that they should elect as their king not his own son Frederick, still a minor, but his nephew, also called Frederick, now thirty years old and, since 1147, the third of the Hohenstaufen family to be Duke of Swabia.

This aspirant to the throne was already politically highly experienced. Frederick, whom the Italians nicknamed 'Barbarossa' because of his luxuriant red beard, was unanimously elected king.

One of his first despatches was sent to Pope Eugene III. In Rome it was seen as a declaration of war. In unmistakeable terms, Frederick declared that 'the Empire had been entrusted by God to him alone'.

In October 1154 Frederick Barbarossa marched south and held court in Lombardy. He also had to do battle with the Milanese, always anti-German, and their allies among the cities of upper Italy. He did not reach Rome until June 1155, and there the new Pope, the English-born Adrian IV, crowned him. During the celebrations a revolt broke out against Pope and Emperor; that same day the Germans were forced to leave the Eternal City, while Adrian barricaded himself in the Castel Sant'Angelo.

Frederick had come to Rome intending that, after his coronation, he would combine with the forces of the Pope and those of his uncle, the Eastern Emperor Manuel, and drove out of southern Italy the Norman barons, against whom the Apulian peasants had rebelled. But Manuel's troops were not ready for action, the 'crack troops' of the besieged Pope were equally unreliable and his own German soldiers were crippled by the unfamiliar climate. They wanted to go home, and the Emperor gave way.

Four years later he was back in Italy. Adrian IV, greatly disappointed by the retreat of the Germans, had in 1156 concluded an agreement with the Norman kingdom of the Two Sicilies. A year later, while Frederick was holding court at Besançon, in the homeland of his second wife Beatrice, Adrian sent him a note packed with political dynamite. He recalled in sharp terms the familiar view of the Curia that 'every Emperor holds his crown in fee from the Pope' and is consequently his vassal.

If the Curia hoped that this threatening gesture would be enough to stir the German princes of the Church or the Guelphs to rise against the King-Emperor, they had miscalculated. Its effect was felt far more strongly in the cities of Lombardy, which by that period was the most important economic region of Europe and was eager to throw off the German yoke. In order to put down this rebellion, Frederick crossed the Alps in the spring of 1158 with at least 100,000 men, an exceptionally strong army for those days, and by 7 September he had forced the stronghold of Milan, the centre of resistance, to capitulate.

Frederick now tried to bring conditions in the city-states of upper Italy up to date by means of a progressive system of constitutional government. But his efforts broke down under continued resistance, especially from the Milanese, who quickly drove out the King's officers, including the Imperial Chancellor Rainald von Dassel.

Frederick's counter-measures proved ineffective, for his forces were split up around the country in an attempt to control the many different cities. Moreover, the King had a piece of bad luck: Adrian IV, who might have compromised with him, died and Alexander III was elected the new Pope. This was the prelate who had carried the note to Besançon and, indeed, may well have drafted it. He came out firmly against the Hohenstaufens, and on 24 March 1160 Frederick was excommunicated.

Milan and Sicily approved of Alexander's action, as was only to be expected; but so did many of the bishops of France, as did those of England, home of Matilda the future wife of Henry the Lion. Frederick was forced to take ruthless measures. Reduced to starvation after months of siege, Milan surrendered in March 1161; the King allowed the city to be sacked.

His true adversary, Alexander III, gained from the episode an army of silent sympathisers, who awaited his signal to rise. In 1164 Frederick tried in vain to out-manoeuvre him by recognizing his ally Cardinal Guido of Crema as anti-Pope Paschal III. The service offered by the Cardinal in return for this was the canonization of Charlemagne, who had for so long embodied the temporal primacy of the Emperor over the Bishop of Rome. The decision that the veneration of the new Saint should be explicitly confined to Aachen 'as a German city' was intended also to counter the French, who were beginning to see in the 'Rex Francorum' in Aachen the ancestor of the King of France, and any

Henry VI in a miniature from the Manesse manuscript.
'Ruthless in the methods he chooses, his eye always
fixed on universal power', as his contemporaries
described him, he acquired the Norman kingdom of
southern Italy by marriage.

Castel del Monte in Puglia, Italy. Built between 1240 and 1250 as a hunting lodge for Frederick II, this remarkable example of medieval architecture may have been designed by the Emperor himself.

claim they might make to the Imperial Crown.

Similar motives lay behind an unexpected treaty of friendship with Henry II of England. Henry had also just broken with the Pope in his quarrel with his Archbishop of Canterbury, Thomas à Becket. The alliance with the Plantagenet King of England, who as Count of Anjou and Duke of Normandy also owned two-fifths of France, was sealed by a marriage between Henry's daughter Matilda and Frederick's cousin Henry the Lion (who was now fully on the side of the Hohenstaufens). This alliance was further strengthened by a marriage settlement between the English King's youngest daughter Eleanor and Frederick's new-born heir, later to become King Henry VI.

On 23 November 1165, Alexander returned in triumph to Rome. Only twenty months later, German troops stormed the Vatican, and Alexander III was forced to take refuge in Norman Benevento. On 1 August 1167 in the Basilica of St Peter, around whose gates there had been bitter fighting only a few days before, anti-Pope Paschal was able to greet Frederick Barbarossa and his Burgundian wife, decked in their insignia of mediaeval Imperial majesty.

But, as at his coronation twelve years before, the glory of the great moment was quickly eclipsed. There was a sudden outbreak of typhus in Rome. The Court and the army both left the Eternal City in a panic. Among the 20,000 Germans who died there, or on the dreary march northwards, were the Emperor's cousin Frederick of Baden and, tragically, the great Imperial Chancellor Rainald von Dassel, who until

then had maintained some sort of order in Italy.

As a consequence of this disaster the Milanese League of cities was revived and Alexander III secured the support of the Republic of Venice, the kingdom of the Two Sicilies and the Byzantine Emperor, to help him to preserve his last possessions in lower Italy. Ever at odds among themselves, they were nevertheless united in their aim of keeping the Germans out of Italy.

It was to be nine years before Frederick undertook another Italian campaign, and this time Henry the Lion was not with him. The Duke was now fully occupied with the extension of his family's power in the area of Slav settlement beyond the Elbe. He saw the great German task to lie, not in the south, but in a systematic colonization towards the east. Lübeck, gateway to the Baltic, was more important to him than Milan. Nevertheless, Frederick risked the march southwards. But he was soon halted; on 20 August 1176 he suffered a crushing defeat at Legnano, on the road from Como to Milan. Frederick Barbarossa himself barely escaped with his life. He was forced to make peace with the Pope, who thereupon released him from excommunication, and met him in Venice on 1 August 1177. Alexander was even able to get the Lombard cities to cease hostilities.

Frederick knew that this could not be a lasting settlement. But for the moment he needed peace and security. For, in Germany, Henry the Lion, who had refused to send his armies into Italy with the Emperor, was engaged in a war on several fronts against his pro-Hohenstaufen neighbours, the Landgrave of

A miniature of Frederick II. This cultured and open-minded son of Henry VI and the Norman Constance of Altavilla was the most complex figure of his dynasty and one of the greatest of medieval Europe.

Thuringia and the archbishops of Magdeburg and Cologne. In consequence, Barbarossa found himself obliged to take their side against the party of the Lion, whom he (unjustly) held responsible for complicity in the catastrophe of Legnano with all its disastrous consequences.

On 18 June 1180 the 'rebel' Lion was outlawed; six months later, his duchy of Saxony was partitioned and Bavaria handed over to Frederick's most loyal paladin, Otto von Wittelsbach, who, during the fighting at Milan had hewn a way of escape for him. To his bitter disappointment, Henry found himself let down by his relatives in France, England and Denmark. He was forced to surrender. At the Diet of Erfurt in November 1181, the Lion received back only his hereditary estates in Brunswick and Lüneburg; and he was exiled for life. He took his family into exile in England.

At the great Imperial festival of Whitsun 1184, with nearly 70,000 knights from Saxony, Swabia and Bavaria, Burgundy and Lorraine, France and Italy gathered before the gates of Mainz, then the geographical centre of Germany, the sixty-two-year-old Emperor stood at the zenith of his power. He planned to extend and secure it as far as possible by marrying his son Henry, now grown to manhood, to Constance, heiress of the Norman kingdom of the Two Sicilies. The very fact that the wedding took place in Milan, now rebuilt, and that this time the Lombards greeted their Emperor with cheers, shows how Barbarossa had re-established his authority in his territories since the death of his great adversary Alexander III in 1181, and had even won back the affection of his subjects.

Frederick's life could have ended thus in peace. But the storming of Jerusalem in 1187 by the Muslim leader Saladin – Jerusalem had become a Christian kingdom in 1099 – inspired him and the other Western monarchs to launch the third Crusade. It proved a complete failure and on 10 June 1190, the Emperor succumbed to a heart attack and was drowned while bathing in Cilicia.

His son Henry VI, called so suddenly to supreme responsibility, was quite another type of man. Even outwardly, he bore little resemblance to his father. The sympathies of the Italians, so painfully won from them by Barbarossa, were lost within two years by Henry when, as an experiment, he was allowed to 'reign' in the South – lost so profoundly that, in 1188, his father hastily recalled him.

Now the great Emperor was dead. His eldest son, Frederick of Swabia, marching on to Acre with a small body of troops, died on 20 January 1191 of a sickness that ravaged the small German contingent. His brother Henry had stayed at home. Now he had to fight for the inheritance of his wife Constance. The Norman barons of Sicily were taking up arms. With the Pope's

Pisans capturing prelates summoned by the Pope to a council in order to depose Frederick II. This was one of the episodes in the almost continuous contest between the Emperor and the Papacy.

agreement, they elected one of Constance's cousins, Prince Tancred, as King of the Two Sicilies, and received support from the English King on his way home from Palestine. Richard Coeur de Lion even used the opportunity to renew former ties with his Norman cousins and to enable his brother-in-law, Henry the Lion, to return to Germany.

Henry VI did not give a thought to the Lion. It was

Italy that attracted him; and there he went through an Imperial coronation by the Roman Curia at Easter 1191, under far from regal conditions. Then he marched on southern Italy and swiftly occupied it; but an epidemic carried off nine-tenths of his army within a few weeks. A siege of Naples, strongly opposed to Hohenstaufen rule had to be abandoned. The Emperor and what remained of his forces, could only manage with difficulty to fight their way back north. Constance had been carried off by a Norman raiding party in Salerno, and Tancred kept her in his custody as a hostage for Henry's withdrawal from Italy.

In Germany an alliance of temporal and spiritual lords waited for the return of the defeated Emperor. They were angered by the murder of Count Albert of Brabant, elected Bishop of Liège, a seat that Henry

Detail of Charlemagne's sarcophagus at Aachen. In 1215 the twenty-one-year-old Frederick II, shortly to receive the German Crown, closed up with his own hands the tomb of the first Emperor.

would have preferred to have seen occupied by the Rhinelander Conrad von Hochstaden. They called on the Emperor to abdicate, accusing him of complicity in the murder and of political incompetence.

The young Emperor was helped once more by a stroke of luck albeit not a very glorious one. In the autumn of 1192, Richard Coeur de Lion made a daring attempt to fight his way from Sicily across the Adriatic and through the chaos that reigned in Germany, to northern France, at that time English territory. Although in disguise, on 21 December 1192 the English king was captured in Styria by the frontier guards of Duke Leopold V of Austria, with whom he had quarrelled in the Holy Land, and was imprisoned in Leopold's stronghold of Dürnstein on the Danube.

Henry VI took advantage of this situation. By threatening to have the prisoner executed for high treason, he was able to hold in check both the German princes and Richard's brother-in-law, Henry the Lion, who was preparing to return to his duchy. The Emperor compelled the English King to do homage, thereby appearing as his feudal lord; then he and Leopold demanded a ransom that today would be worth many millions. Thinking that he had completely secured the sympathies of the imprisoned King, on 2 February 1194 he suddenly released him – and not, as had been feared or planned, to Richard's arch-enemies, the French. One result of this, clearly calculated, move was the reconciliation a few weeks later of the young Emperor with the Lion, now an old man. This, as usual, was sealed by a political marriage between the Duke's son Henry and a cousin of the Emperor – who nevertheless continued to keep the Lion's other two sons, William and Otto (later to become King-Emperor) by him as hostages.

Relieved of these threats, Henry VI could now risk another march to the south, and on 20 November 1194 he entered Palermo. There, on Christmas Day, he received the Crown of King Roger. When on the following day Constance presented him with the longed-for heir to the throne, the future Emperor Frederick II, he and the Sicilians looked upon this as a sign from heaven.

Henry VI's ambition was to make Sicily the strategic and political centre of an Empire in which all the kings of Europe should become the Emperor's vassals, and the countries of the Mediterranean should be reunited into the ancient Roman *orbis terrarum*. He threatened to drive the Moors out of Spain. In the name of Constance, daughter of a Byzantine princess, he demanded that the Eastern Emperor should hand over Greece to him. When a dramatic change of sovereigns occurred in Constantinople, he put forward claims to the rest of the Eastern Roman Empire. In anticipation of future events he demanded homage from the kings of Armenia and Cyprus.

In the autumn of 1196, Henry VI organized a 'crusade', not so much for the liberation of Jerusalem as for the liquidation of the Eastern Roman Empire, which was already beginning to crumble. The concentration of his forces in the Apulian harbours was interrupted by a new rising of the Sicilian nobles. A pitched battle took place between the Emperor's forces and a Sicilian expedition. The Sicilians outnumbered the Germans many times but were nevertheless routed.

In the spring of 1197, Henry VI began again his plans for an Eastern campaign. Advance raiding parties were sent out to the Aegean and to Cyprus, and also appeared before Constantinople to back up German demands that their sovereign be recognized as 'Emperor of the world'. A gigantic plan was taking shape. Within months it was all over. On 28 September 1197 Henry VI, always ailing, died of fever in Messina.

Frederick II was only three when his father died. A year later he lost his mother too. He grew up under the ambivalent guardianship of the Pope. The titles of German and Sicilian kingship, bestowed on him while still in his cradle, weighed him down rather than protected him from the clutches of ambitious pretenders to the throne.

The most dangerous of these was Otto of Brunswick, the twenty-three-year-old son of Henry the

Manfred, King of Sicily, natural son of Frederick II. He fell at Benevento in battle against Charles of Anjou, who later beheaded the young Conradin at Naples.

Lion and nephew of King Richard I of England. To counter Otto's threat, Frederick's uncle Philip of Swabia, elected as Regent by a majority of the German princes, concluded an alliance with Philip II of France on 29 June 1198.

But long before this, Pope Innocent III, arguing that as 'father of Italy' he had also been for centuries feudal lord of the Norman kingdom of the Two Sicilies, had claimed from Constance the guardianship of her little son. Constance, her defence weakened by serious illness, agreed to this. Innocent III was by birth a Lombard aristocrat (namely, Count Lothair of Segnia), and was thus a natural opponent of Hohenstaufen rule in Italy. On the specious grounds that he represented the young Frederick's rights in Sicily, Innocent gave his support to the Guelph Otto and his important ecclesiastical followers, against the Hohenstaufen Philip. The latter had married the daughter of the Byzantine Emperor. With this marriage, Philip was hoping to realize Henry VI's ambition of the reunification of the Eastern and Western Roman Empires under a Hohenstaufen Imperial Crown. After many years of war, during which whole areas of Germany were laid waste, Philip finally gained the upper hand. But, on 21 June 1208, he was assassinated at Bamberg by Otto von Wittelsbach. He died leaving no male heir, and a few days later his wife, fleeing to the castle of the Hohenstaufens, died too in the delivery of a still-born fifth child.

On 4 October 1209 the 'victor', Duke Otto of Saxony, was crowned Emperor Otto IV, in Rome, but he still could only exercise power in north Germany. Just as a majority of German princes had earlier chosen his dead rival Philip as their leader so Otto could not stop them inviting the young Frederick II to receive their homage at a Diet in Mainz in 1212. Nor could he prevent Frederick from making a clandestine return to Germany in December. In his quarrel, Frederick was supported by the King of France, who was engaged in a long-standing feud with Otto IV's English cousins.

At Bouvines, north of Valenciennes, on 27 July 1214, the combined armies of England and the Guelph Emperor suffered a crushing defeat. Otto fled to Brunswick and died in his stronghold of Harzburg in 1218, powerless and almost forgotten.

On 25 August 1215 Frederick, now twenty-one, formally received the German King's Crown. In November of that same year Innocent III achieved the supreme achievement of his papacy with the summoning of the Fourth Lateran Council attended by 400 bishops, 800 abbots and priors and the representatives of the monarchs of Christendom.

Frederick's ideas and character had been formed early, as an orphan in Palermo. There, under the care of his self-appointed guardian Innocent III, he had every reason to appreciate the all-pervading nature of Papal policy, his every step watched over, in an attempt to thwart all possible contact with Germany.

The Prince had been brought up in the colourful world of multi-racial Sicily, where Europe and the Orient met and he gathered around him Arabic, Jewish and Greek mathematicians, astronomers, scientists, doctors and philosophers. This world was also the foundation of scepticism which was to make him the unremitting bane of the ecclesiastical authorities.

After many years of agreement, Frederick's first conflict was with the next Pope, Honorius III, over the question of a new crusade to free the Holy Land from the 'infidels'. Frederick II would have nothing of it. He recalled the catastrophe of 1189–90; but also he made no secret of his high regard for the world of Islam, and no less of his disgust at the hypocrisy of the fourth Crusade of 1204–5. That Crusade had principally been organized by France, with the support of the Pope and the Doge of the Republic of Venice. But Constantinople, not Jerusalem, was the intended goal, in a bid to replace the Byzantine monarchy by a French one, and the Eastern Patriarchate by a legate of the Roman Curia; Venice aimed to put an end to Genoese rivalry on the Bosphorus.

Frederick II was more ready to support a genuine crusade against the Moors in the Iberian Peninsula. Nevertheless, in 1225, he declared himself ready for a campaign in the Near East. But he made his lawyers include so many conditional clauses in the treaty to be drawn up that the next Pope, Gregory IX, a nephew of Innocent III, lost patience and swept the offending paper from the table. Instead he issued a Bull of excommunication against the shifty Hohenstaufen.

In the following year, Frederick II set out on a completely bloodless crusade. Accompanied only by his advisers and a bodyguard of Saracens, he set sail quietly with a small fleet to the East. There, within a few days, he concluded with Malik al-Kamil, nephew of Saladin, Sultan of Egypt, an agreement, prepared in advance through diplomatic channels, for the release of the places of pilgrimage in the Holy Land and a corridor from Jerusalem to the coast for the Christians. Without having had to strike a blow with his sword, the man whom the Pope had excommunicated, was able to crown himself King of Jerusalem in the Church of the Holy Sepulchre. He at once set forth for home.

Frederick II landed in Apulia as unexpectedly as he left, to find his worst fears confirmed: in the few weeks that he was away, a standing army, mostly of mercenaries from Lombardy and the south of France, had marched into lower Italy under the command of John of Brienne. Their intention was to take possession of the Hohenstaufen–Norman lands for the Curia – or for their French representatives. The invaders were swiftly driven out by the Imperial troops.

Doubly defeated, Gregory IX was obliged to withdraw his excommunication of Frederick, who had indeed kept his promises to the full. All oaths of allegiance, of duty and of service, Imperial judgements and charters, were restored to validity in the great Empire, which Frederick II now started to reshape as a modern civil State. This wearer of seven crowns still believed in his father's brave dream of a universal Christian Empire, though all around him, people concerned with their own cultural individualities were fighting for their independence and setting up a new order of national states in Europe.

In the years that followed, Frederick's international Court blossomed in all its glory. He extended his contacts with non-Christian princes and scholars, which displeased the crowned heretic in Rome as much as did his life-style of a half-Oriental, half-Renaissance prince.

In 1239 the 'Sultan of Lucera' was excommunicated for the second time. In reply, he expelled the Dominicans and Franciscans from Germany and in Italy he occupied the Papal State. On 21 October 1241, Pope Gregory died at the age of ninety. His eventual successor was the Lombard-Genoese Count Sinibaldo de'Fieschi of Lavagna, who took the name Innocent IV. On 17 July 1245, from Lyons, he declared Frederick II to be deposed.

In Germany princes contended for the mantle of the excommunicated Emperor, but he was able to stand firm in the south of Italy. Nevertheless he could not prevent the capture of his illegitimate son Enzio by the Bolognese, who kept him in their power until he died in 1272. The blow was the harder for Frederick II to bear since, several years earlier, his eldest son had been persuaded by certain German princes and by the Lombard League to join a rising against his father, and had finally committed suicide.

His youngest son Conrad, King of Germany since 1237, remained loyal to Frederick, But on 13 December 1250, Frederick II died at his estate near Lucera. He passed away in the arms of his illegitimate son, Manfred. In the following autumn Frederick's legitimate son and heir, Conrad IV, crossed the Alps to enter on his unhappy alluring inheritance in the south. As he prepared to march on Rome after the hard-fought capitulation of Naples, he died of an attack of fever on 21 May 1254, only twenty-six years old.

Italy had led him to his fate as it had led so many Germans of his time. Twelve years later his half-brother Manfred, as King of the Two Sicilies, was to fall in battle against Charles of Anjou at Benevento, and in 1268 Charles, the Pope's condottiere, had the last crowned Hohenstaufen, Conrad IV's young son, Conradin, executed in Naples.

The Plantagenets

Heirs of a family holding, they left England
an island state, but their hearts
lay across the water

Kings and nobles in twelfth-century Europe delighted in hunting and the more dangerous sport of war. Among them was Geoffrey the Handsome, whose father was Count of Anjou, in the Loire valley, and of Maine, on the southern border of Normandy. Perhaps it was from planting *genesta*, or broom, as cover for his game that the high-spirited Geoffrey became known as 'Plantagenet'; or perhaps it was from sporting a sprig of the bright yellow blossom in his helm, at a time when it was growing hard to distinguish leaders in battle. Identification would soon be made easier by heraldry, the use of devices on shields, of which our earliest example is provided by Geoffrey himself. In June 1128, aged nearly fifteen, he married Matilda, the only surviving child of Henry I, King of England and Duke of Normandy. A few days before, Henry had knighted the boy and hung from his neck a shield adorned with golden lions. Geoffrey holds just such a shield on an enamel plaque from his tomb, now removed from the cathedral to the museum at Le Mans.

For fourteen reigns and over three hundred years, from 1154 until the accession of Henry Tudor in 1485, England's throne was held by descendants of Geoffrey and Matilda in the male line. Historians often call the first of these kings Angevins, after Geoffrey's country; from 1399 the Crown was disputed between heirs of younger sons, heading the rival Houses of Lancaster and York. In their own day, the earlier kings were often known by personal nicknames and the later ones by their birthplace. All, however, were of the same

family, as the Yorkists recognized when they took Plantagenet as a surname, a generation before their displacement by the Tudors. Heraldry proclaimed the continuity. The lions on Geoffrey's tomb reappeared on a seal of his grandson Prince John. From John's time until our own three lions *passant guardant*, which French heralds called leopards, have remained on the royal arms as the lions of England.

The marriage of 1128 was no love-match. It was a diplomatic move by two unscrupulous feudal houses, which had done well out of the anarchy attending the break-up of the old Frankish Empire and the birth of the Middle Ages. Normans and Angevins were bad neighbours with a common fear of the French king, whose power was growing to the east, around Paris and the Ile-de-France. Matilda had a man's ambition and was in many ways a worthy granddaughter of William the Bastard, the Norman Duke who had conquered England. She was also her own worst enemy, lacking the tact and common sense of the Conqueror or of her father Henry. As the King's heir and a widowed Empress (she had spent most of her youth in Germany, the only land where she was popular), she despised a bridegroom who was ten years her junior and the son of a mere count.

Matilda soon had little cause to look down on Geoffrey, for his father left on crusade to become King of Jerusalem. She need never have doubted the Angevins' spirit. More than any family, they were famous for going to extremes, whether for good or evil. For two hundred years the counts had enriched themselves at the expense of those around, lording it along the Loire and often defying both king and Church. Some of Geoffrey's ancestors had been

The White Tower, the keep of the Tower of London. It was built by William the Conqueror, from whom the Plantagenets were descended in the female line.

remarkably literate, a few had been devout, many had been cruel and impious, all had burned with energy. His grandfather was Fulk Réchin (the Quarrelsome), a drunken debauchee, five times married. His great-grandfather was Fulk Nerra (the Black), notorious for sudden crimes and repentances, who had forced a rebellious son to seek pardon burdened and on all fours, like an animal. It was whispered that one count had brought home a strange and lovely bride, who had rarely gone to mass and always left before the consecration of the Host. When four knights had stood on her cloak to detain her, she had torn free and flown shrieking through the window, since she was none other than Melusine, Satan's daughter, who could not bear to look on the body of Christ. The Angevins were then branded as the devil's brood.

Violent rages were to afflict most of the Plantagenet kings. The sinister fairy tale of Melusine was important enough to be current in the family itself. King Richard Coeur de Lion, Geoffrey's grandson, often said that it was no wonder that sons of such stock should fight among themselves, 'For they had all come from the devil and it was to the devil that they would go'. He had found a good excuse for young Angevins to run wild, in the belief that they were only living up to their reputation. Yet it was not a fit subject for jokes, since a king's success and his people's safety demanded some self-control. So many triumphs were to be won by exceptional vigour, and thrown away through folly, that a demonic streak does seem to have been the curse of the House.

Geoffrey's strength and grace were to pass down through the Plantagenets. Like Geoffrey, many were to have striking reddish-gold hair and would, if they chose, be both charming and generous. They would relish ceremonial and, with their physique, live up to their kingly role. Their gifts would be valuable in gaining the respect of the great barons or magnates with whom they had to work, and in reassuring the people. Nature, however, could not always sustain such excessive energy. Sons, perhaps in reaction, would find entirely different outlets to those of their fathers. Many kings in themselves would prove frighteningly inconsistent: weak ones might suddenly break out, and active ones lapse into strange fits of weariness or indifference. Medieval England was to have a much more conclusive history than France, although without the repeated horrors of invasion. The upheavals would spring from royal failings, often ending in tragedy. At least the Plantagenets in their stormy career were likely to be more colourful than the patient, calculating dynasty fated to be their arch-enemy, the Capetians of France.

For all their faults, the Plantagenets were cultivated. Matilda was honoured by a literary dedication and could presumably write, since her father was nick-

named 'the Clerk' (later, more admiringly, 'Beauclerk'), whereas William the Conqueror had signed himself only with a cross. Geoffrey, who was quick-witted, took care with their children's education; his own grandfather, Fulk Réchin, may have written France's first lay history, and a tenth-century ancestor, Fulk the Good, had been credited with lute-playing, hymn-writing, and telling Louis IV of France that 'an unlettered king is a crowned ass'. Nobles tended to despise book-learning, which they left to the clergy, yet even the first Plantagenet kings could understand Latin and read fluently in French, which helped them to improve and direct the administration. Literacy led to patronage of the arts and often of luxurious novelties. Busy kings, with no time themselves for a quiet life, were to appreciate a learned Court. Unhappy ones would be the keenest patrons, whose work would survive, notably in buildings, to make up for their political failure.

The marriage of Geoffrey and Matilda began so badly that it almost proved barren. Within weeks the haughty bride had been packed off to Normandy, where her father left her for two years before fetching her home. Geoffrey then successfully reclaimed her and in 1133 their elder son Henry was born. Angevins were not popular with Normans and Matilda, because of her sex and her temper, was unwelcome as a future queen of England. On her father's death in 1135 a cousin, Stephen of Blois, stepped in and Matilda had to pursue her claim by force. She crossed to England and battled for years, with see-sawing fortunes, while her husband contented himself with ensuring that Stephen should not have Normandy as well. Geoffrey died of fever, aged only thirty-eight, after rashly plunging into a stream to cool himself. He had already presented Normandy to Henry and left him to try to win England as well.

The boy soon secured the the whole of his mother's inheritance. King Stephen lost heart after his elder son's death, acknowledged the Angevin's right to succeed him, and died a year later. Not content with England and Normandy, the new king then turned on his younger brother, and in defiance of their father's will, robbed him of Anjou and Maine. Henry thus would have held wider sway than any of his ancestors, even if he had not pulled off one of history's most brilliant diplomatic coups by marrying Eleanor of Aquitaine as soon as she was divorced by Louis VII of France. At one stroke, Poitou and the lands southwards to Gascony changed hands, depriving Louis of more than half his subjects and extending Henry's rule down the whole of the western side of France. Brittany, despite fierce local resistance, was later drawn in through the marriage of its heiress to one of Henry's sons. Wales and Ireland, their Celtic chieftains divided and overawed, were forced to admit his overlordship.

So grew up the Angevin Empire, from the damp border-hills of Scotland to the vineyards at the foot of the Pyrenees, covering more of modern France than the domains of her own king. Henry II (reigned 1154–89), the first Plantagenet to rule England, was the foremost prince in Western Christendom. None of his heirs wielded such power overseas. None could forget his example.

One man held together this sprawling Empire. Its boundaries, in the far north and on the continent, were hard to define and harder still to defend. It had, of course, no national basis, in language or law. England had been ruled by French speakers since the Norman Conquest, while France belonged to the teutonized world of customary law and the *langue d'oeil*, contrasting with most of Aquitaine, which used written Roman law and the *langue d'oc*. Such a patchwork was natural in the feudal world, which was divided among families and where society was a pyramid, with small landowners being the vassals of greater ones and the most powerful holding their estates, or fiefs, from the king. As the name Christendom implies, such unity as it enjoyed was derived from the Church, with its use of Latin and its claims on every Christian prince.

The fatal weakness of the Angevin Empire, destroying any chance for it to prosper in peace, was that it did not fit neatly into the feudal pattern. Henry II was soverign only in England. He might be the most powerful man south of the Channel, but for his lands there he was in theory a vassal of the king of France. Such a vassal, backed by English wealth and manpower, posed a deadly threat to the French royal House. There arose constant friction, which could finally have been ended only by the English kings giving up all Continental claims, or by the destruction of the French monarchy. The later Hundred Years War was but part of a long struggle which began when a Norman seized the Crown of England. Rivalry between Plantagenet and Capetian or Valois, punctuated by many hollow treaties, proved the bane of Western Europe throughout the Middle Ages.

'Now in Ireland, now in England, now in Normandy, he must fly rather than sail or ride!' exclaimed the French king, bemused by Henry II's phenomenal energy. Even Henry, who lived in a whirl, was forced to lean on those who would gain most from the Empire's continuance, his own children. A kind of family federation was set up, with Eleanor and, later, their second son Richard in charge of Aquitaine, the eldest son Henry crowned and associated with his father, the third son Geoffrey given Brittany and the youngest, John, made Lord of Ireland. It was a daring experiment, perhaps the only answer but one dependent for its success on his children's loyalty. The Empire was like some glittering piece of jewellery, whose stones rested in a weak setting. It was coveted by neighbours, and if the owners themselves could not agree it would be wrenched apart and the jewels lost.

The Plantagenets' main strength was the English Crown, weakened though it had been under Stephen. The Crown made them responsible for war and justice, under God. It entitled them to deal with the kings of France as equals and its resources made them feared in

Paris. In England the monarchy already enjoyed special prestige, which the dynasty exploited and which has never vanished. The pre-Conquest coronation ceremony, broadly the one in use today, not only bound the ruler to his people but conferred a divinely blessed authority. From that sprang the old claim to have healing powers, which was regularly publicized by touching for the King's Evil. Henry II was soon to exalt his family further by procuring the canonization of King Edward the Confessor, whose heir William the Conqueror had claimed to be. The Capetians would not be able to boast their first saint, Louis IX, for another hundred years.

William the Conqueror had taken over in England a unique local government system bolstered by regular taxes and had managed to parcel out the land among his followers while ensuring their obligations to the Crown. Henry I had strengthened royal power and Henry II's first task was to regain and extend it. Order was restored and he was soon free to press ahead, notably by ensuring that the king's justice was available to all free men. Despite resistance from the clergy, which led to a dramatic quarrel with his old friend Archbishop Thomas à Becket, Henry succeeded. The legal foundations which he laid were never broken up and for that alone the first Plantagenet king,

possibly the greatest, ranks with the Conqueror among the makers of England.

For Henry himself the work in England was merely a means to an end, since he was concerned mainly to keep a grip on his Empire and to cut a figure in Europe. He was not, after all, an Englishman, although Henry I had married a partly English princess and so transmitted to Matilda and all later rulers the blood of the old royal line, going back to the Saxons of the sixth century. Henry II was French bred, with a southern wife. The two sons who followed him were born in England and so were most of their successors, but English was not spoken at Court for another two hundred years. Plantagenets intermingled with the royal Houses of Europe, for Henry II's sons-in-law

ruled Saxony, Sicily, and Castile. No medieval king of England had a native mother before Richard II at the end of the fourteenth century and there was no English-born queen until the last years, in the 1460s.

Henry II's problems, to control and exploit England and assert himself abroad, faced all his heirs. His virtues and faults appeared again, fitfully, in their lives and his priorities in general were followed, although with varying success. It is ironical that the Plantagenets are now remembered mainly for their role in the growth of England's government and the evolution of an island State, when the hearts of so many of them lay across the water.

Thanks to sharp-eyed chroniclers, Henry II stands out more clearly than any other Plantagenet. He was coarser than most in appearance, stocky, of middle height, with reddish hair, freckles, and hard grey eyes which grew bloodshot in rage. It must have been his burning intensity which made him 'one upon whom men gazed a thousand times, yet took occasion to return'. He wore his hair short, strode about in a short cloak which earned him the nick-name 'Curtmantle', did much business standing up, relaxed chiefly when hunting, and talked and fidgeted even in church. With his thirst for facts, hard business instinct, first-class memory and shrewd judgement of character, Henry was one of the ablest men to wear a crown. His roving Court lived in pandemonium.

Equally domineering was the beautiful and hot-blooded Eleanor of Aquitaine, who eagerly made Henry's fortune after parting in contempt with the monkish King Louis. Henry's marriage was in many ways like that of his parents. At nineteen he, too, was younger than his bride but precociously in charge of affairs. Eleanor, like her new husband, was cultivated, impetuous and unable to swallow a slight. She had goaded Louis into adventures, had sailed with him on crusade, and infuriated him by her misconduct. Perhaps at first she was fond of Henry, to whom she bore eight children, but she could not forgive him for being unfaithful. The Queen retired to Poitou, a patroness of literature and courtly love, a match for the touchy nobles and, through her sons, a thorn in Henry's side. With such a woman, there was little hope of a united family.

Obstinacy and hot temper were the undoing of Henry II. In England, he nearly lost his throne after the murder of Becket, carried out by four knights who heard their master rage against the Archbishop. Soon, with his sons growing up, he could never be sure that one or another would not revolt, supported by their mother and the watchful king of France. Henry, readier to grant titles than real power, whetted their appetites and incurred their hatred. In vain did he beat down rebellions and lock up the Queen; the web of intrigue would always be woven again from Paris. As a hammer of the Church he got scant sympathy from chroniclers: Eleanor had been married to his overlord and it seemed right that the greedy father should be punished by his own brood. For a room of his palace at Winchester, the embittered old King ordered a painting of young eagles preying on their parent. With his ungrateful and short-sighted family ranged against him, he was at last forced to seek peace from France's Philip Augustus. He died at Le Mans, a classic and pitiful example of pride laid low, crying 'Shame on a conquered king!'

Richard I (reigned 1189–99), Henry's eldest surviving son, has always been a hero to the English, although he was the least English of all their kings. His mother's favourite, invested with Aquitaine when nearly fifteen, Richard Coeur de Lion belonged to the southern world of the troubadours. He was accomplished, like his parents, passionately musical and perhaps even a writer of verse. A darker side occasionally came out: on crusade he was warned by preachers against homosexual practices and showed a savage streak, unknown in his father, by butchering hostages. As a King he was neglectful, spending but six months of his reign in England and those only to extort the largest possible sums for his armies. The Crusade itself was damaged by affronts to other leaders, notably when he tore down the banner of the Duke of Austria. The wilful King had only himself to blame when shipwreck on the way home placed him in his enemies' power and England had to be bled to pay the ransom. A stupid risk finished him, when he exposed his neck to an archer while furiously besieging a petty French vassal; even then he might have lived had he not snapped off the wooden shaft and left surgeons to probe for the arrow-head in a wound which succumbed to gangrene. Richard was taken to lie beside his parents in the Angevins' abbey of Fontevrault on the Loire, where their elongated stone effigies, now restored, suggest a serenity that none of them knew in life.

How is it that Richard Coeur de Lion, who did so little for England, has eclipsed his father in popular memory? Partly, because in Richard the Plantagenet traits were magnified. Henry is famous for one angry

49

Richard II, the son of the Black Prince, with his first wife, Anne of Bohemia. He ruled in the latter part of the fourteenth century and died tragically after being deposed in favour of his cousin, Henry Bolingbroke.

outburst, which slew Becket, Richard for a headstrong life. Henry was the better man, hard but not wantonly cruel, with no famous victims murdered in his prisons. Above all, although a brave and skilful general, he preferred politics to war. Richard, on the other hand, was a born soldier. He picked the right cause, a crusade to regain Jerusalem, led his knights superbly and touched men's hearts by splendid gestures: lavishing bounty as well as blows, sweating with the troops, gambling with his life, and exchanging gifts with his Muslim opponent, Saladin. Much is forgiven in those who reach for the stars. Writers did not care that the capricious King would himself have made a fine oriental despot. His ambition was vast and his story romantic, which was all that they needed in a hero.

The gilded crusader left all his lands to his brother John (reigned 1199–1216), once painted the blackest of England's kings. The accession of a brother showed that the Crown, for all its mystique, did not yet pass by a fixed rule. Richard, although married in Cyprus, died childless; John was nearest in blood, but the twelve-year-old Arthur of Brittany, born posthumously to the middle brother Geoffrey, who had been killed in a tournament, could claim to be senior in line. John was a slippery man, who had turned against his father at the last and schemed behind Richard's back, yet in England he was readily accepted in preference to a child. Anjou and Maine chose Arthur, Paris gave him

shelter, and the Empire began to break up. Queen Eleanor, now in her eighties, continued to support her one surviving son and in 1202 John pounced on Arthur, who was besieging his grandmother. Some months later the boy was murdered, reputedly felled with a stone by the King himself.

Tales of John's viciousness, beginning with his nephew's death, soon multiplied: of an outspoken archdeacon crushed beneath a cope of lead, of miserly Jews having their teeth pulled out at the rate of one a day, of members of the noble de Braose family left to gnaw each other and starve. Much can be put down to spiteful churchmen, for John, in a dispute over offices, was excommunicated and saw England laid for years under a papal ban or interdict. Unkind names were jealously preserved. John was remembered as 'Lackland', from a paternal joke which had long since ceased to apply, or 'Softsword', from his failure to hold back the French. An odd vein of lethargy certainly helped his enemies but John made up for it in spasms and was never afraid of war. He prowled everywhere, dealing effectively with the Celts and seeing more of his island realm than any other king.

John, embodying too many contradictions, was the most original of his line. Like his father he was strong and of medium height, inquisitive, quick-tempered, impatient even in church. Like Henry, too, he was lustful and like Richard sometimes senselessly cruel. He was accused of wasting whole mornings in bed with a bride who was little more than a child, yet he could lose himself in business and took an almost morbid pleasure in judging lawsuits. He loved gambling and feasting, comfort and splendour, and wore England's earliest recorded dressing-gown. Well educated, in the family tradition, he acquired a monastic collection of books which formed the first royal library. He was in fact a fastidious and high-living man, riddled by suspicion, so mercurial that almost anything might be said about him according to his mood. What earned him such a bad name, and makes him so intriguing today, was his cynicism in an age of faith. Perhaps he could never forget that, as a small boy, he had been destined briefly for the Church.

The King's foibles and vices helped him to lose most of his Empire and to subject him to restraints in the charter of liberties known as Magna Carta. John was unlucky in living at a time when England's baronial rulers were at last being assimilated into the native stock. French remained their language but was spreading downwards to enrich English until, with intermarriage, it became hard to tell a free man's origins. Entrenched landowners grumbled at having to fight for the Plantagenets abroad, until, when Normandy was overrun, all who had a stake on both sides of the Channel were faced with a choice. The families which preferred England were bound in time to think of themselves as English and quick to resent insistent calls to arms. John himself inspired no trust. Quarrels over military service and taxes, which had dogged his father, finally forced him in 1215 to set his seal to Magna Carta.

John failed in his two main inherited tasks but was far too resourceful to admit defeat. Here he may have been right. The final loss of Normandy and Anjou, perhaps inevitable and for England's good, might have been long postponed if a new Continental alliance had beaten King Philip Augustus of France at the hot, dusty battle of Bouvines in 1214. As it was, the Plantagenets held on to part of Aquitaine, paradoxically the most distant and turbulent of their dominions. Around Bordeaux the fiery Gascons, preferring a distant English master to a close French one, kept alive the old dreams of Empire. At home, Magna Carta became a landmark as a precedent, rather than as a binding rule. Order still rested on co-operation between the king and those great lords who recognized his rights, but required him to respect their own.

In private John reacted to Magna Carta with an Angevin frenzy, gnashing his teeth, gnawing sticks like a madman and tearing material to shreds. Outwardly, he expressed content until, within a few months, mutual distrust flared up in civil war, with one party offering the Crown to the French king's son. John

spread terror as he marched to and fro, until familiar rashness cut him short. Weakened by dysentery after a feast, he dashed across the Wash, losing the regalia of England in the quicksands, only to die from gorging on peaches and new cider. His body was carried to Worcester Cathedral, where a tomb in dark Purbeck marble bears the first of England's splendid royal effigies. We have no paintings of these early Plantagenets but it seems that carvers often copied a death-mask. John's likeness was made some twenty years later and is just what we would expect of that wolfish, sardonic, enigmatic man.

The Plantagenets may have been saved by John's gluttony, for his fortunes had been ebbing. Now all his subjects could rally to his nine-year-old son, Henry III (reigned 1216–72), who was hastily crowned with a circlet. The chronicler's well-known warning against the perils of a royal minority for once proved groundless and, in what was almost an early surge of patriotism, the French were expelled and a royal minority ushered in the longest medieval reign.

The next forty years were comparatively placid, noted less for the growth of politics than for the growth of trade, for the friars and their philosophy, and for the first flowering of Gothic architecture. Then, more tension between King and magnates led to Henry's break with his masterful brother-in-law, Simon de Montfort, in the Barons' Wars, when Simon tried to broaden his support by summoning an assembly which included merchants and small landowners. It was a big step to consult such men, who made up, after nobles and clergy, the commons or third estate, although earlier kings had assured them a place in local government. Earl Simon's triumph, however, was short-lived and it was only a stream of later events that allowed Englishmen to celebrate in 1965 the seven hundredth anniversary of Parliament.

Henry III's minority and later trials, like Richard's absence and John's abuses, successfully tested the government machine. Henry himself turned out to be a mediocre King, perceptive but aimless, well served by advisers in his youth and by his son in old age. Although he headed expeditions to Gascony, he was no soldier and thus fortunate in not having to watch over too wide an Empire. By naming his elder son Edward, and choosing the Confesser as his patron saint, he flattered English traditions, yet Henry and his family remained, at heart, cosmopolitan. He advanced foreign churchmen, loved to entertain visiting potentiates, and tried to obtain the throne of Sicily for a younger son. His sister married the dazzling Emperor Frederick II ('the wonder and glory of the world') and his younger brother, Richard, earl of Cornwall, a crusader, later aspired to rule Germany after a disputed election as King of the Romans; Henry himself made a doting husband for Eleanor of Provence, whose favoured relations became dangerously unpopular. In constitution, too, he was a Plantagenet: well-built, handsome, although with a drooping eyelid, inquisitive and touchy. He could never be taken for granted, had a high and rather plaintive sense of what was his due, and brought much trouble on himself by thoughtlessness. Simon de Montfort was among those maddened by the King's sharp tongue.

Henry's tastes are known in unusual detail, from the records of his expenses. Too self-indulgent to be a truly good man, he was at least devout, unlike his father and grandfather. He also grew up fascinated by the arts, on which he lavished time which his forebears would have given to wilder amusements or statecraft. Henry was happiest at courtly banquets, worshipping in beautiful surroundings, and fussing over ornaments or the details of his palaces. To his care we owe the rebuilt chancel and eastern nave of Westminster Abbey, most French of England's Gothic churches, a monastic building which survived the Reformation because it came to be the shrine of royalty. Perhaps, as an onlooker complained, the querulous and free-spending King was too keen on displaying his humility before God. He was at least an affectionate, sensitive man, the first Plantagenet King to be a true connoisseur, and the first to bask in domestic bliss. Squabbles with his more dashing brother were always made up and the strong-willed heir, no doubt exasperated by such an amateur ruler, was fond of him – a political blessing, after the earlier family feuds. Considering the temptations of power, Henry pottered through life remarkably untouched. It would be hard to grudge him the delicately idealized face of gilded bronze on his Westminster tomb.

With Edward I (reigned 1272–1307), 'the best lance in the world', the Crown again took the centre of the stage. Edward, an athlete and soldier who had crushed de Montfort, was returning from crusade at the time of his accession. It was a sign of the monarchy's strength that he did not need to hurry back and that his reign was reckoned from the moment of the old King's death, as has since been the case, rather than from his own coronation: inheritance was virtually automatic. Although already a troubadours' hero, like Richard Coeur de Lion, but Edward was no giddy adventurer. He was a businessman, an administrator, and a lawgiver, who liked to tidy things up. The great statutes in which he codified rights and customs made his reign seem a watershed, when feudal power gave way to a new regime, founded on royal prerogative. In France he held his own and in Wales he lanced a long-festering wound by killing the last native prince, building the huge castles which overawe us today, and starting the practice whereby the English monarch's eldest son is Prince of Wales. Scotland was placed under a new vassal king and might have stayed quiet, if Edward's grasp had not been so rough. The flattering nicknames which he earned, 'the English Justinian' and 'the Hammer of the Scots', are now questioned. The laws were not so revolutionary as they once seemed and Scotland was ablaze at his death. He was, in spite of all, a King who left his mark, vying with Henry II as the most effective of his House.

The career of Edward I has overshadowed the man. We know that he towered head and shoulders above a crowd, being called Longshanks, that he had a good reach for sword-play and muscular legs for riding, and that hunting was his joy. He was a strong if conventional Christian, father of one bastard but devoted to his first Queen, rather old-fashioned in his zest for crusades and chivalrous ideas, deliberately inspiring a cult of King Arthur and the knights of the Round Table. 'The best lance in the world' meant that he was more than just a good fighter; he must have embodied knightly virtues, as elusive as those of the later English 'gentleman', but combining a vaulting ambition with a generous heart. Edward mixed the old Plantagenet spirit with some of his father's piety, a good recipe for success. Energy, however, implied a smouldering temper. The king, once so beside himself that he hurled jewellery into the fire, grew more stubborn and wrathful with age. Stung by defiance, he spent his dying months in efforts to reach the Scots and never gave up, ordering that his bones be carried with the avenging army. Amid the gilded decorations of his family's tombs, he was buried under an almost ostentatiously stark marble slab.

The death of Edward I came almost half-way through the age of the Plantagenet kings. They had held on to a corner of France and weathered many storms in England. Five reigns had spanned one hundred and fifty years, Richard alone had met a violent (and accidental) death, and the line had not been broken. It was a fair record to set beside that of the foxy Capetians in France, where son had succeeded father since the tenth century, but it turned out to be the high-water mark. Nine Plantagenets were to follow, of whom four would be murdered and one, the last, cut down in battle. Their throne was to be shaken ever more violently, until in the fifteenth century its misfortunes would have no parallel. Meanwhile across the Channel, the House of Capet was followed in 1382 by the House of Valois, and every king, despite defeats by English arms, was to die in bed.

Some of the blame for the Plantagenets' tragedy lies with Edward II (reigned 1307–27), known from his Welsh birthplace as Edward of Carnarvon. He is remembered for his humiliation by Robert the Bruce at the battle of Bannockburn, a turning-point in Scotland's fight for independence, and for the blind favouritism which led to his overthrow. Like John, he was seen at the time to be an unworthy king, although Edward's faults were negative. Probably the masterful lawgiver, who was not an understanding parent, had much to answer for.

Outwardly Edward II had his family's regal gifts, for he grew up strong, affable and falsely popular while still in his father's shadow. His Gascon favourite Piers Gaveston, however, had to be sent away and from the moment that the new King brought him back, before marrying the French Princess Isabella, it was clear that

The triumph of the Plantagenets: the marriage of Henry V to Catherine of Valois. By the Treaty of Troyes, Henry became Regent of France and at the death of the French King, the Crown would pass to him and his heirs.

the care of England would take second place to private whims. Gaveston, who strutted in a glittering role at the coronation and was even rumoured to have had his pick of the royal wedding presents, poked fun at the nobles who thought themselves the Crown's natural advisers. Eventually the bumptious foreigner was brought down by a clique, the Lords Ordainers, led by the King's own cousin Thomas of Lancaster. Edward was lazy, as a bishop complained to Rome, and had no heart for war. Careless in guarding against the Scots and with his reputation destroyed by Bruce, he could only wait until strengthened by a middle party. Even then he learned no lesson, for he was lonely, vulnerable and without judgement. New favourites, father and son, both called Hugh Despenser, heaped up riches after Lancaster in his turn had fallen.

There is no proof that Edward II, for all the later gibes, was homosexual. His attraction to Gaveston may have been that of a slow, affectionate, uncertain man for one who brilliantly mocked the world. After Bannockburn a royal messenger was arrested for sneering that it was no use expecting victories from a king who wasted his time in 'digging, making ditches and other indecencies', perhaps a reference only to menial tastes. The gossiping messenger had touched on his master's true weakness, that he shrank from his

own class. Many more recent monarchs have sought relief in simple hobbies: Louis XVI tinkered with clocks at Versailles and the homely George III was good-naturedly called 'Farmer George'. In the fourteenth century a king took risks if he so blatantly stepped outside his role. Nothing made plainer the value of regal behaviour than the fate of the misfit, Edward II.

Edward's fall made a lurid tale, exploited to the full by the Tudor playwright, Christopher Marlowe. The slighted Queen withdrew, ostensibly to mediate with her brother, Charles IV the King of France, and became the mistress of Edward's enemy Roger Mortimer, one of the few prisoners to escape from the Tower of London. After Isabella had secured her elder son Edward, she felt free to denounce the favourites and in the autumn of 1326 she landed to find England at her feet. The melting away of royal support was followed by lynchings, the hunting down of Edward and the Despensers, and a bloody vengeance by 'the she-wolf of France'. A kind of Parliament met in the name of the King and declared him unfit to reign. Edward himself was locked up well away from London. With the medieval sense of theatre, he was dressed in black to be thrust, almost swooning, in front of a deputation which bullied him into submission with the news that his whole family might be swept aside. Too robust to waste away, he was murdered a few months later in a dungeon at Berkeley Castle. Peasants' tales of screams in the night and the absence of any mark on his body gave rise to the story that he died from a red-hot poker. Isabella cynically ordered a splendid funeral at Gloucester Abbey, now the Cathedral. There Edward lies carved in alabaster, with a mournful and puzzled face, amid rich carvings which recall the splendour of which he was stripped.

The revolution of 1326–7 saw England's first rejection of an anointed king. It reflects no credit on anyone: on Edward's shiftless friends, on the foresworn nobility, on the callous Queen and her lover, or the complaisant son. In 1330, when nearly eighteen, Edward III seized power for himself, sending his mother to the country and spurning her pleas to spare Mortimer, but he took only feeble steps against his father's actual killers. There was a bright side for the Plantagenets. Their line continued, the very regality of Edward II had made him too dangerous to be allowed to live (for there had been two rescue attempts), and miracles were reported at his tomb. Yet the divinity which hedged a king had been broken once and would be so again.

For a time Edward III (reigned 1327–77), whose reign began in such squalor, raised his House and England to new heights of glory. In the right of his mother, whose brothers had died childless, the young King refused to accept the junior Capetian line, the Valois, and went far beyond his ancestors to claim

A contemporary portrait of Henry V. By his victory at Agincourt and the Treaty of Troyes, he fulfilled the traditional dreams and Continental ambitions of the Plantagenets, but his success was short-lived.

France itself. The ensuing Hundred Years War opened with unexpected triumphs, for England's resources were one-third of those of France, and rallied popular support. The most stirring victories were at Crécy and Poitiers, gained largely by English archers, and many fortunes were made from plunder. Terrible slaughter in the mud at Poitiers ended in the capture of the French King and, while not bringing his Crown, won the Plantagenets an enlarged Aquitaine, for the first time as a sovereign state. Despite heavy taxes and the ravages of the Black Death, it was only in Edward's old age, with the French nibbling away his conquests, that lustre dimmed and peace was threatened at home.

The secret of Edward III's success was that he lived up to his nobles' ideal. They were glad to follow a monarch so showy, extravagant, and daring. It mattered little that in England everything was sacrificed for the war, or that in France thousands died who by birth could not expect chivalrous treatment. The most famous story of Edward's anger, when he swore to hang six townsmen after the stubborn resistance of Calais, could do no harm to his reputation. He turned his own gallantry to advantage: at a ball to mark the town's capture, he picked up a blue garter dropped by a Court beauty, silencing sniggerers with the words 'Honi soit qui mal y pense', which form the motto of his knightly brotherhood of the Garter. Edward knew how to dazzle Europe by founding what is still the oldest and most exclusive order of chivalry, by his courtesy to high-born (and valuable) prisoners of war, by reconstructing Windsor Castle, where the Garter feasts are kept, and by cultivating a new saint whose scarlet cross became the national emblem, St George.

Edward's eldest son and namesake, called from his armour the Black Prince, closely resembled his father. The victor of Poitiers and, even in French eyes, 'the flower of chivalry', he was brave, athletic, polished and notoriously prodigal. The Prince also had a violent will and, when sick, could not bear to be thwarted; after the city of Limoges had changed sides he was carried in a litter to its siege, which ended in the slaughter of every man, woman and child.

The Black Prince's brothers, although poorer soldiers, also lived on a grand scale. John of Gaunt, Duke of Lancaster, the third son, married a Castilian princess, made a vain bid for her kingdom and left daughters as queens of Castile and Portugal. The Plantagenets, so respected abroad, now were united, and to that extent deserved their good fortune.

All the family was indebted to Edward's Queen, the plump and kindly Philippa of Hainault, whose pleas saved the burghers of Calais. Without some domestic restraint her hot-blooded husband, after such a wretched youth, might have become unbalanced. Although often unfaithful he loved her for forty years and deteriorated, bodily and mentally, after her death. Like his famous forebears, Henry II and Edward I, Edward III reigned too long to die happily. He sank into dotage, a prey to corrupt courtiers, while the country groaned under heavy taxation. Factions manoeuvred and the Black Prince, racked probably by cancer, fought for life. The King followed his heir within a few months, leaving a mistress, Alice Perrers, who stole the rings from his fingers. The prince at Canterbury Cathedral was given a fine but stereotyped effigy, suitably arrayed in full armour. His father rests near the vividly portrayed Philippa at Westminster; the gilded bronze face is long-bearded, old and weary, but with noble features hinting at 'the most valiant prince of this world ... since the days of Julius Caesar or Arthur'.

Many Plantagenets had grown up to be quite different from their fathers. Physical and emotional traits had persisted, while in political capacity the pendulum had swung back and forth from John until Edward III. It then stopped for a generation, only to swing back on the accession of the Black Prince's ten-year-old son, Richard II (reigned 1377–99). Brought up in a hero's shadow, Richard himself longed for peace with France. He was no coward and in 1381 showed his grandfather's flair for the kingly gesture, when he rode out unprotected to calm an enraged mob in the Peasants' Revolt. Envying the authority of the French monarchy, it was on bringing Britain and Ireland to heel and on extravagant patronage of the arts that his heart was set. Richard's was an intelligent if self-interested policy, in advance of the Tudors'. It alarmed the magnates and offended anyone whose pride or pocket might gain from the Hundred Years war. It was ruined by arrogance, for the young king worked through favourites who were soon brought down by the jealousy of a new noble clique, the Lords Appellant. Inspired by his uncle the duke of Gloucester, the lords were merciless in their triumph. When Richard at last regained power by a coup d'état it was to exact vengeance which included Gloucester's life. Thereafter he ruled as an autocrat, a threat to all.

Richard II, resplendent and highly strung, was the most self-conscious of monarchs. His expenses were memorable and ranged from acquiring handkerchiefs and table-forks, perhaps borrowed from the refined French Court which he admired, to rebuilding the Banqueting Hall which still stands at Westminster. His is the earliest royal sign-manual. His, too, are the earliest painted likenesses: crowned and bejewelled, with auburn hair and a pale, aesthete's face, he kneels in red and gold or, as he loved to do, gazes inscrutably from his throne. It is hard to imagine what he suffered, flattered and deserted by attendants, bullied by his family, threatened with Edward II's fate, forced to let his youthful friend Robert de Vere die penniless abroad, unable to save the neck of his old tutor Sir Simon Burley, who had cradled him as a fainting boy during the coronation ceremony. Richard clung to his first Queen, Anne of Bohemia, destroying a wing of the palace where she died and assaulting an imperious noble at her funeral. Even in triumph he felt no peace. He was tall but rather frail, not made for jousting. Perhaps envy prompted his fatal mistake, when he exiled his cousin Henry Bolingbroke, John of Gaunt's son, and struck fear into every property owner by seizing the Lancastrian lands on Gaunt's death.

The rashness of Richard in his last months suggests that his mind was clouded. He lived in splendour, closely guarded by a picked corps of archers and unaware that the foundations of his power had been eaten away. Carelessly, he left for Ireland, leaving the path open for his cousin to claim the Lancastrian estates and then, inevitably, the Crown. Richard, abandoned and probably duped, surrendered in Wales and was led to London, where an assembly recited his misdeeds while rioters urged it on. The childless King was cowed into resignation and later spirited away from the Tower, disguised as a forester. There were rescue plots, as there had been in 1327, which within weeks led to Richard's mysterious death in the Yorkshire castle of Pontefract. The corpse was later moved to a tomb which had been prepared in his lifetime at Westminster, where Richard and Anne, in gilded bronze, once again held hands.

Richard II's brittle glory should not blind us to his menace, for he was more dangerous than any other ill-fated king. It could be argued that his removal was for England's long-term good, but for the Plantagenets it was suicidal. The thread had finally been cut and the throne had been taken by the heir of a third son. Edward III's second son Lionel was represented only by a daughter in 1399 but her line, united with the male descendants of a fourth son, the Duke of York, would later have an excellent claim. The usurper tried to avoid trouble by declaring that the Lancastrians' ancestor, Edmund Crouchback, had been the elder, not the younger, brother of Edward I; by invalidating all the more recent kings he would thus have degraded his family still further, if anyone had believed him. Richard's dethronement could not be excused by his ill-treatment of the Lancastrians and the murder of one of his uncles, an Appellant. In the revolution of 1399 the world's greatest playwright was to see a break with the natural, God-given order, for which crown and nobility would pay in blood for the rest of the Middle Ages. Shakespeare's historical cycle shows the dynasty on its long halting slide into the abyss. No other country could supply such dramatic material.

Henry IV (reigned 1399–1413), with a title so dubious, coveted the aura of divine majesty fostered by Richard. Holy oil, allegedly given by the Virgin Mary to Becket, was conveniently discovered for use at the sumptuous coronation. Yet, within months the new royal family was nearly trapped by rebels in Windsor Castle. French raids were followed by rebellion in Wales and the angry disappointment of the Percies – the Earl of Northumberland and his son Henry Hotspur – who had helped to put the Lancastrians on the throne. Henry IV was never free from slanders, plots and armed outbreaks. He was lucky to have no obvious rival and wise to appease the Church by persecuting its Lollard critics, the forerunners of Protestantism. He wore himself out in a reign that was no more than a holding operation.

After an adventurous youth Henry cut rather a wooden figure. He seemed much older than his cousin, although they were born only three months apart; where Richard II had revelled in the visual arts, the new King studied moral philosophy and sought solace in music. Henry sometimes betrayed his family's headstrong streak but in general he was secretive, resolute and careful. An orthodox man in every way, he would in happier times have made a prudent and conscientious ruler and he did well to come through his trials. His health gratified moralists, for Richard's shrewd and sturdy supplanter died a neurotic. Five years after the usurpation he may have suffered a stroke and later he was often prostrated, probably by mental strain. The King made a suitably pious end: he had learned that he would live until he saw Jerusalem, but collapsed at prayer and expired in one of the Abbot of Westminster's rooms, called from its decorations the Jerusalem Chamber. Even the effigy on Henry's tomb at Canterbury is conventional, although accurate in showing him heavy-featured and middle-aged. No one learned more bitterly that it can be easier to gain a crown than keep it.

Henry V (reigned 1413–22), who followed his father, was the last heroic King. For the Lancastrians his reign was a belated dawn, when the clouds parted, all the more poignant for its stormy sequel and the thought of what might have happened if he had lived. The key was the renewal of the Hundred Years War while France's internal feuds gave Henry his chance. Victory against overwhelming odds at Agincourt was followed by the relentless conquest of Normandy, denied to Edward III but now restored to the Plantagenets after two hundred years. In alliance with the Duke of Burgundy, Henry forced the mad old King of France to offer him his daughter and to disinherit his son. Soon the two crowns would be united. Henry always insisted that his was a war to end all wars and seemed about to justify that dreary and familiar claim. He had come nearer than anyone to realizing the old dynastic ambitions abroad.

Henry V deserved his fame. Edward III and his sons had been showy and slapdash. Henry was a calculating

gambler, rapid yet thorough in thought and action, almost as if he knew that time would be short. He took risks but they were those of one who fancied himself very close to God. The king's portrait reveals the taut face of a bigot, if not a fanatic, explaining a callousness which cannot simply be put down to the waning chivalry of his age. Probably he was all the sterner for being a reformed rake. As a Prince he watched Lollards burn and had one charred heretic, still unrepentant, thrust a second time into the flames. When besieging Harfleur he refused to allow passage for the old and young, driven out by the garrison, and let them die in thousands in the January cold. There was much about Henry that was striking – his manly carriage, his grim resolve, his diplomacy, his judgement – but little that was endearing. Perhaps he was lucky to succumb to dysentery near Paris when only thirty-five, while still expecting to deal French resistance the *coup de grace*. After a hero's funeral he was laid in Westminster Abbey and given an image so costly that it invited despoilment, like his newly-won Empire.

The victor of Agincourt died just before his French father-in-law, leaving Henry VI (reigned 1422–61), the only baby to reign in England, to be proclaimed also as King of France. For a time the tide flooded on under Henry V's brother John, Duke of Bedford, until it turned with Joan of Arc's raising of the siege of

Edward IV, first of the Yorkist Kings and the first Plantagenet King to have an English Queen. Edward was a remarkable King, but the Plantagenets were already hastening to their ruin.

Orléans. By now the ancient dynastic struggle was in reality a national one, where it would have taken a miraculous series of triumphs for the overstretched invaders to hold on. The effect of the Plantagenets' dreams had been to foster patriotism on both sides, as had been recognized in the growing official use of English under Edward III and the care which Henry himself took to advertise his victories. A union of the Crowns was doomed. From the 1430s the French pushed on inexorably towards the sea, until in 1453 they captured even Bordeaux, after three hundred years. Nothing was left of Henry II's Continental Empire and only a foothold at Calais reminded the English of their rulers' old obsession with Europe.

Disgrace abroad stirred unrest at home. Henry V had uncovered plots before victory made him immune, and during the long minority Bedford twice hurried back to keep the peace. Inherited glory might still have saved the family if the ablest of kings had not been followed by the most passive. Henry VI grew up strong enough in body but feeble in will, the only Plantagenet to be dominated by his Queen. As the government floundered and placemen profited, hope inevitably lay in Richard, Duke of York, as heir presumptive. The throne might have passed smoothly to the vigorous Duke, for the unhappy Lancastrians' stock had weakened; Henry's uncle all died childless and his own unpopular marriage to Margaret of Anjou appeared barren. When the King mysteriously collapsed, losing even his memory, York's hour had apparently struck. Margaret, however, bore a son and in 1455 Henry regained enough of his wits for York to have to step down.

There were now two continuing lines, mutually fearful, and England drifted into the Wars of the Roses. The Lancastrians, later symbolized by the red rose, fared worse, although Margaret fought like a tigress for her only child. At least she ensured that York, like John of Gaunt, would be only the father of a king. Duke Richard, who paraded the name Plantagenet with the white rose and the sun of York, was killed and his head was placed on the walls of his own city, mocked with a paper crown.

'The king was a natural fool and would often hold a staff in his hands with a bird on the end, playing therewith as a fool.' Such was the common gossip when Henry VI reached his twenties. Although he was not a complete simpleton no ruler can have proved more disappointing. He suffered from comparison with his father, like Edward II or Richard II, and perhaps also from a harsh upbringing yet only the tainted blood of his Valois mother can perhaps explain why the Plantagenets produced anyone so meek. Henry disapproved of his worldly courtiers, wore plain dark gowns, shuddered at dancing girls and would never fight at the head of any army. When he came of

age, fortune-hunters scrambled to catch his ear. Good-natured weakness, which paralyzed policy and drained the coffers, sprang from utter indifference to the world: a chaplain later described the King's sighs at interruptions with business of State. Henry wondered aloud why anyone should question his title, but in the end his only asset was a saintliness which made it hard to attack him personally. He was the odd man out, for other royal failures had all asserted themselves in some way. The badgered Henry found pleasure only in pious gifts and in buildings. His scholastic foundations of Eton, whose boys he warned against the vices of his own Court, and King's College, Cambridge, grew to be the most distinguished in the land.

The usurper Richard III, perhaps too harshly portrayed by Shakespeare. He was the last Plantagenet to be crowned; the rivalry of York and Lancaster had exhausted the Plantagenet line, and Richard destroyed it.

In his sufferings, as in his defects, Henry VI was alone. He became a pawn to be snatched by one party, then another, until his wife and child abandoned him for France. The only King to be crowned in both Westminster and Paris, he was the only one to linger for years in prison, after the triumphant Yorkists had run him to earth in the north. Granted a second reign, of six months he ruled like 'a crowned calf', from 1470 to 1471, and was the first king to be murdered in London, in the Tower itself. His death followed hard on the capture and killing of his own son Prince Edward, which ended the Lancastrian line. It was the first time that a father and son were removed together, but that step was inevitable once their title had been rejected by a rival branch.

Henry's fortunes were the reverse of those of York's eldest son, Edward IV (reigned 1461–83). Margaret's defeat raised Edward to the throne at the age of nineteen; Edward's quarrel with his chief supporter the Earl of Warwick ('the Kingmaker') ended in frantic flight abroad and Henry's short restoration; Edward's return brought the extinction of Warwick and the House of Lancaster. The Yorkist then reigned with no rival except the young Henry Tudor, whose descent through the Beauforts from John of Gaunt's mistress gave him a laughably weak claim. Edward IV did not need, like Henry V, to seek support by renewing the struggle with France. He might have done so to some profit, with France and Burgundy at loggerheads, and have played a traditional role. Instead he took the field but agreed to be bought off with payments that strengthened him at home and helped him to appear as a forerunner of the centralizing Tudors.

In 1461 the most austere Plantagenet had given way to the worldliest. Edward IV was Henry's exact opposite, a towering and very handsome Prince, with tastes and charm to match. Here was an inspiring leader, a hardened soldier, a clear-sighted administrator and a tough businessman, with an exceptional memory, eye for detail, and gift for subtle diplomacy. England again had a King who relished power. Beneath his graces, however, Edward was hard and coarse, a figure of brass rather than gold. An amoral, almost Italianate, streak led him to drag victims out of sanctuary and promote the use of torture. He also loved luxury and, alone of his family, endangered himself by weakness for women. An impulsive match with Elizabeth Woodville made him the first Plantagenet with an English-born Queen and, when Warwick found out, nearly cost him everything. During Henry VI's restoration, Elizabeth took refuge at Westminster, where she bore an heir, and on her husband's final victory the Woodvilles gathered around him. They had never stood so high as when the King, stricken with appendicitis or worn out by dissipation, died suddenly in 1483, aged forty-three.

Edward IV, with two sons, seemed set to give new life to his dynasty. Yet within less than thirty months of his death the last two Plantagenet reigns were over. The rapid calamity can be traced to Edward's indulgence, for the Woodvilles had lured him into fratricide by turning him against his next brother, the Duke of Clarence. Clarence was a fickle creature, who had joined Warwick in 1470, but his death left the Woodvilles to face the King's youngest brother Richard, Duke of Gloucester. Edward's unpopular marriage could be questioned on the grounds of a betrothal made in his extreme youth. His elder son was proclaimed Edward V, but within weeks Gloucester has seized the leading Woodvilles, overawed London, and cast doubts on the boy's legitimacy. An extra argument, reflecting on the old Duchess of York, was that the late King himself had been a bastard. Amidst these scandals the House of York disintegrated.

Edward V was escorted to the Tower of London in state, as befitted a king awaiting his coronation, and joined there by his brother. The ceremony itself was postponed while Gloucester settled old scores and worked on public opinion until, within a few weeks he felt it safe to assume the Crown. For a few more weeks his nephews were seen playing in the garden and then, more rarely, behind the barred windows; soon there were no more glimpses, and citizens could only shudder at what must have happened to the princes in the Tower.

Richard III (reigned 1483–5), was cast by the Tudors as the proverbial wicked uncle. Later the strained, sensitive face of the last Plantagenet King inspired romantic attempts at whitewash. Richard was not, indeed, the malevolent hunchback of Shakespeare, although less genial than his eldest brother. He had always served Edward loyally and probably had no hand in Clarence's death. Where most princes moved between the palaces and hunting lodges of the south of England, Richard won early experience and lasting popularity among the Northerners. In time he would have made an efficient, hard-working ruler.

Time was not granted, for Richard's usurpation bred such distrust that the power which he had grasped at once began to crumble. Neither victory over a premature rebellion nor the elaborate reburial of Henry VI could stop the rot. Whispers and libels circulated, prominent subjects shipped abroad, and eyes turned to the upstart Henry Tudor in Brittany. The King, after devising an elaborate early warning system with scouts and beacons, was left to wait. His vigil ended when he set out from Nottingham, the centre of his kingdom, to face Henry's much smaller force at Bosworth Field, where treachery tipped the scales. Richard might have escaped but perhaps knew that he could not afford to fly. He fought on to be killed, slung naked across a horse with a noose around

Bosworth, 22 August 1485; Richard III is holding the Crown in his hands after falling from his horse. The victor of this battle, who later married Elizabeth of York, eldest daughter of Edward IV, became King Henry VII.

his neck, and exposed for two days before burial by the Grey Friars at Leicester. No one knows where he lies; he was thrust into an unmarked grave, like his nephews, and, on the Dissolution of the Monasteries fifty years later his bones were tipped into the river.

The Plantagenets, by their rivalries, had long since prepared their own fall. It was jealousy within the Yorkist branch in its triumph, which hastened the end and Richard III who finally destroyed them. For the first and last time a blameless king was removed simply because he stood in someone else's path. The country did not demand a grown man, for it had supported three royal minorities in far worse times than 1483. Richard could easily have rid himself of the Woodvilles and ruled as Protector. In his greed he began to kill off the dynasty, only to lose his only child after a few months and have to consider his sister's son, the Earl of Lincoln, as heir.

So honoured was the blood-stained Plantagenet name that the Tudors dared not ignore it. One of Henry Tudor's first steps was to marry Elizabeth of York, Edward IV's eldest daughter, so linking the medieval line with his own and with the royal family today. There remained challenges from impostors, impersonating the dead Princes, which in time were overcome. There were also threats from Lincoln and other nobles with Plantagenet blood in the female line, who were eliminated during the next half century. One more serious danger also had to be faced: Clarence's son, debarred from the throne by his father's condemnation (which might legally be reversed), survived as the last legitimate descendant in the male line from Geoffrey the Handsome, Count of Anjou.

Few stories are more pathetic than that of Edward Plantagenet, Earl of Warwick. His mother and younger brother died when he was a baby, it was rumoured from poison, and his father when he was three. The boy's mere existence was a menace both to Richard III and Henry VII. Never free from being watched, he was finally imprisoned in the country by Richard and at the age of ten, straight after Bosworth, was shut up in the Tower. Two years later he was allowed out for one day, when Henry decided to scotch malicious gossip by sending him through the streets to hear mass at St Paul's, where several nobles were allowed to chat with him. He then returned to the Tower for another twelve years, until a rescue plot and the urgings of foreign allies made a public end

more than advisable.

On 19 November 1499, one hundred years and seven weeks after Richard II's deposition, Warwick was brought to trail in Westminster Hall. Perhaps onlookers felt that it was no loss, for the young man had been kept 'so long out of all company of men and sight of beasts ... that he could not discern a goose from a capon'. A week later he was beheaded on Tower Hill, guilty in law of having sought to escape, in fact of being by birth the rightful king.

The story of medieval England, from beginning to end, was bound up with the Plantagenets. Their kingdom, spared upheavals in modern times, has unparalleled records of their public activity, and private interests. Outwardly they were a fine regal family, as we can still see from the sad, proud faces and jewelled robes rendered in stone and alabaster, wood and metal, paint and coloured glass. Few of them were likeable individuals, for they had the Angevin spark and were self-willed, rarely content with half measures. Contemporaries, if they had known such a phrase, would have said that the Plantagents had style.

As might be expected of a dynasty which reigned for more than 300 years, it produced a wide variety of characters, national heroes and archetypal villians, soldiers and lawgivers, schemers and adventurers, tyrants and urchins, libertines, spendthrifts and one man who was almost a saint. Most important, for the course of history, were the repeated contrasts between father and son, which made England's politics a switchback, and the continental ambitions that were never abandoned.

Did England gain or lose from rulers who kept Western Europe in a ferment, as they won and lost three empires? At home they could not ignore the great nobility and found that the advanced administration which they built upon developed a strength of its own; parliament, invaluable to a wise king in tune with the country's mood, could weaken one who was out of touch. Strangely, their imperial failures later brought them credit, for they inherited England as a family holding and left it an island State. Their wars forged patriotism and allowed royal warriors to be seen as native champions. Moreover, the first sharing of responsibility with lords and commons meant that the Crown would not be left to bear the whole weight of government. However much kings might resent that fact, it helped the monarchy to endure.

The Hapsburgs

Through territorial expansion and dynastic marriages,
this House dominated European history for over
six hundred years

'When, towards the end of the thirteenth century, the first of the Hapsburgs entered Vienna, the Viennese said: "It can't last",' – so we are told by the Austrian poet Alexander Lernet Holenia, and he adds: 'And, sure enough, by 1918 it was all over.'

The period of nearly six hundred and fifty years so wittily summarized in this epigram is often thought of, even by scholars, as the correct framework enclosing the history of Hapsburg family rule. But we must go back farther and take in another three hundred years. That is, of course, on the assumption that we give no credence to the fantastic pedigrees devised by medieval genealogists, who traced the descent of the Hapsburgs from the Roman family of the Colonnas and so back to Julius Caesar, or tried, skipping the Romans, to furnish them with a Frankish-Trojan origin.

About the middle of the tenth century we hear of one Guntram 'the Rich', who, insofar as he can be identified with that Count Guntram who was punished by the Saxon Emperor Otto I (and all the evidence favours such identification), could be reckoned to be the first of the Hapsburgs. If that is so, the Hapsburgs must have stemmed from the Dukes of Alsace and Lorraine, – a theory that enables us to look on the final absorption of the Hapsburgs into the princely House of Lorraine not as extinction but as a late, almost mystic, reunion.

However, the family did not adopt the name of Hapsburg until the eleventh century. The name was taken from the castle of Habichtsburg or Habsburg ('Hawk Castle'), constructed in 1020 and situated at the confluence of the Aar and the Reuss in what is now Aargau, then on the frontiers of Burgundy. There we find the nickname 'rich' again, in Albert III, 'the Rich', Count of Zurich.

In the twelfth century the Hapsburgs distinguished themselves in support of the great Sicilian-born Hohenstaufen, Frederick II, who was Rudolf of Hapsburg's godfather. They were thus by no means poor nobility, as legend will have it. They belonged to the rich and mighty of ancient Europe; but the unique qualities that were to distinguish the family, from the time that Frederick of Zollern, in the name of the Electors of the Rhine offered the royal Crown to Rudolf of Hapsburg in the camp before Basel in 1273, had not yet manifested themselves. The personal attributes that became so characteristic of the dynasty – physical features such as the drooping underlip, brought into the family by a Polish princess; and mental qualities such as the habit of brooding, breaking off into deep melancholy; the suggestion of doubt and scepticism that made tolerable this special aura of power; the human vulnerability that grandiloquence could not conceal; the taste for outward magnificence contrasted with a personal simplicity, meanness even – all of these belong to a later date. We must picture those first Hapsburgs as vigorous, practical men who governed their territories outstandingly well, introduced modern methods of administration and understood the craft of warfare in all its details.

But it was precisely these qualities – honest, down-to-earth knowledge of life, administration and politics – which not only brought down Dante's censure on the Hapsburgs, but also induced the German princes to elect a Hapsburg as their king.

The Hohenstaufen plans for world domination had collapsed in blood and tears; the Germans had had no luck with outsiders like Richard of Cornwall or Alfonso of Castile; so it was understandable that they should now turn to a wealthy House which would

certainly not squander its strength in political fancies and unnecessary wars. Should the German princes have been suspicious when, after his coronation at Aachen, Rudolf I seemed like a man transformed? 'I am no longer the same man ye knew before,' Grillparzer makes him say. However the princes may have felt, they did not think of the conflict forced on Rudolf with King Ottokar of Bohemia, himself part-Hohenstaufen, as an 'unnecessary war', nor were they made uneasy by Rudolf's determination to convert himself from an 'insatiable warrior' to a guardian of the peace. They knew, too, that if he had avoided the war at any price, Rudolf would have been king only by the grace of Ottokar. Rudolf and Ottokar were fighting over Austria, which Ottokar, although he was married to the sister of the last of the Babenbergs, had wrongfully annexed.

At first Rudolf seemed to acquiesce in Ottokar's move – but in 1278 he assembled his army and marched on Vienna with numerically superior forces.

The Emperor Maximilian I and his wife, Mary of Burgundy, with his son Philip the Fair behind her and, in the foreground, his grandchildren. Portrait by Strigel.

Crossing the Danube, he took the Bohemians by surprise before they had time to regroup or to stage a counter-attack, and Ottokar was killed by the mercenaries. The battle of the Marchfeld was one of the decisive battles of history. If Ottokar had won, he would have ended the institution of the German king as emperor of the Holy Roman Empire; the Great Interregnum – that 'fearful time without an emperor' – would have moved into a new phase; and a Slavic-Austrian-Magyar empire would have established dominion over the disunited German princes. Thus the whole of European history would have taken a different course. As it was, the old system of German liberty was retained, a number of independent areas forming a power balance, and in the course of time twenty Hapsburgs were to occupy the two seats of honour.

But the road to greatness was not to be simple or straight. Rudolf, who died in 1291 at the age of thirty-seven, had not been able to secure the German Crown for his son Albert. It went instead to Adolf of Nassau, and not until Adolf had been deposed and killed in the battle of the Knights at Göllheim – he had little to thank the Crown for – did Albert become king as Albert I. By then, Albert had strengthened his position in the east by crushing a rising in Austria, but meanwhile there had been a weakening of the Hapsburg power in Switzerland that was in time to prove irreparable. As King he pursued one great objective, described as follows by Adam Wandruszka in his definitive work on the Hapsburgs: 'Embracing the body of the Empire in a strong Hapsburg family power in the north-west and north-east, as he already had in the south-west and south-east, weakening the political power of the Electors and so creating a strong hereditary German kingdom of the Hapsburgs.' That was, of course, a radical aim, but in pursuing it even Albert would have submitted himself to a whole series of written and unwritten laws; even he was a child of the system of German liberty. But on 1 May 1308, in front of the castle of Hapsburg, Albert was murdered by his own nephew John Parricida. Schiller introduces this character into his play *William Tell* to emphasize the difference between the justifiable murder of a tyrant and murder from other motives. So clear had Hapsburg ambition become that after the death of Albert, who lacked Rudolf's charisma, no Hapsburg was able to enjoy unlimited royal power for a hundred years.

Nevertheless, during that hundred years the unshakeable conviction, that the royal Crown really belonged to the House of Hapsburg was never forgotten; every decision, every plan, every move can be seen as a step towards this goal. Among these were plans for securing new territories, for strengthening the financial position, for increasing the productive power of the land by new or improved guild laws and the granting of privileges, and the extending of Crown lands, all aimed at increasing the power base of the family. The House law of 1355 made clear the objective of the Hapsburgs: 'that the oldest of you should be like the youngest, living together in affectionate, virtuous, brotherly love'. Albert II, nicknamed both 'the Lame' and 'the Wise', was probably recalling in this law his father, Albert I's terrible end; but equally we can see taking shape in it the conception of the 'House of Austria', a phrase that stood in turn for a family, for a dynasty, for an accumulation of empires – and then again quite simply for a family.

There were, of course other less worthy, less enlightened means used to promote the continuity of the House and the advancement of its glory. For instance, under Rudolf I, a forgery was made of the great Austrian charter from which the titles 'archduke palatine' and 'arch-chief huntsman', as well as the right to the title of archduke, were derived. Such forgeries were common enough in the Middle Ages; but we still need to know why the particular forgery was made. Is it possible to attribute such a barefaced swindle to so honest and essentially straightforward a man as Rudolf I? Have historians allowed themselves to interpolate something, have members of the House added something of their own, to produce evidence which they wanted to believe in, however much they distrusted it? Have they revised the evidence to cancel out the offence, the lack of justice in the Emperor Charles IV's refusal to accept one of them into the college of Electors? An explanation of this sort is supported by the fact that the title of duke was at first only assumed by the line that occupied Carinthia, which had a definite claim to an old ducal title. It was in fact assumed by Ernest, the Iron Duke, the father of Frederick III, who finally legitimized the forged charter in the early fifteenth century and so gave it the status of Imperial law. All this is a little abstruse, but abstruse in the manner of the period, and surely no more abstruse than the frequent thefts of precious relics in the hope that their miraculous powers could be exploited for personal profit.

The chronicle of the king-less, emperor-less period of the Hapsburgs would not be complete if we forgot the game: 'Who has the longest house?', which began in those days and found expression in the Latin verse: *Bella gerant alii, tu felix Austria nube.* This verse was more applicable to advice given in the past than simply as a record of historical truth; most of such gains have to be established by war. The many single and double marriages of the fourteenth century and later times, the countless inheritances, especially those relating to the domain of The Dual Monarchy, proved a terrible problem for schoolchildren in the time of the Old Monarchy, for they were expected to remember them

Charles V, the young man who inherited the greatest Empire in the world, thanks to the far-sighted marriages of his grandfather Maximilian with the heiress of Burgundy, and his father, Philip the Fair, with the heiress of Spain. Portrait by Van Orley.

1439. The subsequent election of Frederick III as Holy Roman Emperor was no mere accident. Long before, it had been decided that the Imperial dignity should devolve upon the Hapsburgs. Thus the son of the Iron Duke Ernest and of Cimburcá of Masovia (the beautiful woman who gave the Hapsburgs the rather loose, pendulous lower lip that persisted so obstinately) reaped what others had sown. Nevertheless, he must have been very proud to know that the greatest and most glorious gift of Christendom had been entrusted to his House. He set out for Rome in 1452 – the last Hapsburg and the last Emperor to be crowned in the Eternal City.

But the glory turned out to be faded, its representative a man of scepticism, doubt and inactivity. Jakob Burckhardt has defended the Emperor nobly: 'Much of the malice directed against Frederick III is just modern national liberalism'. More recently, Edward Crankshaw has tried to excuse him on medical grounds. Only a man with exceptionally low blood pressure could have survived so many disasters and humiliations; they would have killed a more healthy man. This patient, stubborn, thoughtful Emperor had the added problem that he was faced by an opponent who drove through the land like a hurricane, who seemed to succeed in all he undertook: this was the King of Hungary, Matthias Corvinus, who drove Frederick out of his palace in Vienna in 1485. Amid jeers, the Emperor was forced to take refuge in the Tyrol, while his baggage wagons were plundered on the road.

The extraordinary thing about Frederick was that, in good times as in bad, he always seemed so typically Austrian. He showed equanimity, phlegm, scepticism in face of action which always depressed rather than cheered him, a reluctance to take violent measures which lasted so long that eventually such measures became inevitable, and a tendency to remember the defeats rather than the victories – 'Austria's banner is not victorious; my fathers suffered three defeats beneath it,' he said, referring to the battles of Morgarten, Mühldorf and Sempach. He was interested in art and literature, in minutiae, in a domestic way of life. All this greatly distressed his wife, the lovely Eleanor of Portugal, who may well have found the raw Austrian winters and the rather uncomfortable country seats hard to get used to after the bright, sea-girt palaces of Portugal.

Frederick was a mystic, always interested in the black arts and their secrets, he loved setting puzzles and giving them an ironic twist. It would certainly have pleased him to know that the world is still struggling with one of his riddles, the famous letters AEIOU! The usual solution, to which he himself subscribed, reads: *Austriae est imperare orbi universo* ('the whole world must be subject to Austria'). Was the Emperor ever

all correctly if they wanted to pass their examinations. It would perhaps have been enough merely to say that during the fourteenth century an Empire was amassed that stretched from Bohemia to the Adriatic, that an even greater one, taking in Bohemia and Hungary, was beginning to take shape and that the legality of territorial gains was established not so much by the sword as by the bed and the tomb.

The Emperor Albert II wore the Crown for no more than a year when he died fighting against the Turks in

Margaret of Austria, daughter of the Emperor Maximilian, painted by Van Orley in mourning headdress for her husband, John of Aragon, who probably died of consumption and not, as was believed, of an excess of love.

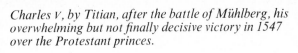

inspired by such a slogan for one single day of his life? Alphons Lhotsky, who has written a treatise on the subject, gives us eighty-six historically verified solutions and says in conclusion: 'It is very probable that he wanted to devise a magic relationship between some specific objects and his own person with the vowels – perhaps they were a protection against destruction. ... Emperor Frederick's AEIOU is thus at best an alphabetical spell or game of mystic numbers.' Feuchtmüller informs us that the five vowels first cropped up after the pilgrimage to the Holy Land; he connects them with the name of God, Jehovah, and goes on to say: 'Hence it is not surprising ... that Frederick III sealed his monuments with the cosmic sign of the coded name of God.'

We have dealt with this problem at some length because it shows how many layers there were to the secrets of this person, whose final triumph on earth was to survive.

Even as we consider this attitude, we must understand that it may have looked quite different to Frederick's contemporaries. They may well have been asking whether the great days of the House were not coming to an end. But with the accession of Frederick's son Maximilian I in 1486, everything was changed at a stroke. There was to be no more 'breaking of the ranks', all his dominions were united under his hand, and his marriage to the Burgundian Princess, Mary, re-established links with the main cultural and political developments of the West. A greater contrast cannot be conceived than that between Frederick and his son Maximilian. Maximilian, moreover, was a new name, after all the Hapsburg and Babenberg names in the family. It was suggested by the Hungarian-Croatian nobleman Nicholas of Ujlak in memory of Maximilian of Cilli, and intended as a reminder of the problem of the Turkish campaign.

Maximilian had a dynamic personality. Can his exciting qualities, his thirst for action, his joy of living, his imagination, his charm that won all hearts at the Court of Burgundy – especially Mary's – be traced back to his Polish grandmother or to her mother, the beautiful, vital Eleanor of Portugal? Were those qualities combined in some way with what was outstanding in Rudolf I of Hapsburg and Rudolf the Founder?

Maximilian was fourteen when, at Trier, he first met his future father-in-law, Charles the Bold, Duke of Burgundy; Charles was negotiating Maximilian's marriage with Frederick III. Frederick brought the negotiations to an abrupt and inconclusive end, it is still not clear why, Charles instead turned to the war with his arch-enemy, the cold-blooded, cunning Louis XI of

France. The Duke was defeated and killed at the battle of Nancy on 5 January 1477, and his body was torn to pieces by wolves. But the engagement between Mary, his only daughter and heiress, and Maximilian miraculously survived, ruining Louis' plan to marry her to the nineteen-year-old Dauphin. Burgundy, a French fief with its capital at Dijon, an Imperial fief with its capital at Besançon, Franche-Comté, with Dôle, Flanders, Brabant and Luxemburg, ceased to be independent powers and became part of the Hapsburg dominions – a generous compensation for the loss of their possessions in Switzerland.

But with the possession of Burgundy, the Hapsburgs inherited something else, something that was to shape European history until Marie Antoinette set out on her fateful journey to Versailles: enmity with France, with the Valois and the Bourbons.

Quite apart from dynastic considerations, the conflict was absolutely inevitable. For we must bear in mind that the natural power of France was increasing, that the French King's revenues were several times greater than those of the German emperor, and that the extension of his territory looked possible only at the expense of Hapsburg lands. Equally, it was impossible for the Hapsburgs to withdraw without compromising their position. France's growing military and economic strength and the unification of its system of government meant that the German princes now found for the first time that they needed, not a weak king, but a strong one. If he were to give way in a matter affecting his own interests, that would hardly be a sign of strength, while if he gave way in a matter affecting Imperial interests, it would be a sign that he was not prepared to employ his strength in the general interest.

How the spirit of an age reacts to the accidents of history, how its evolution is dominated by great figures, has been a perennial theme for historians and philosophers. If the main lines of development for a given period are examined, it is fascinating to see, as it were, what made the wheels go round, what factors helped to bring about changes and how those factors became outworn, until what had seemed humane suddenly became inhuman.

Let us look at this in detail. We have already mentioned that Maximilian married Mary of Burgundy. They were a handsome couple, which meant that prudent State policies could be carried out in a humane way; no wonder Mary never even considered exchanging the fine, attractive Prince for the nineteen-year-old Dauphin. She bore her husband two children, Philip and Margaret, and then she met with a hunting accident near Bruges and died at the age of twenty-five.

The King of France, hoping to make up in the next generation for what had escaped him in this, abducted

Margaret, then only four years old, and married her to the Dauphin. When, shortly afterwards, the Dauphin became king as Charles VIII, he had her brought up as Queen in the rather gloomy castle of Amboise. Meanwhile Maximilian had become betrothed to Anne of Brittany, who was still a minor; the French Court looked on this engagement with suspicion, if not actually with alarm, Anne of Beaujeu, the King's elder sister and Regent, sent her brother to Rennes to bring the thirteen-year-old Anne under her control. Although Maximilian tried to go to the aid of his bride, the German princes would provide neither money nor troops for this task of chivalry. Anne was lost, and Brittany with her.

It was particularly offensive that Charles VIII himself should now marry Anne although he was in theory already married to Margaret, still waiting for him at Amboise – Margaret, the daughter of Maximilian whose bride he had just kidnapped. But the Pope did

not indict the French King for bigamy, and somehow or other the affair was sorted out. Not that the French would have given up Margaret at that time; the young girl, who felt proud of being a Hapsburg, was too valuable a pledge. But after endless negotiations, she was finally freed and married, again in her absence, to John of Aragon. The ship carrying her to her bridegroom ran into a storm, and she composed an elegant couplet:

> *Ci-gît Margot, la gente demoiselle,*
> *Qui eût deux maris, et qui mourut pucelle.*

(Here lies the gentle maid Margaret; she had two husbands, yet died a virgin.)

But the sad lot that she mourned in her verse was soon remedied, for, once again, love followed in the wake of policy and the two young people fell deeply in love with one another. So strong and sympathetic indeed was their mutual attraction that the Queen was advised to

exercise moderation, which she refused to do with the words: 'Whom God hath joined together let no man put asunder.' But only a few months later the Infante was dead. We know now that he must have suffered from consumption, and that in one phase of this disease a heightened erotic urge is not uncommon; he certainly did not die of an excess of love, which in any case would have been checked by nature.

The young Prince's end made a deep and lasting impression on the Hapsburg family. The serene religiosity and unburdened sensuality of the earlier rulers now turned to a mood of gloom and repression. In his carefree days, Maximilian had declared: 'I have paid court to ladies and reaped great pleasure from it, I have laughed long and heartily'; but now there was a puritanical uneasiness abroad. We have letters in which young princes are warned by their fathers against the joys of sex and enjoined to be moderate. Here, in fact, is the origin of that asceticism in personal conduct that contrasts so oddly with outward display, and which can be traced from Charles v to Francis Joseph. Of course, this new feeling was all part of the universal change of attitude that was taking place. The advent of syphilis in Europe, the terrible first appearance of which was recorded by Ulrich von Hutten, further reinforced the anxiety and fear of sex that fed the fanaticism of the Thirty Years War. But in the Hapsburg family this reaction had its own special origin.

Let us return to marriage plans and prospects. Maximilian, a widower so early, now had to find a wife who would increase the glory and the greatness of his House. Maximilian's choice was controversial; he picked Bianca Maria, the daughter of the Duke of Milan. Her grandfather, a rustic condottiere, had dispossessed the Viscontis, and there was a touch of the *parvenu* about the family. All the same, they were *parvenus* of taste. Leonardo da Vinci was entrusted with the task of the artistic organization for the wedding, which was to take place by proxy in Milan. This marriage was solidly based upon *parvenu* wealth; Bianca Maria brought 300,000 ducats in gold with her, while mule-loads of gold, silver, jewels and cloth came over the Brenner Pass.

The Emperor's two wives are potrayed together on the relief in the Golden Dome at Innsbruck. The inscription fails to mention that Maximilian had a double connexion with Spain: Margaret had married John, but in addition, her brother Philip had married Joanna. John and Joanna were both children of Ferdinand and Isabella, known as the 'Catholic' Kings because Aragon and Castile were united under them. Joanna has passed into European history as 'Joan the Mad'. A portrait of her as a child shows a serious, reserved, not unbeautiful girl, her features bespeak a certain stubbornness which later turned to obsession and finally to madness. And Margaret? Naturally, after John's death she had a role to play again in the Hapsburg marriage policies, and she was betrothed to Philibert of Savoy. This was another happy marriage, but Philibert, too, died after a few years.

The exaggerated subtlety of the policy of dynastic marriages, the travesty of normal human relationships that it involved, is illustrated by the Hapsburgs' negotiations with Hungary. Maximilian had signed a treaty with King Ladislas ii of Hungary, whereby the countries of St Stephen's Crown should fall to the Hapsburgs if there was no male heir. But this treaty did not suffice by itself; it had first to be confirmed by altar, table and bed. First, the Emperor gave his grand-daughter Mary as bride to an unborn child. Fortunately it turned out to be a boy, the Crown Prince Louis. Although his mother died in childbirth, Louis was kept alive by being plunged into the bodies of animals freshly killed and cut open. But this was still

not enough, and a double marriage contract was drafted: Louis with Mary, as already arranged, and his sister Anna with one of the Emperor's grandsons, Charles or Ferdinand. Charles, however, was already engaged, and Ferdinand could not leave Spain, where he was being brought up as heir to the throne, so finally the Emperor himself had to step into the breach. Nearly sixty years old, he knelt in St Stephen's Cathedral beside the little Hungarian Princess whom he wanted to marry in case his grandson Ferdinand refused. Beside them, Mary and Louis, aged nine, exchanged rings. In the end Ferdinand did not refuse, so the old man did not have to take the little girls to the marriage bed.

Adult, rational, strong-minded persons, however, who knew their own value, were quite prepared to protest. Margaret, the widow of John of Aragon and of Philibert of Savoy, was drawn once again into the marriage projects of the Hapburgs, but she firmly refused, explaining that she would rather serve the House by bringing up the Emperor's two grandsons, Charles and Ferdinand in her house at Malines. This was very much the house of the future, for Charles and Ferdinand were both to wear the Imperial Crown, while future queens of Denmark, Portugal and Hungary also grew up here. Even Maximilian himself, who in his latter years aspired to the Papal Crown and already signed himself as 'future Pope', had become aware of the unworthiness of excessive entanglement in wordly affairs, whether or not they involved marriage. He wrote to his daughter Margaret: 'Since for various reasons, We do not find it good to marry, We have determined never again to lie beside a naked woman.'

Let us summarize again the genealogy on which so much in this century depended. The Emperor Frederick iii and Eleanor of Portugal had as their son Maximilian. Maximilian married Mary of Burgundy; their son was Philip the Fair, who married Joanna and brought in the Spanish inheritance. Philip and Joanna had two sons, the future Charles v and Ferdinand i, Charles again being married to a Portuguese Princess.

Charles v's reign saw the Hapsburgs at the zenith of their power. This is the Emperor whose personality is remembered with nostalgia, the Emperor to whom countless studies, and books were dedicated. The strength of his Imperial vision, and his readiness to make any sacrifice whatsoever for his vast Empire, are qualities that still move us today. At his Court the great figurative painters flourished, as attested by portraits of the Emperor by Holbein the Younger and by Titian.

What we now find so remarkable is that Charles v who handed over Castile, Aragon and Sicily in 1556, and two years later resigned the Imperial Crown, relinquished power not as a broken man but as one who recognized that there was no solution to the task

Philip II with his second wife, Mary Tudor, Queen of England. Philip later married Elizabeth, the daughter of Henry II of France, and finally his niece, Anna Maria of Austria, daughter of Maximilian II.

The battle of Lepanto between the Turkish and Christian fleets, 7 October 1571. The Christians were led by a Hapsburg, Don John of Austria, the natural son of Charles V and half-brother of Philip II.

before him. That task, in short, comprised three things: first, the maintenance of Christian unity through the strong rule of the House of Hapsburg; second, the defence of the Empire against the threat posed by the growing power of the French King, Francis I; and third, the securing of the West against the Turks, who were probing the defensive capacity of the Christian princes by land and sea. Charles's tragedy lay in the fact that he achieved spectacular successes in all three fields, but that those successes had little permanent effect on the problems he found himself having to solve.

As a beginning, the Imperial troops defeated the French at Pavia in 1525; Francis I was captured and taken to Madrid, where he was held for eight months.

Two years later the army of Pavia, led by the Constable of Bourbon, a cousin of Francis I, marched on Rome, occupied the city in the name of the Emperor and plundered it in the famous 'Sack of Rome'. Although this was the work of mutinous mercenaries, it still put the Pope in the Emperor's power. Charles was duly crowned by him at Bologna in 1530. But the Emperor failed to use this opportunity to heal the religious split in Germany.

Two years later, a fresh onslaught by the Turks brought them as far as Vienna before Charles came to his brother Ferdinand's help with an international body of troops and drove the invaders back. The treaty that followed, whereby Ferdinand demanded a tribute of 30,000 ducats from the Sultan, brought no lasting peace. For combined operations on the North African coast, at Goletta and Algiers, the Emperor sacrificed Württemberg, which could have decisively strengthened and expanded his power in Germany.

But in 1547 the Emperor won a complete victory over the Protestant princes united in the League of Schmalkalden, a victory entirely due to his own efforts. He had relentlessly pursued the army to the Elbe, encouraged his troops, and made his own reconnaissance, discovering the fort from which it would be possible for his horsemen to gain the opposite bank. He convinced his comrades of the certainty of victory, including the hesitant war expert, the Duke of Alba. But did it profit the Emperor that most of his enemies were now in his hands? He treated them formally, with a wounding harshness. He cut short the Elector of Saxony's address at the words: 'Most gracious Lord and Emperor'; he kept the Landgrave of Hesse in uncomfortable captivity; he read out in French a rebuke to the Count Palatine, without even looking at him, and when the humiliated man bent his knee, he did not help him up or even offer him his hand. The Duke of Württemberg fared no better; when the old man, crippled with arthritis, could no longer kneel properly, his councillors had to read their apologies on their knees.

Despite all this he scarcely changed the German situation: the historic princedoms were retained, the Count Palatine was raised to the dignity of Elector, the Electorate of Saxony got a new ruler, Maurice of Saxony, and the imprisonment of the Landgrave of Hesse was not too prolonged. When Maurice of Saxony became Elector, just to show that he was motivated by the functions and dignity of a prince and not by personal considerations, he behaved in a thoroughly Elector-like way, in accordance with the interests of that class: he changed sides. Making common cause with the colleagues he had just been fighting against in the spring of 1552, Maurice marched his forces against Innsbruck, where the Emperor Charles V, King of Spain, Sicily, Naples and Jerusalem, King of the Balearic Islands, the Canaries and the Indies and of the Continent beyond the ocean, Archduke of Austria, Duke of Burgundy and Brabant, Styria, Carinthia and Carniola, Luxemburg, Limburg, Athens and Patras, Count of Hapsburg, Flanders and the Tyrol, Count Palatine of Burgundy, Hainault, Pfirt and Rousillon, Landgrave in Alsace, Count in Swabia, Lord in Asia and Africa, was quite helpless in spite of all his titles, having no army to protect him. He had to make a hurried retreat south across the Brenner, while Maurice, just to show he was in earnest, ordered the storming of the Ehrenburger Monastery. He had no intention, of course, of seizing the Anointed ('I have no cage for such a bird'); instead, he opened negotiations with the Emperor, about betraying his brother Ferdinand, with whom he had never broken off relations. All, as we have said, typical Elector's behaviour.

Thus, Charles V's failures lay primarily in the difficulty of co-ordinating his victories with his policies. Francis I got away from him after Pavia and could not then be prevented from breaking the promises he had given, and setting up a French-Turkish alliance against Spain and the Empire. After his victory over the Pope, Charles failed to bring about a reform of the Church. A reform of the Empire, to include the institution of a common foreign policy and a modern taxation system in place of the 'federal assessment' (*Bundesumlage*), was indeed begun after Mühldorf, but the methods he employed were the old methods of persuasion; the conqueror's power seemed to be ineffectual.

The Emperor's policy had proved successful only when he was in a position, if not to prevent the religious divisions in Germany, at least to moderate the two sides so as to defuse them politically. Moves were made in that direction. The Emperor was much more of a reformer than a counter-reformer. He and his advisers were influenced by Erasmus of Rotterdam, and the Emperor had allowed secret hints to reach the Protestants that he had for long acted according to

Two of Pompeo Leoni's sculptures for Philip II's cenotaph at the Escorial, showing his first wife, Mary of Portugal, and his son Don Carlos, who was imprisoned and perhaps put to death by his father.

Erasmus's dictum: 'One must bear the Lutherans as a plague of the age ... heresy must be cured like a sickness.'

The Schmalkaldic League, however, was not merely a band of rebels; the Council of the League met openly, the League remained loyal to the Turks and to the French and ambassadors were sent to the Emperor to discuss outstanding grievances with him. But when reform of the Church still failed to materialize, religious and political emotions became entangled. The Protestants were afraid that the growing power of the Emperor could be used to coerce them in religious matters, and worked out ways to defend themselves. The Emperor, on learning of this, determined again that the religious community should be excluded altogether from politics – not even the Pope was excepted from this religious-political dialectic. When Charles began to succeed in the conflict against the Schmalkaldic League, the Pope recalled the forces he had sent in support. From the action we can only conclude that he would rather have seen schism than an all-powerful Emperor in Germany. Charles v expressed himself fairly forcibly on the subject of the wearer of the Triple Crown, saying, ambiguously, that, 'young people could be forgiven the French sickness but that it was intolerable in old greybeards'.

And there was something else. The new movements, the new forces that were arising in Europe were far from sympathetic towards the establishment and elaboration of a world monarchy. Friedrich Heer observes about Charles v's ancestor: 'The empire of Frederick I rests like a monstrous fossil, an ancient block hewn from the Carolingian-Ottonian past, amid the currents, the manifold play of forces in a world already grown quite different.' And in his treatise on German history, Hubertus, Prince of Löwenstein, declares: 'When the Emperor hurried home from Spain to be crowned king of the world at Aachen, the sun of unity had already sunk in the evening sky.'

For a long time Charles v had been discussing with his brother a partition of the Hapsburg possessions, no longer governable by a single man. Charles still spoke of 'our House' but Ferdinand already of 'our Houses'. The first treaty of partition was signed in Worms in 1555, but only a year later, in Brussels, they reached another agreement more favourable to Ferdinand.

Ferdinand received the old Hapsburg possessions from Alsace to Hungary, while Charles kept the Burgundian inheritance together with the Spanish Empires and the Italian princedoms. This solution made Ferdinand stronger and enabled him to put forward cogent arguments for his claims to Bohemia and Hungary. 'This Brussels treaty of 1556,' writes Adam Wandruszka, 'is of the greatest significance for the history of the Hapsburgs, and of Europe ... it was already decided in it that the entire house of Hapsburg

*The Emperor Rudolf II taking the waters. In 1607 he
was deposed as head of the family, because of his
mental state, and succeeded by his brother Matthias.
He was a lover of the arts and of science, including
alchemy and astrology.*

... should be divided into a Spanish and a German line
and not into a Burgundian and a Hungarian, which
would presumably have been the final result if the first
partition treaty agreed on at Worms had been
effected.'

It must be asked how could the Hapsburgs rule
justly and effectively in domains carved out, reason-
ably enough indeed from the dynastic point of view,
but with no consideration at all for the countries'
inhabitants, their customs, traditions and historical
memories? The dynasty had never really been fully
identified with the countries over which it now ruled.
Yet it displayed an extraordinary talent for adapting
itself to national customs, for making national saints
its own, much as the Romans had adopted the gods of
foreign peoples in their temples, and for joining in the
pleasures and feasts of the people. The Hapsburgs were
greatly helped in this by a remarkable gift for
languages. Just as Charles V started with Flemish,
French and, of course, Latin, then later learned

Spanish and finally German, so Maxmilian II is
credited with a knowledge not only of Latin, German
and the Romance languages but also of Czech and
Hungarian. A gift for the cultivation and study of
languages has persisted to this day; the present head of
the House – his passport describes him drily as Dr Otto
Hapsburg, since the republic is embarrassed by fancy
names – can converse idiomatically with all the
inhabitants of the former monarchy. But Count
Berchtold, Minister of Foreign Affairs at the outbreak
of the First World War, used to say that the Empress
Elizabeth would talk to him only in Hungarian, since
from the national political standpoint he belonged to
that part of the Empire.

There is one exception to the statement that the
dynasty did not fully identify with any nation. The
later Spanish Hapsburgs were very strongly imprinted
with their national character. This was not the case
with Philip II, Charles V's son. He was the most
influential and powerful prince of his time in Europe

The famous Las Meninas *by Velasquez. In the centre is
the Infanta Margaret Teresa, sister of Charles II, last
of the Spanish Hapsburgs; she later married her uncle,
the Emperor Leopold I.*

and, like Frederick III, in a reign that lasted almost until
the turn of the century, he outlived nearly all his friends
and enemies. Among these were Emperor Ferdinand I,
who died in 1564, and his son, Maximilian II, who
departed this life in 1576. Spain was ahead of other
European countries in acquiring the framework of a
national State, with strong central government. With
the tremendous resources of the American colonies
continually flowing, the country enjoyed great
strength in Europe. Everywhere Spanish arms,
Spanish diplomacy, Spanish money were active, and
behind this activity there always stood the King,
Philip II.

It is not easy to judge fairly this man, honoured by
some as a saint, abused by others as a monster, yet
treated with respect by Schiller in *Don Carlos*. There
were, moreover, secrets in his life that have never been
explained. Did his miserable son die in prison 'of his
own excesses' or did his father have him done away
with? Philip lacked nothing in majesty, in dignity, and

possessed a deep measure of piety – he would have
undergone all sorts of torture rather than miss a single
day's confession. But what did he confess, what sort of
dialogue did he have with God? Did he confess that he
killed men and laid countries waste? Did he say in his
defence that he had not yielded to his English Queen's
demand that he should burn heretics? Was he simply
submitting to the will of God when he calmly accepted
the defeat of the Armada, the Spanish fleet which was to
have landed Spanish troops in England? 'I sent my
ships out against men, not against water and winds.'

It has been said that he continued the development
of the style of life and government fashioned by
Charles V, and so high was the Spanish Court's
reputation that the Emperor Maximilian II sent to him
his two sons, Rudolf and Ernest, as bright young men
are nowadays sent to the country's best universities.
But when the two Archdukes came back it was evident
that the two Courts had grown apart, that the Spanish
life style did not suit the Austrians; a lot of trouble

arose from the attempt to impose this style, this pious manner of living, on other countries. The Venetian ambassador to the Imperial Court, a clever and accurate observer, has identified the difference as a change from the outgoing to the inward: 'These princes have also brought something with them from their education in Spain ... a certain hauteur, not only in their demeanour but in every other aspect of their behaviour, which makes them – I should prefer to avoid the disagreeable word "hated", but at any rate much less beloved than they could be. For their manner is quite contrary to the custom of this country, which expects in the prince a somewhat familiar way of speaking ... and when they came back from Spain, His Majesty noticed this and drew their attention to it and told them to mend their manners ... and since that had little or no effect, he was forced one day, to save their face, to say laughingly that they behaved like that even with him – implying that it was not pride that made them behave as they did. ...' But it was not 'the custom of this country' that prevailed; the Spanish Hapsburg style persisted in Austria up to the time of Leopold I and Charles VI, and it was only Maria Theresa who

once again recalled the warm-hearted directness of Maximilian I and II.

Whatever we may think of Philip II as an individual, we can only really recognize the greatness and forcefulness of his personality as a ruler if we look at the decay of Spanish power under his successors. There are a number of general reasons for that: other European nations grew stronger, with increased economic power; the flow of gold and silver from the colonies was not an unmixed blessing, and communications became insecure as English sea-power gained strength. But the decline was hastened by the weakness of Philip's successors, their dependence on favourites such as the Duke of Lerma and Count Olivares, mediocre people whom Philip had kept well away from himself. In addition, his successors could not avoid the renewal of the struggle with France, how could they insist that the Spanish subsidies sent to Vienna were spent as Madrid wished them to be spent.

People often talk glibly about in-breeding and degeneration; in fact, the experience of animal breeders has shown that for the development of certain qualities this process is essential, and even from the

Investiture of the military order of Maria Theresa at the Viennese Court. The order had been introduced in 1757 to celebrate a victory of the Austrian army during the Seven Years War.

Maria Theresa, in mourning for the death of Francis of Lorraine, with four of her sixteen children, among them the Emperors Joseph II and Leopold II. Of her daughters, Marie Antoinette became Queen in France and Maria Carolina, Queen in Naples.

time of the Pharaohs there is no record of any injurious consequences of in-breeding. But when we look at the hundred years or so of Hapsburg rule in Spain, we cannot fail to conclude that the frequent marriages of near relatives led to an inferior vintage. Among the last of such was the marriage of Ferdinand III's daughter Maria Anna with Philip IV, then a widower. The Emperor had hoped for a double wedding, with his son, the Archduke Ferdinand, marrying Philip's eldest daughter Maria Theresa. But there must have been a short circuit in the arrangements between the two Houses, for when the Archduke and heir to the throne arrived with his sister at Rovereto, the city that marked the boundary between the territories administered by Vienna and those administered by Madrid, he was told that the Infanta's hand had already been given elsewhere. The lucky bridegroom was Louis XIV of France, whose mother was yet another Hapsburg. The rejection had world-wide political significance, for it was this marriage with the Sun King that led to the War of the Spanish Succession. Hundreds of thou-

sands of young Europeans were to perish on the battlefields; France appeared to have won, but the sacrifices, privations and burdens that she had to bear brought closer the day of the French Revolution.

Until the end of the seventeenth century the Austrian Hapsburgs had to deal with two tremendous problems, externally with the threat from the 'Sublime Porte', from the Turkish Sultan's powerful Moslem army, and internally with schism. Looked at broadly, the two phenomena might seem to be inter-dependent: Hapsburgs were for now prepared to tolerate the Protestants, and to safeguard their rights, when the danger-signals were threatening in the East, and far less so when their relationship with the Sublime Porte appeared more peaceful. But looked at more closely, the situation was certainly far more complex, and changed as the rulers changed.

Ferdinand I was a strict Catholic, but showed tolerance toward the Lutherans and was always anxious to reach a settlement with them. The Emperor had difficulties with his son, based to some extent on

the partition treaty which provided for an alternation of the Imperial dignity between Spain and Austria. This treaty would have sent Maximilian away empty-handed, and he thus opposed it. In any case, the German princes were not at all prepared to make a 'Spaniard' their Emperor. Moreover, there was a good deal in Protestantism that Maximilian found attractive. Quarrels broke out between father and son; Maximilian finally gave way and in 1562 swore an oath that he would live and die a Catholic.

In that same year he was elected King of the Romans at Frankfurt, and two years later, on Ferdinand's death, he became Emperor, reigning for twelve years. During that time he remained close to many Protestants. He did not, however, get on too well with his wife, his cousin Maria from Spain, a severe-looking woman with a big nose, who wore her hair combed back. Despite their mutual dislike, she bore her husband four sons, of whom two were to wear the Imperial Crown. There was a distressing scene at Regensburg as Maximilian lay on his deathbed; he

refused to have a priest brought and would not receive extreme unction. His unloved wife, his sister, his younger son, the Papal nuncio and the Spanish ambassador all reasoned with him about what they called his 'salvation'. But the Emperor remained firm; his priest, he said, was in heaven.

The obduracy of the Emperor, who had once said that religious questions could never be solved by fire and the sword, but only by Christian understanding and justice, was certainly attributable to the fact that he had seen how Catholic monarchs, who would never take a single step without their father confessors, could still act in certain circumstances. There was, for instance, the report of the Massacre of St Bartholomew's Eve in Paris, which was so terrible that at first the Emperor refused to believe it; it distressed him the more because his daughter was married to Charles IX of France.

He was even more deeply shocked by the fate of Don Carlos, the son of Philip II, whom his father had had imprisoned and, as many believed, murdered. Don

A meeting between the 'enlightened despots', Joseph II and Catherine II of Russia. The Emperor's rationalist reformism lacked the tolerance which tempered his mother's exceptional energy.

Carlos had been bethrothed to Maximilian's favourite daughter, the lovely Archduchess Anna, and it must have caused the Emperor the deepest mental anguish to determine where his duty lay when the unhappy bridegroom's father – possibly even his murderer – now put himself forward in his son's place as a suitor for the twenty-one-year-old girl. In the end Maximilian agreed to it and the wedding took place in 1570. But when the Emperor lay on his deathbed, six years later, his accumulated disgust at the amalgam of spiritual and temporal power, of bigotry and un-scrupulousness, once more found forceful expression when he refused to allow a priest to be brought to his bedside.

That an Emperor like Maximilian II should be followed by such a man as Rudolf II is one of the greatest tragedies of European history. In his veins the blood of 'Joan the Mad' flowed from two sources – his father, the son of Ferdinand I, was her grandson and his mother, daughter of Charles V, her granddaughter. Rudolf was irresolute but stubborn, intolerant but ineffectual, more interested in his horological clock than in politics. By letting affairs drift, he hastened the polarization of his inheritance, the Protestant Union facing the Catholic League, so that it was just a matter of time when the great clash would come.

Meanwhile Henry IV of France, the former Henry of Navarre, was showing the world how quickly a nation under tolerant rule – ruled under such policies as Maximilian II had adopted – could blossom and gain in strength and power. The Edict of Nantes gave the Huguenots back all their old rights and guaranteed freedom of conscience throughout the land. Henry's great plan was to combine with the Protestants in Germany and found a new French Empire in Europe.

Rudolf, the man most closely concerned with the plan, was scarcely even aware of it, shut up in his castle in Prague. It might well have been put into effect had not Henry fallen victim to the murderous attack of Ravaillac in 1610.

All the same, Rudolf II was not such an uninteresting figure. Prague, where he lived, became a centre of cultural and artistic endeavour. The Emperor was a first-class collector; the Breughels and Correggios that now hang in Vienna attest his artistic taste. His interest in science, his special feeling for alchemy, were certainly mingled with superstition, but he not only sent for Tycho Brahe from Denmark but also allowed the Protestant Kepler to work as his assistant. However, astronomy and the history of art, not to mention astrology, are not really the hallmarks of active kingship. Rudolf II increasingly cut himself off from the world, a world in which catastrophes, which it should have been his task to prevent, began to loom up ever more clearly. He shut himself away completely in the Imperial palace above the Moldau; the boundaries between the real and the unreal began to become blurred, and exotic animals inhabited the great halls of Hradčany.

The Emperor's brother Matthias had already assumed the government several years earlier, and when Rudolf II died in 1612 he succeeded him in the Imperial dignity, which he was to enjoy for seven years. He was more tolerant than his predecessor; but what could have saved the situation at that moment was tolerance coupled with firmness, vigour and wisdom. All Matthias could manage, however, was, in Grillparzer's phrase, 'to struggle haltingly along half-roads, using half-measures to achieve half-deeds'.

As happened so often in history, after a period of uncertain rule, of constant hesitation and unfulfilled intentions, a man of quite the opposite type, strong-willed and fanatically resolute, met at first with hardly any opposition. Such a man was Ferdinand, Duke of Styria, to whom his cousin Matthias had ceded the kingdoms of Bohemia and Hungary in order to give him a good starting point for election as King and Emperor. Ferdinand was a tall man with sandy hair and a charming manner. In Styria he had persecuted the Protestants, who made up more than half of the population and he continued to do so in Bohemia and Hungary. But yet once more it turned out that success for a man of this sort was limited to the range of his personal charisma; he could not prevent the alliance of outlying powers nor avoid dreadful wars of attrition.

The outlying powers in this instance were France and Sweden, the dreadful war of attrition was the Thirty Years War – strictly speaking a whole series of wars and campaigns, of periods of rest and renewed struggles, of starvation and epidemics, which reduced the population of Germany to a fraction of its former

The misfortunes of a Hapsburg in France: Marie
Antoinette, daughter of Maria Theresa, married the
Dauphin and later became Queen, but died on the
guillotine on 16 October 1793.

numbers and set the whole of Europe back a hundred
years.

This tragedy had begun with a brilliant victory at the
battle of the White Mountain, where on 8 November
1620, the Imperial commander-in-chief Tilly destroyed
the army of the 'Winter King', the Elector Palatine,
Frederick v, who wanted to take the Crown of
Bohemia from the Emperor. The flower of Bohemian
nobility perished. The Emperor Ferdinand II is said to
have hesitated long before signing the death warrant
of the leaders of the national movement. Sweat stood

on his brow, as he pushed the parchment away from
him, he wanted to speak with his father confessor first.
Then the executions were carried out on the
Altstädterring and the heads of the leaders were
impaled above the tall gate of the Karlsbrücke. But if
that was terrible, far more terrible things were to
follow.

Until recently, twentieth-century historians and
publicists have not evinced much sympathy for the
House of Hapsburg; they gave little consideration to
the fact that the Hapsburgs were an international

family, that they never tried to deprive peoples of their national character, that they were sympathetic to local traditions and adopted the language and grammar of the peoples and races under their rule. Only in the last decade has this verdict been revised somewhat and, especially in Italy, some thought given to a fairer valuation. Strangely enough, in the general condemnation hardly anyone has referred to the events in Bohemia of the months and years that followed the battle of the White Mountain. Gradually the whole of the old Bohemian nobility, the entire leadership of the country, was dispossessed and often liquidated; hardly a single Czech name survived and untold wealth was piled up in the hands of a few families that occupied the country, notably the Liechtensteins. Details can be found in Golo Mann's huge biography of Albert von Wallenstein.

Wallenstein, a Catholic nobleman (though originally from a Protestant family), was one of the beneficiaries of the reallocation of lands. He was wealthy enough to raise his own army, was employed, dismissed, employed again and finally, suspected of high treason, was assassinated. The leadership of the Imperial House now passed to a Spanish Infante, who proved to be courageous and extremely capable. Ferdinand II died in 1637, eleven years before the Peace of Westphalia. He had lived to witness the war going from bad to worse, and to see how mercenary armies driven by greed and fear were marching through the land, how the peasants' buffer system was breaking down, how noble principles were being abandoned, as people began to think of no more than grabbing a little piece of exhausted land or a ruined city. All the great objects for which the Hapsburgs had gone to war now proved to be impracticable; Germany was more firmly and finally divided; now it was a war merely about personal property, about keeping what originally no one had wanted to fight about.

There remained the satisfaction that the True Faith had triumphed in the hereditary lands, the faith that in the years to come was to bring forth the *pietas Austriaca*, the piety of the Hapsburg Austrians with processions, Holy Trinity columns, images of the Virgin, House-Crowns, Imperial rooms, memorial tablets and confessional boxes. But that satisfaction could not suffice by itself to overcome the feelings of emptiness, of fruitlessness, of political hangover left by the Peace of Westphalia.

However, Fate had still kept one heroic trial in store for the Hapsburgs, a war that was necessary, and inevitable – a war from which they were to emerge strengthened and revitalized. Hero of this conflict was an ugly little man with weak bones and decayed teeth, musical, shy, and originally destined for the service of God. ... No, not Prince Eugene of Savoy, but the Emperor Leopold I. Two years younger than his great

opponent Louis XIV, he was elected Emperor in 1658 and married, first, Margaret Theresa, the younger daughter of Philip IV, who died in childbirth when she was twenty-two, next an Austrian Archduchess, and finally a German Princess, Eleanor of Pfalz-Neuburg, who bore him two future Emperors, Joseph I and Charles VI.

The threat from Turkey had been manifest for some time. Intelligence reports made it clear that the Sultan had assembled a huge army, but for a long time people in Vienna simply refused to believe it. They just rejected the bad news – 'It can't be as bad as that' – so that they had to renew the city's fortifications at the very last moment. By 1683 a Turkish army of over 250,000 men had crossed the Balkans and broken into the Tisza Plain; in July it stood before the gates of Vienna. Some of the Hungarian magnates had come to an agreement with the Turks; not only the King of Transylvania, but also the Draskovichs, the Nadastys and the Esterhazys had entered the Turkish camp before Vienna to be allowed to kiss the hem of the Grand Vizier's robe.

But to the peasants and craftsmen of Lower Austria, to the prisoners of war, to the merchants, the invaders meant nothing but fear and ruin. This was not a fear, often exaggerated, of foreign soldiers; we know from Turkish sources, including the diary of the Turkish master of ceremonies who took part in the siege, that thousands of prisoners were beheaded and that many who had been promised quarter were massacred. 'The pasha in command had a red carpet laid amid the ruins of the main square of Perchtoldsdorf and demanded that they bring him the key of the church together with a fair young virgin, who was to carry a white flag and wear a wreath of flowers. The seventeen-year-old daughter of the mayor was chosen ... when the villagers came out they were disarmed and made prisoner. The men were cut down on the spot. The pasha reserved for himself the pleasure of killing the unfortunate girl with his own hands.'

Leopold resisted the temptation to put himself at the head of his army – he would not have known much about how to lead it. He escaped first to Innsbruck, then to Passau; he convened a Diet at Regensburg and was tireless and inventive in organizing help for the beleaguered city. The German princes, who were gradually awakening from the nightmare of the Thirty Years War, called up troops; the King of Poland swept down from Cracow with an army; volunteers from all over Europe reported in Passau, so that a special uniform for foreign princes was designed (one of them, who came from the House of Savoy and rejoiced in the name of Eugene, found it too expensive).

The relieving army arrived in the nick of time; on 12 September the troops streamed across the slopes of the Vienna woods, which the Turks had not occupied. The

*The misfortune of a Hapsburg in France: Marie
Louise, in a portrait by G. B. Borghesi. The daughter of
the Emperor Francis II, she married Napoleon
Bonaparte and after his exile she became Duchess of
Parma and Piacenza.*

armed superiority of the Christians in single combat had its effect and the Turkish army took flight, leaving their silken tents, their gardens, their concubines and exotic animals behind them. But the little man from Savoy had had his baptism of fire. Only fourteen years later, as Imperial commander-in-chief at Zenta, he overwhelmed a huge Turkish army which he had been able to intercept by crossing the Tisza. Thirty-four years later, he not only captured Belgrade but routed the Turkish army, a feat of arms recalled to this day in the Song of the Noble Knight: 'He had a bridge made/So that men could cross/With the army for the city!'

These three dates, 1683, 1697 and 1717, tower over the disasters of the Turkish war, with its endless skirmishes, exaction of tribute and running battles. To the first victories the Emperor made one significant contribution, it was he who recognized the quality of Eugene, made him commander-in-chief and gave him a free hand.

In 1705 the Emperor died; Emperor Joseph I succeeded him but reigned for only six years before he died of cholera in 1711. The throne then passed to Charles VI, and it was under him that the victory of Belgrade was won. With it, the threat from Turkey was finally banished. The nation breathed again; the old eternal awareness that armies of barbarians could suddenly break in from the East and South East to murder, plunder and ravage, driving pitilessly into the very heart of Europe, was ended at last; the nightmare haunted by so many dreaded names – Huns, Avars, Mongols and Turks – seemed to have vanished.

Austria, where, as Musil once declared, 'genius and initiative in private persons are looked on as provocation and presumption', had certainly profited from the brilliance of the Prince of Savoy, who became the embodiment of a new spirit, exuberant, elegant, expressive, reaching up to heaven but rooted in the earth. Great architects appeared at this period, enriching and transforming city and surroundings in the Emperor's service and building palaces for the Prince of Savoy – Johann Bernhard Fischer von Erlach, architect of the Karlskirche, Lukas von Hildebrandt, who designed the Belvedere, Jakob Brandtauer, who was responsible for the gigantic Benedictine Abbey of Melk on its cliff overhanging the Danube.

So far we have said nothing about the campaigns, with their great battles, that were fought against the Emperor's cousin, Louis XIV – himself half a Hapsburg – at the same time as the Turkish wars. The great victory of Höchstädt (the British call it Blenheim), for instance, was won in 1704, seven years after Zenta and thirteen years before Belgrade; Malplaquet took place in 1709, twelve years after Zenta and eight years before Belgrade; but also of the highest interest were the victories that Eugene gained in Italy over the French marshals Catinat, Villeroy and Vendôme, and his great action before Turin.

However, we are concerned here with the effect that external events had on the Hapsburgs, not with the events themselves; our task is to show how those events shaped and changed the members of the House and how, in turn, the changes in the House influenced events. We have already mentioned that the Emperor Leopold died in 1705, that Joseph I then reigned for six years and was succeeded on the throne by Charles VI, who had originally been destined only for the throne of Spain.

In most histories, even today, it is alleged that it was the death of Joseph that was responsible for Britain's departure from the grand alliance against France. In fact, this volte-face is constantly quoted as an example of the policy of the 'balance of power'. But, if we examine British sources, we soon find that the war was already regarded as having gone on too long and for some time there had been strong opposition to the alliance. The instrigues that led to Britain's withdrawal were going on while the health of the Emperor – who was only thirty-three when he died – was giving no cause for alarm.

Charles VI, who in appearance already looked more like one of the Spanish Hapsburgs who came after Philip II, had set his heart on the Spanish throne. Even the Peace of Utrecht and Rastatt could not convince him that the game was over; he lived in Vienna like an *emigré* Spanish monarch, insisted on Spanish ceremonial, surrounded himself with Spanish advisers (which naturally aroused complaints) and relaxed only while listening to music or shooting. In this last activity, however, he had the misfortune to shoot accidentally the Prince Schwarzenberg.

As a sign of his nostalgia for Spain, he began to convert Klosterneuburg into a monastery-residence on the lines of the Escorial; the enterprise was never completed, but we can still see the Imperial crown and Archducal hat on the cupolas of the Emperor's folly.

The entry in the Emperor's diary about the death of Prince Eugene strikes one as remarkably mean: 'At half past eight news that prince Eugene of Savoy, in the service of my house since '83, who gave great service in the field in command of battles since '97 and became president of the council of war in 1703, who has served me in everything since 1711, was found dead in his bed after a long illness. God have mercy on his soul. In his seventy-third year.' And to this entry – which has to be read closely to make sure it is not simply about some trusty personal servant – there are added the terse words: 'Now to see everything put right, in better order', which give the impression that the Prince of Savoy had long been regarded as a tiresome has-been and that the Emperor thought he could run the nation's affairs better without him. In that he certainly deceived himself.

However senile Eugene might have been, however easily he nodded off in the middle of a conversation, his urgent advice that, in view of the rapacity of the European princes, the 'Pragmatic Sanction', which guaranteed rule over all the Hapsburg lands to Charles VI's daughter Maria Theresa, and which virtually every European prince had signed, would be worth no more than the army that stood ready to defend her, proved to be absolutely right. But the army that Eugene had begun to build up was disbanded. This cutting down of forces can be understood only as one aspect of a wider process, a process of sagging willpower, of a national political potency that was exhausted. Instead, all energies were concentrated on those legal-intellectual-diplomatic games which the 'Pragmatic Sanction', especially through its acceptance by Prussia and Germany, was intended to secure. But every sacrifice – the giving up of the East India Company, participation in two unsuccessful wars and the projected withdrawal from certain areas – proved quite unavailing.

Maria Theresa was twenty-three when she succeeded to an Empire whose cohesion had been put in serious doubt in the last years of her father's government. At what age is a woman most beautiful, when does she exercise the greatest fascination? We have a portrait of Maria Theresa painted before she came to the throne. Her features are young, attractive, a little timid; she seems to be asking the world what it holds in store for her and to be just a little afraid of the answer. These features are not yet lit by the radiance of a fulfilled woman. She was the last of the old Hapsburg rulers; with her, half a millennium came to an end; but she was also the first ruler of a new Austria that was to blossom and develop, an Austria of reform and reorganization, shaking off the last traces of the Middle Ages. Her mother, Princess Elizabeth Christina of Brunswick-Lüneburg-Wolfenbüttel, was a Guelph, and her grandmother, too, had been a German Princess, of the House of Pfalz-Neuburg. A long line of marriages between the same families had now come to an end, and one cannot help thinking that the Empress's tremendous vitality and creative power may well have been due to this influx of new blood – the complete reconstruction of a nation, which would never have been possible without her participation, and an active family life in which she helped with her sixteen children's education and, in later life, kept in touch with them by letter.

The Empress was thus related not only to the Bourbons but also to most of the German princely houses. It did her little good.

The first attack came from an unexpected quarter, from the rapacious Frederick of Prussia, hardly four years her elder – Frederick, whom Prince Eugene had defended, and who had lived for years with Imperial support. Clearly the Prussian King supposed he would have very little trouble with the young woman who had described herself to Count Khevenhüller as 'a king abandoned by the whole world', and who had to tell her advisers crossly 'not to discourage the poor queen any more but to help and advise her'. But Maria Theresa had a generous share of her father's traditional courage in adversity; she involved Frederick in endless wars and more than once his end seemed to be near. To his conception of a monarch, cold, unscrupulous, ironic, she contrasted hers. 'The world is now so thoughtless, so unkind. Everything is made to look ridiculous ... our Germans are losing the best qualities they possessed in this way: a little awkward, a little rough, but at the same time honest and hardworking. For myself, I do not like all that which men call irony. No man will ever be improved by it, but will rather be offended, and I think it incompatible with love for one's neighbour.' But she could be hard if she had to be. After the loss of Prague she wrote to Prince Kinsky: 'I would see all my armies destroyed rather than surrender anything. The critical moment has come at last; let the country take care to seize it. Help the soldier to do his duty and spare nothing. ... You will say that I am cruel. It is true; but I know that for all the cruelties that I now demand in order to save my country I will be able to make amends a hundredfold. And so I will; but now I must shut my heart to pity.'

What would have happened if the Empress had not had to face the senseless, useless wars sparked off by the greed of the King of Prussia, the Wittelsbachs' nostalgia for the Imperial dignity, and the French hope of cashing in on the liquidation of the Hapsburgs – wars which finally turned into mere sideshows of the great Anglo-French struggle for sea-power and new world empires? The Empress was just thirty-one years old when she signed the Peace of Aachen in 1748. The

actually feeble-minded has never really been established. The dry humour that Francis II had possessed, was not entirely missing in him. When, after his abdication in 1848, Ferdinand heard in Prague the news of the Italian disaster, his only comment is said to have been (in a thick Viennese accent): 'I could have managed that'. What made the situation untenable after 1835, however, and what prevented reforms and made the emotional tide rise ever higher until 1848, was not so much the character or the intellectual capacity of Ferdinand as a testamentary instruction of Emperor Francis, who had given a position in the Council of State to Count Kolowrat, a man compared with whom Metternich, whom he openly disliked, could still be regarded as a liberal.

Sophia of Bavaria, wife of the Archduke Francis Charles, renounced the title of Empress, to ensure that her son, the eighteen-year-old Francis Joseph should succeed to the Imperial Crown in 1848. Youth was felt to be an asset – Francis Joseph would not be hampered by the errors of the past, he could be relied on for an absolutely fresh start. Who could steel his heart against this handsome, brave young Prince? In one respect, the length of his reign, Francis Joseph put all other monarchs of his dynasty in the shade, Frederick III and Francis II alike; no one ever achieved anything like his sixty-eight years. But his longevity brought no triumph; in all those years, the dark clouds never cleared, the end of the dynasty seemed at hand. The Emperor, indeed, lived to survive most of his adversaries, but they were always replaced by new, more obstinate, more wicked men.

At the start of the epoch, Imperial arms were victorious when Jellačić and Radetzky suppressed the revolutions in Prague, Austria, Hungary and Italy; Russian military assistance was needed only in Hungary. But those were to be the last victories of the dynasty. It must have been most distressing to a man who felt himself so closely bound up with the army that every subsequent campaign ended in defeat. Certainly the army fought bravely in later years: the fact that they did not break at Sadowa, despite the technical superiority of the Prussian army, and were able to join up with the successful southern army must be reckoned as a battle honour equal with many successful actions in the First World War. But these battles did not end in victory; they brought no final decision. They merely added to the Emperor's burdens the duties which he had taken on as constitutional monarch, and which he took very seriously. The Imperial Council could not consider a conflict with Prussia; there was simply no money for breech-loading rifles, which were, of course, not made in Prussia but in England. Later the Emperor, who was completely dominated by traditional concepts of war, failed to make use of technical possibilities which might have proved significant.

While he never had any success in the one field to which the whole of his concern, his attention and his vigilance was devoted, the events and the changes that took place elsewhere in those sixty-eight years were astonishing. The technical revolution, from the railway to the motor-car, was perhaps not pursued so vigorously as it was in other countries, but something more humane, more intellectual took its place. Austrian industry could never make up its mind between free trade and protection; it wanted the one on ideological grounds, the other on practical.

Old bonds were constantly being broken, new movements, new unrest were developing which were soon permeated by nationalist sentiments. Many people hold the view that the Dual Monarchy collapsed through a lack of will to solve the problem of nationalities, that only the dynasty stood above the nations, and failed to take its character from any one of them, although even this by itself would not have been sufficient to save the monarchy.

This view overlooks one critical aspect of events: the people who were demanding independence could only see that independence in the historical framework they had inherited. The Bohemians, for instance, saw it within the context of the Bohemian Crown, the Hungarians within the extent of the Crown of St Stephen and of the lands that they felt belonged to them, as it were, by divine dispensation. But while the Hapsburgs had allowed the different peoples their own language, customs and traditions, the Magyars were busy trying to 'Magyarize' the Croats, to attract the Croatian nobles to Hungary, to change their names

and ways of thought. The conflict of nationalities was thus insoluble – and not because of any lack of goodwill on the part of the Hapsburgs, but as a result of internal contradictions.

The heir to the throne, Francis Ferdinand, did indeed try to reach a solution with 'trialism', which would have been juster and more rational than the existing structure of the Empire. The question remains how such a solution could ever have obtained the agreement of Budapest. But while there was bickering within the Imperial Council, while students demonstrated, and the language problem spread until it was as much as the army could do to preserve German as its service language, the nations were meeting in friendly, reasonable conversation, exchanging experiences for the first time; higher educational standards meant that for the first time they were really able to communicate

The heir who never reigned: the Archduke Rudolf, son of Francis Joseph, with his wife Stephanie of Belgium. Rudolf committed suicide at Mayerling in mysterious circumstances.

with each other. The result was astounding. At the turn of the century in Vienna there occurred what can only be described as an explosion of talent, the effects of which are still with us today. The brilliance of the Poles, the intellectual sharpness of the Hungarians, the speculative ability of the Eastern Jews, highly cultivated in centuries of isolation, the Romance peoples' gift for form and the Slavs' poetry and imagery, all these were here met together. Freud's parents came from Moravia, but the family could be traced back to Galicia; Joseph Roth was of Polish descent; Rilke and Kafka came from Prague, Italo Svevo from Trieste, Wittgenstein from Vienna, and Trakl from Salzburg. But in Hofmannsthal we seem to have a combination of blood from all parts of the old monarchy: of Jewish descent from one grandfather, and Lombard from that patrician's daughter from Milan; on his mother's side, dignitaries, peasants, innkeepers, craftsmen from Lower Austria. If all these extraordinary talents are lined up, we get an astonishing array – Schnitzler, Beer-Hoffmann, Mahler, Schiele, Klimt and Kokoschka, Semmelweiss, Musil, Adler, Markus Meier, Wagner Jauregg and Karl Kraus.

If now we look back at that period, we can hardly see the tremendous turbulence; to us it seems a time of respectability, of an ordered existence, of assured values. But the Emperor's own life, with its many tragedies and afflictions, does not fit into that pattern. His son and heir committed suicide, his brother was

shot in Mexico, his wife was stabbed in Geneva, the next heir to the throne was murdered at Sarajevo. He was spared nothing. Yet our nostalgia is not usually extended from the age at which Francis Joseph lived to his own person. If anyone is asked about Francis Joseph, they will probably ponder and then remember that he was a humourless, dry bureaucrat, conscientious but unimaginative, a boring unsympathetic husband, a father who made no effort to understand his son and heir and who kept the next in line to the throne, Francis Ferdinand Este, at arm's length and excluded him from State affairs.

There is a little truth in all this – a little, but not too much. It is strange, for a start, that he should be thought of as lacking in humour, though this cliché constantly recurs. From many of his papers speaks that same dry wit that we recognized in Francis II, and the inconspicuous poke in the ribs with which he woke one of his aides who had gone to sleep on his shoulder hardly suggests a lack of sympathy. He was certainly a bureaucrat, and if he shared many of the opinions of his great uncle, the Field Marshal Archduke Albert, who had revived the concept of the 'unique position of the dynasty', he also comprehended 'kingship as a public service'. He even described himself in a questionnaire as an 'independent official', hardly a sign of lack of humour.

But the problem of his relationship with his son Rudolf was far from simple. Rudolf was impetuous, passionate, felt attracted by liberal ideas, and wrote articles for the newspapers (though they did not appear under his name). How could his father, holding quite different views, have influenced him in what opinions he ought to hold? Was it not best to remain at a friendly distance and allow Rudolf every conceivable freedom? We still know little about Rudolf's suicide; the mystery of this nineteenth-century Don Carlos remains unsolved. The Empress Elizabeth had deposited a strongbox with a lawyer in Brno which, according to instructions, was not to be opened until years after the Second World War. But when it was opened, the Czech authorities announced that it was empty! We have to believe them. What we do have are the police papers, found on a heap of rubble in Berlin after the Second World War. They make the tragedy even more terrible. For instance, Rudolf and Maria Vetsera did not die one after the other; the Crown Prince lived for some hours after his mistress was already dead. But is there any sign that the tragedy could have been prevented by anything that his father could have done? Was not the Empress more to blame? Rudolf had not forigven her for a quarrel in England, and after that she only saw him very rarely.

This brings us back to the Emperor as husband; certainly as a boy he may have been neglected and not corrected often enough by his mother. But Francis

The heir who never reigned: the Archduke Francis Ferdinand with his wife, Sophia Chotek. He was assassinated at Sarajevo shortly after this photograph was taken.

Joseph's letters show another side: he was also a great lover, wooing, swearing, pleading over and over again, yet it availed him not at all, for nothing proved so hard as to win his own woman.

Let us turn to Francis Ferdinand Este, that self-willed, dominating, in many ways noble Hapsburg. Francis Joseph had handed over the Belvedere to him and he lived there as a second ruler, maintained his own military chancery, was kept informed about all army matters, and even collected a circle of independent men around him so that he could crystallize his ideas in conversation with them. It cannot be denied that the Emperor opposed the plan for his heir to marry the non-royal Countess Chotek, but he gave way in the end. It was certainly a political error, when the Archduke and his wife were murdered at Sarajevo, not to invite heads of State to the funeral, but to have the ceremony held quietly in private. Some ignoble details – for instance, the coffin of the morganatic wife was placed lower at the lying-in-state to emphasize the difference in rank – can probably be laid at the door of Count Montenuovo, himself also the child of a morganatic marriage.

And what of the Emperor's imagination? Did not Francis Joseph predict the end, did he not fear for the fate of the dynasty, did he not try to smother his endlessly torturing doubt in work, and work, and more work?

The First World War was already some two years old when Charles I succeeded to the throne. He came to power too late; affairs were too much in a state of flux. He tried every expedient but could make no impression – for this he must be given credit. Even the final effort to make peace through the mediation of Prince Sixtus of Bourbon Parma was blamed by the Germans more on his wife, Princess Zita of Bourbon Parma, than on him. It may be said that all his actions were carried out with a certain dignity and humanity, that he never needlessly shed blood, that he never showed harshness where harshness would achieve nothing. There is something touching about Charles I, so obvious were his good intentions, his efforts to serve mankind. Only hardened monarchists find anything to criticize in him: he ought to have had a regiment of soldiers parading in front of him, marching and shooting, then everything would have been all right. Such statements are always heard at moments of change.

In November 1918, 640 years after Rudolf I had raised his banner in Vienna, Charles laid down the Crown and released his people from the rule of the Dual Monarchy. He did not lack initiative and courage – this was shown by his unsuccessful attempt to stage a restoration in Hungary. The nightmare of the Czech historian Palacký was gradually coming true. The successor States became caricatures of the old monarchy; only in Czechoslovakia was a workable democracy established, and that was brought to an end, first by Hitler, then by Stalin, then by Stalin's successors.

Austria, whose name had so long been identified with the House of Hapsburg, took an ungracious leave of its ancient dynasty. It is perhaps understandable that the young republic should wish to keep its former ruling House at a distance. It is regrettable that it could not have done so with the grace and good temper of Weimar. It is unpardonable that it not only demanded that those members of the House who did not wish to leave their homeland and lose their property should renounce any claim to sovereignty, but went so far as to require them to relinquish membership of their House.

The English took the Emperor to Madeira, where he lived for several years, not wholly free from material cares. In 1922 he felt the first onset of his fatal illness. His first thought was to spare his children the sight of a man fighting for his life. But then he sent for his eldest son. 'Let him see how an emperor dies'.

First Interlude

THE LONGEVITY OF MONARCHS

Even kings respect the demographic and statistical laws that affect the rest of humanity. The average lifespan for monarchs, as for others, has increased in recent centuries, thanks to improved living conditions and medical progress. Of the ten longest-surviving monarchs, eight lived during the last three centuries, and the other two only take seventh and eighth place on the list. It is the eighteenth and nineteenth centuries that have seen the longest reigns. The twentieth century offers very few cases of long reigns, but this is for historical rather than biological reasons; in our century, opportunities have increasingly arisen of ending a reign without waiting for the natural death of the sovereign.

Among the ten longest reigning monarchs in European history we find as many as three from the French Bourbon dynasty: Louis XIV, his grandson, Philip of Anjou (King of Spain as Philip V and founder of the Spanish Bourbons), and his great-grandson, Louis XV. Louis XIV was in fact the longest reigning monarch: from 1643 to 1715, seventy-two years. However, Louis XIV had the advantage of coming to the throne at only five years old. His reign was more than twice the average for most of the other European dynasties.

In second place is the Austrian Emperor Francis Joseph, ruling from 1848 to 1916, sixty-eight years. Unlike Louis XIV, Francis Joseph was not helped by a precocious succession to the throne, being crowned after his eighteenth birthday. It is also worth noting that while Louis' long reign coincided with the greatest splendour of his dynasty, Francis Joseph's reign was linked to the slow but inexorable decline of the Hapsburgs and was punctuated by defeats (the war against France and Piedmont in 1859, the war against Prussia in 1866, and the First World War), ending just before the dynasty's final collapse.

Victoria, of the Hanover–Windsor dynasty, reigned in Britain from 1837 to 1901, sixty-four years. Her reign, like Louis XIV's, coincided with a period of great national prosperity: the time of the Industrial Revolution and of Britain's control of the seas and world domination. She gave her name to an epoch, a style, a culture. The much less brilliant reign of her grandfather, George III, was not much shorter than her own, sixty years from 1760 to 1820.

Four more sovereigns reigned longer than half a century: Louis XV, the great-grandson of Louis XIV, ruled France for fifty-nine years from 1715 to 1774; Peter II of Braganza was Emperor of Brazil from 1831 to 1889, fifty-eight years; and two members of the Plantagenet dynasty, Henry III, 1216 to 1272, a fifty-six-year reign, and Edward III, 1327 to 1377, a fifty-year-reign. Many sovereigns reigned for more than forty years: Philip V (Bourbons of Spain), Frederick II (Hohenzollern) and Victor Emmanuel III (Savoy), all for forty-six years; the Tudor Elizabeth I for forty-five years; Louis IX (Capetians) and John V (Braganza) for forty-four years; Charles Emmanuel III (Savoy) and Frederick William III (Hohenzollern) for forty-three years and Charles VI (Valois) for forty-two years.

DURATION AND PRESTIGE

A dynasty's prestige would seem to be linked above all to its age, but when we analyze a few facts relating to the great European families, we notice that this is not really the case. Undoubtedly, the Hapsburg dynasty is the most outstanding, not only the longest, with about a thousand years of documented existence, but also succeeding longest in preserving its power. After having held the Crown of the Holy Roman Empire for short periods with Rudolf I (1273–91) and Albert I (1298–1308), the Hapsburgs again took possession of it with Albert V in 1437 and never again lost it. They later passed without a break from the title of Holy Roman Emperor to that of Emperor of Austria in 1806, and Austro-Hungarian Emperor in 1862 and were not over-thrown until 1918, at the end of the First World War, after 481 years of uninterrupted power. In total the Austrian Hapsburgs reigned for 509 years and the Spanish branch for 184; the dynasty can therefore boast of 693 years of rule, almost seven centuries. But if the Hapsburgs are excluded, the equation between duration and prestige no longer holds. Often long-lasting dynasties have had uneventful histories, while ephemeral ones have given their names to the most outstanding moments of European history.

The Capetians, the longest dynasty after the Hapsburgs, reigning for 341 years, from Hugh Capet (987–96) to Charles IV, the Fair (1322–8), are not remembered for any moment of exceptional splendour. The Plantagenet dynasty, lasting 331 years, from Henry II to Richard III (1483–5), ended ignominiously after being defeated by the French in the Hundred Years War and torn apart in the civil war known as the Wars of the

Roses. The Stuarts reigned for more than three centuries, 343 years, but for 232 of them their dynasty was confined to the small and poor kingdom of Scotland. Only in the last 111 years, from James I (1603–25) to Anne (1702–14), did they enjoy the much more important kingdom of England, and even this short period was marred by the execution of Charles I. The Romanovs ruled for a slightly shorter length of time, 304 years – from Michael III (1613–45) to Nicholas II (1894–1917), but their name is linked with Russia's appearance on the European scene and to the birth of a powerful Empire. The Braganzas vegetated for as long as 337 years, from John IV (1640–56) to Manuel II (1908–10), on the outskirts of Europe, in the small kingdom of Portugal and in Brazil, from 1822 to 1889. On the other hand, the 262 years of rule by the Hanover-Windsors were identified with the most glorious period of Britain's Empire and its control of the seas, from George I (1714–27) to Elizabeth II who is still reigning. The Valois, who reigned for 261 years, from Philip VI (1328–50) to Henry III (1574–89), won the Hundred Years War and were the creators of the modern French nation; under their rule a powerful army was created capable of facing the challenge of the Imperial Hapsburg army. Among the European dynasties included in this volume, the other four that enjoyed more than two centuries of rule are the Spanish Bourbons, reigning for 231 years, from Philip V (1700–46) to Alfonso XIII (1886–1931); the House of Savoy, first on the throne of Sardinia, from Victor Amadeus II (1720–30) to Victor Emmanuel II (1849–61), and later on that of Italy, from Victor Emmanuel II (1861–78) to Umberto II (1946); the French Bourbons, from Henry IV (1589–1610) to Louis XVI (1774–92) and, after the dramatic interruption of the French Revolution, from Louis XVIII (1814–24) to Charles X (1824–30); and finally the Hohenzollerns, reigning for 217 years, first in Prussia, from 1701 to 1871, then in the German Empire, from 1871 to 1918.

Nevertheless, the dynasties that came to the forefront of history for a briefer period, a century or even just a few decades, had their moments of great splendour: the Tudors, reigning for 188 years in England, from 1485 to 1603, and the Hohenstaufens, who held the Imperial crown for 116 years, from 1138 to 1254. The Bourbons of Naples ruled longer than these dynasties, 126 years, but during one of the most obscure periods of Southern Italian history. Finally, the Bonapartes in their brief periods of European prominence at the beginning of the nineteenth century with Napoleon I and his brothers, and from 1852 to 1870 with Napoleon III, can compete in their achievements with the longer-lasting European dynasties.

KINGDOMS, KINGDOMS, KINGDOMS. . . .

Though the House of Bonaparte reigned for the least number of years (54 altogether), as a family it does hold a record: the most crowns held. The Bonapartes in fact reigned over six different states (even though this occurred in the same period). Napoleon I held the Imperial Crown of France (1804–14 and 1815) and was King of Italy (1805–14), while his brothers Joseph, Louis and Jerome divided the other four thrones between them: first it was Joseph's turn to rule Naples (1806–8), then Spain (1808–13); Louis held the Dutch Crown (1808–10) and Jerome ruled West-phalia (1807–13). Later, the French throne was once again occupied by a Bonaparte, from 1852 to 1870: this was Napoleon III, Louis' son.

The runners-up in this scale are the house of Savoy (though it is difficult to decide, because it is debatable which thrones corresponded to actual power and which were merely nominal, or 'legitimist' throw-backs to a past now superseded by the events of history; for example, the last of the Stuarts left the House of Savoy his right to the English Crown, which, however, he had lost long ago). The House of Savoy held many kingdoms throughout the different eras of their dynastic heyday. They were rulers of Sardinia and later Italy, also of Sicily and Spain (not to mention Albania, Croatia and Ethiopia). Victor Amadeus II obtained the kingdom of Sicily with the treaty of Utrecht in 1713, after the wars of the Spanish Succession; he had initially sided with the French, but in 1703 made a sudden volte-face and signed an alliance with Austria, on condition of notable rewards. When the conflict was over, however, instead of coveted Lombardy, he was offered Sicily which seven years later, in 1720, he was obliged to hand over to Austria in exchange for Sardinia. The Spanish throne was held by Amadeus, the second-born of Victor Emanuel II, for just two years: he succeeded in 1871 in place of Leopold of Hohenzollern-Sigmaringen, whose nomination had unleashed the Franco-Prussian war, and he decided to abdicate in 1873, after clerical, republican and Carlist uprisings, and various attempts on his life.

The other dynasties which can boast more than one crown to their credit are the Hapsburgs, who embraced the thrones of the Holy Roman Empire, the Austrian Empire (later Austro-Hungarian) and Spain (with the later addition of Portugal from 1580 to 1640); the Stuarts were sovereigns of the 'precious trefoil': England, Scotland and Ireland; the Bourbons ruled France, Spain and the kingdom of Naples; the Hohenzollerns were first kings of Prussia, then sovereigns of the German Empire; the Braganza line governed Brazil as well as Portugal; and the House of Hanover-Windsor, besides the English throne, right up until 1866, held the land of their origin, the electoral principate, later the kingdom of Hanover.

Charles V (1364–80), the third Valois to be King of France, knighting Bertrand du Guesclin, the military leader who provided the King with the 'first reconquest' against the English invaders.

On the following pages: Paris at the beginning of the reign of the mad Charles VI. The gate on the right is that of the Rue Saint Jacques, and in the centre are the towers of Notre-Dame.

The Valois

Heir of the Capets, protagonist of the
Hundred Years War and the religious wars
of France, this dynasty saw the rise
of a national spirit

The Valois dynasty was a younger branch of the Capetians. It ruled France for 261 years, from 1328 to 1589, often in the midst of tragic circumstances, beginning with the Hundred Years War and ending with religious wars which threatened national unity.

Although he left three sons, Philip IV, known as Philip the Fair, was to see his male lineage die out. The eldest, Louis X (the Quarrelsome), had had by his wife Margaret of Burgundy a daughter of dubious legitimacy. He died in 1316 leaving his second wife, Clémence of Hungary, pregnant with a son, John I, who only lived for five days. At that time the law of succession to the throne, which had been honoured for three centuries, would have given the Crown to Margaret of Burgundy's daughter. However, Louis X's brother, Philip, who had already been appointed Regent, was chosen as King under the provisions of a law unearthed by the jurists – the Salic Law excluding women from the succession. As Philip V left only daughters, his brother Charles IV, the Fair, succeeded him, but died in 1328 also without a male heir. When Edward III, King of England and grandson of Philip the Fair, claimed the Crown, the jurists gave preference to the son of Charles of Valois, Philip's younger brother.

Charles of Valois, son and brother of kings, was also the father of a king. In his own right, he had himself been invested by the Pope with the kingdoms of Valence and Aragon and the earldom of Barcelona. Later, the Pope appointed him Emperor of Constantinople. Whilst he was unable to profit from these titles, he nevertheless used them to play an important part in government, especially during the reign of Louis X.

It was this influence which facilitated his son Philip's accession both to the regency on the death of Charles

IV and to the French throne when Charles's Queen gave birth posthumously to a daughter.

Philip of Valois became King in 1328 and his reign opened brilliantly. France occupied a dominant position in Europe and the establishment of the Papacy at Avignon strengthened her power. It began with a remarkable series of feats of arms: the victory over the Flemish at Cassel on 13 August 1328, the liege-homage offered to him by the English King in 1331, and his appointment as commander-in-chief of a crusade in 1334.

Philip then decided to acquire the English possessions in south-west France, and he instigated disturbances there, at the same time strengthening his fleet so as to attempt a landing in England. The scheme miscarried and the French fleet was destroyed at the Battle of Sluys on 24 June 1340. Henceforth the English were in command; they landed at St-Vaast la Hougue and marched on Paris. Philip VI, who was at that time attacking Guienne, went to meet them and was routed at Crecy in 1346.

The fall of Calais, renowned for the famous episode of 'The Burghers of Calais', marked the end of hostilities and a truce was signed in 1347. In the same year Philip annexed Dauphiné, subject to the heir to the French throne taking the title of Dauphin. Two years later Montpellier was secured. These important acquisitions nevertheless left France in a critical situation at the time of Philip's death in 1350.

John II the second Valois King, was a man of few talents. He came to the throne during difficult times for France: the black death had killed a third of the population, and the truce with England was to run out in 1351. Treason was rife in the kingdom at this time. The King had to have his Constable, the Count of Eu beheaded as the latter had surrendered Guisnes to the

Joan of Arc marching towards Chinon where she urged
the Dauphin, later Charles VII, to liberate France. The
Dauphin's father, Charles VI, had surrendered the
country and the Crown to the English.

English. He then had to fight against Charles the Bad,
his son-in-law and Louis x's grandson.

War had begun again in the south, although no
declaration had been made. A raid by the Black Prince,
Edward III's son, laid waste the Languedoc from
Toulouse to Nîmes. The King, compelled to raise
troops to secure the defence of the country, asked the
Estates-General for credits. He was opposed by
Etienne Marcel, provost of the Paris merchants, who
claimed for the Estates the right to control taxation.

Lacking money, John II set out for war with
insufficient troops. At Poitiers he ran right into the
Black Prince's forces and, after a heroic stand, he was
defeated and taken prisoner by the English.

His capture was to bring about a crisis in government. The regency had been secured by the Dauphin,
the future Charles V, and he proceeded to convene the
Estates-General. Led by Etienne Marcel, the Estates
rebelled and enacted the *Grande Ordonnance* which
established constitutional monarchy with a form of
government by assembly. The Dauphin's chief advisers, the Marshals of Champagne and Normandy,
were put to death before his eyes. Meanwhile Etienne
Marcel set himself up as the Crown's protector, by
dressing the young Prince in his colours. The Dauphin
had the good sense to leave Paris and organize the
defence of the Crown. Etienne Marcel appealed for
assistance from the English, which led to his assassination by his followers.

While his son was returning victorious to the capital,
John II, a prisoner in London, was negotiating the
Treaty of Bretigny which, whilst it gave him back his
liberty, sanctioned a substantial dismemberment of his
kingdom. Fate seemed to make up for his sacrifices by
restoring Burgundy to him – it had been enfeoffed to
the descendants of Robert the Pious. He gave it as a
perquisite to his fourth son Philip the Bold. This was
subsequently to have consequences. John's sons,
whom he had left as hostages, escaped and, unable to
pay the ransom required by the English the French
King returned to his imprisonment in London. There
he died in 1364.

Charles V was to come close to rectifying the
national circumstances so seriously endangered by his
father and his grandfather. Having kept up the maletolt
and salt taxes, the special taxes which had been levied to
provide for the payment of John II's ransom, he then
added a hearth tax – forerunner of rates and tax on
rents. With his finances in good order, he was able to
train regular troops and reconstitute a navy. He was
supported by an exceptional military leader, Bertrand
du Guesclin, Constable of France.

The latter had secured the control of the Seine
through his victory at Cocherel in 1365. He then fought
Montfort for Brittany, but was taken prisoner. Once
free, he rid France of the free companies by putting

them at the service of Henry of Trastamara, illegitimate son of the King of Castile, who was fighting his
half-brother, Pedro the Cruel, an ally of the English.
Indirectly this represented a renewal of the war against
Edward III, but on foreign soil. Du Guesclin was taken
prisoner at the battle of Nájera on 3 April 1367, and
the resources of the whole of France were brought
together to pay his ransom. With royal support he
attempted the conquest of Provence, hoping to reunite
Languedoc with Dauphiné. Although he was not
successful in this, du Guesclin nonetheless achieved
other important successes: at the battle of Pontvallain
he reconquered the west of France, and he likewise
recovered Normandy assisted by the fleet which had
been rebuilt and led by the Admiral Jean of Vienne. He
was supported throughout by the King. What Charles
V achieved was so important that it is known as 'the
first reconquest'.

Yet Charles V's undeniable military successes were
counterbalanced by the bad results of his diplomacy
and monetary policies. In particular, in order to hinder
the planned marriage between Margaret the daughter
of the Count of Flanders, and one of the sons of
Edward III, he married this Princess to his brother
Philip the Bold, the Duke of Burgundy. To obtain the
parties' consent he was obliged to return the conquests
made by Philip the Fair, in particular Lille and Douai.
The King had thought that by allying Flanders with
Burgundy he would gallicize Flanders. But the
opposite occurred and Burgundy came under Flemish
influence, its Dukes preferring to live in Bruges rather
than in Dijon. Thus, for France, the Burgundian
marriage was the cause of the difficulties from which
she almost perished in the following century.

108

Charles v's religious policy seems to have been equally unfortunate. France had acquired great prestige through the setting up of the Papacy at Avignon. But under the influence of St Catherine of Siena, the Popes of Avignon contemplated returning to Rome. At the Synod of 1378 the Conclave, meeting in Rome, chose Cardinal Prignano as Pope, and he took the name Urban VI. Siding with the French cardinals, Charles v encouraged the election of an anti-pope, Robert of Geneva, known as Clement VII. Without the support of the King of France this anti-Pope was powerless; but with it, he appeared to flourish. The Catholic Church was split into two factions, until 1415 when the Synod of Constance restored unity.

A last act completes the portrait of Charles v; this King who had instituted a budget and who had endowed the Crown with solid financial foundation, experienced towards the end of his short life doubts as to whether the taxes he had established were just. Out of scruple he abolished them before his death in 1380. This was to leave a situation all the more difficult as he was succeeded by an heir only twelve years of age, a succession that carried with it all the risks inherent in regencies.

In spite of these mistakes, Charles v has a good reputation; in part due to the eulogies of his chroniclers, and still more to the fact that he put an end to the anarchy that he had found. This anarchy was to revive after his death, with the result that the interlude that was his reign, enjoys a reputation that might be considered exaggerated.

The reign of Charles VI, which lasted for forty-two years, is one of the saddest periods in the history of France. Charles v, a widower, had entrusted the regency to one of his brothers, Louis, the Duke of Anjou; but the latter was compelled to share his powers with his other brothers, the Dukes of Burgundy and Berry, with whom the Duke of Bourbon, brother of the late Queen, had allied himself. This oligarchy wished to invest itself with all the positions of power; it re-established the taxes which led to rebellions in the provinces and to disturbances by the *Maillotins* in Paris. In addition a Flemish attack had to be countered, but this was crushed at Roosebeke on 27 November 1382.

The position of the young King appeared to be strengthened by this success, but he allowed himself to be dominated by his uncle Philip, the Duke of Burgundy. Philip inveigled him into an expedition to south Germany, which resulted in Charles VI's marriage to Isabella of Bavaria, the most disasterous of the queens of France. Although the marriage began well, the King felt himself too dominated by his uncles. While they were planning revenge against England, he preferred entente with Richard II. He thanked his uncles, sent them back to their apanages and recalled Charles v's old ministers, known derisively as the *Marmousets*. Rid of the cares of government, the King threw himself into a sumptuous life-style under the bad influence of his brother Louis, the Duke of Orléans.

In 1393, Charles VI led a punitive expedition against the Duke of Brittany. As he was going through the forest of Le Mans on a scorching summer's day, a stranger dressed in rags shot out of a thicket and leapt at the sovereign's bridle crying: 'King, you are betrayed.' Charles appeared very shaken by this incident. The march continued, a page dropped a lance on a helmet, the King woke up with a start shouting:

November 1407. Then, in alliance with Queen Isabella, he became the actual head of government. This divided France into two camps – the party known as the Armagnacs opposing the Burgundians of John the Fearless. For several years, France was torn by civil war and Henry v of England, took advantage of this to resume the hostilities which had been broken off since the time of du Guesclin. He landed at St-Adresse on 12 August 1415 and two months later, on 25 October, completely defeated the French forces at Agincourt.

The Armagnacs led the resistance against the invader but they were defeated and massacred by the Burgundians. The Dauphin Charles countered by having John the Fearless murdered at Montereau on 18 Spetember 1419. This crime achieved him nothing. Dominated by Isabella of Bavaria, Charles VI surrendered his powers to Philip the Good – son of the murdered John. Philip negotiated the Convention of Arras with the English; this was the prelude to the Treaty of Troyes, signed on 22 May 1420, which surrendered France to Henry v. Under the Treaty, Charles VI's daughter, Catherine of France, had to marry the English King, and was to succeed her father when he died. The Dauphin Charles tried to resist this dispossession of his inheritance; he raised troops, defeated the English at Baugé in 1421 and established his capital at Bourges.

Henry v and Charles VI died within three months of each other in 1422. On Charles VI's death, Henry v's one-year-old son, Henry VI, was proclaimed King of France in place of the Dauphin, the legitimate heir. The latter took the name Charles VII.

The situation confronting Charles was tragic: it seemed impossible that he would be able to reconquer his kingdom. In fact it took a real miracle, a figure unique in world history – Joan of Arc.

She was the daughter of a shepherd from Lorraine. Born in the village of Domrémy in 1412, she was

'Death to the traitors', charged with his horse and killed four of his own followers. Sun-stroke had made him lose his reason, and he became lucid only sporadically and for short periods. His uncles resumed power. The following year, during a Court ball, the cloth covering several masquers caught fire. The screams of this 'burning ball' brought about a new crisis of madness in the King, who had up till then been feeling better. This time the madness was permanent.

Charles's policy of entente with England was, nevertheless, continued by the marriage of his daughter Isabelle to Richard II. However, Richard II was dethroned by his cousin, Henry Bolingbroke, Duke of Lancaster, in 1349, and this was soon to upset French policy.

Other difficulties had arisen as a result of the Italian ambitions of the Duke of Orléans – who was married to Valentina Visconti. With the onset of the King's madness, Louis shared the regency with Philip of Burgundy. After the latter's death in 1404, the new Duke of Burgundy, John the Fearless, quarrelled badly with his cousin and had him assassinated on 23

Agnes Sorel, the celebrated mistress of Charles VII.
Lady of Beauté, a castle given her by the King, and
commonly known as Beauté du diable, *she was the first*
of the many official mistresses of French kings.

tending the sheep there when heavenly voices bade her to go to save the kingdom. She managed to have herself taken to the château of Chinon and there she recognized the Dauphin, who had hidden himself in a crowd of courtiers.

Charles VII took this recognition as a sign of the lawfulness of his claim to the throne. He believed in Joan of Arc's mission, had her examined by a group of theologians and entrusted her with an army which liberated Orléans on 8 May 1429. The effect on morale was such that the Maid was able to open up the road to Rheims and have the King crowned there on 17 July.

At this juncture she considered her mission accomplished. But she reckoned without politics; there was in the King's entourage a Burgundian faction which had little wish to see the lawful monarchy triumph. Joan was compelled to resume military operations and, after a few localized successes, she fell into the hands of the Burgundians, who handed her over to the English.

Her trial remains one of the moving episodes of history. Joan defended herself with honour but was nonetheless sentenced to imprisonment for life. Then, as she insisted that she must continue to wear men's clothes which protected her from the attentions of the English soldiers, she was declared a heretic by Pierre Cauchon, the Bishop of Beauvais, who had conducted her trial. She was taken to the stake at Rouen in 1431. When she had breathed her last there was a moment of stupor and the English said: 'We are lost, we have burned a saint.' In fact she had triumphed, but long years had to pass before her victory could be honoured. Charles VII, having abandoned her to her fate, had her good name re-established only in 1457.

After the death of Joan of Arc the English had remained immovable and Henry VI was crowned in Paris. The Duke of Burgundy sought a settlement and negotiated a truce at Chinon. Peace negotiations took place but the claims of the English were such that Charles VII rejected them and resumed hostilities. On 13 April 1436 the Constable, de Richemont, re-captured Paris. The reconquest of Guienne was undertaken, and England had to demand a truce in 1444.

Three years later the English resumed hostilities in Normandy and Charles VII defeated them at Formigny in 1450. He then made towards Guienne and fought a decisive battle at Castillon on 16 July 1453. In the same year Constantinople was captured by the Turks, an event often considered as the beginning of modern history.

The last years of Charles VII's reign were devoted to putting France to rights. When he had come to power the country was ruined, devastated and starving. When his son succeeded him in 1461 the country was restored in its essentials. It now had an administrative and financial framework. Charles VII was nicknamed 'the Well Served' and he was surrounded by a remarkable body of men.

Military reforms commanded priority of attention: Charles VII created standing armies by the ordinances of 1439, and the reform of 1445. The regular companies already formed a professional army, a distant forerunner of the Royal Gendarmerie. He added infantry – the corps of the free archers. He had the Bureau brothers and the Grand Master Bessonneau organize an artillery which became the best in Europe.

Financial reforms were essential to maintain a regular army. These were carried into effect by making indirect taxation permanent and by the establishment of *aides*, salt tax and tallage, the foundation of the modern system of taxation. Administrative reform kept pace with financial arrangements. Charles VII founded provincial *parlements* by the *Grande Ordonnance* of Montils-lez-Tours in 1454. It was necessary to find an honourable and lasting rule of conduct for the holders of the newly-created offices.

They were, therefore, made part of the nobility, but not without provoking opposition from the hereditary nobles. The revolt of the hereditary nobles, known as the Praguerie, was led to a large extent by the Dauphin, the future Louis XI, who often proved himself a rebellious son and who was encouraged in these revolts by Philip the Good, Duke of Burgundy.

Louis XI is the most interesting of the Valois kings. He has aroused severe judgements, and the criticisms are reasonable. As a man he was violent, vindictive and cruel; he lacked moderation in his actions. But his perseverance achieved notable results, and he is among the kings who significantly enlarged French territory.

At first Louis XI gave weight to religious affairs, repudiating the action of his father, author of the Pragmatic Sanction of Bourges of 1438, which had made the French bishoprics open to election. He signed a Concordat with Pope Sixtus IV, which permitted him to nominate the holders of bishoprics himself.

He dismissed all his father's advisers and replaced them with people of humble birth.

He began by raising taxes in order to pay his debts to Philip the Good, of Burgundy, from whom he had snatched the sale of towns in Picardy. These measures made him so unpopular that the hereditary nobility, led by his own brother, the Duke of Berry, united against him. They were supported by Charles the Bold, the Burgundian heir to the throne. After an indecisive battle at Montlhéry, Louis XI was obliged to make a settlement and, by the treaties of Conflans and St-Maur, he agreed to return without compensation to Charles the Bold the towns that his father had acquired. But, in order not to hand them over, he convened the Estates-General in 1468. Since the Estates refused to ratify the treaties, there were renewed difficulties with the Duke of Burgundy. The King stirred up a revolt in Ghent against the Duke, but to distract him he proposed a conference at Péronne. Whilst it was taking place, Charles learned of the rising in Ghent. To punish Louis XI's treachery, he kept him prisoner and then compelled him to give assistance against Ghent. Finally, because of the strength of his position, the Duke of Burgundy had the disputed treaties enforced.

This adventure seriously diminished Louis XI's standing. Had he died at that time, his reign would have been judged as disastrous as that of Charles VI. But he was not a man to lose hope and the Estates, convened in Tours in 1470, declared themselves once again against the enforcement of the treaties. Next, the King took advantage of the dynastic troubles in England to buy the services of Warwick the Kingmaker. But the scheme ended suddenly because Edward IV was able to win back the throne of England and to overthrow Warwick. Moreover, he made preparations to come to the aid of Charles the Bold, who was married to his sister, Margaret of York, in the war which the Duke wished to wage against France.

Luck would have it that Charles the Bold had gone to lay seige to the town of Neuss and Louis XI was able to take advantage of the diversion to propose a financial arrangement to Edward IV. The latter agreed to sign the Treaty of Picquigny on 29 August 1475 in exchange for compensation and an annuity. This Treaty marked the true end of the Hundred Years War. Once the threat from the King of England had been neutralized, Louis XI established a coalition with his own sons. The Duke of Burgundy, at risk between two enemies, made his first attacks to the east. He was defeated by the Swiss at Grandson on 2 March 1476 and at Morat on 22 June 1476. After attacking Lorraine, he sustained a third defeat at Nancy on 5 January 1477, where he met his death.

As Charles the Bold had no sons, Burgundy was at last restored to France. But Louis, flushed with victory, made the mistake of wishing to push his success too far by claiming the portion which reverted to Charles the Bold's daughter, Mary of Burgundy. After five years of war a settlement was concluded: Mary of Burgundy's daughter would become engaged to marry the Dauphin Charles. It was a long-term plan which could not be successfully concluded once the King was dead.

Louis XI did not live to see these consequences, and regency entrusted to his elder daughter, Anne of overshadowed by the astonishing successes which marked the end of his reign. For, to the annexation of Burgundy, the option on Artois and other considerable acquisitions were to be added. The King's brother, the Duke of Berry, had had to exchange his apanage of Champagne for that of Guienne; this important territory reverted to the Crown when the Duke died without an heir. In 1480 the death of King René, last heir of the branch of Anjou of the line of John the Good, brought to France Maine and Anjou, and Provence. This completed French rule in the Mediterranean. These enormous enlargements were to be permanent, for the example of Burgundy had at last made the French kings understand the dangers inherent in apanages.

In domestic policy, Louis XI strengthened the institutions founded by Charles VII. By convening the Estates-General, he derived a source of personal power from contact with the people, and this permitted him to increase taxation and to maintain a standing army equipped with good artillery.

Louis XI died in 1483. Although his son was legally old enough to become King, Louis XI had arranged a regency entrusted to his elder daughter Anne of Beaujeu, who was married to one of his Bourbon cousins. The regency was justified because of the backward intellectual development of the new King who had had a late and difficult puberty. But the

Francis I with his second wife Eleanor of Austria, elder sister of Charles V. The marriage was arranged by the Treaty of Madrid, which Francis was compelled to sign.

regency caused aggravation because Louis Duke of Orléans, the husband of Jeanne of France, sister of both the new King and of Anne of Beaujeu, was annoyed at only being the Lieutenant-General of the kingdom. He demanded the convening of the Estates of Languedoïl with the intention of grabbing all its powers. When the Estates met, numerous disagreements came to light. Anne of Beaujeu settled their differences and then, once the Estates had been dissolved, regained enough power to try to have the Duke of Orléans arrested. The latter fled, but, assisted by the Duke of Brittany, he stirred up a revolt known as 'the Mad War'. The rebels were defeated at St Aubin du Cormier on 14 July 1488 and the Duke of Orléans was imprisoned under very harsh conditions. But Charles VIII, when he began to rule, set his cousin free and reconciled him with Anne of Beaujeu.

Louis of Orléans offered his help in negotiating the marriage of Charles VIII to the Duchess Anne, heiress to Brittany. However, she was engaged to Maximilian of Austria, while the King was engaged to Maximilian's daugher, Margaret. Both engagements were broken off, compelling Charles to restore Artois and Franche-Comté to the Holy Roman Empire. But it was considered that the possession of Brittany was worth

113

Francis I, by Jean Clouet. He succeeded to the throne at the age of twenty and acquired great prestige by his early, but not lasting, successes, and posthumous fame for his artistic taste.

The battle of Pavia, 1525. Francis I was defeated by the Constable of Bourbon, then in the service of Charles V; he wrote to his mother Louise of Savoy: 'Nothing remains to me except my honour and my life, which have been spared.'

this sacrifice, and to avoid future loss, a provision was drawn up stating that if Charles VIII died childless, the Duchess of Brittany would marry his successor.

The King cherished dreams of crusades. To carry out his plans he wanted to make sure of his bases in Italy. In this he was encouraged by the Duke of Orléans, who claimed rights over Milan, at that time in the hands of a usurper, Ludovico Moro.

Charles VIII crossed the Alps at the head of an army of 30,000 men, thus beginning an extraordinary venture which was to last for half a century. It was not so much a war as a triumphal march, especially at Florence where Savonarola greeted the King of France as a liberator. At Rome, the Pope Alexander VI Borgia was reticent but he nevertheless granted free passage to the French troops. The advance continued beyond Naples as the King intended to reassert the rights of the House of Anjou. Having advanced too far down the peninsula, Charles VIII was rather late in perceiving that Europe was uniting against him behind his back. Ludovico Moro, who had become the father-in-law of the Emperor Maximilian, did his utmost to encircle the King of France.

Charles withdrew rapidly and was able to break through the lines of the allies at Fornoue on 6 July 1495. After this negative success he crossed back over the Alps and, intoxicated by Italian art, he made new plans to recapture his conquests in Italy. But he did not have the time to carry them out. In 1498, on the way to play tennis in the moats of his castle at Amboise he ran into the lintel of a low door and died shortly afterwards, aged only twenty-eight. The Crown reverted to his cousin and brother-in-law, Louis, of Orléans.

Louis was at that time in a delicate situation, for he was involved once more in intrigues. Consequently, when the royal messenger arrived at the château of Montil-lez-Blois where he was established, he thought he was going to be arrested. When he learned that he had succeeded to the Crown, which in any account posed problems for a collateral heir, he acted quickly, and, at a stroke, he rallied all his opponents and laid the basis for his popularity. This popularity was so well established that it did not decline when he started separation proceedings against his wife, the pious and physically unfortunate Jeanne of France. Having obtained an annulment on grounds of non-consummation, he married Charles VIII's widow, the Duchess of Brittany, in order to keep Brittany for France.

115

Louis XII then returned to the Italian plans of his predecessor and sent an army of 24,000 men commanded by Trivulzio. He seized Milan and drove out Ludovico Moro. When he came in person to take possession of his conquest in 1500, he found that Ludovico was trying to retake Milan. Louis had him defeated by Trivulzio and confined him for life in the fortress of Lys St Georges in Berry. Milan was thus annexed. Louis then began the conquest of the kingdom of Naples but this was thwarted by the treachery of the King of Aragon.

At that moment, Louis XII fell ill and lost consciousness. Queen Anne therefore signed the Treaty of Blois by which she gave her daughter, Claude of France, in marriage to the future Emperor Charles V. Louis duly recovered and had the Treaty annulled by the Estates-General, which met at Tours on 14 May 1506. The Estates showed their satisfaction by bestowing on Louis XII the nickname 'Father of the People'. This marked about the only period in history when France declared itself satisfied with its government. In addition, the Estates had the arrangements for the marriage of Claude of France broken off and expressed the wish that she be engaged to the Duke of Angoulême, cousin to the King and heir presumptive to the Crown, should the sovereign have no male heir. These dynastic difficulties thus resolved, the King, with the full approval of the French people, resumed his designs on Italy.

To counter the Emperor Maximilian, he sent Trivulzio to support the Venetians. When the Venetians proved treacherous Louis XII broke off his alliance and signed the League of Cambrai with Pope Julius II, Alexander VI's successor, on 10 December 1508. To begin with, the alliance brought success and Louis XII crushed the Venetians at Agnadello on 14 May 1509. But Julius II became uneasy about the successes of the King of France and changed camps. Allying himself with the Venetians, he formed the Holy League and offered the kingdom of France to the English King, Henry VIII.

There was no other solution open to Louis XII but to make war with the Pope. The campaign, which was to become legendary, was led by Gaston de Foix, Duke of Nemours and nephew of the King. Having captured Brescia and Bologna, Gaston de Foix died at the seige of Ravenna in 1512. Fortunes were reversed and the relief army, led by Trémoille, was overwhelmed at Novara on 6 June 1513. Milan was lost, and it was necessary to cross back over the Alps again. The death of Julius II enabled the King of France to sign a truce and to oppose an attempted invasion by the English led by Henry VIII, who had landed at Calais and taken possession of Guisnes.

Whilst this was going on Anne of Brittany died. Louis XII, in order to effect a settlement with Henry VIII

of England, married the latter's sister Mary Tudor, who was aged only seventeen. The King displayed such amorous affection towards his young bride that he died on 1 January 1515, two and a half months after his marriage. The Crown reverted to his son-in-law and cousin, François de Valois-Angoulême, who took the title Francis I.

King Francis I enjoys great prestige: he owes this to his gigantic stature, to the successes which marked the beginning of his reign, and still more to his taste for the arts and his love of literature.

Two advisers helped the twenty-year-old King to direct policymaking: his mother, Louise of Savoy, and his minister Duprat, first President of the Parlement of Paris, and before long Chancellor and Cardinal.

In order to face the danger presented by Charles V, heir to the thrones of Austria and Spain, a considerable army was fitted out to reconquer Milan. The Duke of Bourbon, son-in-law to Anne of Beaujeu, was appointed Constable of France. Francis and his army crossed the Alps at the Larche Pass and a brilliant victory at Marignano on 13/14 September 1515 settled the outcome of the campaign. The King's reputation was greatly enhanced, for he slept on a gun-carriage and had himself dubbed knight by Bayard.

The consequences of the success at Marignano were considerable: first, it established permanent peace with the Swiss which has never been renounced: second, a Concordat was signed with Pope Leo X which remained in force until the Civil Constitution of the Clergy in 1790. This Concordat put the property of the clergy at the disposal of the Crown and made it possible for the Crown to award bishoprics to nominees of its own choice, a power which soon was to lead to abuse. A Treaty signed at Cambrai in 1517 completed these arrangements by having Charles V and Henry VIII of England declare their respective possessions. But just when the principle of the balance of power in Europe was being established, everything was thrown into confusion.

The deaths of the Emperor Maximilian and of Ferdinand of Aragon made their grandson, Charles V, the most powerful ruler in the world and the equal of Charlemagne. To offset the danger of France being encircled, Francis I decided to assert his rights as a rival and he submitted his candidature to the Empire. This gesture, one of the most significant in French history, was momentous in its consequences. But Francis' campaign for election was clumsily executed, and Charles V easily added to his many titles that of Emperor.

The arbiter of this situation was henceforth to be the King of England, capable with his support to tilt the scales in favour of an ally. 'Whoever I support is master,' he declared proudly. A meeting between Henry VIII and Francis I at the famous Field of the

The double spiral staircase in the château of Chambord, built for Francis I. It is said that Leonardo da Vinci had a hand in the designs for this splendid Renaissance building.

Cloth of Gold in 1520 did not result in the settlement which Francis had hoped for. The King of England instead offered his support to Charles V.

France was surrounded and found herself compelled to make war with her two most formidable adversaries. To make matters worse, the King was betrayed by the Constable of Bourbon, whose grievance was a dispute over inheritance. This revolt, the last of the feudal era, opened up the centre of France to the Anglo-Imperial allies. Bayard checked the invasion in the north and went to assist Bonnivet, only to die at Sesia before the Constable. Bourbon invaded Provence to coincide with the French King's march south across the Alps by Mont-Genèvre. A flanking movement towards Gênes would have surrounded Bourbon, but Francis I chose to lay seige to Pavia in 1525. Bourbon went to attack him there, the French suffered total defeat and Francis I was taken prisoner.

The King found himself in the same situation as John the Good after the battle of Poitiers. Kept in captivity in Madrid, Francis I was able to make an alliance with the Sultan, Suleiman the Magnificent, who was to attack Charles V from the rear and to put Vienna to seige in 1529. But first the disastrous Treaty of Madrid had to be signed, giving Burgundy to Charles V and obliging Francis I to leave his sons hostage in Madrid.

On his return to France, Francis I had himself released from his promises by an assembly of leading citizens and found sufficient support in Europe to compel Charles V, who was being threatened by Suleiman, to make a compromise peace by the Treaty of Cambrai of 1529, also called the *Paix des Dames*.

The rest of Francis I's reign can only be understood if the Reformation is taken into account. A monk, Martin Luther, protested against the sale of indulgences. Condemned by the Pope and anathematized by the Emperor Charles V, Luther nonetheless had the support of a large body of German princes who formed a league against the Emperor at Schmalkalden. Francis I helped the princes, a move which was logical from the point of view of French interests, but made the Emperor the true defender of the Catholic faith. Under Francis I the Reformation, however, caused no serious trouble in France. On the other hand, England drifted into schism but, for very particular reasons, did not embrace Lutheranism.

The war against Charles V dragged on, interrupted by periods of truce, for the last ten years of the reign. In 1536 Savoy, Bugey, Bresse and Piedmont were conquered for France, but Charles V countered with an attack on Provence, which was laid to waste. An armistice was made at Nice and Francis I met Charles V under the walls of Aigues-Mortes in 1538. But the entente was short-lived because Charles V appointed his brother as King of the Romans, an appointment which led to the title of Emperor being made hereditary. Charles V called Henry VIII into play; France was once more under attack on all fronts. The Duke of Enghien won a victory in Italy at Ceresole in 1543 but this did not remove the danger of English and Imperial troops moving on Paris. Once more, Francis I set Suleiman onto Charles V's rearguard and the Emperor chose to parley. By the Treaty of Crépy-en-Laonnois on 18 September 1544, France renounced its conquests in Italy and Charles V his claims to Burgundy. At the peace of Ardres in 1546, Henry VIII surrendered Boulogne to France in return for a large indemnity.

The reputation of Francis I's reign does not merely rest on military feats, political and artistic activity must also be taken into account. First and most important,

the marriage was arranged of the Dauphin to the niece of Pope Clement VII; the bride was Catherine de' Medici, who was to manage French politics for nearly half a century. Francis' prolific domestic policy is also noteworthy. In 1539 justice was centralized by the Ordinnance of Villers-Cotterets, the use of French was made obligatory in legal documents and the Collége de France was founded. In the social sphere, Francis I abolished the old feudal lordships, and by his seizure of the wealth of the Constable of Bourbon put an end to apanages. Thus he united national territory.

Francis also encouraged conquests of distant foreign lands, and the pioneers of the discovery of North America departed from the port of Havre de Grâce, which he had founded in 1517. Verrazano discovered the Bay of New York, Jacques Ango

pioneered the discovery of the East Indies and Jacques Cartier explored Canada.

But it was in the sphere of the arts that Francis I created the greatest innovations. This ostentatious King, with his dazzling mistresses, Madame de Châteaubriant and the Duchess of Etampes, was largely responsible for the introduction of Italian Renaissance art into France. At Amboise he received Leonardo da Vinci and bought from him the *Mona Lisa*. At Blois, Chambord and Chaumont he revived the art of building châteaux. Associated with his reign are some of the great architects Primaticcio, Serlio, Boccadoro and the sculptor Jean Goujon.

Henry II was a very different figure from his father, marked as he was by the sadness of his childhood captivity in Madrid. He was little enamoured with his wife, Catherine de' Medici, although she bore him six children. Instead, he was dominated by a favourite twenty years older than himself – the famous Diane de Poitiers, who was to play a political role and who was to urge her lover to persecute the Protestants. Henry II, already dominated by a mistress, was also dominated by a minister, the Constable de Montmorency, who came to wield great influence. De Montmorency was supported by his nephews, the Châtillons, the eldest of whom is best known under the name of Admiral de Coligny.

The opening years of Henry II's reign were to prove difficult because Francis I had neglected the country's finances. The increase in salt tax led to riots and in Guienne, Montmorency had to use force to suppress them. A new arrival at Court, the Duke of Guise,

Henry II was mortally wounded in this tournament, held on 29 June 1559 to celebrate the marriage of his daughter Elizabeth to Philip II of Spain after the Peace of Cateau-Cambrésis.

seemed happy to pacify Saintonge.

Once Charles V had defeated the Schmalkaldic League, he was able to set himself up as federal leader of Europe. He was opposed by Henry II, who held the view that it was necessary 'to have German affairs under one's control and in as much difficulty as they possibly could be'. Henry II continued the entente with the Turks, gave assurances to the Protestant princes and renewed the treaty with the Swiss cantons. With the aid of Maurice of Saxony, Henry II became Protector of the towns of Toul, Metz and Verdun – the Three Bishoprics. Henry entrusted the regency to Catherine de' Medici and set off towards Germany to 'water his horses in the Rhine'. During this expedition the King set up a regency at Nancy and appeared for a moment to get the better of the Emperor. But his success was short-lived, Charles V laid siege to Metz; and the town was only saved by the resistance of Francis, Duke of Guise.

The struggle continued in Italy and on the Mediterranean. English mediation led to Henry II's acceptance of a truce at Vaucelles in 1555, which restored Piedmont to France and assured him possession of the Three Bishoprics. But again success was precarious. Charles V retired from the world to the monastery of Yuste, giving Bohemia and Hungary to his brother Ferdinand, and Spain to his son Philip.

Encouraged by Pope Paul IV, who wished to destroy the Imperial influence in Italy, Henry II made an alliance with him and the war started again. Montmorency was so severely defeated at St-Quentin on 10 August 1557 that Philip II came close to entering Paris. But the King of Spain did not take advantage of his success and Francis of Guise, appointed Lieutenant-General, succeeded in recapturing Calais from the English allies of Spain on 8 January 1558. The treaty of Câteau-Cambrésis on 2 April 1559 put an end to hostilities. Henry II kept Calais but finally gave up his dream of Italian conquests. To seal the agreement he gave his daughter Elizabeth in marriage to Philip II. In celebration of this peace, Henry II provided for a series of entertainments at Court. He took a leading part in these and, during a joust with Montmorency, he was wounded by his adversary's lance which struck the

120

visor of his helmet. After nine days in a coma Henry II died at the age of forty-one leaving the throne to his eldest son Francis II, a sickly child of sixteen. This premature succession was the first of a series of sad events for France.

Queen Catherine de' Medici was to dominate the thirty years that marked the reigns of Henry II's three sons. This extraordinary woman, who had acted several times as Regent proved to be a wily politician rather than a great policy-maker. Her volte-faces were to provoke dramatic events.

Of Francis II, her eldest son, there is little to say except that he was Mary Stuart's husband and that the sensual attachment which she inspired in him hastened his end. During his eighteen-month-reign, the Crown had to face a Protestant plot known as the Amboise Conspiracy, which was savagely repressed.

The Guises, uncles of the young Queen, exercised some power and represented a Catholic faction which was to conflict with the Protestant faction of the Coligny-Châtillons, and even more, with that of the Bourbons. Anthony, leader of the Bourbons, King of Navarre by his marriage to Jeanne d'Albret, and brother of Condé, was heir presumptive to the throne in the event of the failure of the Valoise line.

The reign of Charles IX began in 1560, when he was still a sickly child. It was marked from the outset by confrontation between Catholics and Protestants. Catherine de' Medici's chancellor, Michel de L'Hôpital wished to bring about a settlement; this failed at the Colloquy of Poissy, but the Edict of St-Germain promulgated on 17 January 1562, gave the Protestants the right to practise their religion.

The peace was of short duration; on 1 March 1562 followers of the Duke of Guise, who were passing through the town of Wassy, had a violent scuffle with the Protestants and this unleashed civil war. Eight distinct struggles have been classified, but they are only episodes of the same war, as the balance of power swung from one side to the other. The first of these episodes began with the victory in 1562 of the Duke of Guise over Condé and Coligny at Dreux; the victory was followed by the assassination of the Duke of Guise and the death of Anthony of Bourbon. The two factions, having lost their respective leaders, made peace at Troyes in 1564.

Charles IX came of age and devoted eighteen months to a tour of France, taking with him Henry of Navarre, Anthony of Bourbon's son. On his return civil war resumed. It came to an end at the battle of St-Denis where the Constable de Montmorency met his death. A third phase of war followed, during the course of which the Duke of Anjou, younger brother of Charles IX and the future Henry III, proved himself to be a good fighter at the battles of Jarnac and Moncontour in 1569.

The Peace of St-Germain in 1570 seemed to indicate a general reconciliation. Charles IX then made large concessions to the Protestants and took their leader, Admiral de Coligny, as his adviser. They decided that Henry of Navarre should marry Marguerite, the King's sister. But at the time of the marriage, celebrated on 19 August 1572, a disagreement arose between Catherine de' Medici and Coligny. The Guises attempted to have the Admiral killed.

Catherine de' Medici, still fearing Coligny's influence, persuaded her weak son that there was a Protestant plot to bring down the Crown and she begged him to order the massacre of the Protestants. After some hesitation, the King spoke the famous words: 'Kill them all so that not one of them remains to reproach me.' This massacre, know as the St Bartholemew's Day Massacre of 23–24 August 1572, still tarnishes Charles IX's reputation. It rekindled the civil war for the fourth time.

But the King did not see the end of the war, for he died of pneumonia at the beginning of 1574, leaving only the Duke of Auvergne, an illegitimate son by his

The Dominican Jacques Clément assassinating Henry III. Before dying, the last Valois named Henry of Navarre as his successor, urging him to become a Catholic.

favourite Marie Touchet. The Crown reverted to his brother the Duke of Anjou, who had been chosen King of Poland in preference to the Czar Ivan the Terrible. He returned hurriedly from his capital at Cracow and took the French throne under the title Henry III. Few kings in history have attracted so much discussion. Henry III distinguished himself by his habits which earned him the name 'Prince of Sodom'. He lived surrounded by beautiful men known as the 'mignons'. Nevertheless, he got on well with his wife Louise de Mercoeur.

The new King had to face a difficult situation, from which he extracted himself several times with tact and determination. He found the country in a state of civil war and threatened by the invasion of *Reiters* hired by Condé. These were defeated at Dormans by Henry of Guise, son of Francis of Guise, and henceforth the Duke of Guise was to prove to be a powerful rival to the Crown.

By the Edict of Beaulieu in 1576, Henry III bestowed freedom of worship on the Protestants. In response to this, the Duke of Guise formed a Catholic party called The League. Henry III, with great skill assumed the leadership of this party. This did not prevent three civil wars in succession, the details of which matter little. What was important was that on the death in 1584 of the Duke of Alençon, the youngest son of Henry II, Henry of Navarre, leader of the Protestants, became the heir presumptive to the Crown. Henry of Navarre's right to the throne was challenged, because of his religious adherence, and this fired Henry of Guise's ambitions, for he claimed descent from the Carolingians and coveted the Crown.

An eighth religious war known as the 'Three Henrys' was the result. Henry of Navarre, a clever soldier, won the first great victory of the Protestants over the Catholics at Coutras on 20 October 1587. To counter this, Henry of Guise twice prevented the invasion of the *Reiters* at Vimory and Auneau, and in so doing acquired such popularity that The League controlled Paris. Henry III then forebade the Duke of Guise to enter the capital. When the Duke defied the prohibition, the barricades went up in Paris and on 12 May 1588, the King was forced to flee to Blois.

The Estates-General were convened at Blois. The King was quickly taken to task by the nobility, who rallied to the Duke of Guise. Henry III wavered no longer; on 23 December 1588 he had the Duke of Guise assassinated. A few days later, Catherine de' Medici died.

The League called up armies and rose up against the King. Henry III could find no other solution than

reconciliation with Henry of Navarre, for he saw in him the only possibility for dynastic continuity. On 16 April 1589 a meeting took place at Plessis-lez-Tours. The King of France and the King of Navarre joined forces and went to St-Cloud to lay siege to Paris.

The League recognized the hopelessness of their situation, and sent a fanatical Dominican monk, Jacques Clément, to the King, carrying credentials. Taken into the presence of the King, Jacques Clément stabbed him in the stomach with a knife. As the monk was then thrown out of the window, we are left in the dark as to the motives for his action.

Before dying on 2 August 1589, the King had Henry of Navarre summoned and beseeched him for the last time to become a Catholic. His dying words to him were: 'My brother, I well know that it is your turn to inherit the throne and I have laboured to protect for you that which God has given you.' With this magnificent gesture, which secured the continuity of the dynasty, Henry III died. The Valois of the legitimate line died with him. The Duke of Auvergne, illegitimate son of Charles IX, died only in 1650. He had taken as his second wife, late in life Françoise de Mareuil, and she lived long enough to become in 1708 godmother to a young Belloy. He lived to be one hundred, and as Cardinal-Archbishop of Paris officiated at the consecration of Napoleon. Thus it is that the French Emperor received the blessing of the godchild of Charles IX's daughter-in-law.

123

The Stuarts

Traditionally fond of losers, the English people
have a special place in their hearts for
this ill-fated family

The Stuarts (or 'Stewarts'), as their name implies, were by origin hereditary High Stewards to the medieval kings of Scotland. But in 1315 Walter, the sixth Steward, married Marjorie, daughter of King Robert Bruce, the hero of the Scots War of Independence against England, and she bore him a son, also named Robert. When Bruce's son, King David II, died childless in 1371, his Stuart nephew ascended the throne as Robert II.

The first hundred years of the dynasty were embattled and precarious. Scotland was a weak, wild and backward country hampered by its continuing feud with England; governmental institutions were rudimentary, and the King no more than the tolerated spokesman of a lawless and quarrelsome aristocracy. It is significant that of the first five Stuart kings to bear the family name 'James', whose reigns spanned the years 1406–1542, all of them came to the throne as children, and only one died in his bed. And the premature death of James V in 1542 ushered in the longest minority yet, for his daughter Mary was only a week old. When they brought him the news of her birth, he turned his face to the wall and summed up his family's history in the bitter words: 'It came with a lass, and it will pass with a lass.'

In fact, Mary Queen of Scots (reigned 1542–67) grew up to be one of the most celebrated of the Stuarts, her name a by-word for sexual adventure and ill-starred romance. She had a French mother, Mary of Guise, and she was raised at the French Court. She did not return to Edinburgh until 1561, with one marriage already behind her, to King Francis II of France, who had died the previous year. But as the throne of France receded, that of England beckoned; for Queen Elizabeth, the last surviving child of Henry VIII, had

announced that she would never marry. This left Mary as the next in line, for she was the granddaughter of Henry VIII's elder sister Margaret, who had married James IV of Scotland.

Unfortunately, hampered as she was by her staunch Catholicism, she could not consolidate a power base in Scotland. In the maelstrom of Scots politics she could at first use her outstanding sexual charm and the promise of her hand to play off one nobleman against another; but she threw away this weapon when she married Lord Darnley in 1565. She bore him a son the following year, but the marriage then broke down in spectacular fashion, and when Darnley was mysteriously killed in 1567 she was at once the prime suspect. Her subsequent elopement with an unsavoury adventurer, James Hepburn, Earl of Bothwell, was held to demean the dignity of the Crown, and she was deposed by a sudden *coup d'état* in favour of her one-year-old son, now King James VI. In 1568 she escaped from custody and crossed into England, only to find that she had made her imprisonment permanent. Queen Elizabeth was delighted to have the heir to the throne under her control, but she was too dangerous to be liberated, and the unresolved suspicion that she had murdered her husband still hung over her. Her religion naturally made her the focus for a series of Catholic plots against Elizabeth, and in 1587 the Queen finally bowed to pressure from Parliament and her ministers for her execution.

By this time James VI was twenty-one, and had been reigning somewhat precariously for five years. He wasted few regrets on a mother he had never known, and whom he had been raised to regard as a Popish whore. Instead, he concluded an agreement with Elizabeth which safeguarded his rights of succession,

125

Mary Queen of Scots returning to Edinburgh after her flight following Rizzio's murder. She has become a tragic figure famous for her misfortunes in love and her death on the scaffold.

and in the 1590s set out to impose his rule on Scotland; he did not intend to make his mother's mistake. And he triumphantly succeeded, despite his own personal timorousness, the wretched poverty of the Crown, the absence of a royal army. He used guile and diplomacy to subdue a nobility exhausted by generations of internecine strife, and held them down by encouraging the middle classes to show their independence; he secured complete control of Parliament, then enhanced its role in government. Finally, he safeguarded the succession by marrying Anne of Denmark in 1589, and, though even at this age his sexual inclinations lay another way, siring three promising children, the youngest, the future Charles I, born in 1600. By then he had had the title of the greatest King of Scotland since Robert Bruce. The death of Elizabeth in 1603 called him to London and the English throne.

Unfortunately, James I of England (reigned 1603–25) could not repeat James VI's success. He was unlucky in his predecessor. Even as an old woman Elizabeth had projected enormous glamour and power over those around her; she had 'style', that undefinable rightness in looks, bearing and speech which all the Tudors and the Stuarts had, except James I. He was uncouth, clumsy and undignified, and a congenital weakness in the legs made it difficult for him to walk or even stand well. His humdrum familiarity disconcerted a Court accustomed to the oracular majesty of the old Queen. It was doubly unfortunate that his first task was to dismantle the spectacular and exciting apparatus of war emergency over which Elizabeth had presided with such *éclat*. Peace with Spain was vitally necessary, but it brought James no credit; his favourite motto, *beati pacifici*, was ill received by a nation still dreaming of bellicose adventures, and his well-known fear of cold steel was a joke.

The successful techniques he brought with him were not transferable. The sophistication and complexity of English administration was beyond him; he leaned heavily on Robert Cecil, Earl of Salisbury, the chief minister he had inherited from Elizabeth, and on his death in 1612 found him irreplaceable. The politics of Scotland was the politics of small group situations; James had trained himself in face-to-face negotiation with men he knew well, and he had the pace and timing required. He would have made a superb industrial arbitrator today. But he could not begin to handle a large inchoate body like the House of Commons, to which he was denied direct access; he was disconcerted, too, to find that the English nobility, though wealthy enough, were proportionately small in numbers and weak in authority compared with the Scots nobility. On their side, the Commons were suspicious of an experienced male ruler, the first for fifty years, who was a public advocate of Divine Right, and they proved darkly jealous of their rights and privileges. In

an attempt to gain contact James resorted to long, pedantic, condescending speeches, and when he was thwarted, indulged in petulant outbursts which had authoritarian undertones.

The most important result was that he could never secure from Parliament the additional income the Crown desparately needed in an era of mounting inflation; a need exacerbated by James's extravagance, and his rather pathetic attempts to rival his fellow monarchs in public display, notably through the great masques, staged by Inigo Jones, which were a feature of his reign. His inability to handle money was proverbial, and Parliament was not anxious to indulge his spectacular tastes; moreover, it still suspected his motives. After a long series of abortive negotiations they parted in 1611 on the worst of terms.

From then on the reign ran downhill, with a bankrupt and ageing King at the wheel, and its career punctuated by resounding explosions: the aptly-named Addled Parliament of 1614, which provoked James to remark: 'I am surprised my ancestors permitted such an institution to come into existence'; the Overbury scandal of 1616, which involved his favourite, the Earl of Somerset, in charges of murder and witchcraft; and in 1618 the execution of that great Elizabethan folk hero, Sir Walter Raleigh, to appease the Spanish government.

But there was further discredit to be endured. Up to now James's obvious homosexual tendencies had been largely disregarded; his beaux were expensive and greedy, but they had no influence on State policy (unlike Queen Elizabeth's). But this ended with the advent in 1616 of the handsome and ambitious young *parvenu* George Villiers, successively Earl, Marquis and Duke of Buckingham, the love of the King's old age. The surrender to him of complete governmental control, in patronage as well as policy, deeply alienated the ruling classes, particularly the nobility; and Buckingham's unexpected influence with the young Prince Charles ensured the perpetuation of his power.

Buckingham seized the first opportunity to recreate the glamorous war situation of Elizabeth's reign, but in the changed conditions of the 1620s he failed, and his failure ultimately engulfed Charles I. In 1618 Bohemia revolted against the Hapsburgs, and James's son-in-law, the Elector Palatine, unwisely accepted the offer of the Crown, only to be ejected in 1620 by Spanish and Imperialist forces. The nation clamoured for war on behalf of the popular Princess Elizabeth and her husband, but a new Parliament called in 1621 would not vote the necessary money; instead it impeached the Lord Chancellor, Francis Bacon, and quarrelled furiously with the King over freedom of speech. In a last attempt at 'appeasement', James allowed Charles to go with Buckingham to Madrid to negotiate a marriage alliance. They returned deeply humiliated

127

without a Spanish princess and, with the aid of another jingoistic (though still penny-wise) Parliament summoned in 1624, overrode James's cherished peace policy, and launched the nation into war.

James died in 1625, a disappointed and disillusioned man. Even his statesmanlike plan of uniting Scotland and England had been rejected. But the extent of the disaster is often exaggerated. He was a pliant man, with a talent for defusing explosive situations. For instance, by his genius for face-to-face negotiation, at the Hampton Court Conference in 1604 he settled the Puritan problem, which his son found intractable. Again, though his relations with Parliament were never good, he avoided direct confrontation until 1621. One wry epitaph on him reads: 'He was (take him altogether and not in pieces) such a king I wish this kingdom never have any worse, on the condition, nor any better.'

Charles I (reigned 1625–49) was manifestly better; or at least, he was in complete contrast to his father. Graceful in his movements, measured in his speech, handsome and elegant, he had to an eminent degree that 'style' which James could never aspire to. His manners were dignified, if a trifle stilted, and he was restrained in his pleasures. He was almost unique amongst contemporary monarchs in that no breath of sexual scandal ever touched his name. The atmosphere at Whitehall changed overnight; henceforward ceremonial would still be expensive, but at least it was sober and decorous.

But he had embarked on a war with Spain which Parliament had applauded but would not pay for, and which Buckingham, as self-constituted war leader, could not wage effectively. Buckingham started with a disastrous expedition against Cadiz in 1625, then turned his hand to diplomacy; with the result that England was soon at war with France as well. This had unfortunate repercussions on the King's private life, for he had now married Henrietta Maria, sister of Louis XIII.

As for Parliament, it found him a different man from his father. He lacked resilience and a sense of humour, his anger was quick to rise, and hard to deflect. He shared James's belief in the God-given ascendancy of kings, and he was not willing to compromise. The Commons regarded him with a wary obstructiveness from the beginning, and their relations with each other soon acquired a sharp cutting edge unknown in the previous reign. He leaped to the conclusion that there was a deliberate plot afoot to restrict his authority; the Commons feared he would seize the first opportunity to dispense with them altogether. Both sides adopted the tactics of confrontation. The Parliament of 1625 was abruptly dissolved; the Parliament of 1626 suffered the same fate when it tried to impeach Buckingham, and Charles then embarked on what was

effectively a direct confrontation with the whole ruling class by levying forced loans from the nobility and gentry and imprisoning those who refused. Buckingham's military incompetence wasted the fruits of this policy, and in 1628 another Parliament forced the King to accept the Petition of Right by which he formally surrendered the right to levy taxes on his own initiative. The assassination of Buckingham in August 1628 cleared the air, but in 1629 there was another full-scale confrontation ending in a stormy dissolution, though this time Parliament was clearly the aggressor.

Charles now fulfilled his threats; he slashed expenditure by pulling England out of the war, and proceeded to rule without Parliament. In this he was successful. His rule was probably unpopular, but he met with no overt opposition, and he and his new Archbishop of Canterbury, William Laud, laboured to suppress Puritanism and impose on the Church a rigid Anglican uniformity. (It was at once Charles's glory, and his misfortune, that he was the first English monarch to be raised in the Church of England.) England seemed to be moving, though less purposefully, in the same direction as France under Cardinal Richelieu. Many thought this deliberate, but Charles made no attempt to form an army, though he did refit the navy with the aid of a controversial new tax, ship money, which his opponents unsuccessfully contested in the courts.

Meanwhile Charles had found a new serenity. The death of Buckingham brought a reconciliation with Henrietta Maria which was a lasting source of happiness. It is possible that the marriage had not even been consummated before; but the future Charles II was born in 1630, in 1631 the Princess Mary (later Princess of Orange and mother to William III), and in 1633 the future James II. But the Queen's aggressive devotion to Rome prejudiced the King's reputation, in the absence of Parliaments the gap between Court and Country widened, and he never found a servant to replace Buckingham. Even to the Court Charles became an aloof, hieratic figure, locked in connubial bliss and encircled by an impenetrable wall of etiquette. With his most loyal servants he had nothing in common; the Earl of Strafford he sent to Ireland, and Archbishop Laud later wrote regretfully of his master: 'He was a mild and gracious prince who knew not how to be, or be made, great.' It is remarkable that the great Van Dyck portraits of the 1630s possess a brooding tragedy not evident in his last portrait, in 1648. When they sent Bernini a Van Dyck in 1637 so that he could make a portrait bust, he said, 'Never have I beheld a countenance so unfortunate.'

Misfortune struck with startling suddenness. An attempt to impose the English prayer book on the Presbyterian Scots, who had been remarkably quiescent under long-range rule from London, provoked a

James I of England (VI of Scotland) attending a sermon in St Paul's Churchyard in London. James became King of England in 1603 on the death of his Tudor cousin Elizabeth I.

nationalist revolt in 1638 which Charles had neither the money nor the men to cope with. The Long Parliament, which met in 1640, had been given an unlooked-for chance, and they were determined not to squander it. They sent Strafford to the block, put Laud in the Tower and dismantled the whole structure of Church discipline, giving Puritanism its head. They then passed a stream of statutes curbing the regal power, including one which made it impossible for the King to dissolve them. Compromise and peace were still theoretically possible, but both sides, understandably, were now more wedded than ever to the 'conspiracy theory' of politics. The King was freely blamed for the Irish Rebellion in November 1641, and neither side would trust the other to raise an army to suppress it. Charles confirmed Parliament's worst fears by an abortive attempt at a *coup d'état*, and in January 1642 he left London. After a series of pronunciamentos on both sides, civil war broke out in August.

Strangely enough, Charles's popularity and moral authority steadily rose from then on. He fought a hard war, and to defeat him Parliament had to call on the Scots again, and then raise an expensive professional army, the New Model, under Oliver Cromwell. His defeat in 1646 ushered in a complex series of negotiations between Charles on the one hand, and Parliament, the Army and the Scots on the other. Those concerned in these negotiations found their distrust of him handsomely confirmed, but to a disillusioned public he became increasingly an unfortunate but worthy neutral surrounded by power-crazy intriguers. Holding out for the re-establishment of the Church and determined to retain control of State policy, Charles got the best terms from the Scots; they invaded England in 1648, only to be annihilated by Cromwell at Preston.

The needless bloodshed of this second civil war infuriated the Army. The occupied London and coerced Parliament into bringing Charles to trial for high treason; he refused to plead, was declared guilty, and beheaded on 30 January 1649. England was declared a republic.

This supereme act of stupidity was calculated to make Charles a martyr; and it did. His supreme sacrifice on behalf (it was said) of the Church of England and of law and order had repercussions lasting for generations. His execution was high melodrama. For some time he had had a foreknowledge of doom (towards which his own policy was carrying him anyway), and he rose to the occasion admirably. His dignity, forbearance and grace were so overwhelming as to lead his more hysterical supporters to blasphemous comparisons between him and the Saviour of the World.

The iron rule of the Army only confirmed the nation in its royalism, and once Cromwell's grip was relaxed in 1658 it was a matter of time before Charles's son was triumphantly recalled to the throne. Monarchy and Church were both restored in 1660.

Charles II (reigned 1660–85) had one of the most comprehensive upbringings of any English king. Titular commander in the West in 1645, aged fifteen, he retired abroad at the end of the first civil war, and assumed the responsibilities of kingship-in-exile in 1649. Enraged at Charles I's death, the Scots invited him to Edinburgh and at the age of twenty-one he led an army into England. After his defeat at Worcester he lived for six weeks on the run, amongst the common people and one of them, until his escape to France.

Exile toughened him, emotionally and physically, but it left him callous and cynical. It also left him little time for learning, and despite his patronage of the Royal Society, founded in 1662, and of men like Hobbes and Dryden, his intellectuality was superficial. But he had a practical gift for handling men, of all kinds and all ages; like his grandfather James I, he had a talent for negotiation, and he was the only man who could consistently outwit that practised diplomatist, Louis XIV of France.

Amateur genetics is a dangerous pastime, but it is difficult not to see in him at the same time a great deal of his other grandfather, Henry IV of France; in his immediate practical ability, his easy charm, his cynicism and his essential frivolity. He had something of Henry's looks, too; he was a tall, swarthy man, with dark, curly hair, dark eyes, and a relaxed swinging gait; a considerable athlete who rode his own horse to victory at Newmarket quite late in life. He was not considered handsome – in the seventeenth century male beauty partook of the feminine, as with Charles I – but he was immensely attractive to women, and they to him. An exact count of his conquests can never be made, but *The Complete Peerage* lists fourteen known illegitimate children, beginning with James Crofts, later Duke of Monmouth, in 1649. On his return in 1660 he openly paraded his liaison with Barbara, Countess of Castlemaine, and his patronage of the theatre soon brought a procession of young actresses to his bed, headed by the famous Nell Gwynne. Not until the late 1670s did he settle down in something like regular domesticity with the Frenchwoman Louise de Kéroualle, Duchess of Portsmouth.

In short, he had 'style' to an unusual degree; he was able, witty and distinguished; but he was never really respected, as even his unpopular father had been. And though he must count as the most successful member of the dynasty, no one thought of him as a great king. There was an essential shallowness to his character, and though his informality was appreciated after the glacial humours of Charles I, it too easily degenerated

*Charles I, by Van Dyck. As Archbishop Laud wrote,
'He was a mild and gracious prince who knew not how
to be, or be made, great.' He was the only English King
to be executed.*

into frivolity. When the poet Rochester penned some scurrilous lines ending,

Here lies a pretty witty prince, whose word no man relies on;
He never said a foolish thing, nor ever did a wise one.

Charles imperturbably replied: 'Quite so. My words are my own; my actions belong to my ministers.' Such *bons mots* are better appreciated by his contemporaries than by posterity.

Not only was he frivolous, he was shifty; men trusted him no more than they had trusted his father. Looking at his reign as a whole, we can detect no positive long-term policy, just a series of brilliant short-term improvizations. He often said he was determined not to go 'on his travels' again, and his attitude can be summed up in the word 'survivalism'. A determined and consistent man could have used the overwhelming revulsion of feeling in favour of the monarchy in 1660 to win back some of the ground lost by Charles I in the 1640s, perhaps even to move towards an autocracy on the Continental model. Instead, Charles frittered away his advantages, then tried to recoup them by a war on Holland which ended in 1667 with humiliating defeat and an empty Treasury. Nor did the Plague of 1665 and the Great Fire of London of 1666 help; it was natural, if unfair, that such natural disasters should be blamed on the government. Switching course, Charles then signed the notorious Treaty of Dover with France in 1670, and

joined her in another attack on Holland, which was again abortive.

By this time, he had virtually created an opposition in Parliament which had been non-existent in 1661, and he was strongly suspected of Catholicism, as his father had been. His favour to Catholics was blatant, and he had married a Catholic princess, Catherine of Braganza. Worse still, Catherine proved sterile, which meant that the Crown must devolve on his unpopular brother, James, Duke of York. In 1673 a suspicious Parliament passed a Test Act to exclude Catholics from public life, and the first to resign was James himself. At this stage Charles's policy blew up in his face. The opposition 'Country Party', strengthened by the adhesion of many of Charles's former supporters and servants, forced him out of the war. For the next six years he lived a hand-to-mouth existence, playing

off France against Holland in an over-clever and ultimately unsuccessful foreign policy, while at home his chief minister, Lord Danby, struggled to control Parliament and rally the nation to the King in the unlikely role of Defender of the (Anglican) Faith. Danby's greatest *coup* was to marry James's elder daughter, Princess Mary, to William III of Orange in 1677, a match which was to have unforeseen consequences.

In 1678 and 1679 the monarchy nearly collapsed again. Parliament and the nation were stampeded by a number of mendacious informers, who pretended to reveal a 'Popish Plot' to assassinate Charles and put his brother on the throne. Danby was swept into the Tower, James was forced into exile, and three disorderly Parliaments met in two years, all clamouring for the Duke's exclusion from the succession. The

133

A painting by Duncan of the 'Young Pretender', Charles Edward Stuart, entering Edinburgh in 1745 after the battle of Prestonpans. His was the most serious attempt to restore the Stuarts to the English throne.

King's bastard son, Monmouth, ran as an alternative candidate, and the nation was on the verge of civil war.

But, fortunately, Europe was at peace, and Charles was at his most brilliant in a crisis which called for tactical, day-to-day improvization. He refused to be rattled – as he told James: 'They will never kill me to make you king' – he gave his opponents plenty of rope, and they duly hanged themselves. The intemperance and irresponsibility of the 'Exclusionists', or 'Whigs', alarmed a nation which had already experienced civil war in that century. Led by the Church, conservative opinion rallied to the monarchy, indifferent now to whether it was Catholic or not. On the flood-tide of reaction the Whig leaders were destroyed, their puppet Monmouth was exiled, and after 1681 Parliament did not meet again.

It was Charles's second chance to consolidate the power of the monarchy; unquestioning royalism was the order of the day, and with the steady increase of overseas trade the Crown's income was rising too. But Charles, typically, was content to leave such initiatives to his brother James, now a strong ally of the Anglican Church and very much the coming man. (Although Charles more than once observed that he would not last three years once he came to the throne.) Charles lived out his life in peace at Newmarket or Windsor, in the company of a few select 'yes-men' and his bevy of increasingly middle-aged mistresses. He died in February 1685 of a coronary thrombosis, but not before he was admitted to the Catholic Church, at the very last moment.

James II (reigned 1685–8) had fought with distinction in the French and the Spanish armies in the 1650s, and after the Restoration, in common with other generals of this generation, he went to sea; in the Dutch Wars of his brother's reign he led the English fleet in several testing though indecisive battles. Much of his inflexibility, his naivety and his political clumsiness falls into place if we think of him as a retired professional soldier taking up politics in late middle age, an Eisenhower or a Franco; so does his insistence on unquestioning obedience, and his impatience with criticism or opposition.

Yet he had a long apprenticeship to civil government; for most of his brother's reign he was a member of all councils, privy to all decisions. Unfortunately, he learned the wrong lessons from his experience. He believed that his brother's flexibility – and his father's, for he was an earnest student of recent history – had seriously endangered the monarchy, and the Exclusion Crisis confirmed him in the soldierly belief that attack was the best means of defence, and retreat was a sign of weakness. When it was suggested that he pardon the Seven Bishops in 1688 he refused, 'bringing forward the example of the late king his father and the king his brother, who had weakened their authority – and in his father's case brought on his own death – by showing undue leniency'. The Duke of Lauderdale's comment was: 'This good prince has all the weaknesses of his father without the strength.'

For a bluff, open, physical man his character is strangely elusive. He had the Stuart 'style', the grace of bearing and the knack with clothes. In his youth he was very fair, and more conventionally good-looking than Charles. He liked to be painted in armour, naturally. He was highly-sexed, like his brother, but at the same time something of a Puritan; Charles once remarked that his mistresses were so ugly they must be a penance. As King he imposed rigid standards of morality and decorum on the Court, but he had to resort to a hair-shirt and self-flagellation to keep himself in line. His most famous mistress was Arabella Churchill, sister to John, Duke of Marlborough; she bore him a famous son, James Fitzjames, Duke of Berwick, later Marshal of France. His first marriage, with Anne Hyde, daughter to the Earl of Clarendon, arose from an illicit pregnancy; it was typical that he should sweep aside his mother's objections and 'do the right thing'. She bore him two daughters, Mary and Anne, both Queens of England.

His conversion to Rome in 1668 came out of the blue; hitherto his interest in any kind of religion had been minimal. Being James, of course, he never wavered in his new faith, but his attempts to convert others to it were strangely tentative, almost shy. He had few Catholic friends, and one of his weaknesses as a Catholic king is that he was curiously out of touch with the English Catholic community, and his partiality for the Society of Jesus ensured that he remained so. On the other hand, he was almost entirely ignorant of European Catholicism, and he shared the 'siege mentality' typical of the English Catholics down to the present day.

His first marriage gave him a close relationship with the Anglican upper classes, which he maintained; despite his conversion, he was a strong public supporter of the Anglican Church, and many regarded his politico-religious attitude as more honest and more reliable than his brother's. In the aftermath of the Popish Plot he became a rallying point for reaction, even the leader of the Anglican interest.

On his first wife's death he had married an Italian Catholic, Mary of Modena, but she remained childless. He was fifty-two in 1685, an old man by contemporary standards, and both his daughters had been raised as firm Protestants and married to Protestants: Mary to William of Orange, Anne to Prince George of Denmark. With a short reign in prospect, and one likely to be conservative-Anglican in tone, his accession was generally welcomed, and the Parliament he immediately called granted him the unprecedented income of two million pounds a year. It is ironic that

James was the first Stuart monarch who had no substantial money worries.

But the rot set in almost at once. Charles II's son Monmouth raised a rebellion in the west that summer; it was easily crushed, but James announced that he intended to keep on foot the army of 20,000 men he had raised, and to retain certain Catholic officers he had commissioned in defiance of the Test Act. This led to a direct confrontation with Parliament in November, and it did not meet again. He then quarrelled with his principal allies, the leaders of the Anglican Church. In 1686 he suspended Bishop Compton of London, and early in 1687 he dismissed his Anglican ministers, including his brothers-in-law, Lawrence Hyde, Earl of Rochester, and Henry Hyde, Earl of Clarendon. Meanwhile he was giving every encouragement to the Catholic priesthood, in defiance of the law, and in April 1687 he suspended the penal laws by public proclamation.

His real aims are a matter for speculation, but it is not surprising that many Englishmen, with the example before them of Louis XIV and other European rulers, believed that James was working towards a Catholic despotism maintained by armed force. The crisis deepened when the Queen became pregnant in 1687 and on 10 June 1688 gave birth to a son, James Francis Edward, bringing the prospect of a Catholic dynasty in perpetuity. James chose this moment to prosecute the Archbishop of Canterbury and six of his bishops for seditious libel; a maladroit act which ended in fiasco when they were acquitted. On 30 June seven leading English politicians, the 'Immortal Seven', despatched an invitation to William of Orange, who only landed in England with an army on 5 November.

William was husband of the heiress-presumptive (if James's son were ignored, as he increasingly was); moreover, he was a grandson of Charles I through his mother, Mary of Orange. But his immediate role was merely to summon a new Parliament and investigate the birth of James Francis Edward. Had James stayed for a confrontation, he could have saved his throne, but in this crisis his physical courage, the only quality his bitterest enemies had always allowed him, melted away. Obsessed by fears of assassination, he dwelt often on the fate of Edward II, Richard II and Henry VI, and it is strange that this most unintellectual of men should have been betrayed by his interest in history. He disbanded his army without a fight and fled to France, preceded by his wife and son.

James's sudden exit left a gap which had to be filled, especially since a new European war was now raging into which England would soon be dragged. A Parliament hastily convened in January 1689 decided, with some hesitation, that James had by implication abdicated, ignored his son's claims, and offered the Crown jointly to William and Mary.

James II's 'after-history' was melancholy, and unexpectedly prolonged. He landed in Ireland in 1689, but in 1690 he was defeated by William at the battle of the Boyne, where he again showed a distinct lack of resolution, and returned to France. In 1692 he was scheduled to lead a French invasion force against England, but it was destroyed by Admiral Russell off Barfleur before it could get to sea. James, watching from the shore, is supposed to have applauded the bravery of 'his' English sailors. After that he fell increasingly under the influence of his wife, and devoted much of his time to pietistic exercises. He died in 1701, aged sixty-eight.

Mary II (reigned 1689–94) was an unusual Stuart: graceful and lovely, but also decorous, docile, unadventurous and chaste. She was overshadowed by her husband, William III (reigned 1689–1702), and perfectly content that this should be so. As the wife of the Stadtholder she was not expected to take any part in politics or government, and when she came to the English throne it was too late for her to learn. She acted as Regent during William's absences abroad, but then she relied entirely on the ministers appointed by him.

She won the sincere and unreserved affection of the English people, but her reign was far from happy: her childlessness was a bitter cross; she was deeply troubled by the implications of her conduct towards her father; and her last years were embittered by a quarrel with her sister Anne. There were faults on both sides, and this is the only occasion on which she showed the Stuart temper. She died of smallpox in 1694, aged thirty-two, to the deep grief of the whole nation, whatever their political complexion.

Like her sister Mary, Anne (reigned 1702–14) was no ordinary Stuart. She had an aggressive and regal personality, but her dumpy plainness was the despair of portrait painters. She was a limited woman, and defective vision prevented her broadening her mind by reading. Her husband, George of Denmark, was even duller.

She remained in the background at Charles II's and James II's Courts, repelled by her uncle's frivolity and by her father's religion, for on Charles's orders she had been raised a strict and pious Anglican. Lacking an effective mate, her personal life hinged on her passionate friendship with Sarah, wife of John Churchill, later Duke of Marlborough. It was Marlborough's disgrace in 1692 which precipitated her quarrel with her sister, but she also found it humiliating that King William (like his predecessors) refused to employ her husband in any capacity, however nominal. She lived to regret the undertaking, given at the Revolution, that if Mary predeceased her husband he should continue as King, and she came to the throne at last in 1702 a disappointed, frustrated and fretful woman; the more so since her last surviving child, William, Duke of Gloucester, had died in 1700, and Parliament had fixed the succession on the Hanoverians, descended from James I's daughter Elizabeth.

The War of the Spanish Succession broke out almost immediately; and while this covered her reign with military glory – Blenheim, Vigo, Ramillies, Oudenarde, Gibraltar and the rest – it necessarily limited the role she could play. Historians are now inclined to regard her political role with much more seriousness than before, and she was certainly not a *fainéante* ruler, whose co-operation could be taken for granted. But she lacked the application to detail, the mastery of documentation, which was now becoming essential to the exercise of authority, and she was overshadowed by a succession of brilliant and commanding servants who might well have outfaced a successful male ruler: Marlborough himself, indisputably the greatest captain of the age, Godolphin, her Lord Treasurer, Robert Harley, Earl of Oxford, and Henry St John, the mercurial Lord Bolingbroke, to mention only the most prominent.

But the few decisions she made for herself were of abiding importance. When it became clear that the war had dragged on too long, that the nation desperately needed peace, she could face a final parting with her life-long friends, the Marlboroughs, and put Harley in the saddle to negotiate the Treaty of Utrecht. She hated the Hanoverians, and felt little but guilt for the Revolution, but she was steadfast in her defence of the Protestant Succession. On her deathbed in 1714, friendless and alone, she handed the white staff of Lord Treasurer not to the Jacobite Bolingbroke but to the Duke of Shrewsbury, whom she knew would usher in the reign of George I. She took as her motto that of the great Queen Elizabeth, *semper eadem*, and she proved not unworthy of it.

Henceforward the Stuart title to the thrones of England and Scotland was maintained by a succession of kings in exile, whose public credibility steadily declined as the eighteenth century progressed. As rulers, it is difficult to assess them because they never enjoyed more than a nominal executive power.

James Francis Edward, 'James III', 'the Old Pretender', left England when he was a few months old, and it is remarkable that he was able to retain something of the speech and manners of his native land. A handsome man of considerable charm, he had the Stuart weakness of obstinacy coupled with ingrowing piety. Had he been willing to turn Protestant in 1714, there is little doubt that he could have regained the throne, or at least made a serious attempt on it. As it was, he made a brief appearance in Scotland during the Rebellion of 1715, when his irresolution, and his prompt withdrawal, made a poor impression. Under the influence of his wife, Maria Sobieska of Poland, he grew even more bigoted, and his decision to settle in Rome after 1719 did little to help his cause. He died in 1766, and rather ironically his 'reign' was the longest of any English monarch.

Charles Edward, 'Charles III', or 'the Young Pretender', was a young man of great promise; intelligent, charming, talented and enterprising. He showed all these qualities in 1745, when he landed in Scotland with a token following and succeeded in taking over the whole country; he even invaded England and got as far as Derby. As 'Bonnie Prince Charlie' he has an assured place in legend, song and romance, but in the real world he could not withstand the wealth and power of Hanoverian Britain. His army annihilated by the Duke of Cumberland at Culloden in 1746, he returned to what was now permanent exile. His character deteriorated; his fondness for the bottle became an addiction, and his failure to beget an heir was the final frustration. He made no further attempt to regain the throne, and died in 1788.

His brother Henry, Duke of York, titular Henry IX, took orders in the Roman Church, and with him the main line of the Stuarts came to an end, though the Dukes of Savoy and their descendents down to the present day preserve a technical claim through Henrietta-Anne, youngest daughter of Charles I. The Cardinal of York was driven from Rome by the Napoleonic invasions, and received financial assistance from George III. In gratitude, on his death in 1807 he left his papers and the English crown jewels to the Prince Regent.

The Stuarts were an ill-fated and in many ways an incompetent family, but they continue to enjoy a special place in the affections of the English people, who are traditionally fond of losers, particularly romantic and attractive losers. There is still a flourishing society, the Royal Stuart Society, engaged in keeping their memory alive. More successful dynasties, most notably the Tudors, have no equivalent.

The Tudors

Although their suzerainty over England lasted
only three generations, these monarchs knew
prosperity, success and glory

King Harry of the golden crown, our loved one,
conquers.
Poets are in better heart, that the world prospers
And little Richard is killed.

Thus a Welsh bard welcomed the victory at Bosworth
in 1485: the last of the Plantagent kings had been
struck down for his wrongdoings, and his mutilated
corpse was displayed naked on the orders of Henry
Tudor, before burial in an unmarked grave. Few could
have anticipated Richard III's death. The expedition
led by Henry had been mounted by Charles VIII of
France to rid himself of some tiresome English exiles
and, perhaps by doing so, to irritate Richard III. The
small force from France had gathered few supporters
after its landing in south Wales, and its steady march
towards London almost certainly reflected more upon
the determination of its leader to please his French
backer than upon hope of success. Henry's relations
and their followers did not rally to his side until victory
had made him King, and then all England acclaimed
him. Henry VII had gambled: he was never to take such
a risk again, but the qualities shown by him in
preparing and captaining the expedition were not
transient, as they were to set the tone of his reign.

Henry VII (reigned 1485–1509) was a usurper.
Despite the claims made later on his behalf, he had no
right to the throne that he took by force. His
grandfather Owen ap Mereddydd ap Tudur had come
from a minor Welsh family in which Henry V had taken

*The Thames and London Bridge in a map of 1616. Over
the gateway to the bridge can be seen the heads of those
executed for treason.*

an interest, and through the King's good will he had
procured a post in the royal household. On the death of
Henry V, his widow Catherine of Valois had married
Owen and by him she had several children. The eldest
of these, Edmund, was married, at the wish of his half-
brother, Henry VI, to the heiress Margaret Beaufort,
who could claim royal descent, but whose ancestors
had been specifically denied the royal dignity.
Margaret gave birth to Henry Tudor at Pembroke
Castle on 28 January 1457, three months after her
husband's premature death. She was then only thirteen
years old, and the birth was a difficult one, the baby
almost certainly being delivered by cæsarian section.
She was to live another fifty-two years and to remarry
twice, but Henry was to be her only child.

Although Henry's early childhood was evidently
spent with his mother, his upbringing was entrusted in
1462 to an earl who cared for him for seven years, after
which he was brought up by his paternal uncle Jasper,
Earl of Pembroke. His uncle Pembroke's political
sympathies were to drive both of them into exile for
thirteen years and efforts by the last Plantagenets to get
hold of his person were unsuccessful. It was from this
exile that he returned in 1485.

Had Henry VII claimed the throne by descent, then it
would not have been he but his mother who should
have succeeded. But he did not. She, who had plotted
for his return, was rewarded, and given status in the
new reign as befitted a king's mother: she was deferred
to, but the role that she played was a limited one. In
two spheres, those of religion and education, she was
given free rein, and it is on her efforts in these that her
fame rests. A model of piety, she understood that
knowledge could be the hand-maiden of faith and
encouraged teachers, especially those of the humanist

139

persuasion, by gifts, preferment and the establishment of colleges at the university of Cambridge.

Henry VII entrusted to her care some of the heirs to the great estates, and magnates asked her to supervize the rearing of their sons. She was not the first in England to appreciate the value of learning, but her zeal for education was influential in bringing the country abreast of changes on the Continent and in enabling Englishmen to meet their associates abroad on an equal footing. The care she lavished on her projects and protégés perhaps compensated her for the lack of love between her and her son: their relationship was correct, but without feeling.

Henry VII was a slim man, well-built and strong, being above average height. His face was pale and his hair red, as was that of many of his dynasty. He made some capital out of his Welsh ancestry: he flew the red dragon banner and adopted the red dragon with the white greyhound as supporters for his shield. His purpose was to suggest that he was the heir to the British folk hero King Arthur, come to restore the golden age. Calling his first-born Arthur was part of this scheme, but such allusions probably did little to strengthen his position. However, a revival in antiquarian studies in the sixteenth century, and the fashionable pretence of noblemen to be able to trace their lineage from those who had opposed the Romans and the Anglo-Saxons, benefited the dynasty and provides a key to the great celebration of Henry VII's granddaughter Elizabeth in Spenser's *Faerie Queene*.

Before entering London, Henry VII arrested Richard III's nephew, Edward Plantagenet, the ten-year-old Earl of Warwick, whom he imprisoned in the Tower. He released from captivity his bride-to-be, Elizabeth of York, one of Richard III's nieces and Edward IV's eldest daughter. Doubt had been thrown upon her legitimacy, but Henry persisted in his avowed intention. As the pair were distantly related, a dispensation was required for their marriage, but before this was issued he had been crowned and called his first Parliament. Thus by the time of the wedding he was the King by conquest, by sacrament and in law, and in no way could it be said that his rule depended on his wife's better claim. The marriage was meant to heal the divisions that beset the kingdom, and love-knots symbolizing this union enjoyed a vogue: the device of a double-petalled red (Lancaster) and white (York) rose adopted by the dynasty served as a more permanent reminder. The birth of Prince Arthur made the gesture a reality, and this, as much as anything, spelled doom for the subjects who took arms against him in 1487.

Henry VII sought to maintain peace and prevent the renewal of the strife that had marred the reigns of his predecessors. In doing this he proved himself to be a better ruler than they had been, and his family were to follow his example. Rival claimants to the throne were treated with generosity, unless, mistaking this for weakness, they conspired against him. There was no question as to who was in authority. He and his family ruled, and expected obedience. However, this expectation did not mean tyranny, as the Crown lacked the resources to act independently of its subjects: the decisions of the Tudors met the requirements of those upon whom their power rested, and despite statements to the contrary rarely went in opposition. The dynasty possessed the ability to identify its interests with those of its subjects, and this trait was first apparent in its founder.

At his accession Henry VII was unprepared for kingship. As a boy he had shown an aptitude for learning that astonished his tutors, but his education had been halted on his uncle's flight abroad. He could speak several languages. In exile he had tasted of poverty and learned the shallowness of promises. He had shown himself to be tenacious, but he lacked any experience in management. It is not surprising, therefore, that at first he did not appreciate some of the achievements of his predecessors, although he retained the services of those responsible for their innovations. He was not unaware of the deficiency in himself, and sought to remedy it by diligence. Aided by a remarkable memory, he presided over his Council and scrutinized the principal documents of State, correcting and signing them as they passed through his hands. Much, mistakenly jettisoned, was restored as he became convinced of its worth, and with time the

reforms which had been interrupted on his accession were resumed.

In about 1500 both his health and sight began to fail. This enforced his retirement from day-to-day administration, but he had chosen his men well and government continued to move along the lines he had determined until his death. His aim, whether in domestic or in foreign affairs, was to preserve his dynasty so as to preserve the State, and in this he succeeded. He died solvent, a remarkable achievement which no English king had managed for three centuries, leaving a small fortune to Henry VIII. It was in diplomacy that he achieved his greatest triumph. As an usurper he had been coolly received by his fellow-kings, but by his death he had been recognized as a man not to be lightly dismissed, and this he had managed without undue recourse to war. The marriage-alliance he arranged between his daughter Margaret and James IV of Scotland was to prove decisive, as from it came the eventual heir to the English throne on the extinction of the Tudors.

Henry VII's Court lacked the opulence of those of the Continent, not on account of stinginess but because England was not a wealthy country. He was accessible, cheerful and hospitable. He rebuilt his favourite palace at Richmond. His zest for the good life did not preclude sincere religious convictions. He supported the Franciscans Observant and promoted the canonization of his uncle Henry VI, rebuilding the Lady Chapel at Westminster Abbey to house the intended shrine. In the event, Henry VI was not reburied there, but the chapel which is Henry VII's finest memorial was to be his own final resting place.

Henry VII's successor was not his first-born. The precocious and promising Prince Arthur had been married to Catherine, a daughter of the King of Aragon, and to help prepare him as heir-apparent he had been sent to the Marches of Wales to head the Council responsible for their administration. There, in 1502, he had died unexpectedly without issue, leaving his only surviving brother, a boy of eleven, as heir to the throne. Prince Henry had been overshadowed by Arthur, but he too possessed a nimble mind. Although Erasmus doubted his talent, as a man he showed a fluent command of Latin and French, and knew some Italian and perhaps some Spanish. Long after his formal education was over, he had sufficient interest in the newly fashionable language of Greek to receive some instruction in it. He had an avid interest in theology and a passion for mathematics and astronomy. Above all he was a gifted, enthusiastic musician, dancer and composer, some of whose works are still sung. He excelled as a sportsman, both in the mock warfare of the Court as well as in the aristocratic accomplishments of riding, hunting and hawking. Tall, well-built and handsome, he was the epitome of the Renaissance courtier described by Castiglione. Yet at his coming to the throne in 1509 he was no more prepared than his father had been twenty-four years before: after the death of Arthur he had not undergone the same vigorous training, but had been left to indulge in the pleasures available at Court. He was never to forsake the pursuit of pleasure.

The accession of Henry VIII (reigned 1509–47) was unopposed, and almost all the councillors who had helped his father remained on to rule in the young King's name. The fate of the two men dropped from the royal Council was the first indication of the ingratitude to be shown by him towards others. Richard Empson and Edmund Dudley, the unpopular agents of his father's fiscal policy, were sacrificed so as to gain for him yet more golden opinions: they had served their time and their new master no longer had any use for them. This was also to be the fate of Cardinal Wolsey in 1529 and of Thomas Cromwell in 1540, and, had not the King's own death intervened, it would have been that of the Duke of Norfolk in 1547.

The business of government was left to others and until 1540 he ruled through a minister, first Wolsey, then Cromwell. This pattern would perhaps have been repeated in the closing years of his reign had there been an equally outstanding figure not overawed by the King, but his councillors at that time had either grown old with him or were his juniors. He could rarely be persuaded to take an interest in routine administration and not infrequently State papers awaited his signature for days: in the 1540s the difficulty in obtaining his signature became so great that a stamp was made to replace it. In temperament as well as in physique he resembled his maternal grandfather Edward IV more than his father. Henry VIII was by nature indolent and fitful, rarely conscientious, but despite the blemishes in

his make-up he commanded respect and was to be affectionately remembered by his subjects.

His father had given England peace but in steadfastly avoiding war he had not covered the country with glory. Henry VIII sought to remedy this omission and, by demonstrating his martial prowess, to emphasize his superiority over his pacific father. The re-entry of England into Continental hostilities achieved that end, but having taken that step he was unable to free his kingdom from foreign entanglements, and frequent warfare emptied his coffers. His intrusion in Scotland in 1542 was to burden his subjects and to prove a fateful heritage for his heir. The enormous expenditure and barren fruits of his early military experiences did not deter him from standing for election as Holy Roman Emperor in 1519, or from

personal rivalries with Charles V who defeated him at the Imperial poll, or with Francis I of France. He wished to surpass his rivals in every sphere. The ostentation that marked his encounter with Francis at the Field of Cloth of Gold in 1520 was for him a way of life. Both he and his Court adopted each change in fashion. Outmoded palaces gave way to more stylish replacements: Richmond was superseded by Bridewell and New Hall, these in their turn by Whitehall and Hampton Court, and all by Nonsuch. He wooed some of the more distinguished artists of his day to England, his most notable catch being Holbein, but his purse was no match for those of Charles V and of Francis I. By contrast with their brilliant assemblies, his Court was somewhat lustreless.

By the late 1520s Henry VIII could no longer

Henry VIII on his death-bed, handing on the succession to his son Edward VI. Edward, the son of Jane Seymour, died aged fifteen and his cousin Lady Jane Grey then reigned for thirteen days.

overlook one notable failure, his lack of a male heir to secure the succession and to perpetuate the dynasty. In 1509 he had married with Papal approval his elder brother's widow Catherine of Aragon, some five years older than himself. Although she had borne him several children, only one daughter, Mary, survived infancy: there were miscarriages, and after 1518 no further pregnancies. For Catherine this was a misfortune, for Henry VIII a disaster. A son was deemed a necessity and to bear one a new wife was evidently a prerequisite after 1525. Before either was possible Henry VIII's marriage had to be formally dissolved either by Catherine's withdrawal into a nunnery or by divorce. Despite her piety, Catherine would not consider taking religious orders. Divorce was not common in the sixteenth century but it was procurable for the more influential, if the grounds were reasonable.

Henry VIII's need would doubtless have been accepted as sufficient reason had he not become enmeshed in Italian politics and alienated Catherine's nephew, the Emperor Charles V, into whose power the Pope fell in 1527. When petitions and cajoling failed, the King turned to threats. Discontent with the Church in England had come to a head on the fall of Cardinal Wolsey, the victim of his own 'many words without deeds'. The King had previously shown himself an opponent to reform and for his book attacking Protestantism he had been called *Fidei Defensor*, the Defender of the Faith, by a grateful Pope, but in 1529 it suited him to allow his subjects to voice their resentment, in the hope that the Pope and Emperor would bend. Their refusal to concede was to bring about the destruction of Catholicism and of the monastic orders in England, a prospect never contemplated by the King when he started the divorce

proceedings. The chance of an heir to be borne by Anne Boleyn forced the King's hand, and after the annulment of his first marriage by Archbishop Cranmer he married Anne in 1533. This act of defiance not only united Henry VIII to his second Queen but also to the religious hopes of many of his subjects, and under the guidance of Thomas Cromwell the changes so long sought after became a reality. The English clergy had already acknowledged the royal supremacy with reservations, but Cromwell obtained the recognition that 'this realm of England is an empire ... governed by one Supreme Head and King'. Anne's child was a girl, christened Elizabeth, but this disappointment apart her birth assured that there would be no going back to the old order as long as Henry VIII lived, and her longevity enabled the Reformed faith to become established in England.

Henry VIII's ardour for Anne abated when no son followed Princess Elizabeth. A miscarriage, indiscreet behaviour and the King's dalliance with one of her ladies-in-waiting ended her three-year ascendancy and brought her to the Tower and to the block. Catherine's death in straitened circumstances several months earlier removed any obstacle to the legality of the King's third marriage, to Jane Seymour who produced the long desired son in 1537 but who died as a result of the delivery. The advent of Prince Edward delighted the King and postponed his remarriage, but the realization that all his realm's hopes should not be pinned on one frail boy persuaded him to remarry thrice: in 1540 came Anne of Cleves to cement a Protestant alliance, but a mutual antipathy and the fall of Cromwell, who had engineered the alliance, led to their separation; in 1540 also Catherine Howard, a young cousin of Anne Boleyn, whose equally senseless indiscretions brought her to the same fate; and in 1543 Catherine Parr, a widow who had outlived two husbands and survived the King to take a fourth.

These last three unions were childless, and this dearth obliged Henry VIII to rely increasingly upon statute to prevent a disputed succession at his death. The King's incapacity to father healthy offspring brought down those in whom the blood of the Plantagenets still flowed. Royal descent has usually been a matter for pride, but Henry saw in it a threat to his and his family's throne. Others not so related to him, like Sir Thomas More, Bishop Fisher and the Carthusian monks, died victims of the same wrath, not because their convictions were abhorrent to the King but because these possibly threatened the succession. The problem gnawed into Henry VIII's soul and came to obsess him. His endeavours to resolve it transformed his kingdom, but in their main objective they were in the long run to fail.

Henry VIII died on 28 January 1547 and was succeeded by his son Edward VI, a boy of nine years

old. The King's death was kept secret for three days, the reason being that although he had revised his will a month earlier, he had probably not signed it. He had intended to lay down guidelines for the government of England during his son's minority, but perhaps even before he died his proposals were realized to be unworkable. One feature was preserved on the setting up of the Protectorate under Edward VI's maternal uncle, the Duke of Somerset: the more conservative of his father's councillors were excluded and this made possible the establishment of a Protestant Church in England. Despite his excommunication and the changes wrought by him, Henry VIII had remained at heart a Catholic, but the decision taken shortly before his death determined the course of change for the next six years in the favour of Protestantism.

Edward VI (reigned 1547–53) was hailed as God's 'high gift' under whose rule the dawn of 'true religion' would break: the mass was abolished and divine services were ordered to be held in English. The enforcement of Protestantism added to the discontent already fed by social unrest and inflation. The legacy of war with Scotland prevented due consideration of these domestic problems until the conclusion of peace in 1550. By that time, the King's consumption was evident, and uncertainty as to the future hamstrung any attempt at a solution.

Edward VI's education as a boy had been entrusted to two eminent teachers, Richard Cox and John Cheke. Their purpose was to set on the throne a cultured Christian prince, and in their precocious pupil they came near their mark. By 1547 he was well grounded in French, Greek and Latin, scripture, philosophy and the liberal sciences, and in music unusually gifted. On his accesion his instruction was not discontinued but it was gradually modified to prepare him for the assumption of power. Under guidance he was encouraged from 1549 to keep a daily record of events and to assess contemporary issues. He was not deprived of company, as a group of noblemen's sons were educated with him, but with only one, Barnaby Fitzpatrick, did he form a friendship. However, the prospect of a favourite emerging from the schoolroom apparently persuaded the Council to post Fitzpatrick abroad. Edward VI appears to have sensed the isolation of his position and the danger of showing partiality. When his uncles, the Lord Admiral Seymour and the Protector Somerset, were executed he did not grieve for them as to have done so would have offended his councillors. His loneliness made him vulnerable and when the Lord Admiral Seymour had sought political ascendancy, he tried to gain his nephew's trust by gifts and by affection. To strangers he was courteous, but a foreign physician noted, 'he carried himself like an old man'.

The issue of a wife for Edward VI preoccupied his

Northumberland proclaimed his equally young daughter-in-law Queen.

Lady Jane Grey was the granddaughter of Henry VIII's younger sister Mary, who had been married briefly to Louis XII of France and then to a man of her own choosing, the Duke of Suffolk. Although a Grey by name, in appearance and temperament Jane was a Tudor. She grew up a paragon of learning and of Protestantism. By thirteen she was fluent in Greek, Hebrew and Latin as well as several contemporary languages, and a correspondent with leading religious thinkers both in England and on the Continent.

Jane's accession precipitated a crisis, for Princess Mary was determined to assert her claim, which rested upon Henry VIII's will and statute. Northumberland tried to rally the country in Jane's name, but doubts as to his purpose persuaded most people to hold back until the outcome was clear. To settle the issue, Northumberland tried to take Mary captive, but she eluded him. An upturn in Mary's popularity brought not her, but Northumberland, a prisoner to the Tower and on 19 July 1553 she was proclaimed Queen in London (reigned 1553–8). Mary ignored the fact that England had ostensibly been ruled in Jane's name for thirteen days, and although Jane was condemned to death the Queen spared her life, until early in the following year when Jane's father joined a rebellion.

In 1553 Mary was thirty-seven and unmarried. She was thin and slightly built with a prematurely lined face but a still youthful complexion. Her grey eyes were so short-sighted that she could only read by holding books or papers close to her face. She had been taught French, Greek and Latin, knew a little Italian and understood Spanish. From her father she had inherited his musical ability. Despite sickness, her early years had been happy, but the separation of her father from Catherine of Aragon brought misery and loneliness. Declared a bastard in 1534, legitimacy was restored to her ten years later when made next in succession to her half-brother. Although this recognition brought her some comfort, it did not end her sufferings. Her Catholicism prevented her from subscribing to either the Henrician or Edwardian Reformation and led her to believe that only her cousin the Emperor Charles V could 'provide a remedy' for England. She saw as her duty the birth of an heir and the restoration of Catholicism. Both objects were linked in her mind with Charles V, and it seemed obvious to her to marry Charles's son Philip. Neither her Council nor her subjects welcomed this alliance, an English marriage being suggested as an alternative, but she was not prepared to consider either the last two Plantagenet heirs, the Earl of Devon and Reginald, later Cardinal Pole, or anyone else. The divisions caused by this determination did not heal until her death. Although in almost every respect she was a conscientious ruler,

councillors until his illness could no longer be overlooked. At first it was hoped that he would marry his cousin, Mary Queen of Scots, and by his marriage unite two kingdoms as his grandfather had united two factions. Later a French princess was considered a likely match.

The decline in his health became marked in 1552 and entries in his journal stop after November of that year. His death threatened the future of Protestantism, and perhaps more significantly that of the Duke of Northumberland, who had replaced Somerset as minister. To safeguard Protestantism the claim of Princess Mary to the throne had to be passed over; to maintain Northumberland's ascendancy, that of the strong-willed Princess Elizabeth had also to be dismissed. The solution was simple: Edward VI exercised the traditional right of English kings to designate a successor, and with the minister's assistance he chose a cousin, Lady Jane Grey, to whom Northumberland hastily married his son Guilford. On 6 July 1553 Edward VI died, aged fifteen, and

Elizabeth I presiding over Parliament. The last of the Tudors was popular during her long reign and her fame grew in the seventeenth century, when hers was remembered as a golden age.

she failed to make her presence felt in government after securing her Crown and marriage. Mary's personal courage during an uprising in 1554 when the rebels entered the outskirts of London saved the hour, but as a monarch she rarely gave a lead. The contemporary opinion of her as 'a good woman but an ill prince' was a fair assessment. The achievement of her reign was limited to the administrative and financial recovery set in motion before 1553.

While Philip was in England, Mary and he were 'never apart or out of sight', but their union was barren. Although Philip was never crowned King, he behaved as feared, taking a lead in government, fomenting faction and referring matters to his father. Philip's own succession to the throne of Spain in 1556 entangled England in a war of Spanish making, which gained Mary little credit and lost her Calais, the last remnant of the Plantagenet Empire in France. The reintroduction of Catholicism met with opposition, but measures restoring England to the Papal obedience were pushed through by over-zealous subjects, regardless of the toleration advocated by Mary and by Cardinal Pole. The burning of Protestants, although not comparable with their persecution on the Continent, sickened would-be sympathizers and harmed the future of Catholicism. Her designation of her Protestant half-sister as heir shortly before her death on 17 November 1558 was an admission of failure, but it was also a final assertion of her will, for, while confirming her father's intentions, it excluded Mary Queen of Scots whom some hoped to see as the next Queen of England.

At her accession Elizabeth (reigned 1558–1603) was twenty-five. In appearance she took more after Henry VII than her father. On her mother's execution in 1536, Henry VIII had denied her legitimacy, but in a kinder and more practical mood eight years later he had reinstated her and acknowledged her as one of his heirs. Her closeness to the throne had involved the young Princess in the hopes and plans of others, and, even though her part in these was uncertain, she had spent some time in the Tower in 1554 and had remained under close surveillance after her release. As a girl she had delighted her tutors by her quickness of mind, her application and love of learning. She grew up with as fluent a command of French, Greek, Italian and Latin as of English, and with a moderate understanding of Spanish. Like her father she was a skilful musician and a keen dancer. She shared his enthusiasm for riding, hunting and cards, but unlike him she enjoyed chess. She had been brought up as a Protestant, and nothing had shaken her faith.

Elizabeth inherited a war and she was to bequeath an unresolved conflict to her successor. The cost of keeping an army and navy prevented her from building new palaces and forced her to lean heavily upon others for entertainment. Her royal ancestors had made occasional progresses through the country, but Elizabeth made such journeys nearly every summer. Those qualified by rank and wealth to entertain her spared no expense, and the houses they erected in anticipation of her arrival took on an almost fabulous character. The extraordinary demands upon her income did not stop her from investing in the newfangled joint-stock companies, so she had an interest in many commercial ventures, including Sir Francis Drake's circumnavigation of the globe from 1577 to 1580. She did not invest in potentially profitless schemes and put nothing into those for settling North America.

There were years when England was not at war and when Englishmen were not fighting somewhere in Europe, off Africa or in the Americas, but the periods of so-called peace were never free from the threat of renewed hostilities. These were not originally of England's making, but Queen Mary's entry into the rivalry between France and Spain involved the country in that rivalry's repercussions for the remainder of the century. The lustreless campaign of 1557 had been an expense England could ill afford and the loss of Calais in 1558 had been a blow to the country's prestige, although it relieved the country of an increasingly burdensome outpost.

Elizabeth appreciated the folly of this way and evidently she determined not to repeat her half-sister's mistake. But the choice was not often hers to make: the international situation sometimes called for English intervention, and this she undertook, most unwillingly. To annoy her the French put forward the claim of Mary Queen of Scots to the English throne and encouraged the Scottish Queen's marriage to her English-born cousin Henry, Lord Darnley, to strengthen her claim, for as a foreigner Mary had no title under English law. As Queen of Scotland Mary proved incompetent, and in 1568 she turned to Elizabeth for help to regain her own throne. It was not in Elizabeth's interest to do this and she kept her rival in captivity in England for nineteen years. Despite Mary's inadequacy and known adultery she became the focus of conspiracies to kill Elizabeth, but rather than gain a name as a regicide Elizabeth spared her life as long as possible. But the rebellion of The Netherlands against their Spanish overlord eventually drew Elizabeth into war with Spain, although she declined the offered Crown. Her former brother-in-law Philip reacted by preparing an invasion and by supporting the Scottish Queen's claim, and in 1587 Mary was executed. In 1588 Philip sent the Armada to conquer England. To this threat Elizabeth did not outwardly weaken, but responded with what was undoubtedly the most commanding example of the leadership that she gave throughout her reign when she addressed the English fleet at Tilbury.

The Armada had already been defeated when she spoke but at the time this was not known. The threat was averted, but, because she lacked the resources, Elizabeth could not bring the war to a successful conclusion. This was undoubtedly a failure, but it should not be allowed to obscure her real achievement: against overwhlming odds she had remained Queen, preserved her country and her throne and passed both intact to the successor.

It is against the background of war that Elizabeth's handling of the religious issue, her marriage and the succession must be considered. The uncertainty over religion in England in 1558 called for immediate attention. Under Mary the mass had been reintroduced, divine service in English abolished and a handful of monastic houses refounded. These changes were considered reactionary by some, but they may have been accepted had not their enforcement been accompanied by an intolerance which drove not a few eminent figures to seek safety, charity and co-religionists abroad. Men of different persuasions looked to see how Elizabeth would act. Her request that the Host should not be elevated in her presence

149

delighted the Protestants, but they were disappointed by her evident wish to go no further than the re-establishment of the Church as it had been in January 1547. In Parliament it became clear that this was not enough and Elizabeth agreed to a restoration of nearly all the changes introduced during Edward VI's reign. Once Parliament had spoken and she had conceded, the settlement had to be enforced. This she did with leniency and with the assistance of Archbishop Parker, who shared her dislike for extremes. As 'supreme governor' of the Church of England, she resisted the appeals of Catholics and the demands of Protestants to modify the settlement which, despite the way it had emerged, satisfied almost no one. A rebellion in 1569, her excommunication in 1570, followed first by threats, then by war with Catholic States, ended the kindness initially shown to her Catholic subjects, whom successive popes ordered to rebel, and whose encouragement of seminary priests suspected of spying could not easily be distinguished from treason. The same events persuaded Protestants to accept the settlement, and the preservation of the Anglican Church became identified with the survival of the Queen and of England. Thus what had begun as a matter of expedience became established, and its moderation was the cornerstone of Elizabeth's achievement.

On the deaths, without issue, of the Earl of Devon in 1556 and of Cardinal Pole in 1558 the Plantagenet claim to the throne was extinguished. Their deaths removed a threat which had hung over the dynasty since 1485, but the problem of the succession remained. To prevent a contest and to keep the Crown in her family, Elizabeth's marriage was a prerequisite, but, despite the pleas of her advisers and the string of candidates offering themselves as bridegrooms, she remained unmarried. Before her accession she had declined several advantageous offers, presumably because she realized the dangers of an ill-considered Continental alliance. It is possible that her neglect as a child, or her later experience of improper approaches by Lord Admiral Seymour, made any close relationship with a man distasteful to her, but the way she put her possible marriage to use in diplomacy suggests that she sacrificed her emotion to the preservation of her kingdom.

Her brother-in-law Philip offered himself, so did a Swedish prince, two Imperial archdukes, a German duke, two French princes, a Scottish earl, as well as several of her own subjects. With only one of these, Robert Dudley, was there any real sign of affection, but as an ambitious man, and the son of the Duke of Northumberland and grandson of Edmund Dudley, his intentions were questionable, and the death of his neglected wife in suspicious circumstances added to the general incredulity. To have married Dudley would have been to risk her throne. Despite the rumours about their intimacy she valued the significance of her purity as a counter in marriage negotiations, and it would have been out of character for her to have hazarded all for love.

Elizabeth's enforced necessity was praised and her steadfastness became a symbol for her kingdom in the face of its numerous enemies. It was to England she declared herself wedded. Elizabeth's relationship with her subjects was conceived as a love-affair. In their eyes 'Gloriana' remained for ever youthful, and to cover the ravages of sickness and of age she used all the deceptions of dress, jewellery and cosmetics. Her encouragement of the cult of Gloriana helped to nurture a flowering of the arts that placed England in the forefront of European culture.

In Elizabeth's honour the first English colony in America was called Virginia. But having denied herself the joys of marriage and of motherhood, she resented others enjoying them, and those who did so without her approval felt her displeasure. The clandestine marriages of Lady Jane Grey's sisters and the behaviour of other English relatives made them unacceptable as Elizabeth's heirs, leaving Mary Queen of Scots' son, the Protestant James VI, as successor in 1603.

The complexity of the problems during her reign meant that Elizabeth's advisers were rarely in agreement. The decisions taken, sometimes after prevarication, were hers, and not infrequently went against the advice given by her Council. She was fortunate to have in Sir William Cecil, later Lord Burghley, an astute statesman and a kindred spirit, but she so rarely confided in him that even he was usually unaware of her intentions. Burghley's death in 1598 ended a forty-year-old partnership, and no one replaced him. During the years remaining to her, Elizabeth was not unfairly described as 'a lady whom time had surprised'. She remained firmly in control, but her fatigue became increasingly obvious. Although she had made mistakes earlier, none compared with her disastrous encouragement of Robert Devereux, Earl of Essex, which ended with his exectuion in 1601. The less flamboyant Robert Cecil, hunchbacked son of Burghley, was then left unrivalled on her Council, and it was he who welcomed James VI from Scotland after her death on 24 March 1603.

Elizabeth was buried with most of her dynasty in the family mausoleum, Henry VII's chapel at Westminster Abbey. Although some had complained 'her Majesty did all by halves', her worth became obvious by the contrast with her Stuart successors and, as the last of a talented family, her memory was increasingly revered in the seventeenth century.

The Bourbons of France

A younger branch of the Capets, this House took
control of France at a time of despair and
raised her to the height of grandeur and success

The Bourbons form a younger branch of the Capetian dynasty, and are descended from Robert of Clermont, the sixth son of St Louis. At the time of the Renaissance, when this branch of the family had been separated from the direct line for nearly ten generations, it was represented by Charles, Duke of Vendôme, who had four children: Anthony, Duke of Bourbon, husband of Jeanne d'Albret and father of Henry of Navarre; Francis, Count of Enghien; Charles, Cardinal of Bourbon; and Louis, Prince of Condé, the founder of the line of Condé, who was killed in the battle of Jarnac. When Henry III was assassinated in 1589 by the monk Jacques Clément, Henry of Navarre became King of France as Henry IV.

The fact that Henry of Navarre was Protestant, and therefore not entitled to consecration, led to serious difficulties; these were resolved by a five-year civil war which devastated France. Henry IV ultimately won through, thanks to his skill and personal qualities. The assessment of his character has, to say the least, been oversimplified. He cut the picturesque figure of a warrior with a great taste for women, but he also had a good head for politics, a profound knowledge of human nature, and an ability to cultivate his popularity. He put an exhausted France back on her feet, bringing unity and restoring prosperity.

In his youth he was forced into marriage with Marguerite, the sister of the last Valois kings, but he abandoned her for his favourites and devoted himself to war, displaying his military skills in the victory he won at the battle of Coutras in 1587. Then, with the unity of the nation at heart, he consented to reconciliation with Henry III and the latter, on his death-bed, named him successor to the throne.

This same concern for unity made him vow to reconquer the entire kingdom, to which the League of Sixteen and various foreign powers were laying claim. In order to obtain reinforcements from Elizabeth I of England, Henry IV liberated the Channel coastline in the battle of Arques, 21 September 1589, which gave him control over Dieppe. Then, backed up by assurances of England's solidarity, he headed down towards Paris, opened up the route to the capital at the battle of Ivry, 13–14 March 1590 and laid siege to Paris. But the capital was relieved by Alexander Farnese, Duke of Parma. Paris was held by the League of Sixteen which had proclaimed the Cardinal of Bourbon, Henry's uncle, as King under the name of Charles X. Upon his death in 1590, however, no one could further challenge Henry's right to the Crown.

Yet the struggle continued for a further four years. In Paris, the League was responsible for countless atrocities, and the French began to fear that their territory would be hacked to pieces. In 1593, the League summoned the Estates-General. Henry IV seized the opportunity: he proclaimed his rights and declared himself ready to abjure the Protestant faith. On 25 July 1593, he abjured his first faith at St-Denis and on 15 February 1594, he was crowned and consecrated in Chartres Cathedral. His famous phrase, 'Paris is well worth a mass', neatly summed up the matter, for the gates of the capital were opened on 22 March 1594.

The fall of Paris failed to put an end to hostilities with the Spanish. The King defeated them at Fontaine-Française, 5 June 1595, but the Peace agreement was not signed until 2 May 1598 at Vervins.

This year of 1598, which marked an end to

Among Louis XII's retinue, on the white horse, can be seen Charles III, Duke of Bourbon, later Constable of France and finally general in the service of Charles V. By his marriage to a cousin he united the properties, almost a state in themselves in central France, of the two branches of the family, which descended from a son of St Louis. He, however, died without issue.

Rome at the time of its sacking in 1527; Charles III of Bourbon died in the assault on the city. The title was then conferred on Charles, Duke of Vendôme, the grandfather of Henry IV.

hostilities, saw the proclamation of the most important act of the reign: the Edict of Nantes, which settled the Protestant problem on French territory. It had been preceded by the King's reconciliation with the Papacy. The religious settlement was not obtained without lengthy discussions, and in order to secure it, Henry IV was forced to grant the Protestants 'places of security', forming a virtual state within the State. But Henry IV wished to be obeyed, and he was capable of realizing this aim.

The problem of the dynasty remained to be solved. Henry IV lived with a mistress, Gabrielle d'Estrées, whom he had promised to marry. But when she died suddenly in 1599, the King requested the annulment of his marriage to 'Queen Margot' and agreed to marry Marie de' Medici, the niece of the Grand Duke of Tuscany. This diplomatic marriage did not prevent the King from dallying with another favourite, Henriette d'Entragues, the daughter of Marie Touchet. This attachment, one of many, caused him numerous problems. Nevertheless, this unfortunate and extravagant behaviour in his private life, which earned him the nickname of *Vert Galant*, did not impair his success in reconstructing the State.

He was admirably supported in this task by Maximilian de Béthune, the Duke of Sully. The latter, when appointed Minister of Finance in 1597, with responsibility also for other ministerial offices, found that the treasury was empty and heavily in debt. He undertook to pay off the National Debt, and gradually increased the taxes, thus raising the State revenue by fifty per cent. His major idea was to boost agriculture and aided by the agriculturalist, Olivier de Serres, he succeeded in adapting agricultural production to the needs of the nation. He also implemented a remarkable colonial policy and, in particular, with Samuel Champlain he established strong bases in Canada.

Foreign relations were not altogether peaceful, particularly in Savoy. Sully led the operations there, and by the Treaty of Lyons in 1601, France annexed Bresse and Bugey.

However, Henry IV's popularity began to decline rather rapidly, while France, though now much wealthier, failed to realize how much she owed to his political skills. His private life was criticized and public opinion was scandalized by his love for the young Charlotte de Montmorency, whom he had married to the Prince of Condé. This flirtation coincided with a political event of prime importance – the death of the ruler of Cleves and Jülich, early in 1610. The Emperor Rudolf II seized these lands, which constituted a strategic outpost facing the Eastern Marches. But Henry IV refused to countenance this annexation and prepared for war, drawing up armies on three fronts. Before marching at the head of his troops to the Low Countries, he decided to entrust the Regency to Marie

de' Medici, who was consecrated at his orders on 13 May 1610.

Speculation was rife as to the intentions of the King, and there were widespread rumours of a possible assassination. Impassioned monks remorselessly accused the King of waging war for love of the beautiful Charlotte de Montmorency and of favouring Protestant causes. These arguments had a powerful effect on an Angoulême schoolmaster named Ravaillac, who, with dagger in pocket, set off for Paris.

On 14 May, the eve of his departure for war, Henry IV went to visit Sully in the Arsenal. The carriage was halted by an obstacle, possibly deliberately, in the Rue de la Ferronnerie. Ravaillac, who was following the team, jumped onto the hub of the wheel and twice plunged his dagger into the King's breast. Henry IV died instantly.

Ravaillac was torn limb from limb after a rapid trial, which made it possible to distract the search for accomplices from sources which seem today to be likely, and to concentrate instead on implicating

154

former members of the League of Sixteen.

The Regency which followed upon the death of Henry IV was a troubled period. Marie de' Medici dismissed Sully as early as 1611, and bestowed the power upon a favourite, Concini, the husband of her lady-in-waiting, Eleonora Galigai. Concini, now the Marquis of Ancre and Marshal of France, was an avaricious man, but not without political sense. He ordered the occupation of the town of Jülich, thus saving the honour of the French, and arranged a marriage between Henry IV's little son by Marie de' Medici, Louis XIII, and Anne of Austria. But he came up against the hostility of the princes and nobles and was forced to make costly concessions including, in particular, the summoning of the Estates-General. This session, the last to be held before 1789, took place in 1614; it was characterized by the hostility of the three Orders, each one towards the others and by the whims of constitutional monarchy. Nonetheless it ended with a triumph for royal power. This meeting of the Estates also brought into the limelight a spokes-man for the clergy, Armand-Jean du Plessis de Richelieu. Thereupon, Concini dismissed Henry IV's ministers, consigned Condé to the Bastille, and brought the aristocrats to heel.

These measures were to be countered by an unforeseen event. The young Louis XIII, who had now grown to maturity, hated Concini and felt no love for the Queen, his own mother, Marie de' Medici. Urged on by his favourite, Charles d'Albert de Luynes, in 1617 he gave orders to the Captain of the Guard, Vitry, to arrest Concini and, if necessary, to put him to death – orders which were promptly carried out.

Luynes became head of the government, a Duke and Constable; he recalled Henry IV's ministers and chased out Richelieu. But the new favourite embarked upon a power struggle with Marie de' Medici, which led to civil war; Richelieu, who had taken the Queen Mother's part, made peace at the Treaty of the Ponts-de-Cé in August 1620.

The situation abroad was soon seen to be extremely serious. As a result of religious unrest in Bohemia, the

Emperor Ferdinand II was in difficulties, and appealed for help to the King of France. The latter unsuccessfully attempted to mediate, and the Emperor, having won a victory over the Bohemians at the battle of the White Mountain on 8 November 1620, began to threaten French policy abroad.

Domestic policy was also proving a problem, as a result of the Protestant uprising led by the Duke of Rohan, Sully's son-in-law. The King was forced to confirm the status of the Protestants by the Treaty of Montpellier on 18 October 1622, while Luynes, having suffered a setback at Montauban, died of purple fever.

These events led to a period of instability which helped Richelieu's rise to power. Once he had become a Minister he eliminated all those who stood in his way, and for eighteen years, he was to be the real master of France. Richelieu represents a unique case in the history of France: the dictatorship of a Prime Minister, with the approval – occasionally qualified – of a King. This was a crucial period, in which political continuity was successfully established with far-reaching consequences for the future.

Richelieu was a man of fine bearing, intimidating, seductive and artful. The King appears somewhat dwarfed by this figure, but the way in which he generally supported the Cardinal's policies implies that the two men saw eye to eye over most things. Richelieu himself summed up his political programme in three points: 'to destroy the Huguenot cause, to subdue the nobility, and to enhance the King's prestige abroad'.

Rarely has a programme been implemented with greater skill and success. The Huguenot problem was the first to be resolved. The Protestants had established links with England through the port of La Rochelle, and were in a position to create an independent state in Western France. In order to eliminate this risk, Richelieu besieged and captured La Rochelle from October 1627 to October 1628. He then concentrated his efforts on the Languedoc. He captured Privas on 27 May 1629 and Montauban on 20 August 1629. After the first of these successes, he made Louis XIII sign the 'Grâce d'Alais', which reestablished the Edict of Nantes as a measure granting freedom of worship, but withdrew from the Protestants all political and military privileges. It was a total success.

The task of subduing the nobility proved more troublesome and occupied the entire reign. Gaston of Orléans, Louis XIII's brother, was behind most of the intrigues, which, for the most part, aimed at getting rid of the Cardinal.

The most illustrious victim was the Queen, Marie de' Medici. She took advantage of her son's ill health to demand the dismissal of the Cardinal; she very nearly succeeded in her purpose, but Richelieu acted a fraction more swiftly than she, and sent her into exile. This became known as the Day of Dupes, 11 November 1630. Gaston of Orléans was forced into hiding, the Duke of Guise was exiled, Bassompierre was relegated to the Bastille and Marillac was to meet his fate at the hand of the public executioner. Gaston of Orléans reacted to this show of authority by rallying to his cause the Governor of Languedoc, Henry, Duke of Montmorency, who stirred up the provinces from the Rhône to the Garonne. But he was defeated at Castelnaudary and executed in 1632 in the courtyard of the Capitole at Toulouse, Louis XIII having refused to grant him a pardon.

There remains one conspiracy worthy of mention, organized by Gaston of Orléans with the aid of the Marquis of Cinq-Mars. It involved treason, since they planned to deliver the Cardinal into the hands of the Spanish. Richelieu, then on his deathbed, retaliated in terrible fashion. He executed Cinq-Mars, although he had been the King's favourite, together with his friend Thou, who was guilty of failing to denounce the plot.

This rather frightening aspect of Cardinal Richelieu's character should not obscure his very considerable merits.

Richelieu's finest achievement was his foreign policy. At first he intervened only indirectly in the Thirty Years War. Opposing German unity, which would be to the advantage of the Hapsburgs, he demanded the withdrawal of the condottiere Wallenstein and signed a treaty with the champion of the Protestant cause, King Gustavus II Adolphus of Sweden. When the latter was killed at the battle of Lützen on 16 November 1632, and Wallenstein was assassinated two years later, only then did Richelieu commit himself and made Louis XIII declare war on Spain in 1635. The initial stages of the war were hard, with France invaded as far as Corbie in 1636. But retaliation came promptly. Arras was taken after a long siege in 1640 and Turenne received his baptism of fire on the Rhine.

Richelieu died at the end of 1642. The death of Louis XIII followed on 14 May 1643, shortly after that of his great minister.

The King's conjugal life had been most unusual, with no offspring for twenty years. He vowed to dedicate France to the Virgin should he beget a child. The miracle took place and Anne of Austria gave birth to two children, the future Louis XIV, born in 1638, and Philip, Duke of Orléans, born in 1640.

Before his death, Louis XIII had made provision for maximum restrictions to be laid upon the powers of the Queen, who was named Regent. The Power was put into the hands of a former secretary of Richelieu, Cardinal Jules Mazarin. Although an Italian by birth, he became one of France's greatest statesmen. The Queen made the *parlements* confer considerable power upon her, and she ruled with a strong hand, aided by Mazarin.

The presentation of Marie de' Medici's portrait to Henry IV, the first of the Bourbons to succeed to the French throne. The painting is part of a series by Rubens celebrating the life of the Queen.

A ball at the Court of Henry IV, by Caulery. The first Bourbon King is credited with having restored unity and prosperity to a country exhausted by religious wars.

The fortunes of war now began to turn in favour of France. Five days after the death of Louis XIII, the Duke of Enghien crushed the Spanish at Rocroi. But the last act of the Thirty Years War did not take place for another six years, with the victory at Lens in August 1648, which compelled the Emperor to sue for peace. The Treaty of Westphalia was signed at Münster and Osnabrück in October 1648. It was to be the charter for Europe until the French Revolution. Germany was divided up into 343 principalities, and Alsace was handed over to France, making her hopeful of completing the hexagon.

Mazarin's financial policy, the resistance of the *parlements*, and the rebellion of the nobles, had plunged the country into civil war. The Queen, Mazarin and the young King had to flee from Paris, and take up residence first at Rueil, then at St-Germain.

Condé laid siege to Paris, while Turenne tried to stir up the army against the King. But Turenne had no following and the revolt, known as the 'Parliamentary Fronde', ended in failure. The peace, however, was short-lived. Mazarin arrested Condé, but Gaston of Orléans intervened and exiled Mazarin, who fled to Germany. The country was thrown into disorder; Condé appealed to the Spanish and established himself at Bordeaux.

The Queen then proclaimed that Louis XIV had come of age and recalled Mazarin. When he returned, he had to deal with Condé, who was occupying Paris. Turenne returned to the service of the Crown, but met with difficulties in the fighting in the Faubourg St-Antoine. On 4 July 1652, the Paris *parlement* was besieged by the troops of the Fronde and the Hôtel de Ville was burned down. Peace was then restored. Although Louis XIV promised an amnesty, this did nothing to diminish the severity of the repression which followed. This civil war, known as the 'Fronde of the Princes', had ruined

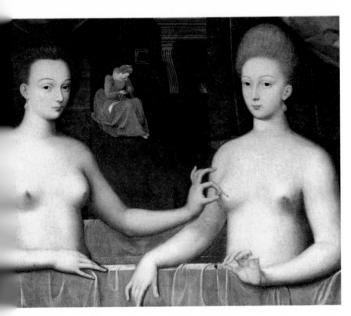

the country and many years were to pass before prosperity was restored.

From 1653 to 1661, Louis XIV allowed Mazarin to enforce a true dictatorship. In order to defeat the Spanish, Mazarin did not hesitate to make an alliance with Oliver Cromwell, although the latter was guilty of regicide, and a Protestant. Military operations lasted until 1658, when Condé was defeated by Turenne at the battle of Dunes, near Dunkirk. By the Treaty of the Pyrenees in 1659, France gained part of Roussillon, Artois and isolated strongholds in Flanders, and Louis XIV married Maria Teresa, the Infanta of Spain and the eldest daughter of Philip IV.

In 1661, Mazarin died and the King announced to his Council that from henceforth he intended to govern personally, which he was indeed to do, in magnificent style, for fifty-four years.

Louis XIV was a man of short stature, though he appeared taller with the aid of high heels and monumental wigs. He had hard eyes, an aquiline nose and a fat, sloping chin, but his appearance gave total effect of incredible majesty; it deeply impressed his contemporaries, who baptized him 'the Sun King' and summed up his philosophy in the formula, 'I am the State.'

Louis was a bad husband, and remains famous for his amorous adventures. When he was approaching forty-five years of age, the King became infatuated with the governess of his royal bastards, Françoise d'Aubigné, the widow of the poet Scarron. He married her morganatically and made her the Marchioness of Maintenon; she was a staunch counsellor, playing an important role in politics for the last thirty years of the reign.

Louis XIV began his personal reign by subduing those who had grown powerful through their wealth at the expense of the nobility, who had been crushed by Richelieu. The King also attacked thinkers known to be somewhat too independent in their ideas, particularly at Port-Royal. Then, by repeated insults regarding mere breaches of etiquette, he humiliated first England, then the Papacy, Turkey and the Holy Roman Empire in turn. He also tamed the nobility, a move which, in the long run, was to destroy the very backbone of the country.

But, with the aid of two key ministers, Colbert and Louvois, he dealt skilfully with financial policy and military organization. For Colbert, the son of a Rheims draper, the economy took priority over politics; in the space of ten years he succeeded in balancing the budget. Although he ruined the peasantry by lowering the price of agricultural produce, his idea of the balance of payments was an innovation. He greatly encouraged industry, giving aid to St-Gobain, the Savonnerie and the Gobelins, founding large commercial companies and giving France a

Victory crowning Louis XIII, by Philippe de Champaigne. Henry IV's son was overshadowed by the personality of the greatest of France's ministers, Richelieu.

foothold in Louisiana and Santo Domingo. He was also a great Minister of the Marine, a canny legislator, and the founder of the Academies of Science and of Inscriptions. Side by side with Colbert, Louvois was forging an army which was to remain invincible for many years, while Vauban was constructing citadels to make the borders impenetrable.

It was hardly surprising, given the existence of such forces, that Louis XIV should embark upon wars of conquest. On the death of King Philip IV of Spain, Louis demanded his wife's dowry, which had never been paid, and declared war. This campaign, known as the War of Devolution, began with an attack on Flanders; Belgium was occupied from May to November 1667. Europe retaliated: England, Holland and Sweden formed an alliance against France.

While the alliance was being built up, Condé attacked Franche-Comté, a Spanish stronghold, and took it within a fortnight. Louis XIV offered Spain a choice between Flanders and Franche-Comté. Spain handed over the latter, and in addition, ceded Lille, Douai and Armentières, by the Treaty of Aix-la-Chapelle on 2 May 1668. But Louis XIV, displeased with the attitude of the Dutch, spent four years preparing his revenge. He plunged Holland into diplomatic isolation by neutralizing Sweden and England by the Treaty of Dover, 1670.

In April 1672, the King launched a devastating attack, which was marked by the famous episode of the Passage of the Rhine at the Tolhuys ford. Although Louis could easily have pushed on as far as Amsterdam, he persisted in conducting sieges. The Dutch put up an astonishing fight; they entrusted the government to William of Orange and opened up the dykes which held back the sea. The Dutch resistance paved the way for a coalition between Holland and a number of European States against Louis XIV.

The war continued for six years, marked by the victories of Condé at Senef in 1674, and of Turenne at Turckheim in 1675, and also by the naval successes at Duquesne. But, in spite of the Treaty of Nijmegen in 1678, which confirmed the tenure of Franche-Comté and secured Valenciennes, Maubeuge and Cambrai, Louis XIV had not secured total victory. Holland remained intact and retained the right to hold garrisons in the Spanish Netherlands, thereby forming a series of fortifications known as the Barrier.

In order to further his conquests, Louis XIV renounced the pursuit of war and initiated a series of peaceful annexations which gave him mastery over Montbéliard, Sarrebourg, Pont à Mousson and Casal. This campaign culminated in the annexation of the free town of Strasbourg in 1681. Louis had all but completed the hexagon, since Lorraine was wedged in and likely to fall prey, while the northern and eastern borders closely corresponded to the dreams of his Capetian forebears. Royal administration had been remodelled, royal powers were exercised by the intendants, and material prosperity was at its zenith.

But this was also a dominant period in two other domains: philosophy and the arts. At no other time has France known such an abundance of geniuses. The most remarkable achievement of the reign was the Palace of Versailles. In 1682 Louis XIV moved his government to this new capital on a permanent basis.

The move to Versailles was an effective turning-point in the reign. It was marked by the death of Queen Maria Teresa and the King's morganatic marriage to Madame de Maintenon. It also saw the Truce of Regensburg in 1684, when a twenty-year peace was offered to Austria, who had been shaken by the siege of Vienna when the Turkish threat had been averted by John Sobieski. The Truce of Regensberg should, logically, have allowed Louis XIV to enjoy the last years of his reign in peace. But his religious policy upset all this, and resulted in problems of very different kinds.

First there were numerous conflicts with the Papacy: as absolute monarch, Louis XIV was unwilling for the spiritual to intrude upon the temporal. The 1682 Assembly which proclaimed the existence of a Gallic Church, led to the secret excommunication of the King. For years, the French bishoprics were unprovided for when they fell vacant. The Comtat-Venaissin was occupied by French troops. Finally Pope Innocent XII settled their disagreement, but Louis was obliged to yield.

A tournament for the marriage of Louis XIII and Anne of Austria in 1612. When left a widow, the Queen ruled through the Italian-born Mazarin, considered one of France's greatest statesmen.

The other problems arose for the opposite reason: the King, in the belief that he was serving Catholic interests, made the most unfortunate decision of his entire reign by signing, on 18 October 1685, the Edict of Fontainebleau, which revoked the Edict of Nantes. Louis could tolerate no opposition, and the failure of certain subjects to practise the State religion was interpreted as opposition to his wishes. Thus he had first made considerable restrictions in his enforcement of the Edict of Nantes, then, after the Treaty of Nijmegen, he believed himself sufficiently strong to compel the Protestants to abjure their faith. Repressive measures, including the famous *dragonnades*, were frequently enforced with cruelty. In order to flatter the King, certain ministers convinced him that a mass conversion of the Protestants had taken place, and that a negligible number remained unconverted.

Madame de Maintenon, born a Protestant, was now an ardent defender of the Catholic faith, and urged her royal spouse to revoke the Edict. The consequences of this decision were disastrous, for this outrageously intolerant act provoked a mass exodus, with half a million citizens settling in neighbouring Protestant States. It even led to the civil war of the Camisards,

which raged throughout Bas-Languedoc from 1702 to 1705, taking a heavy toll. But the immediate consequence was far more serious, for the Revocation was one of the causes of a European war which was to last nine years: the War of the League of Augsburg.

The League of Augsburg, formed in 1686, brought together Brandenburg, the Hapsburg Emperor, Venice, Muscovy and Poland. It was later expanded by the addition of Spain, Sweden, Bavaria and Holland. Louis XIV attempted at first to negotiate, by handing over the inheritance of his sister-in-law, the Princess of the Palatine, in exchange for the prolongation of the Truce of Regensburg. As a precautionary measure, Louvois invaded and devastated the Palatinate and Louis occupied the left bank of the Rhine. Just when France's strategic situation appeared to be very strong, her fortunes were reversed by the Revolution of 1688, which placed William of Orange on the English throne and brought Britain into the Augsburg Coalition.

By the Treaty of Ryswick signed in 1697, France, having been spared invasion, was forced to recognize William of Orange as the legitimate English sovereign. The Barrier was reinforced, and of all her administrative annexations, France retained only Strasbourg.

But a new conflict was threatening to set Europe alight: Charles II of Spain, although a chronically ailing monarch, had nonetheless reigned for thirty-five years. On 1 November 1700 he died, bequeathing all his lands to Louis XIV's grandson, the Duke of Anjou. Louis accepted the succession, although he was fully aware that Europe would retaliate if no concessions were made.

Louis XIV was old; he had no wish to wage war. The financial situation had changed; coins were frequently reminted, it had been necessary to introduce personal taxation, known as *capitation*, which struck at the privileged classes, and loans were alarmingly on the increase. But, however reluctantly, the decision to fight had to be made. Villars and Berwick were brilliant leaders in the initial stages. Villars pressed on as far as Ulm, and triumphed at Höchstadt on 20 September 1703, but was defeated at the same place the following year by Prince Eugene of Savoy and the Duke of Marlborough.

The retreat had to be called. The French were forced onto the defensive and nearly collapsed at Ramillies on 23 May 1706, where Marshal Villeroy was crushed by Marlborough. The situation was no happier at sea, where the Count of Toulouse, Louis' bastard son and Grand Admiral of France, was defeated at Velez Malaga. The English took advantage of this success to occupy Gibraltar, and then blockaded the French fleet in the port of Toulon, where it was scuttled in 1707.

France's northern border was threatened by Prince Eugene, who captured Lille. Villars, however, stopped the offensive in the indecisive and bloody battle of Malplaquet on 11 September 1709. The situation gradually deteriorated. In 1712, Prince Eugene captured Quesnoy, then surrounded Landrecies, the last fortress guarding the approach to Paris.

At that stage Louis XIV ordered Villars to go into battle for the last time. Villars' resounding success at Denain, 18 July 1712, redressed the situation and opened the way for the invasion of the Palatinate.

The peace settlement, created by the Treaties of Utrecht and Rastatt in 1713–14, exacted heavy concessions from France. Above all, the Crowns of France and Spain had to be separated once and for all. This posed a succession problem, for Louis XIV, in the last sad years of his reign, had seen the successive deaths of his son, the Great Dauphin, in 1711, his grandson, the Duke of Burgundy, who became Dauphin in 1712, and finally the Duke of Brittany, the heir presumptive. Only one child was left to ensure the continuity of the dynasty, his great-grandson, the future Louis XV, born in 1710. In order to avoid the possible dearth of heirs and to close the way to his nephew, the Duke of Orléans, Louis XIV took the desperate step in July 1714 of authorizing the royal bastards to succeed him.

The following year, in early August, feeling unwell, the King drew up his will. On 1 September 1715 he died, and the Regency of Louis XV's minority began.

The general atrophy produced by Louis XIV's reign inevitably led to a reaction. This was the work of the Sun King's nephew, Philip of Orléans. A man of great intelligence, with a wide knowledge and an open mind, his exceptional gifts were undervalued because of the bad reputation which a dissolute life had given him.

A soon as Louis XIV was dead, Philip of Orléans dared to ask the *parlement* for the annulment of the great King's will, on the grounds that it ran counter to the fundamental laws of the kingdom. His request was granted, but only after he had put himself at the mercy of the members of the *parlement*.

He replaced the ministers in office by small councils, headed by the Council of the Regency; this form of oligarchy has retained the name of 'polysynod'. It was, in effect, the revenge of the old nobility over the new nobility of bourgeois origin, which had assisted Louis XIV. The results of the change were not successful and the Duke of Noailles, who was Minister of Finance, soon proved unequal to the task.

The Regent then listened to the advice of a Scottish financier, John Law, who held advanced ideas regarding the economy, and advocated that coinage should be replaced by paper money, with a view to speeding up payments. He consolidated the system by founding colonial companies whose shares rapidly shot to dizzy heights, but the system collapsed when the first dividend fell due; the result was total bankruptcy.

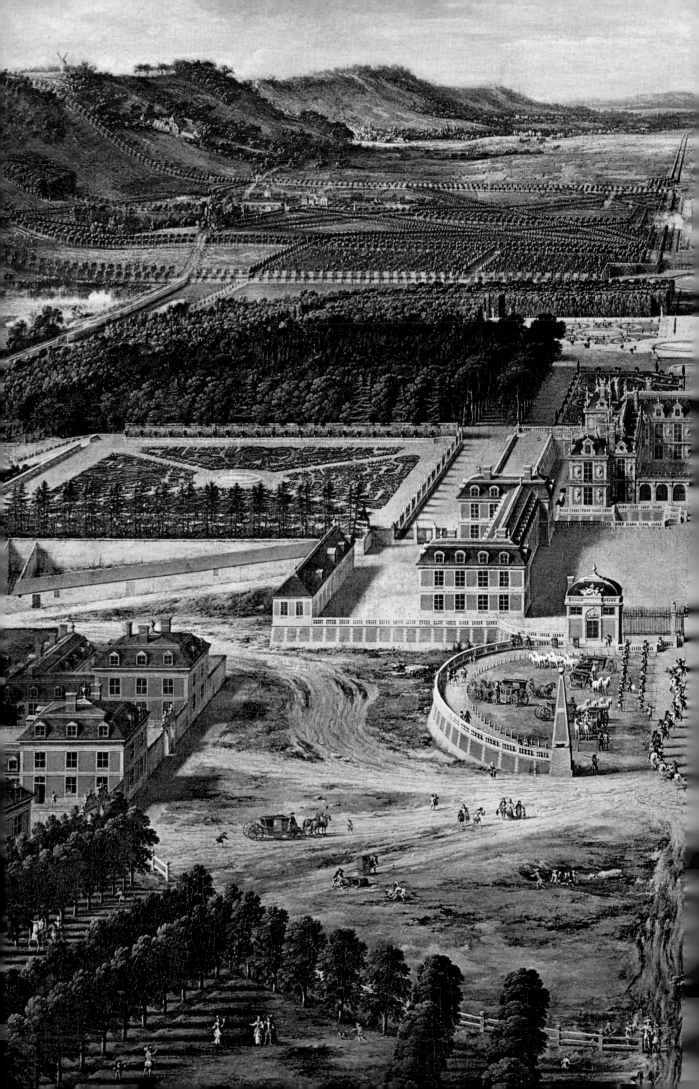

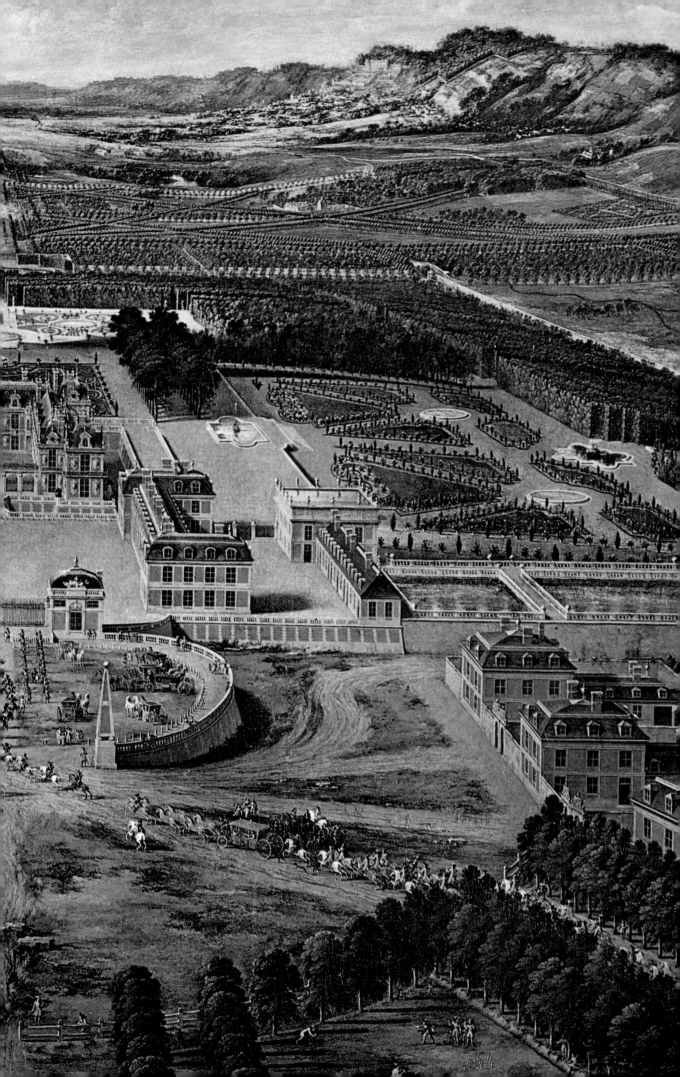

The pleasures of life at the Court of Versailles: Louis
XIV playing billiards with some intimates. In 1682 the
monarchy settled permanently in the fantastic residence
that was to prove its tomb.

The Regent's foreign policy led him to form an alliance with England, which was then reinforced by an agreement with Holland and Austria. This coalition was organized by the Minister for Foreign Affairs, the devious Cardinal Dubois, and it led to an absurd war with Spain, a short-lived conflict that ended in a reconciliation with Philip v and an Anglo-French agreement supported by Spain, aiming to resist Austria. The significant result of these various manoeuvres was a twenty-year peace with England, which led to the infiltration of English freemasonry into France.

Louis xv officially reached his majority in 1723. The Regent became Prime Minister but immediately died of apoplexy. His place was taken by the Duke of Bourbon, whose first move was to marry Louis xv to Maria Leczinska, the daughter of the dethroned King of Poland. The marriage was initially a happy one; but for two-thirds of his reign the king was dominated by favourites.

Louis xv is one of the most controversial kings in French history. In fact, he was a shy character, and rather hard-hearted where the good of the State was concerned. Although somewhat lazy, he attended to State affairs conscientiously and kept well informed on all matters, being aided initially by his tutor, and then by favourites. His personal reign was not really to begin until 1743.

From the death of the Duke of Bourbon, in 1726, until 1743 power was effectively held by Cardinal Fleury, Bishop of Fréjus and former tutor to the King. He was an old man of seventy-three, a model of wisdom and discernment. In religious policy, he proved himself to be the adversary of the Jansenists, whom he finally broke at the Council of Embrun in 1729. His financial policy seems to have been remarkable. He fixed the price of the louis at twenty-four livres, which meant that the value of money remained stable throughout the century. He then reintroduced the system of farming taxes, on the basis of a fixed annual amount, to be regularly increased at intervals of six years. With the aid of the Minister of Finance, Orry, he founded the public roads service (Ponts et Chaussées). His colonial policy was wise, and it was due to him that commerce was introduced into the Caribbean and into Louisiana.

In foreign policy, Fleury was a dedicated spokesman for peace. He was, however, forced into war over the

A painting attributed to Largillière, showing Louis XIV, seated, with his son, the Great Dauphin, behind him, and the latter's wife, Maria Anna Christina of Bavaria, and on the right, his grandson, the Duke of Burgundy.

question of the Polish succession, which Stanislas Leczinski, the father of the Queen, was plotting to secure. Stanislas was elected King of Poland, but failed to take possession of the throne, which was also laid claim to by Augustus III of Saxony. To save national honour, France declared war on Austria, while England remained neutral, on condition that Belgium was left untouched. After a vain attack on Danzig, the war moved to Italy, where Villars took Milan. After his death, the French marched on into the Trentino, while Marshal Berwick advanced powerfully through Germany. An armistice was called in 1735 and was consolidated by the Treaty of Vienna in 1738, marking the apogee of the reign.

The main provision of the Treaty was that the Duke of Lorraine should exchange his duchy for Tuscany, and that Stanislas Leczinski should become Duke of Lorraine, on condition that this province should be returned to France after his death. The hexagon was nearly complete. At the same time, a dispute having arisen between Austria and Turkey, Fleury sent aid to Turkey and recovered a traditional ally in the East.

It was now 1740, a critical turning-point in European eighteenth-century politics. On the death of

Emperor Charles VI, in that year his daughter Maria Theresa succeeded to the throne by virtue of the Pragmatic Sanction. When Frederick William I of Prussia died in the same year, his son Frederick II succeeded him, while in Russia, Elisabeth, the daughter of Peter the Great, became Czarina. Immediately, Frederick II attacked Silesia claiming it as a reward for his allegiance to the Pragmatic Sanction.

An anti-Austrian faction developed in France, under the leadership of Fouquet's grandson Marshal Belle-Isle. The Elector of Bavaria was made Emperor and France supported his cause, in spite of Fleury's efforts to prevent war. Belle-Isle captured Prague in brilliant style, but failed to reach Vienna. Maria Theresa negotiated with Frederick II, and handed Silesia over to him. Fleury, growing feeble with age, clumsily approached Maria Theresa over an agreement which he was then forced to disavow. He died shortly after, on 29 January 1743.

Louis XV thereupon declared that he would appoint no Prime Minister and would content himself merely with advice. The King was going through a moral crisis and embarking upon his first amorous attachments to the Nesle sisters, the most beautiful of whom was made the Duchess of Châteauroux.

The French had to evacuate Prague, but the army remained in Germany. Marshal Noailles was defeated at Dettingen, but Maurice of Saxony came to the defence of Alsace. Frederick II, disturbed by this defensive victory, contracted an alliance with France, which led to a declaration of war upon England. The campaign got off to a good start with the capture of Menin, Ypres and Furnes. But the Austrians counter-attacked at Saverne. Entrusting Belgium to Maurice of Saxony, the King moved on to Metz, where he fell seriously ill, and was feared to be close to death. He asked for the Last Sacraments, made amends and dismissed the Duchess of Châteauroux. All France prayed for the monarch's recovery and nicknamed him *le Bien-Aimé* (the Beloved). Louis XV duly recovered and, with Lowendal as his second-in-command, he led the attack on Freiburg in Brisgau.

On 20 January 1745, the Bavarian Emperor died at Munich, and Francis of Lorraine, the husband of Maria Theresa of Austria, was elected Emperor. This could have led to a compromise treaty, had Frederick II not resumed hostilities.

In this same year of 1745, Louis XV took an official mistress, from the bourgeoisie: Jeanne le Normant d'Etioles, née Poisson, who was to become famous under the name of Madame de Pompadour. This attachment, which considerably irritated the nobility, was of great importance, for the favourite was a woman of exceptional qualities, who patronized literature and the arts, and who played quite a significant role in politics.

The campaign continued in Belgium, and was marked by the victory of Maurice of Saxony at Fontenoy on 11 May 1745. Frederick II then signed a separate peace treaty with Austria, forcing France to continue the war single-handed. On 20 February 1746, Maurice of Saxony took Brussels, which could have led to peace-talks if the Stuart Pretender had not been crushed by the Duke of Cumberland at Culloden on 16 April 1746. Encouraged by this success at home, England returned to the offensive in Belgium. Maurice of Saxony captured Antwerp and won resounding victories at Raucoux, 1746, and Lawfeld, 1747, crowning the campaign with the capture of Maastricht, in the spring of 1748.

Unfortunately, the war had not been so successful in the colonial territories, and the English had won substantial victories in India over Dupleix and La Bourdonnais, and in Canada. Moreover, the Treaty of Aix-la-Chapelle proved extremely disappointing. But, in fact, the gains were mutually restored.

France was prospering, her territory having been spared the hostilities; this was a period when châteaux were being enriched and the Place de la Concorde and

the Military School were being laid out. But financial difficulties arose, and an astute minister, Machault d'Arnouville, tried in vain to impose equality of taxation by introducing a five per cent income tax known as the *vingtième*. The Clergy succeeded in evading the *vingtième*, thereby making a nonsense of fiscal equality, but since the King's conduct had strained his relations with the Church, he was forced to give way.

After the Treaty of Aix-la-Chapelle the situation slowly deteriorated. England pursued her plan of capturing the French colonies. Louis attempted to avert the approaching danger, and, failing to obtain an alliance with Spain, he assigned Cardinal Bernis, Minister of Foreign Affairs, to the task of negotiating an agreement with Austria; Prussia, for her part, had signed a peace treaty with England. This complicated jig, known as 'the upheaval of the alliances', was to be at the origin of the disastrous Seven Years War.

The war began successfully with the capture of Minorca and the occupation of Hanover by Marshal Richelieu, but then French fortunes suffered a reversal. Frederick II took the upper hand when he defeated the French army at Rossbach, 5 November 1757, and the Russian army at Leuthen, 5 December 1757.

The war continued indecisively in Europe until 1763. It was elsewhere that the real disasters took place: the loss of Canada, where Montcalm was killed at the storming of Quebec in 1759, and the loss of India, with the defeat of Lally-Tollendal. The naval campaign was marked by the defeats of Lagos in 1757, and of Les Cardinaux, near Quiberon, in 1759.

At this stage the need for a strong fleet was keenly felt; it was supplied by the Family Pact, an alliance between all the Bourbons of Europe, negotiated in 1762 by the greatest minister of the period, the Duke of Choiseul.

The death of the Czarina Elisabeth was the turning-point of the war; her mediocre successor, Peter III, entered into negotiations with the Prussian King, whom he greatly admired. By the Treaty of Hubertsburg, Maria Theresa handed over Silesia, while France was forced to sign the disastrous Treaty of Paris in 1763, which sealed the loss of Canada and India.

Naturally Louis XV, with the aid of Choiseul, began to prepare his revenge and to build up the navy, but he gave precedence to internal problems and the last years of his reign are marked by an attempt to destroy the *parlements* and to restore absolutism. This attempt coincides with the King's last amorous attachment, when he invited to his bed a lady of easy virtue, the Comtesse du Barry. Her sole political intervention apparently consisted of obtaining the dismissal of Choiseul, that minister having just secured Corsica for France.

The struggle with the *parlements* became a desperate one; the King, in the session known as the Flagellation, had declared that he alone held power, an outdated concept at a time when a desire for constitutional monarchy was beginning to emerge from the general confusion.

In 1768, Louis XV appointed President Maupéou as Chancellor. This man was supported by Abbé Terray, the Minister of Finance and, after the fall of Choiseul, the Duke of Aiguillon joined the team to form the 'Triumvirate'. On 20 January 1771, Maupéou, in accordance with the King's wishes, called on the members of the *parlement* to register an edict giving full powers to the sovereign. Upon their refusal, *parlement* was disbanded and its members exiled. On 10 February, the King created a new law court, whose members were to be appointed to office and remunerated; recourse to law was now to be made free and former costs reimbursed to the appropriate persons.

Terray's financial policy proved adequate and established greater equality in taxation. But Aiguillon's foreign policy was discredited by the first division of Poland, which caused great bloodshed, and represented the failure of the policy known as the 'King's Secret', which was to have been Louis XV's personal solution to the Polish question.

Louis was growing old and lived in constant fear of death. He was worried for the succession, his son having died in 1765, while his grandson, the Dauphin, was young, inexperienced and married to a light-hearted Princess, the Archduchess Marie Antoinette, the daughter of the Empress Maria Theresa.

On 27 April 1774, Louis XV fell ill at the Trianon, where he was residing in the company of Madame du Barry. He was brought back to Versailles, where his physicians recognized the symptoms of smallpox. The King lay in agony for ten days and died on 10 May 1774.

The reign of Louis XVI, which was so disastrous for the Bourbon dynasty, nevertheless made a promising start. The first nine years can even be thought brilliantly successful, rising gradually to their zenith with the Treaty of Versailles, in 1783. Then the curve began to slope downwards, the path leading to the scaffold in 1793.

The young twenty-year-old King who succeeded to Louis XV was a mixture of the lymphatic hesitancy of the Leczinskis and of the Germanic stolidity of his mother, Maria Josepha of Saxony. He was a dull-witted adolescent, with a puffy face and protruding, short-sighted eyes. He was extremely well informed, with a lively taste for hunting and manual work, but his brain was slow and indecisive; he had little intuition and less personality. In addition, a slight physical malformation prevented the consummation of his

Jeanne le Normant d'Etioles, née Poisson, a bourgeoise with rare qualities, better known as Madame de Pompadour, to whom Louis XV became attached in 1745. She is painted here with her brother by A. Roslin.

marriage for several years – Marie Antoinette suffered in consequence. She was a majestic young woman, stiff-mannered, very proud and bitingly sarcastic. Having been put aside as a wife, she attempted to lead a life of her own, exposing her to calumny and making her unpopular.

Louis XVI felt too young to govern. He sought guidance from Louis XV's former minister, the Count of Maurepas, who very quickly acquired the authority of a Prime Minister. He destroyed the Duke of Aiguillon, then, as he wished to reconstitute the *parlements*, Maupéou and Terray retired from the scene. It was risky returning to the former state of affairs, and the monarchy was to perish as a result of this retrograde step.

Maurepas had nonetheless surrounded himself with worthy men; Malesherbes, the Minister of the Maison du Roi; Miromesnil, the Keeper of the Seals; Vergennes, the Minister for Foreign Affairs; and Turgot, the Minister of Finance. The two last-mentioned ministers were to play vital roles. Vergennes immediately saw that France, given the decline of her prestige in Europe since the Treaty of Paris, would sink into total insignificance if she completely withdrew from the scene of possible conflicts. He had thirteen years in which to bring his foreign policy to a successful conclusion.

Turgot's ministerial career, on the other hand, was very brief. He proved to be innovative with his proposals for a property tax, and for the abolition of forced labour and torture. His major idea was to establish free trade in grain, but this decision rebounded on him, and led to the troubles known as the 'flour war'. Turgot fell into disgrace and, upon leaving his post on 12 May 1776, dared to address Louis XVI with a phrase that was to become famous: 'Remember, Sire, that it was weakness put Charles I's head on the block'.

Turgot was replaced by a financier from Geneva, Jacques Necker. As a foreigner and a Protestant, he could not enter the Council, although this did not prevent him from tackling some bold reforms. He would probably have cleared up the financial chaos if the nation had not had to contribute financially towards the American War of Independence. This war is the crucial event of the first part of the reign.

The thirteen English colonies of North America were facing taxation problems with their mother country; these were seriously aggravated by the Boston Tea Party in 1773 and bloodshed began with a military engagement at Lexington on 19 April 1775. Convinced of their inability to win through single-handed, the Americans appealed to France for aid. Shortly after, they declared independence, on 4 July 1776, and formed the United States of North America.

A young Frenchman, the Marquis of Lafayette, signed a pledge to Benjamin Franklin, the American delegate in France, to the effect that he would rejoin the American army, which he did in the spring of 1777. He was officially rebuked by Louis XVI, but the King and Vergennes secretly approved of his conduct, for it coincided with their underlying policies. Aid to America could take the form of vengeance against England, and a victory might eradicate the consequences of the Treaty of Paris.

An American victory at Saratoga in October 1777 decided the issue. In spite of a crisis in Europe over the problem of the Bavarian succession, the treaty of alliance with America was signed in Paris on 6 February 1778, leading to war with England. After varying fortunes, the war was brought to a head in 1780 by the dispatch to America of an expeditionary force led by Rochambeau, who cooperated with the Commander-in-Chief of the American forces, General Washington. In 1781, Marshal Castries, the Minister of the Marine, sent the reinforcements requested by

Rochambeau: one fleet under Admiral de Grasse went to America, another, under Bailli de Suffren, to India. The victory of Yorktown on 19 October 1781 marked the beginning of success in America.

But the war was expensive and financial difficulties were becoming a cause for concern. Necker dealt a heavy blow by publishing the *Compte-rendu* disclosing the secrets of the budget, and indicating the percentage of State funds apportioned to the Court for expenses and allowances. This had a shattering effect. Necker was forced to resign, but retained such popularity that his recall was inevitable at a time when the financial crisis had become insoluble.

The Treaty of Versailles on 3 September 1783 proclaimed the independence of the United States. This was a significant victory for France, but did not, unfortunately, bring any material gains other than the Isle of Tobago and the restitution of Louisiana, which never in fact took place. While Vergennes' foreign policy was restoring France to a lofty status, the country was internally ravaged by a political crisis from a number of causes.

The disturbances were partly the result of the organization of society, which divided the French into castes of unequal privilege. The highest posts in the Army and Church were reserved for the nobility, a source of bitterness. Contact with American democracy had led to a dangerous spreading of ideas on freedom. The Crown was involved in scandals, in particular the bankruptcy of Prince Rohan-Guéménée and the Affair of the Queen's Necklace.

Vergennes was growing old and proved to be less resolute in negotiations. In 1786 he signed a commercial treaty with England, which brought few advantages to French industry. He refused to support Turkey in 1785 and Holland in 1786.

But the basic cause of France's increasing weakness was the financial crisis, which made it impossible to carry projects through to the end. The Minister of Finance, Calonne, who had served since 1783, saw clearly what had to be done. But he lost three years trying to obtain the good graces of the Court for the furtherance of his plans. In August 1786, he presented the King with a programme of financial reform which indicated that the servicing of the National Debt absorbed half the budget. It was necessary to envisage a substantial loan which would grant the necessary respite for setting up a new programme of taxation. In order to obtain acceptance for views which seemed revolutionary to him, the King, early in 1787, called an Assembly of Notables, who rejected the reforms proposed by Calonne on the grounds that they restricted their privileges. Calonne was forced to resign and was replaced by the Archbishop of Toulouse, Cardinal Loménie de Brienne. He obtained the vote for new taxation, but, as the Notables had expected,

the *parlement* rejected the proposal and demanded an Assembly of the Estates-General.

Louis XVI retaliated by exiling the *parlement* to Troyes. Brienne negotiated with the members and obtained assurances that the loan would be granted; in return, he promised that the Estates would be convened. These measures seemed misleadingly innovative, but they nevertheless alarmed the aristocracy who prepared a revolt, led by the Duke of Orléans, the head of the younger branch of the Bourbons. When the registration of the edicts was to have taken place, the Duke voiced his protest and received the following reply from Louis XVI: 'It is legal because I desire it to be so.' The voice of absolutism had spoken for the last time. Subsequently the situation was to degenerate very rapidly.

Louis XVI found himself in agreement with Loménie de Brienne on the need to fight back. He destroyed the *parlements* which he had restored at the beginning of his reign. The Paris *parlement* revolted. The King took a vacation and instituted a plenary court to serve in his absence. But Louis was not long able to follow his whims; he was obliged first to allow Loménie de Brienne, by the decree of 8 August 1788, to convene the Estates-General for 1789, and then accept the resignation of his chief minister, who had been unable to meet State debts payable by the end of August 1788. At this stage, Louis XVI recalled Necker, a decision which momentarily strengthened credit. While dealing with current problems, Necker postponed the drawing-up of all other plans until the meeting of the Estates-General.

A new session of the Assembly of Notables decided on the election procedure for the Estates. This was not observed by Louis, who, together with Necker, decided on double representation for the Third Estate, without, however, indicating whether voting was to be by head or by Order. This was the confused atmosphere in which the Estates-General met at Versailles, on 5 May 1789. The consultation granted by Louis XVI might have saved the royalty; to the surprise of all, it was to change the destiny of the nation.

The grievances listed in the books of the various electoral committees contained only three demands in common: the necessity for national consent for loans and taxation, the confirmation of the rights of property, and the respect of individual freedom. These claims were most reasonable and Louis XVI could have accepted them without trouble. It would have been enough for the King to agree to these demands, vote the necessary credit to obtain the liberating loan and the necessary taxes to pay it off.

Unfortunately, Louis XVI and Necker made speeches that were too vague, and left the Estates-General to their own devices. The three Orders separately verified their powers, then the Third Estate initiated a move to

Louis XVI, by J. S. Duplessis. Cultured, with a taste for hunting and manual work, but with a slow and indecisive mind, he lacked strength of character and had the misfortune to have to face the Revolution.

14 July 1789: the taking of the Bastille. Two years earlier, Louis XVI had said about an edict, 'It is legal because I desire it.' This was to be his last expression of absolutism.

act as a united body. Since the two privileged Orders did not respond to the appeal, the Third Estate, acting on the proposals of Abbé-Siéyès, on 17 June declared itself to be the National Assembly. Considering this attitude to be rebellious, Louis announced a royal session for 23 June at which he would make his will known. On 20 June, the deputies of the Third Estate assembled in the covered tennis court at Versailles and solemnly swore that they would not disband until they had provided the country with a constitution.

The session of 23 June opened in a stormy atmosphere. The King commanded the Orders to separate, annulled the decrees made by the National Assembly and made the single concession of granting the tax vote to the representatives of the people. Then he ordered the deputies of the Third Estate to leave the Assembly Room. When the Marquis of Dreux-Brézé came to execute the royal order, he was met with this famous retort: 'Go and tell those who sent you that we are here at the will of the people and we will leave only at the point of the bayonet.'

Louis XVI refused to use violence. On 27 June 1789, he commanded the three Orders to sit together, which effectively established constitutional monarchy. The meeting of the three Orders took the name of the Constituent Assembly and set to work to provide France with a constitution.

But Louis XVI's refusal to use violence alarmed the Court. The King, in order to placate his entourage, concentrated troops around Paris, in the hope, too, that he might dissolve the Assembly. He dismissed Necker and ordered the Baron of Breteuil to form an emergency Ministry. At this stage Paris revolted, bands of armed men stormed and captured the fortress of the Bastille, symbol of arbitrary rule, and then murdered the Governor, de Launay on 14 July 1789.

Louis XVI accepted the situation. He exiled those who had been most compromised, recalled Necker, and went to Paris, where he was presented with the tricoloured cockade by Bailly the Mayor, and Lafayette, who had been appointed Commander of the National Guard.

For the following two months, Louis XVI hesitantly moved troops to Versailles, alarming public opinion. On the 5 and 6 October, rioters from Paris attacked the Palace of Versailles. The King and Queen, virtually made prisoner, were forced to move to Paris where they were lodged at the Tuileries, under tight and permanent surveillance. Sordid intrigues became the centre of Louis XVI's existence. Mirabeau advised him to leave Paris and dissolve the Assembly, but this body remained vigilant and active, determined to carry its mission through to the end.

In order to raise fresh money, Talleyrand proposed that the property of the Clergy should be confiscated, and certificates of payment, known as *assignats*, issued

in security. Next the ecclesiastical vows were abolished, and the Civil Constitution of the Clergy was drawn up.

By the time of the Federation Fête, on 14 July 1790, tempers seemed to have calmed down. Louis XVI swore loyalty to the Constitution, while making mental reservations. In particular, he refused to accept the Civil Constitution of the Clergy.

Meanwhile, he charged the Baron of Breteuil with the mission of contacting *emigré* nobles; his long-term plan was to obtain the re-establishment of absolute monarchy in France with the aid of his fellow European sovereigns. This double-dealing was suspected by the Assembly, which intervened in 1791 to compel Louis to take Easter Communion administered by a constitutional priest. Louis pretended to comply, but organized his escape, which took place on the night of the 20–21 June 1791. Paris was amazed by this move believing that the King wished to cross the border. Lafayette took the initiative by announcing that the King had been abducted, and issued a warrant for his arrest. Louis XVI was taken at Varennes and brought back to Paris, where he was stripped of his powers.

But the Constituent Assembly revoked its decision and reinstated the King with slightly wider powers, on condition that he swore loyalty to the Constitution, which he did on 14 September 1791. The Constituent was disbanded, to be replaced by an assembly of entirely new men, the Legislative. This immediately came into conflict with the King on the issue of the struggle against the clergy and the émigrés. These latter, led by the Count of Provence and the Count of Artois, younger brothers of Louis XVI, had installed themselves at Coblenz, where they were stirring up dangerous intrigues, and setting Europe against France. Severe measures were brought against them, and Louis was forced, on 20 April 1792, to take the radical decision of declaring war on the Emperor Francis II, Marie Antoinette's own nephew.

The hostilities began with setbacks, but the members of the coalition improved their organization, and

conferred the command of their troops on the Duke of Brunswick. Louis XVI continued to struggle with terrible problems at home. On 20 June 1792, the crowd invaded the Tuileries, in order to obtain the removal of the King's veto from the decree banishing refractory priests. The King faced up to the situation with courage and dignity, slightly improving his position. But a manifesto issued by the Duke of Brunswick, threatening Paris with invasion if the royal family were harmed, set passions alight once more. On 10 August

1792, the Commune of Paris attacked the Tuileries. Louis XVI refused to defend himself; he entrusted himself to the good will of the Assembly, which handed him over to the Commune. The King and his family were imprisoned in the tower of the Temple. The Legislative Assembly was disbanded and the country elected a National Convention, whose first move was to abolish royalty on 21 September 1792. On the same day, at the Mill of Valmy, General Dumouriez, former Minister to Louis XVI, and General Kellermann halted the Duke of Brunswick's troops and forced them to retreat.

The Convention deemed it fitting to bring the King to justice for high treason. The issue was open to argument since the Constitution rendered him inviolate. This point was ignored, since a hiding-place in the Tuileries, a metal wardrobe, had revealed 'documents that were irrefutable proof of the King's collusion with the *émigrés*'.

Louis XVI's trial opened on 26 December 1792. It was to be full of moving episodes. The defence was led by Malesherbes, Tronchet and Desèze. The last-mentioned reminded the members of the Convention that, 'History would judge their verdict.' The Convention nevertheless took the vote in January 1793. By a very slender majority the King was condemned to death.

On 21 January 1793, Louis XVI, who showed great dignity, was conveyed to the Place de la Concorde where the guillotine had been erected. Marie Antoinette was soon to join him, for she in turn was executed on 16 October 1793.

Louis XVI left an eight-year-old son, imprisoned like his father in the Temple. His upbringing had been entrusted by the Convention to a kindly but ignorant man of the people, Simon the shoemaker.

Although the Crown had been officially abolished by the Convention, the legitimacy of this Assembly, elected on only ten per cent of the votes, was so doubtful that Louis XVII represented the continuity of the monarchy. But the fate of the little King remains shrouded in mystery. It is generally believed that Louis XVII died in the tower of the Temple on 8 June 1795, the official date of his decease. But so many impostors have arisen – more than a hundred, from Hervagault to Naundorf – claiming to be the sons of Louis XVI, that doubt has been sown in many minds. Indeed, some people still believe that the dynasty has not died out.

It seems likely that the little King, long before the official date of his death, had fallen victim to a sickly constitution, aggravated by rough treatment, and had been replaced by a scrofulous child who was walled up alive so that the substitution would not be discovered.

Upon the announcement of Louis XVI's execution, the Count of Provence, who was residing at Hamm in Westphalia, had declared himself Regent and took up his duties, as far as this was possible in exile. At Verona he learned of his nephew's death, and proclaimed himself King under the name of Louis XVIII.

For nineteen years, he was to insist upon his title without a throne, transferring his retinue in turn from Blankenbourg, the home of the Duke of Brunswick, to Mitau in Courlande, to Warsaw, then to Mitau again, and finally to England, where he resided first at Gosfield and then at Hartwell. His political Cabinet was directed by Marshal Castries from 1793 to 1800, then by Saint-Priest, and finally by the favourites d'Avaray and Blacas. In 1804, he launched, with the support of his family, a protest from the Castle of Kalmar in Sweden against the crowning of Napoleon as Emperor. Dated 2 December 1804, the day of the Emperor's coronation, his manifesto met with total indifference on the part of other European sovereigns.

The fall of Napoleon in 1814 immediately revived all his hopes. While his brother, the Count of Artois, was on his way to Paris, Louis XVIII left Hartwell with all

honour due to a sovereign, and disembarked at Calais on 24 April 1814. On 2 May, he spoke with the representatives of the Imperial Senate at St-Ouen, and informed them that he was recovering his throne by virtue of the divine right, but that he was prepared to grant his people a constitutional charter in accordance with their aspirations.

While the charter was being drawn up, Louis XVIII negotiated the Treaty of Paris with the Allies. Signed on 30 May 1814, this Treaty left France virtually untouched, as compared with the France of 1792. She even made a few territorial gains: the Comtat-Venaissin, Savoy and the line of the Queich with Landau.

When the Treaty had been signed, Louis XVIII published the charter, appointed a Chamber of Peers, which consisted partly of the former Imperial Senate,

and retained Napoleon's Chamber of Deputies. The financial situation was not desperately bad and the Finance Minister, Baron Louis, succeeded in redressing it with a minimum of taxation. Discontent, however, sprang from other causes: many officers were put on half-pay and administrative personnel was reduced, whereas new posts were created for the nobility, who had been ruined, and the *émigrés*. Louis XVIII was preoccupied elsewhere with serious problems and he was therefore inclined to neglect matters which he considered to be of minor importance. In particular he was concerned with the remodelling of Europe at the Congress of Vienna, where Talleyrand was defending French interests.

While Talleyrand was recovering France's status in Europe, the astonished nation learned that Napoleon had left the Isle of Elba, landed at the Gulf of Juan and was marching on Paris. 'The Eagle with its national colours will fly from belfry to belfry until it alights on the towers of Notre-Dame.'

The Emperor was correct in his predictions. On the night of 19 March 1815, the day before Napoleon made his victorious entry into Paris, Louis XVIII left the Tuileries and set off for Belgium. Having installed himself at Ghent, Louis set up a provisional government and waited for the next round of events.

These took place rapidly. Napoleon was defeated at Waterloo on 18 June, and was forced to abdicate shortly after. Louis XVIII rushed back to Paris, where he was forced to make serious concessions in order to retrieve his throne. France was thrown into turmoil by a royalist counter-revolution known as the 'White Terror'. At the same time, Louis was forced to take strong action against those who had betrayed him during the Hundred Days of Napoleon's return to power. There was a full-scale administrative purge, the Chamber of Paris was reorganized and a number of executions took place, the most notable of which was that of Marshal Ney.

Needing the support of Czar Alexander I to negotiate with the Allies, Louis XVIII dismissed Talleyrand and Fouché, who had facilitated the restoration of the monarchy, and entrusted the ministry to a friend of the Russian sovereign, the Duke of Richelieu. Before Richelieu's arrival at the ministry, elections had been held on the basis of a poll that was heavily restricted by a property qualification (cens). The elected chamber was so completely royalist that Louis baptized it la Chambre Introuvable (the Incomparable Assembly). He was, however, not long in falling out with this Assembly; it was even more royalist than the King, and he was forced to dissolve it rapidly.

Richelieu's major concern was with the terms of the Second Treaty of Paris, in which France stood to suffer heavy territorial losses, notably Savoy. But even more irksome was the scheduled three-year occupation of her territory, and a heavy war indemnity. Richelieu held step-by-step negotiations with the Allies. At the Congress of Aix-la-Chapelle in 1818, he obtained a reduction in the costs of the occupation, and the total liberation of French territory. This Congress was part of a system known as the Holy Alliance, the vehicle devised by the great European nations for keeping a close watch on French politics.

Richelieu was then replaced by Louis XVIII's favourite, the Count of Decazes, the Minister of Police. Decazes, an open-minded man, believed that the monarchy's only chance lay in liberalism and he made a great effort to convince the King of this. The latter was involved in constant disputes with his brother, the Count of Artois, a belated supporter of the *ancien régime*, and hostile to all concessions. Since he was strongly supported by the King, Decazes would probably have fulfilled his aims had not a dramatic event taken place. The Duke of Berry, the son of the Count of Artois, was assassinated by a fanatic named Louvel as he was leaving the Opera on 13 February 1820. A Court clique, led by the Count of Artois, laid the responsibility for the crime firmly upon Decazes and Louis XVIII mournfully acknowledged the need to sacrifice his favourite, whom he made duke, and appointed ambassador to London. He recalled Richelieu, who agreed to return only on condition that the Count of Artois support his policies.

On 28 September 1820, a posthumous son was born to the Duke of Berry; he received the title of Duke of Bordeaux and the nation assigned to him as a gift the Château of Chambord. Suddenly, it seemed that the dynasty was reviving. However, plots within the country indicated that the opposition was still alive. This was a liberal movement, whose fundamental aim was to create a republic which would, in all probability, have been entrusted to Lafayette.

In order to counteract this liberalism, Louis XVIII, under the influence of the Count of Artois, began to favour ultra-royalism. Richelieu was forced to allow the leader of the Ultras, the Count of Villèle, to enter his ministry. Villèle then supplanted Richelieu, who had been abandoned by the Count of Artois. Villèle, who was a pacifist by nature and by conviction, was to find himself forced to declare war. The King of Spain, Ferdinand VII, having experienced difficulties with his *Cortes*, gave his backing to an insurrectional Junta aiming to restore his rights as absolute monarch. The French Minister for Foreign Affairs, Mathieu de Montmorency, was imprudent enough to have arms sent to the Junta, which had set up headquarters at Seo de Urgel. Next, at the Congress of the Holy Alliance which met at Verona in 1823, he supported the idea of intervention in Spain. Villèle did not approve of intervention, but he had to give way to the wish of the King, who also appointed Châteaubriand as successor to Montmorency. Châteaubriand, the most illustrious writer of the day, viewed the war of Spain as an almost private matter. The expedition, led by the Duke of Angoulême, son of the Count of Artois, was no more than a military parade. It ended with the battle of the Trocadero on 31 August 1823, which opened the gates of Cadiz, where Ferdinand VII was virtually being held prisoner by the *Cortes*.

To put this success to best advantage, Louis XVIII decided to call general elections, which took place on 26 February and 6 March 1824. These elections, conducted without undue restraint, returned such an enormous majority that Louis XVIII could declare 'C'est la Chambre retrouvée.'

He was not long able to reap the benefits of these elections, for the last months of his reign were marked by his declining faculties. These became particularly evident when the sudden disgrace of Châteaubriand turned the latter into a feared opponent. Louis XVIII died of an infectious gangrene on 16 September 1824. He was to be the last of the Bourbon Kings to die in power. He had transformed France from a ruined nation into a wealthy one; he had restored the humiliated country to her pride of place in Europe. But he had not, perhaps, made sufficient provision for a future which the incompetence of his brother and successor, Charles X, was soon to turn into tragedy.

The new King was an agreeable and charismatic leader, but hardly intelligent. He had never come to terms with the Revolution of 1789, and, at sixty-seven years of age, he was not likely to reconsider his prejudices.

During the first days of his reign, however, he made a favourable impression, with his graciousness, elegance and affability. He began by granting freedom of the Press, but the truce was short-lived. The King violently clashed with public opinion by voting laws that were considered reactionary.

In order to stem criticism of his policies, Charles X brought back censorship. Next he dissolved the Chamber, a move which reduced his majority, and led to the retirement of Villèle. The latter was replaced by the Count of Martignac, an agreeable man, who held no illusions about the difficulty of his task.

Charles X was convinced that parliamentary monarchy would not work. He therefore resolutely turned his back on the realities of the situation and called to the ministry one of his most faithful friends, Prince Jules of Polignac, a veritable remnant of the *ancien régime*. Polignac was devoted body and soul to the King, and had vowed him total obedience. With Charles's consent, he organized an expedition to conquer Algiers and to consolidate the victory which had been won over the Turks at the battle of Navarino in 1827 and the expedition to the Peloponnese of 1828, which had freed Greece from the yoke of the Ottoman Empire. He believed that a new victory would consolidate the policies favoured by Charles X.

Unfortunately, the over-confident King made an exceptionally tactless speech from the throne on 19 March 1830, in which he openly threatened to dissolve the Chamber of Deputies if they did not blindly obey him. The Chamber reacted immediately, and a censure of the address from the throne was signed by 221 deputies. The King retaliated by dissolving the Chamber. Elections were begun in June and the first results were very unfavourable to the government. But the news of the capture of Algiers strengthened Charles X in his purpose. When the voting had been completed, the Chamber was found to consist of two hundred and twenty members of the opposition, as against only one hundred and fifty ministerial deputies. It would have

been wise to bow to the facts and govern with the opposition. But Charles X did not wish to do so, and, on 26 July 1830, he promulgated the Five Ordinances, dissolving the new Chamber before its first session, modifying the electoral law, calling new elections for September, and suppressing the freedom of the Press.

This flagrant violation of the charter, despite the fact that Charles X had protected himself by the charter's fourteenth article, immediately led to revolution in Paris. Barricades were erected. The man in charge of restoring order, Marshal Marmont, was soon overwhelmed. Polignac was not quick enough to realize the seriousness of the situation, for the deputies had sided with the people, and public opinion was wavering between monarchy and republic.

Charles X, at last aware of the situation, withdrew the Ordinances and entrusted the ministry to the Duke of Mortemart, who was well liked by the opposition. But his appointment came too late. At the Hôtel de Ville in Paris, the presidency of the Republic was offered to Lafayette. He refused, and, on the balcony of the Hôtel de Ville, acclaimed the Duke of Orléans, head of the younger branch of the Bourbon dynasty.

Charles X had no alternative but to take the road to exile. He retreated to England, then to Austria and died at Goritz, in November 1836, at the age of seventy-nine. No other member of the Bourbon dynasty had ever enjoyed such longevity.

It seems fitting to include Louis-Philippe among the Bourbons. He belonged to the younger branch of the dynasty, separated for more than a century from the direct line, and descended from Philip of Orléans, the brother of Louis XIV. In the line of succession, the King came immediately after the Dukes of Angoulême and Bordeaux, since the Spanish line had not been eligible for the French throne since the Treaty of Utrecht.

The succession of Louis-Philippe is particularly interesting in the fact that, with him, the monarchy again became elective, as it had been during the time of the Capets. In effect, as Thiers, the man really responsible for putting forward Louis-Philippe, had recognized, it was a question of substituting an old atrophied branch for a younger one, more dynamic and better equipped to understand contemporary problems. But the negotiators of the substitution failed to see that they were about to divide the royalist party into two factions so irreconcilable that it would be impossible to re-establish the monarchy in France.

None of this could be seen when, in August 1830, Louis-Philippe was invested by a vote in the Chamber, where he obtained 219 votes from the 253 deputies present, who represented the 428 elected to the National Assembly. The vote was ratified in the Chamber of Peers by a special minority. On 9 August, he accepted the elective Crown; to mark the break with the Bourbons, he took the name of Louis-Philippe I.

The beginning of the reign was troublesome. The former ministers of Charles x had to be tried, and sentenced to life-imprisonment. It was also necessary to get rid of Lafayette, now too important a figure as Commander of the National Guard, and to neutralize Laffitte, the representative of the Movement party, since he was resolved upon large-scale reforms which terrified the conservative sovereign.

Louis-Philippe showed great wisdom in refusing to annex Belgium, although he did gain an indirect hold over the country by marrying one of his daughters to the new King of the Belgians, Leopold of Saxe-Coburg. In Paris the civil order was constantly shattered: the Archbishop's Palace was sacked in 1831; and fighting took place in the Rue Transnonain and in the cloisters of St-Merry.

Louis-Philippe began truly to govern with his energetic President of the Council, Casimir-Périer, who strengthened France's position abroad by sending French troops to Portugal and to the Italian Marches, and by making a military intervention in Belgium, capturing Antwerp in 1831. On the other hand, Casimir-Périer totally failed to understand the problem of the working class, as shown in his handling of the troubles in Lyons in 1831. Even now unfortunately, the President of the Council, who was capable of great things, never was to realize his full potential, for he died of cholera in 1832.

The King, who had greatly respected Casimir-Périer, was now free to act as he wished. For the next four years he had enough experience of the difficulties of the parliamentary system to wish to bypass it altogether. In this respect, he was to react very much as had Charles x. In 1836, however, he was forced to work with Adolph Thiers and the Movement party, although thanks to the skill of the King, the experience was short-lived. Louis-Philippe soon dissociated himself from the belligerent attitudes of Thiers, and called to the ministry a man whom he esteemed above all others, the Count of Molé. Molé had to deal with a Bonapartist uprising, during which the Pretender Louis-Napoleon, nephew of the great Emperor, attempted to take over the garrison at Strasbourg. Louis-Philippe confined his revenge to dispatching the Pretender off to America.

Molé remained in power for nearly three years, not without encountering difficulties, since he had to face a coalition consisting of Thiers, Guizot and Odilon Barrot. When Molé fell, his departure led to a terrible crisis, aggravated by a revolt instigated by Blanqui. After an interlude with Marshal Soult in office, Louis-Philippe had, once more, to hand the government over to Thiers.

A crisis, precipitated by the Eastern Question and involving the whole of Europe, provoked Thiers yet again into making violent threats which gave Louis-Philippe a pretext for dismissing him. But Thiers had meanwhile initiated the decision to return Napoleon i's ashes to Les Invalides. The ceremony coincided with a new Bonapartist uprising led by Louis-Napoleon, at Boulogne in 1840. On this occasion, Louis-Napoleon was brought before the Chamber of Peers and sentenced to life imprisonment. He was interned at the fortress of Ham, from which he was to make a spectacular escape in 1846.

Louis-Philippe had now held power for more than ten years. He was weary of parliamentarianism, and opted for the policies of immobility, placing all his confidence in his minister, Guizot. This immobility of policy did not prevent the King from making important moves in Algeria. Under his orders, Constantine was taken in 1837, and Marshal Bugeaud was entrusted with conquering Algerian territory, a task which, seven years later, was all but complete. This conquest was to be the major achievement of Louis-Philippe's reign.

But his reign was also marked by achievements in industry, in particular the construction of the first railways, the extension of the electric telegraph, and the repair-work carried out to secondary roads. To these achievements must be added the development of primary education, which was made compulsory in 1833. In foreign policy, Guizot won a notable victory when he signed the Straits Convention, a measure concerning the Eastern Question, in which the Russian fleet was forced back into the Black Sea.

But from thereon, the reign was afflicted with bad luck. On 13 July 1842, Ferdinand, the Duke of Orléans, heir to the throne, was killed in a road accident at Neuilly. A Regency now seemed inevitable, given the advanced age of the King, and there followed a bitter dispute over who should be entrusted with the Regency, with the Duchess of Orléans, formerly of Mecklenburg-Schwein, on the one side, and on the other the Duke of Nemours, one of the King's sons. The latter was to be successful.

The Count of Chambord, the grandson of Charles x, took advantage of these troubles to make his presence felt, and, much to the fury of Louis-Philippe, he called a meeting of the legitimist royalists at Belgrave Square in London, presided over by Châteaubriand. Queen Victoria disowned the Count of Chambord, since she was friendly to Louis-Philippe and supported the Entente Cordiale. But this Entente was to be broken by Louis-Philippe himself, in the Affair of the Spanish Marriages, when the Duke of Montpensier, the King's youngest son, married Luisa Fernanda, the sister of Queen Isabella of Spain.

The regime was undermined by a series of scandals which shook its very foundations. A struggle had begun for the extension of the vote, while a campaign known as 'the Banquets', led in part by Lamartine, indicated the existence of a growing opposition. Louis-Philippe faced this opposition with an uncompromising and tactless speech from the throne, towards the end of December 1847. With as much overbearing pride as Louis xiv, he proclaimed himself to be the only defender of political truth.

A minor incident was now enough to start off the troubles; the banning of a banquet in Paris was the spark which set light to the revolution. Guizot, under pressure from the street-fighters, was forced to depart. The King in vain called upon Molé, then Thiers. The uprising swept through Paris and on the morning of 24 February 1848, it seemed likely that the Tuileries would fall into the hands of the insurgents.

Louis-Philippe was forced by circumstances to sign an act of abdication, and miserably resorted to flight.

His son and his daughter-in-law, the Duke and Duchess of Nemours, tried in vain to establish the Regency. As they were pleading their cause, the Chamber was invaded by a band of insurgents. The Republic was duly proclaimed at the Hôtel de Ville in the evening of the same day.

Louis-Philippe took up residence in England, at Claremont, where he died two and a half years later. The constitutional monarchy had collapsed as suddenly as had the monarchy of divine right in 1830.

The fall of Louis-Philippe opened up the way for the legitimate Bourbon heir, the Count of Chambord, but he was unable to seize the opportunity, even though the Chamber of the Second Republic had an overwhelming royalist majority.

The Pretender Louis-Napoleon was appointed President of the Republic; he was to be Emperor from 1852 until his fall in September 1870, after the surrender of Sedan.

Strangely, Chambord forbade royalists to hold public office as long as Louis-Napoleon governed France. The result was a total loss of posts and the political destruction of a whole generation. After the fall of the Empire, the Chamber, which was elected on 8 February 1871, consisted of a nearly two-thirds majority of royalists. This majority aimed to restore the monarchy in the person of the Count of Chambord, who would become King under the name of Henry V. The Count, in an unwise manifesto launched at Chambord in July 1871, declared that he would not accept the Crown unless it was accompanied by the old white flag of the Bourbons. This demand was so reactionary that his cause was abandoned.

Two years later, on 24 May 1873, a parliamentary manoeuvre led by the Duke of Broglie brought about the fall of Thiers, who had been virtual President of the Republic. Thiers was replaced by Marshal MacMahon. It was agreed that MacMahon should consider himself to be Regent only, and be willing to vacate his place for the Count of Chambord. But the latter was to prove a bitter disappointment to his followers. In spite of a reconciliation with the Count of Paris, Louis-Philippe's grandson, which guaranteed the unity of the royalist party, the Count of Chambord, after much persuasion, merely repeated his manifesto and his demand for the white flag.

The disappointed royalists then planned to obtain an extension of Marshal MacMahon's powers until such time as Chambord should have disappeared from the scene. Chambord, having been informed of this plan, took a surprising step; he made a secret journey to Versailles and asked to see MacMahon, hoping that the latter would take him to the Assembly and proclaim him King in the face of all opposition. Since this was contrary to his presidential oath, MacMahon refused. He obtained an extension of his powers for seven years, and the Count returned to the solitude of Frohsdorf, in Austria, where he had lived since 1842.

On his deathbed in 1883, the Count of Chambord, while admitting the Princes of Orléans to his presence, did not explicitly name the Count of Paris as his

successor. Having seen for himself how the idea of monarchy had fallen into disrepute in nineteenth-century France, Chambord seems to have refused to become a constitutional monarch, subject to the whim of assembly and electorate.

The direct line of the Bourbons ended with the Count of Chambord. The line of Orléans, now the senior branch, today represents the continuity of the great dynasty which, in 1589, took control of France at a time of despair, and succeeded in raising her to the height of grandeur and success.

The unhappy events of subsequent years do nothing to blot out these magnificent achievements, which live on in human memory and are symbolized by a sublime series of architectural glories such as the Plâce des Vosges, the Plâce Vendôme, Les Invalides, the Place de la Concorde, the Military School, the Panthéon, the Palace of Compiègne, and the dominating splendours of Versailles and of the Trianons.

Second Interlude

Some sovereigns have established a kind of negative record, ruling for less than a year rather than for forty or fifty years. Edward VIII succeeded his father George V on the British throne in January 1936, and abdicated in December of the same year. His reason for abdicating was the decision to marry Wallis Simpson, a rich American divorcee. This proposal met with firm resistance from the Prime Minister, Stanley Baldwin, and the Church. British public opinion was divided; many favouring the marriage, but others opposed. Finally, Edward decided to abdicate and the Crown passed to his brother, George VI.

Czar Peter III reigned for only six months in 1762; he came to the throne in January and was overthrown in June in a palace revolution instigated by his wife, Princess Sophia Augusta of Anhalt-Zerbst, later Catherine II, and her favourite, Orlov. The Czar was imprisoned and died mysteriously in July of that year, probably murdered on the orders of his wife.

A similarly tragic fate befell the boy-King Edward V, who succeeded his father, Edward IV, on the English throne when barely thirteen. Edward, who belonged to the House of York, the younger branch of the Plantagenets, was crowned on 9 April 1483, and a few days later fell into the hands of his uncle, Richard of Gloucester, who declared him illegitimate and imprisoned him together with his brother Richard in the Tower of London. On 25 June, a tame Parliament proclaimed Richard of Gloucester King and Edward was murdered in the Tower.

Umberto II of Savoy, the last King of Italy, known as 'the May King', reigned from 8 May to 2 June 1946, for twenty-six days. He came to the throne when Victor Emmanuel III decided to abdicate; the old King hoped this action would save the monarchy, which had been deeply compromised by fascism, by presenting it with 'a new face' to the decision of the institutional referendum on 2 June. But this manouvre was unsuccessful; the Republic won the referendum and Umberto II, after vainly attempting to contest the validity of the result, went into exile.

The reign of Jane Grey, great-niece of Henry VIII, was even shorter. In 1551, John Dudley, Duke of Northumberland, succeeded in convincing Edward VI to name Jane Grey, the King's second cousin, as heir to the throne; the Crown should have gone to Mary, Edward's elder half-sister, had she not been declared illegitimate in 1544, as the daughter of Henry's marriage to Catherine of Aragon. So Jane Grey came to the throne on Edward's death, but her reign lasted only a few days. Mary, with popular support, overthrew her and eventually had her executed with her supporters.

However, the shortest reign of all is that of the Capetian John I, who was King in 1316 for five days, the first and only five days of his life.

SOVEREIGNS CAPTURED IN BATTLE

France holds a rather unenviable record, that of the most kings – three, two Valois and one Bonaparte – who have undergone the indignity of being captured in battle. The first was John the Good, King from 1350 to 1364; his reign coincided with the first phase of the Hundred Years War, when the English troops were on the offensive, a revolt by the people of Paris, the explosion of the Jacquerie, and the spread of the plague. The battle of Poitiers in 1356 ended in a terrible defeat for the French and John was taken prisoner and brought to London, where he was imprisoned until 1360.

After less than two centuries the same fate overtook Francis I (1514–47) during the long struggle between France and the Empire of Charles V. Three years after the commencement of hostilities, in 1524, Francis I decided to go in person to Italy, the centre of the war, at the head of a strong force. But at Pavia on 25 February 1525, his army was overcome by the Imperial forces. The French King was in fact defeated by a Frenchman, Charles of Bourbon, who, with the Marquis of Pescara, commanded the Imperial troops. Charles of Bourbon, one of the most powerful French nobles, angered by the confiscation of some family estates, had conspired against his sovereign in 1523, and when the conspiracy was discovered had abandoned the French camp and passed into the Emperor's service. Francis I remained almost a year in prison, the price of his freedom, obtained on 14 January 1526, being the signing of a humiliating Peace treaty.

Napoleon III, Emperor of the French from 1852, and nephew of the great Napoleon – whose strategic skills he unfortunately did not inherit – was defeated and captured during the Franco-Prussian War of 1870. The Prussians attacked with lightning speed, breaking the French army in two. The Emperor was taken prisoner at Sedan on 2 September 1870, little more than a month after the beginning of the war, together with his army of 120,000 men, while attempting to join Bazaine's army besieged by the Prussians at Metz. This defeat cost Napoleon III his Crown; on 4 September, forty-eight hours after the disaster at Sedan, the Republic was proclaimed.

ASSASSINATIONS

The art of regicide has many variations, poison, dagger, bomb or pistol, but still seems to illustrate certain constant factors, rules dictated by history. For instance, in the Middle Ages kings were almost always assassinated only after being deposed and imprisoned in some dungeon. During the period of religious wars, it was the daggers of fanatical defenders of the faith that cut short the lives of monarchs. At the end of last century, the more reactionary sovereigns were assassinated by anarchists.

It seems as if at certain moments or in certain places the regular flow of dynastic succession was arrested by a wave that swept away an incredible number of crowned heads. One of these, in England, took place in the fourteenth and fifteenth centuries. The Plantagenet Edward II, who had come to the throne in 1307, fell into disgrace when his disastrous policies allowed Scotland to become independent in 1314, and in 1327, Parliament forced him to abdicate in favour of his son, Edward III; he was assassinated in prison a few months later. His great-grandson, Richard II, suffered a similar fate in 1399 and once again it was Parliament, in collusion with Henry of Lancaster, of a younger branch of the Plantagenets, that deposed him. He was imprisoned in Pontefract Castle and assassinated. But the Lancastrian Henry IV's rise to the throne was soon followed by the extremely bloody civil war of the 'Two Roses': the red rose of Lancaster and the white rose of York. During the thirty years of war from 1455 to 1485, four sovereigns came to the throne and three of these were assassinated. The Lancastrian Henry VI, King from 1422 to 1461 and from 1470 to 1471, was imprisoned in the Tower of London by his rival, Edward of York, and murdered there. Edward V, son of Edward of York, who succeeded his father to the throne at thirteen, was deposed and eliminated by his uncle, Richard of Gloucester, who assumed the Crown with the title of Richard III (1483–5), but was himself killed at the battle of Bosworth on 24 August 1485 by Henry Tudor, who then became King as Henry VII.

Further north, in Scotland, the Stuart kings fell as the victims of a destiny not without a certain pattern. James I, King in 1406 and then from 1424 to 1437, was assassinated at the instigation of two nobles, Sir Robert Stewart and Sir Robert Graham. James II (1437–60)

fell in battle while assaulting an English fortress. James III (1460–88) was assassinated during a rebellion of the nobility. Finally, James IV (1488–1513) died at the battle of Flodden on 13 September 1513, fighting against the English. The tragic series of this unlucky dynasty was completed with Mary Stuart (1552–68) who was overcome by the opposition of the nobles and forced to take refuge in England in 1568, where Elizabeth Tudor kept her prisoner for many years and finally had her condemned to death, accusing her of having taken part in conspiracies. The unfortunate Mary was decapitated in February 1587.

Two French sovereigns were stabbed to death within the space of twenty years. Henry III, the last of the Valois, was assassinated on 2 August 1589 by the monk Jacques Clément, who wished to avenge the killing of Henry of Guise, ordered a year earlier by the King. Henry III was succeeded by Henry IV, the founder of the Bourbon dynasty, who ended his days on 14 May 1610 at the hand of an ex-monk, François Ravaillac. It is probably more than just coincidence that these assassinations took place in a period when the Jesuits were upholding the legitimacy of regicide as the people's weapon against the heresy of kings.

The Romanov dynasty was notably prone to palace revolutions, two of which ended tragically. In 1762, Catherine II deposed her husband Peter III and probably had him assassinated. Czar Paul I was killed on the night of 11–12 March 1801 by officers of the Imperial Guard. Czar Alexander II's death was also due to political motives, but of a different kind; on 13 March 1881 in St Petersburg, the monarch, who had already escaped two previous attempts on his life, was killed by a bomb planted by nihilists.

Umberto I of Savoy suffered a similar fate, killed by four shots fired by an anarchist, Gaetano Bresci, while leaving a gymnastic display at Monza on 29 July 1900 in his carriage. Bresci later declared that he had wanted to revenge the massacre carried out by General Bava Beccaris in Milan in 1898.

EXECUTIONS

Only three sovereigns, instead of being killed in battle or by the hand of rivals, relatives or conspirators, were tried and condemned to death. These three executions coincide with the three major revolutions of modern Europe: the English Civil War, the French Revolution and the Russian Revolution. After his defeat by Oliver Cromwell in the Civil War, Charles I was beheaded on 9 February 1649. Louis XVI was guillotined on 21 January 1793. Nicholas, the last Czar of Russia, was shot at Ekaterinburg on 16 July 1918.

Michael Romanov on horseback, in a contemporary portrait. At sixteen he was elected Czar by an assembly in 1613, and was the first member of the dynasty which ruled Russia for three hundred and four years, up to the Revolution.

The Romanovs

Three hundred and four years of rule in a
country which at first was, for Europe, a
remote entity but became a great power

Between 1604 and 1613, Russia suffered one of the
most serious crises in her history: 'the Time of
Troubles'. The old dynasty died out in 1598 with Fedor
I, the son of Ivan the Terrible. Three usurpers followed
in quick succession: Boris Godunov; Dmitri 'the self-
styled'; and Basil Shuisky, the Boyar. The struggles
between the factions led to civil war, and the torn
country was ravaged by the Swedes who held
Smolensk, and the Poles, who were in Moscow. Nobles
committed treachery, resistance fighters were imprisoned. A legitimate Czar was needed to save Russia.

Then, from the depths of his dungeon, the Patriarch
Hermogen appealed to the cities to 'save Russia'. His
voice was heard by Kuzma Minin, a butcher-alderman
of Nizhni-Novgorod, and by Prince Pozharsky who
ruled Jaroslavl. Courageous and bold both, the
plebeian and the patrician armed patriotic militia. 'The
whole land rose up,' say the annals: Russia incarnate
in her sons. The Poles were driven from the Kremlin. A
National Assembly – Zemski Sobor – was set up, and,
in an attempt to form a link between the old dynasty
and the new, five hundred delegates from all over the
country elected Michael Fedorovitch Romanov,
second cousin of Czar Fedor. As he was related
(though distantly) to the old sovereigns, this sixteen-
year-old adolescent would have seemed to be the only
'natural' czar to the nation. The first Romanov, legally
elected by delegates from all over the country, could
count on them to work with him in his efforts to rebuild
and establish peace.

The Romanovs were to reign over the Russian
Empire from the day the first of them was sought out at
the Ipatiev Monastery at Kaluga and offered the
ancient crown, 'the cap of Monomakh', until the night
the last was murdered in Ipatiev House at Ekaterinburg. 13 March 1613 to 19 March 1917: three hundred
and four years and six days. . . .

Michael I's parents had both been forced to go into
religious orders by Godunov, who was jealous of them.
Then his father, Fedor Romanov ('the Reverend
Philaret'), had been taken captive by the Poles.
Michael had grown up in solitude and ignorance, but
he was mild and gentle. He was in no way prepared for
his high vocation and he sought advice from his
Council on everything. Under their guidance, he
signed a truce with Sweden and then with Poland in
1618, which enabled his father to return. Philaret
became Patriarch and 'Co-Emperor', and his ability
was to make up for the lack of it in his son. He curbed
corruption, levied taxes, encouraged the colonization
of Siberia and welcomed foreigners. British, German
and Dutch engaged in commerce, built factories and
opened up mines. Thus the West began to infiltrate.

Philaret died in 1623. He had never felt the need to
call the Assembly, but Michael was entirely different.
Though he had received the title of 'Autocrat', at the
time it simply meant that the Czar was the guarantee of
national unity. It would be up to the other Romanovs
to give this word the meaning of 'absolute power'.
Michael I began to call the 'men from the whole land'
together again and no Russian monarch would ever
consult his Sobor so seriously and with so much
respect; never would the nation's representatives give
their advice so freely and with so much confidence.

But when Michael died aged forty-nine in 1645, he
had only achieved half of his plans. For the treaty with
Sweden had taken away Russia's access to the Baltic,
one of her 'lungs': she had only a single port,
Archangel, which was frozen in winter. She was in
danger of suffocating. . . .

This painting by Abraham Storck depicts the naval review at Amsterdam for the visit of Peter the Great. The Czar is on board the little ship flying the Russian flag.

Michael I left a son, Alexis, 'elected successor' by the Assembly; a pure formality, since there was no quarrel over the succession. Alexis I was then sixteen. Unlike his father, he had been prepared for his reign by his tutor, Boyar Morozov, an energetic and learned man. The young Czar was open to new ideas whilst at the same time remaining piously attached to the rigorous precepts of the Orthodox Church – the last Russian sovereign to be faithful to the image of the devout prince of the old days. Paradoxically, he took pleasure in visiting 'heretical' lands overseas. Forward looking, yet at the same time a guardian of the old Russia, he stood between the past and the future.

A conciliatory, debonair and trusting man, Alexis would prove well worthy of being called 'the Very Peaceful' but these qualities also led him to close his eyes to the vices of his friends. Morozov took enormous advantage of the situation and, with a handful of acolytes, he oppressed the country. He was shrewd, greedy and fabulously rich, his extortions were enormous. Suddenly the people burst forth in anger demanding the heads of the prevaricators. Alexis was afraid and had the guilty boyars executed, but saved his favourite. Nevertheless, the revolt had opened his eyes on the state of the country, the many abuses and the antiquated structures. He called together the *Sobor* to prepare a Law Code, revising and modernizing that of Ivan III, dating from 1497. Alexis' Code of 1649, called the *uloshenie*, was an important landmark in seventeenth-century Russia, and it was to last until the middle of the nineteenth century. However, above all it strengthened the power of the State, and, although it stated that 'every Muscovite, from the greatest to the smallest, should enjoy the same justice', this did not counterbalance the monstrous law on serfdom, which attached the serf to his master for the whole of his life, from whom he could only be separated if he was sold or exchanged.

During the reign of Alexis I there were wars and popular uprisings which lasted for twenty years. A war was fought against Poland, over the Ukraine, and there were popular riots over economic matters. In the south, a Cossack, Stephen Razin, led a group of malcontents: law-breakers, deserters, escaped serfs, even people from towns and villages that had been ruined by taxes. Razin raised his banner for the oppressed, promised to exterminate the boyars, squires and priests, and to suppress 'taxes and serfdom'. Along the Volga he seized forty of the Czar's ships and three cities. It was to be four years before he met his end, and only then because he was betrayed. In 1671, he was beheaded in Red Square, but the insolent bravery of his 'crusade' made him a popular hero, fighting to relieve the distress of the Russian people.

Troubled by his wars and their various outcomes, and by the poor state of the economy, Alexis did not know which way to turn. He tried to strike a balance between the 'radicals' and the 'traditionalists'. Although he gave in to the latter and confined all foreigners to the 'German Quarter' – *Niemetskaya Slobod* – on the outskirts of Moscow, he often visited the 'European' home of the Boyar Matveev, who had a Scottish wife. There he met their ward, Natalia Naryshkina, who thought and dressed in the Western manner. Alexis fell in love with her and married her on the death of his first wife, Maria Miloslavna, a pious and dull recluse of the *Terem*. Natalia brought bold changes to the Kremlin: the Czarina was no longer cloistered, and her soirées were joyous occasions, free from hieratic etiquette. Foreign newspapers were read, and German and French actors were encouraged to

190

put on profane plays. In private, the Czar dressed in 'German style' clothes.

His thirst for progress led Alexis I to consent to the religious reforms put forward by his friend and adviser, Nikon, Patriarch of all the Russias. The day was to come when the Czar grew tired of Nikon's authoritarianism, but in the meantime this reformer overturned the Church and the nation. But the majority of believers and clergy felt any change to be wrong: to alter or to suppress a ritual gesture or a verse resulted in damnation. Even though Nikon was not concerned with dogmas and only wanted to return to the primitive purity of the texts, which had parted from the original over the centuries, the Great Schism (*Raskol*) divided the country in two. The 'Old Believers', led by the priest Avvakum, and the convinced 'Nikonians' believed each other to be heretics. Alexis handed the adversaries over to the secular power and schismatics were sent to the stake in their thousands. It was a cruel and sterile contest which tore Russia apart, and its consequences were to be felt for centuries.

When Alexis I died on 30 January 1676, aged forty-seven, at his bedside were not only the children of Maria Miloslavna, but also Natalia Naryshkina with her son. His legitimate successor was Fedor, sixteen years old, very gentle and with a fine mind. He had been well educated by Simon de Polotsky, a theologian and eminent poet, but, weak in health, he was to have neither the strength nor the time to carry out his

Detail of a painting by Hersent, in which Peter the Great, in an overly familiar gesture, is holding the young King Louis XV in his arms during his visit to the French Court.

numerous projects. However, he managed to establish the first Slav-Greek-Latin Academy in Moscow, and he abolished the archaic institution of precedences which placed the ancestry of a boyar family and the birthright of its members above personal merit. Fedor III died in 1682, and the battle for succession amongst the Romanovs began.

There were two princes, one from each family, to choose from: Ivan, Alexis' son by his first wife, was weak and feeble-minded; Peter, Natalia's son, was handsome and strong and, though only ten, he already looked older than his sixteen-year-old half-brother. Princess Sophia, eldest daughter of Alexis by Marie Miloslavna, was a determined character, not bound by convention, and declared Ivan to be the 'natural heir', which was in theory true. But the people, the clergy and the nobles were in no doubt as they poured into the Kremlin to acclaim their 'Czar Peter'. Mad with rage, Sophia went in search of the garrison of Moscow, the *streltsi*, leading them to believe that the Naryshkins had assassinated Ivan. Natalia appeared, holding the two princes, Ivan and Peter, by the hand, but too late: the soldiers massacred Peter's family before his very eyes. Sophia then found a compromise: Ivan v would

be the 'first Czar' and Peter I, the 'second'. Sophia declared herself Regent, fully intending to rule by herself before long. She married off Ivan and banished him to the Kolomenskoe Palace on the outskirts of Moscow, and she then exiled Peter and his mother to the village of Preobrazhenskoe, near the capital.

This was to prove a fortunate exile, for Peter here learnt from the book of life. Close by, lay the 'German Quarter', where he became a frequent visitor, and here he met Westerners who taught him the ideas that he needed to know in his future reign – something that he did not doubt for a moment would happen. He also formed gangs of soldier playmates, later to become the nucleus of the élite Guards regiments.

The Regent observed these 'childish fantasies' from the Kremlin and mocked them. In fact, Sophia was already preparing for her coronation as Czarina. Peter did not worry her, for she never realized that he was growing up and beginning to assert himself. She did not understand that her ugly face was a constant reminder to her half-brother of the evil she had done him in 1682, seven years before. Suddenly he defied her: appearing in Moscow, making enquiries, having himself acclaimed in the street. Sophia had drafted her inaugural manifesto, but she was already losing control. She engaged a company of *streltsi* to burn Preobrazhenskoe, ordering them to kill Peter and his mother if they tried to escape. That evening, the fate of Peter I and, therefore, of Russia, rested upon a humble musketeer, named Sukharev, who was taken with pity. He ran to the village, awoke the Czar and warned him of the danger. Peter escaped in his night-shirt and hid in a wood, where clothes and a horse were brought to him. In the early hours, he arrived, exhausted, at the Trinity Monastery, an Orthodox stronghold, where the Abbot took him in. Perfectly lucid, he took control of himself, and like every man who has an exceptional vocation, he recognized his moment when it arrived. His 'merry' gangs began to arrive, all of them now real soldiers; the *streltsi* came to side with him. He pardoned them, for at the opportune moment it was with them that he was to conquer Azov. The clergy and the Patriarch Joachim recognized him as the 'only sovereign'. No-one spared a thought for poor Ivan v. As for Sophia, Peter ordered her to retire to a convent.

However, the Czar felt that he was not yet ready to reign and, leaving the Regency to his mother and to the Patriarch, he set off on his apprenticeship. His obsession was to open up Russia to the north and the south. His passion was the navy. He had his first flotilla built and launched on Lake Pereyaslavl, installed a naval dockyard at Archangel, and built his first war-ship. In 1695, he attacked the fortress of Azov. Although the expedition failed, it taught Peter a hard lesson. He realized that he had quickly to build thirty ships, and a thousand boats. Within a year came

*The crown used at Peter the Great's coronation.
Extremely precious, with a large uncut ruby below the
cross, it was created especially for the occasion,
together with the one for Peter's half-brother, Ivan V.*

victory, and the news of it sounded all over Europe, much louder than that of the death of Ivan v, making Peter sole master of the whole of Russia.

Everything about Peter the Great was colossal: his physique; his projects; his capacity for work; his thirst for pleasure. He enjoyed himself in the German Quarter with his Russian and foreign friends, such as Alexander Menshikov, a former pastry-cook. His mother had arranged his marriage with an old-fashioned girl, Eudoxia Lopukhina, who gave him a son, Alexis. But he did not care for her or for the child, enjoying himself instead with his mistress, Anna Mons, the daughter of a German jeweller. He loved women, drink, friends; but at the same time his first love was Russia and the job he had to do: to transform his Empire and to let in Western civilization.

Thus, in 1697, he took his tour abroad in order to learn. He took with him a group of two hundred people so that they might discover 'the secret of power in other countries', and so that he might learn for himself and be able to direct affairs personally. Never before had a Russian Orthodox Czar left his country and gone amongst 'unbelievers'. The scandal amongst tradition-alist circles was enormous, but Peter took no notice. After a year, having amassed a great store of practical knowledge, for Peter was neither a dreamer nor an ideologist, he set off for home, taking with him a large number of specialists in many different fields. On his journey, he received a warm welcome in Vienna from the Emperor Leopold I. But when he was about to leave for Venice, he heard that the *streltsi* had been secretly recalled from Azov by Sophia and had revolted against him. For the third time, the ex-Regent had tried to get rid of her brother.

Although Patrick Gordon had already put an end to the rebellion, on his return the Czar set about an atrocious repression, taking part personally in the interrogations and executions. The massacre of the *streltsi* is one of the most bloody episodes in the history of the Romanov dynasty. But since childhood Peter had seen so much violence, borne so many grudges. In his view, all those bodies in Red Square avenged those of his family who had been cut down in the same square in May 1682. Hatred bred hatred, and he was never to forgive anyone for anything. When Alexis, his son, plotted against him, in the name of a retrograde and declining Russia, he was to have him killed without pity. That was his harsh, implacable side; but, on the other hand, there was his faith in the future of his people to whom he dedicated his life, without ever sparing of himself. At Poltava he conquered the greatest leader of his time: Charles XII of Sweden. At last he could 'let Russia breathe through one of her lungs', the Baltic, and open a window onto Europe: ('the great window through which Russia looks into Europe', as Algarotti wrote).

In the midst of the war, he took a fancy to the mistress of Menshikov, who was not only his closest companion, minister and factotum but also a very clever rogue. Martha Skavronska, a young Lithuanian servant and a Protestant, was voluptuous, generous, and discerning. She accompanied the Czar on all his campaigns, sleeping rough, and sharing in his successes and his failures. She bore him four children, of whom only Anna and Elizabeth survived. When she was received into the Orthodox Church, she took the name 'Catherine', and Peter married her, although Eudoxia was still alive and had been forced to retire to a nunnery. The Czar was committing bigamy. In 1717 Peter wanted to form an alliance with France. He went to Versailles and offered the hand of his daughter Elizabeth to the young Louis XV. But Cardinal Dubois mistrusted 'Russian barbarians' and rejected the idea.

The Russians, barbarians? To a great extent, they were. It was because he was made to suffer for this fact that Peter the Great resolved to become the reformer. He had to reform everything, in all provinces, to

Westernize habits, customs, institutions, to make new men. But he was in too much of a hurry, and his reforms were a terrible shock. For this reason, this genius was considered by many to be an 'evil genius', a frantic destroyer. However, he was a visionary, constructing for the future. The new capital of his Empire, 'the Palmyra of the North', founded in 1703, without doubt represented the most daring of all his enterprises. For new Russia needed a new city, Moscow was out of date, retrograde, sluggish. Whilst the mighty Neva flowing through St Petersburg would enable technical knowledge, goods and ideas to be exchanged with the West. 'They will all sail in to see us,' said Peter I, in the words of the poet, Pushkin.

Peter the Great died too soon. Deprived of his stimulating and exacting personality, the 'young eagles' that he had raised could achieve no more than mediocrity, or else they became megalomaniacs.

The Czar had caught cold whilst rescuing some sailors in difficulties. He, who was never ill, was carried off in three days. On his death-bed, he wanted to dictate his wishes to his elder daughter, Anna. He sighed: 'I give all to . . .', and died on 27 January 1725. Once he had gone, everything was uncertain. For seventeen years, the sceptre of the Empire, whose reforms were so very far from complete, was to pass from the hands of one woman to another. The age of the female autocrats had arrived.

When the Czarevitch, Alexis, had risen up against his father, Peter had had him executed and then changed the rule of primogeniture. The revolutionary new decree declared that henceforth every Czar could give his heritage to whomsoever he wished and take it away from any successor who seemed to him to be unworthy or incapable. In 1724, he had crowned Catherine 'for her many and important services', and declared her heiress in writing. But he destroyed this paper when Catherine had deceived him with Mons, her estate manager. Her lover's head had been cut off and had then adorned her bedroom for some time under a glass bowl. It was assumed that he no longer considered her 'worthy'. To whom, then, should 'all be given'? To the Czar's grandson, Peter, the son of Alexis? To Anna, the daughter of Ivan V? But the

*Peter III with his wife and son Paul in a painting by A.
R. Lisiewski. His wife (later Catherine II the Great)
was a German Princess, Sophia of Anhalt-Zerbst.*

Diamonds and pink topazes, set in gold and silver, for
the brooch and earrings which formed part of a parure
made for Catherine II. This ambitious German Princess
gained the Russian throne through her marriage.

associates of Peter I, and the army, thought that
Catherine alone could take on this heavy burden. At
dawn on 28 January, the Guards regiments, led by
Menshikov, shouted below the windows of the Winter
Palace: 'Long live our little mother, Catherine I'. The
Preobrazhenskoe and Semenovskoe Regiments had
lifted the widow of their founder onto the throne, and
from then on they became the arbiters of power.

Catherine I was the first woman to reign over all the
Russias. Entrusted with limitless authority, she was
described by the diplomats of the day as 'the most
powerful woman in the world'. She was sincere in her
resolve to continue with unfinished projects, and not to
allow herself to be led by anyone. Unfortunately, her
taste for drink, first acquired in the bivouacs, her
successive infatuations for members of the Court, and
her irregular life-style, all left Menskikov's hands free;
Menshikov who was now Prince and Most Serene! He
stripped the Senate and the Synod of their authority,
oppressed the Supreme Council, from which he
expelled the Empress's son-in-law, the Duke of
Holstein, and sent him back to his ducal seat with his
wife, the Princess Anna. Meanwhile, Catherine
devoted all her attention to achieving what Peter had
begun: the marriage of Princess Elizabeth with Louis
XV. But at Versailles she was treated with contempt.
So, humiliated and discouraged, she decided to form
an alliance with Austria, the enemy of France. After
that she let herself go. She put on weight, her health
deteriorated; and her mind began to go. Seeing that
she had not long to live, Emperor Charles VI, bribed
Menshikov to get Catherine to name the son of the
Czarevitch Alexis as her successor, since he was
connected through his mother to the Hapsburgs. The
Empress signed a document handing over the Russian
Empire to a twelve-year-old boy. Nevertheless, at the
last moment, she placed her two daughters after their
first cousin in the order of succession. Soon afterwards,
in 1727, she died, having reigned without glory for two
years. As for Elizabeth: her dream of becoming Queen
of France had vanished, but she could not have
guessed that the King who refused her today, would
tomorrow help her to become Empress.

Peter II was thus 'installed' by Menshikov, who set
himself up as a dictator. To strengthen his position, he
betrothed the new Czar to his daughter, Maria. But in
the eyes of the old nobility, the son of the unfortunate
Alexis was the symbol of the Russia before Peter I,
before 'the Flood'. The princes of the old aristocracy,
the Dolgorukys, the Golitsyns, seized power, got rid of
the 'young eagles', and sent Menshikov and his family
to Siberia. Peter II did not react. High-spirited and
frivolous, he was interested only in pleasure and
hunting, with no thoughts for his Empire, for affairs of
State and for politics. Next, the oligarchs transferred
the Court to Moscow, thus marking a return to the

past. But there the work of these boyars came to an
end; they, incompetent like their ancestors, proved as
incapable of initiative as their young sovereign. Peter II
allowed himself to become betrothed to Catherine
Dolgoruky, just as he had accepted Maria Menshikov.
On the eve of his wedding in February 1730, Peter II
died of smallpox, at the age of fifteen.

The succession was wide open. No-one bothered
about the will of Catherine I. Anna, Duchess of
Holstein, had died in childbirth, leaving only a baby
son. If he were to become Czar, it would have been
necessary to put up with the Regency of his father, a
foreigner. Elizabeth was the obvious candidate, but the
oligarchs protested that she was too strong-willed.
They wanted to be in sole charge, so they chose Anna,
the daughter of Ivan V, and the widow of the Duke of
Courland. She was thirty-seven, living in poverty in
Mitau with her lover, Ernest Bühren, who had changed
his name to Biron. The princes were so sure that Anna
would submit to their rule that they drew up a charter
limiting her power. But the Council of Ministers and

the army realized what was happening and warned the Duchess. Though lazy and irresolute, she was cunning. She signed the document, appeared in Moscow determined to defend herself, but she was plotting in secret and, on 8 March 1730, she gave an audience to the 'representatives of the people'. They begged her 'spontaneously' to 'rule as an autocrat like her ancestors'. The officers of the Guard intervened, of course, and threatened to kill anyone who dictated the law to their sovereign. Tearing up the charter, Anna announced that by 'inheriting' the title of Empress (which was not untrue, since she was the heiress of the eldest branch of the family) she was 'keeping within the law of the Empire which has always been ruled by an absolute sovereign' (which was less true). From that day forward, for ten years, Anna I was determined to make Russia suffer, in the hands of her favourite, and a crowd of Germans who held all the key positions. Biron ruled with an iron hand, and this reign was to be known as the *Bironstchina* – 'The Age of Biron'. Nevertheless, he acted with the approval of his Imperial lover, and this unworthy couple devoted themselves to despotism, proscription and execution, while at the same time raiding the treasury to finance their stupendous extravagances. Meanwhile, the war against France, over the Polish succession, led Count Münnich and the Russian army as far as the Rhine. This surprising event made the King of France think that a renewal of relations would be a good thing. After all, the Czarina was a German. Elizabeth's hour rang out at last at the Trianon, and Louis XV sent the Marquis de la Chétardie to St Petersburg to make contact with her. The ambassador lost no time in discovering that she lived an isolated and sheltered existence, and that 'she was generally loved by the Nation that groans under the Germans'.

In October 1740, the Empress Anna died, leaving the throne to a child a few months old, the son of her niece, Anna of Mecklenburg, whom she had adopted and married to the Prince of Brunswick. By choosing Ivan VI, a descendant of Ivan V, she had kept the Romanov Crown with the eldest branch of the family. Biron was made Regent and thus the country was handed over yet again to this tyrant. The mother of the Czar was put in custody, but she rebelled and plotted. Within a month the Guards had arrived to arrest the Regent. Princess Anna had won, for a little while, at least.

Meanwhile Elizabeth, Peter the Great's surviving daughter, was no longer closely guarded and appeared in St Petersburg, and she was acclaimed and received soldiers of all ranks in her Summer Palace. The French ambassador was plotting with her, promising that Louis XV would do all he could to put her on the throne. The Regent Anna was warned by her spies, but La Chétardie, who had his own, warned Elizabeth that her cousin was going to lock her away in a convent. On the freezing night of 24 November, she went to the Guards barracks and asked the troops to help her to seize a Crown 'that was hers by right'. The Sovereign and the Nation were one, just as they had been for her father. The Guards shouted, 'Long live our little mother, Elizabeth!', and she replied, 'Let us go and make our Country happy!' The *coup d'état* was achieved without a single drop of blood being spilt or a shot being fired, the Brunswick family was merely woken up and escorted away. Elizabeth I was Empress and Russia was 'to return to herself'.

Elizabeth was going to let Russia live again, and to assure her of twenty happy years, by her enlightened statecraft, by establishing a regular Court, similar to that of Versailles, and by taking part in everything that went on in Europe with an 'obstinate clairvoyance'. Beautiful, passionate and captivating, she loved to dance and to wear fashionable clothes. But her exuberant nature made her equally conscious of her duty as of her pleasure-seeking, as equally capable of doing business with an ambassador as of dancing a minuet with him. If she had been only a magnificent bird in fine feathers, would Louis XV, Frederick II and

200

Maria Theresa have shown friendship or hostility towards her in their foreign policy? Like Peter the Great, she wanted Russia to be truly Russian but at the same time open to the West, independent but also a friend to other nations. Although she was high-spirited rather than reflective, she knew how to get down to work when she had to, and she chose her collaborators well. Her chief adviser was her lover, and later her morganatic husband, Alexis Razunovsky. Though much loved, he nevertheless remained discreetly in the background, an unusual occurrence during the age of the female autocrats, since this was also the time of greedy and arrogant favourites.

Was Elizabeth I the legitimate successor to Anna I? Without doubt the Crown should have gone to young Peter, the son of her elder sister, Anna, or to Ivan VI, who, even though he was three-quarters German, was nevertheless the grandson of Ivan V. Elizabeth condemned the child-Czar she had dethroned to perpetual prison, because she was worried. When she hurriedly summoned her nephew, Peter of Holstein-Gottorp, to Russia to proclaim him as her heir, it was because she was examining her conscience. But this young man proved a surprise: ignorant, badly brought up and surly, he was not interested in Russia, the throne or the Orthodox Church. Although he was a grandson of Peter the Great, he was interested only in the King of Prussia. Elizabeth was heart-broken but could do nothing except arrange for the marriage of the monster, because her work had to have continuity.

Sophia of Anhalt-Zerbst, an obscure little German princess without a penny to her name, was burning with ambition. To be Empress of Russia; what a dream! Intelligent and cultivated, cunning and shrewd, she would ask for nothing more than to be taught by the Empress, who devoted herself to fashioning and polishing the future Catherine the Great. In return, the ungrateful girl was to do all she could to cast Elizabeth the Great into oblivion.

Having been received into the Orthodox Church and renamed the Grand Duchess Catherine, Sophia devoted herself to Russia. She did not like her fiancé, but in order to be Empress one day she would put up with anything. The marriage was not consummated. Elizabeth was distressed, but like a true daughter of her father she sacrificed morality for the sake of the State and threw the frustrated and seductive Catherine into the arms of the most handsome man at the Court, Count Sergius Saltykov, whilst Peter carried out 'a little intervention' in the nick of time. As a result, no-one will ever know who was the father of little Paul, born in 1754. Some attribute paternity to Peter, but reading between the lines in Catherine's *Memoirs*, it seems very doubtful. The succession assured, Elizabeth took the child into her apartments and Catherine, forsaken now, threw herself into politics

with her new lover, Stanislaus Poniatowski, the future King of Poland, who had been presented by the British ambassador. She dabbled in British politics, whilst her husband became involved with Prussia as a sort of secret agent for Frederick II, Russia's enemy. Meanwhile, the Empress had entered the Seven Years War on the Franco-Austrian side – a disinterested act, but very beneficial to the morale of the allies and for the outcome of the hostilities. Like her father, Elizabeth died too soon for the good of her Empire. She passed away at Christmas 1761 as a result of an apoplectic fit. Without this calamity, the emerging strength of Prussia and the House of Brandenburg would have been crushed.

Whether Paul I was the son of Peter III or of Saltykov, Elizabeth was the last true Romanov. Henceforth it was to be the Holstein-Gottorp family who were to reign over Russia, sovereigns who became less and less Russian and more and more German through their maternal line. But they took the name of Romanov in some way, in order to proclaim their spiritual ascendancy and their strong moral heritage. Physiologically, they had very little Romanov blood. Even if Paul I was the son of Peter III, it can be calculated that the blood in his veins was only one-sixteenth Russian.

The first act of the new Emperor, Peter III, was to sign a treaty of alliance with his 'idol', his 'master', Frederick II, even though the Russian army was in Berlin. Once again Russia was to suffer a 'Germanic invasion'; the army was taken over by Prussians, while the Russian nobility were scoffed at. Unbalanced and vicious, Peter III had no thoughts for the past and he turned against his subjects and his wife. He detested Catherine, intending to reject her to marry his mistress, Elizabeth Vorontsova. But Catherine was 'loved and respected by all, whilst her husband was loathed and mistrusted'.

The reign of this mediocre little tyrant was to be brief. Like Peter the Great and Elizabeth before her, the young Empress was to strike when her adversary believed her unarmed, and she was to take him by surprise. In fact, she was well armed, for her third lover, Gregory, and his brother, Alexis Orlov, were officers of the Guard; she had the nobility with her. She had learned Elizabeth's lesson well, and the action that took place on 28 June 1762 echoed the earlier *coup*. Catherine was acclaimed by the troops, 'Long live our little mother, Catherine', and proclaimed 'Sovereign and Autocrat' by the Archbishop. Catherine then galloped to Oranienbaum at the head of a regiment to obtain the abdication of the Emperor, who crawled at her feet. She had him confined to a manor-house at Ropsha, where he soon died, strangled by Alexis Orlov. The tradition of assassinations by a third party was maintained: Peter I had his son, Alexis, murdered;

Catherine had her husband murdered, one for the 'security of the Empire', the other for her own security. 'A necessary crime!' Frederick II would say. And she was to allow the hapless Ivan VI to be beaten to death, whilst an attempt was being made to release him from the dungeon, where he had been languishing for twenty years. He had troubled her, like Peter II. They were both natural Czars and she an intruder with no more right than to be Regent until Paul came of age! But she was never to hand over the throne to her son, and she was to make him bitter and spiteful. However, neither this legerdemain nor her crimes were to do her any harm in the eyes of Europe: from then on she was always to be, 'the Semiramis of the North'. One of Napoleon's generals said: 'Our moral standards are not so easily applicable to unusual destinies.'

Capable of anything, the Empress was immensely intelligent and well educated. A friend of the Enlightenment, a philosopher and an opportunist, she had a keen instinct, almost a genius, for government. As 'Arbiter of Europe', a collector and a patron of the arts, like Peter I, she was constantly in search of knowledge. Her methods were more subtle, but like him she bubbled with new ideas and knew how to inspire all those who wanted to share in the enormous task of building a great nation. She had such a virile mind, that the Prince de Ligne named her 'Catherine the Great'. Endowed with a nature with as many facets as a prized diamond, she had an enormous diversity of interests and, consequently, a vast field of action. Even though she worked fifteen hours a day for thirty-four years, it is astonishing the amount she achieved. And what a love life! Her sex life has always added spice to her story: her lovers were numerous, all of them handsome and young but they never deflected her from her work. Potemkin was the favourite. Carnal and intellectual sympathies bound them together, and Potemkin became first her lover, and then, possibly, her morganatic husband. Together they worked to enlarge the Empire – a project which was taken too far with the three partitions of Poland. There is a marked contrast between the Empress's 'axioms to throw down the walls' and their application. Thus, she did not suppress serfdom and, though she declared herself to love 'independent souls', she imprisoned two of the finest minds of her time, Radishchev and Novikov, for their satirical works. It is true that the French Revolution had frightened her; apart from the Pugachev revolt from 1773 to 1775, which had seriously threatened her throne, this was the greatest fear of her life. Nevertheless, although neither a Russian nor a Romanov, she remained faithful to her great model, Peter I, and, through her conquests and her diplomacy, she made Russia powerful. She placed Russia once and for all on the European map and gave her her 'second lung', the Black Sea, fertile plains and new cities in the south, which she called 'the New Russia'.

When Catherine II died on 7 November 1796, this was the end of an age. She intended to leave her heritage to her adored grandson, Alexander, but she died before publishing the manifesto setting her son Paul aside. Alexander knew of the existence of this explosive document, but he did not dare to say anything. Paul I put on the Crown at the age of forty-two, but he had waited too long. A muddled thinker, who was a prey to fantasies, he became a cruel tyrant, plunging Russia into the shadows with his deportations, arbitrary executions and abhorrent decrees. He was hated and feared and, the victim of a military plot, he was ignominiously struck down on 11 March 1801 in the palace-stronghold that he had had built to be safe from assassins.

Paul's son, Alexander I, knew nothing of the conspiracy, but believed, or wanted to believe that the conspirators would obtain the abdication of his father without bloodshed. He was always to regret that terrible night and it was to be the cause of his black moods. It is difficult to sum up this handsome, charming and retiring 'Sphinx of the North'. He had the ability both to charm and to disturb. He was sincere and yet false, determined yet fanciful, fearless yet cowardly, and always subject to his illusions. At first, he joyfully indulged in hazy projects for the rebuilding of Russia. But soon the grandiose reforms were set aside, and instead the Czar tried his hand at diplomacy. He listened to no-one; and his personal infatuations drew him away from the common good. For the sake of his Czarina, Louise, he formed an alliance with Prussia; this proved a disaster, and he then embarked on the War of the Third Coalition against France. The Austerlitz catastrophe took place: the Czar playing at strategy, and not following the advice of the great Kutuzov! More defeats followed: Eylau and Friedland in 1807, and suddenly friendship with Napoleon, with hugs and kisses all round at Tilsit. This effusive *entente cordiale* displeased the Russians. Although the agreement with Napoleon was confirmed at Erfurt in 1808, Alexander was more reticent and Franco-Russian relations were to deteriorate gradually for a variety of reasons. On 4 June 1812 Napoleon's Great Army crossed the Niemen, and advanced rapidly, whilst the Russians retreated. In September came the defeat of Borodino and Moscow. Alexander recognized that the fate of the world rested upon this duel between the two Emperors. Napoleon offered to make peace, but he would not give in; instead he would carry on to the end. Napoleon's

The achievements and death of Alexander II: below right, the emancipation of a serf by the reform of 1861; below left, the bomb of the terrorist Ryssakov which killed the Emperor on 1 March 1881.

troops left Moscow and were driven to their final destruction by the clever tactics of Kutuzov. As they rushed towards the Berezina, Alexander decided to go farther. He led his allies – Austria, Britain and Prussia – from victory to victory, taking them as far as Paris, where he made a triumphal entry and aroused enthusiasm for the leniency he showed towards France.

Next came the Congress of Vienna, suddenly brought to a close by the return of Napoleon. For Alexander I there followed his period of mysticism, influenced by a celebrated lady, Baroness Krüdener, when he conceived the idea of a Holy Alliance. This would enable the people of the allied nations to claim what was promised to them: fundamental liberties and a constitution, with the result that the Blessed (according to the Russians), the Emperor of Europe (according to the West) as well as his 'crowned brothers' would take fear and 'defend their rights'. The Holy Alliance was to become a league of monarchs against their subjects. When the Czar returned home, he was tired and worn out. Having given of his all, he had reached his peak and was already on the way down. Leaving Russia in the hands of the dreadful General Arakcheiv, who brought oppression throughout the domain, he went from congress to congress, each one marking a stiffening of reactionary policies in the face of the spread of popular national movements. Alexander I came more and more under the ultra-conservative influence of Metternich. The news of the insurrection of a Guards regiment, which reached him at Troppau, alarmed him so much that from then on he saw subversion everywhere, at home just as in Europe. For him the game was over. He fled from the capital and retired with the sick Empress, to whom he had

returned, after neglecting her for years, to a small town on the Black Sea: Taganrod. Subsequent events remain a mystery. Did he contract pneumonia during a tour of the Crimea? He did take the opportunity of acquiring a property, which was perhaps proof of his intention to abdicate: though he confessed this to those close to him, they did not believe him. Did he leave to become a hermit in Siberia, or a monk on Mount Athos? All we can say is that he disappeared on 13 November 1825, there is nothing to prove that it is his body that rests in the Peter and Paul Cathedral in St Petersburg–Leningrad. What is certain is that his unexpected end was the cause of a troubled interregnum.

Alexander's Crown was passed back and forth by his younger brothers, Constantine and Nicholas. Constantine had secretly abdicated his claim to the throne in 1822, but Nicholas did not realize this. He hesitated, disappeared and finally proclaimed himself ruler. But, taking advantage of this interlude, a group of young officers, all of them veterans of the Napoleonic campaigns, tried to incite the garrison and to demand from the new Czar a constitution, the abolition of serfdom and freedom of the Press. If this had succeeded, it would, in fact, have been the first Russian Revolution. But the December rising failed. Though patriotic and determined, its leaders were ideologists, theorists, amateurs, who did not know how to conduct a *coup d'état*. They were not plotting a revolution; they did not plan in advance. The uprising of 26 December 1825 in Senate Square, St Petersburg, was brought to an end with hundreds of arrests, a long trial, five hangings and a hundred and twenty life

*The Crown Prince Nicholas and his future wife,
Alexandra of Hesse. The last Czar came to the throne
at the death of his father, when the Imperial train was
derailed in the Crimea in 1894.*

archaic conception of an *Imperator*.

Alexander II inherited a Russia that was bleeding to death. His first task was to bring the war to an end. He succeeded in this, but the Treaty of Paris hardly resounded to his glory. After freeing what remained of the Decembrists after thirty years in Siberia, he faced an enormous task: the liberation of the serfs. For four years, committees were to be involved with the most colossal of reforms and on 3 March 1861, Alexander II, henceforth known as 'the Czar Liberator', signed the decree of emancipation. But, despite his fine appearance, he was weak, influenced by opposing views and doctrines. Enthusiastic one minute, discouraged the next, humouring everyone, he achieved only half a reform, half an emancipation. He had not pleased the liberals, the intelligentsia, the students; he had stirred up a lot of dissatisfaction, frustrated and driven the peasant to despair. He reacted against 'so much ingratitude', reinstating the police and ordering massssive arrests; from then on the opposition opted for open battle. Under the banner of Chernyshevsky, Bakunin and Lavrov, young populists engaged in cruel rioting, using guns, bombs, and dynamite, and derailing trains; there was even an attempt to blow up the Winter Palace. Alexander II escaped all the attempts on his life, but those who became terrorists, who had formed organized revolutionary parties, such as the People's Will, had condemned him to death! Alexander alternated between anger and depression, and finished up by listening to his minister, Loris-Melikov, who recommended a 'dictatorship of the heart'. On Sunday, 13 March 1881, he confided to the woman he loved passionately, for many years his mistress and now his wife, Princess Catherine Dolgoruky, that he was having a constitutional project drawn up. Then he went to a parade. On the way back a bomb exploded under his sledge, thrown by a terrorist named Ryssakov, a member of the 'Revolutionary Executive Committee'. The Czar got out of the sledge, but a second bomb maimed him. He was left lying helpless in the snow until a group of officer-cadets passed by. They picked him up and took him, half dead, to the Winter Palace, where he died that evening.

It has been said that this all happened 'with the inevitability of a Shakespearian tragedy'. In that case, Alexander III, an unintelligent, bearded giant of a man, played the penultimate act. His intentions were known in advance from his Inaugural Manifesto, in which he declared himself to be 'an autocrat in accordance with the vocation received from God', and promised to 'strengthen the power of the autocracy for the good of his people'. Although he was a good, frugal husband and father, he was a 'bourgeois', with a horror of ideas and culture. Dominated since childhood by his tutor, Constantine Pobiedonotsev, the evil Procurator of

sentences, depriving Russia of her best sons.

Nicholas I, a handsome man with an icy glare, would neither forgive nor forget this rebellion. He built up a bureaucratic Russia, controlled by the army and the police, crushed by an unswerving and pitiless absolutism. The Czar created his own personal arm of the government, the infamous Third Section, a political police force, with its executive, the Gendarmes Corps. Surveillance and repression had been institutionalized. Although Nicholas I was known as the 'Crowned Corporal' and 'Nicholas the Stick', he was also called the 'Gendarme of Europe'. He mistrusted Louis-Philippe, whom he called 'the King of the Barricades'. When Poland arose to free herself from Russian tyranny, there followed the blood bath of 1830 and the famous message: 'Order reigns in Warsaw!' In 1848, frightened by 'the mad subversion which is all around', he swore to halt it at the frontiers of his Empire. He, therefore, rushed to the aid of Francis Joseph to help him crush the Hungarians. However, neither the gendarmes nor the prisons could prevent the spread of free ideas, and a secret, clandestine opposition was developing. The university students, the intelligentsia, refused to be subjected to the Czar's triple slogan: 'Autocracy, Orthodoxy, Nationalism'.

Provoked by Nicholas I, war broke out in the Crimea, a disastrous war that was lost from the start through lack of competence, foresight and organization. The glorious days of the victorious Romanovs were over, and Russia's heroic defence of Sevastopol, Alma, and Malakoff proved useless. The Czar had been convinced that France 'would be incapable', that Great Britain 'would not move', and that Austria would be at his side. He was wrong from start to finish. The Gendarme of Europe, the invincible autocrat, found himself face to face with disaster. When he died on 2 March 1855, apparently of a cold, there was talk of poison, of suicide. Having thrust his nation into a wasp's nest, it is possible that this Czar, who wore the mask of a Roman Emperor, might have wanted to 'die like a Roman'. That would have fitted in well with his

'I intend to maintain the autocracy, because I think that representation is bad for the people whom God has given to me!' So wrote Nicholas II, the last of the Czars, in his diary.

His son Nicholas II was chosen to play in the final act of the monarchy. He was hesitant and indecisive, well brought up and with average intelligence, but without any political education, initiative, or imagination. His diary reveals his immaturity, his blindness. But he showed enormous determination to take up the fatal *leitmotiv* of his father, his grandfather and his great-grandfather: autocratic rule for the good of the people.

Incompetent and apathetic, he yielded to those who intimidated him: his uncles, his wife, Alexandra Fedorovna, Princess of Hesse-Darmstadt, and Rasputin. He could not tolerate intelligent or superior people and, unfortunately for Russia, certain ministers, such as Witte, were dismissed. He allowed himself to be drawn into a senseless war against Japan in 1904–5 because he was under pressure from his uncles, the Grand Dukes. It was lost for very much the same reasons as the Crimean War had been lost. The year 1905 was very eventful; full of omens. The century was yet young, and so was the Revolution. It can be said to have started with the Bloody Sunday of 22 January. A hundred and fifty thousand workers, women and children, carrying banners, icons and petitions, were singing hymns and praising the Czar, when they were fired upon. The Decembrists and the People's Will revolutionaries had wanted everything. These did not want to live as slaves and animals, they wanted to be treated as men. Shots were fired from all round, leaving a thousand dead. Alongside the peaceful petitioners, the dynasty, too, had died. There was a sudden eruption, the end of an almost superstitious loyalty. It was only to return for a brief moment, on 1 August 1914, the day war was declared: ten thousand people, gathered together in Palace Square, acclaimed the Czar and, he, much moved, blessed them – the last fervent gesture of a nation towards her last sovereign.

But Nicholas II learnt nothing from 1905, nor from Bloody Sunday, nor from the assassination of his uncle, Grand Duke Sergius, nor from the mutiny on board the battleship *Potemkin*. The revolutionary movement was increasing in strength, strikes were multiplying and spreading. Reluctantly, the Czar listened to advice and decided to form a parliament, a Duma.

There can be no denying that the Czarina, who was both physically and mentally sick, had an unfortunate influence on Nicholas. There can be no denying that, to a certain extent, all his policies originated in his children's school-room, where a charlatan monk, by the name of Rasputin, was treated as a saint and a thaumaturge because he had convinced a doting mother that without him, Alexis, her only son, the heir to the throne, would die. For ten years Rasputin dominated the Empress and, through her (as well as directly), the Emperor. Then came the First World War and defeats for Russia, although it is true that

the Synod, he was fundamentally convinced of the benefits of an intransigent and nationalistic absolutism, in the style of his grandfather, Nicholas I. He authorized pogroms and 'Russified' the Baltic provinces, Finland and Poland with a vengeance. Only in his foreign policy did he show any liberalism, since he had a genuine desire for peace. Thus, despite his prejudice against 'republican, anti-clerical France', he sealed the Franco-Russian alliance for the sake of peace in Europe. The French fleet arrived in Kronstadt in 1891, something that would have pleased Peter I who had said: 'They will all sail in to see us'. And Catherine II would have smiled at the sight of this despot standing to attention to the sound of the *Marseillaise*! The Russian fleet went to Toulon, the Russian sovereigns visited Paris, and it was all an enormous success. Alexander III has been called many unkind names, such as 'the Illustrious Fool', but he is worthy of the honourable title of Alexander 'the Peaceful'. He died in the Crimea, as a result of the derailment of the Imperial train in 1894.

Nicholas wanted nothing to do with it. In 1916, in view of Rasputin's increasing power, Prince Yusupov and Grand Duke Dmitri assassinated him. The demise of this extraordinary personality was almost immediately followed by the demise of the Romanovs. In February 1917, the capital was hungry; the news from the front was disastrous; there were demonstrations, Cossack charges; finally, the Guards regiments mutinied and went over 'to the other side'. The capital was now in the grip of the Revolution. Prince Lvov formed a provisional government; a Soviet Committee of workers and soldiers was installed at the Smolny Institute; Kerensky, a Socialist barrister, became Minister of Justice. What of the Czar? He just did not understand. When the President of the Duma wired him at Headquarters, 'Anarchy in the Capital', he replied, 'Absurd!' and dissolved the Duma. It was his last act as Czar. His abdication took place on 15 March in a railway carriage. He then returned to his family at Tsarskoe Selo, to the empty Palace, and to leave-takings. 'Treason, cowardice, deceit!' he cried, lucid at last. Then came the banishment to Tobolsk, and finally the dreadful massacre at Ekaterinburg on 16 July 1918.

We often hear of the 'curse of the Romanovs', but what is this? It was a misconception that each one carried within him: the sacrosanct idea of his own imperial 'self'. Brought up in a tradition of opaque conservatism, almost all of them believed in their own absolute power. Practically all of them were convinced that they were working for the good of their Empire by keeping it locked within a rigorous framework of immobility. To them autocracy was God-given. The revered image of the hieratic sovereign wearing a long robe of gold and sable, with the cap of Monomakh, filigreed in gold and precious stones, and holding the jewel-studded orb and sceptre did gradually alter. Such a Czar, a character rather than a person, could not survive in a world that was forever changing. But the first Romanovs were more aware of the changes taking place in the West, and more realistic. The last dreaded any change and were dedicated either to becoming what they could not be, or finishing in the abyss.

The Braganzas

Descendant from the Avis dynasty, this
family gained the throne when Portugal
threw off the Spanish yoke

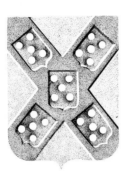

The dynasty of Braganza, which ruled Portugal from 1640 to 1910, was founded when John, the eighth Duke of Braganza, was acclaimed as king. The revolt of the Portuguese nobility against the rule of King Philip IV of Spain and III of Portugal placed the Duke on the throne as King John IV on 1 December 1640. The Portuguese have since then commemorated the restoration of their independence on this day.

The Duke was descended from the kings of the dynasty of Avis through two lines of male ancestry, his own and that of his paternal grandmother, the Infanta Catherine. His father, the seventh Duke, Teodosio II, was the grandson of the first Duke of Braganza, Alfonso, the natural son of King John I, founder of the dynasty of Avis which ruled Portugal from 1356 to 1580.

Before ascending to the throne, the Dukes of Braganza already led a regal life and were thus a very important ducal dynasty.

The Braganza royal family can be described as having its origins in a double illegitimacy. King John I was the natural son of King Peter I by Theresa Lourenço. Before ascending to the throne and marrying Queen Philippa of Lancaster, John had two illegitimate children by Inês Pires Esteves, Beatrice and Alfonso, both of whom he made legitimate. Beatrice married the Earl of Arundel in England in 1405 and had no offspring. Alfonso was made Count of Barcelos

The prison tower of the castle of Braganza. The small city, in the north-east corner of Portugal, was created a Duchy in 1442 for Alfonso, the natural son of King John I.

and later Duke of Braganza, with the title of Alfonso I. He was the founder of the ducal dynasty of Braganza.

It is, therefore, with Alfonso I, Count of Barcelos and Duke of Braganza, that the genealogical outline of the great ducal House begins. He was probably born in 1377 and died in the town of Chaves in 1461. He was brought up by his tutor, Gomes Martins de Lemos, and lived with him in Leiria until 1400, when he was legitimized by his father. He was immediately granted the title of Count of Barcelos and given gifts, the beginning of the many privileges which gradually contributed to the greatness of the House of Braganza. Alfonso remains a highly controversial figure in the history of Portugal. In prestige and deeds he failed to match his father's legitimate sons. He married twice: his first wife, Beatrice Pereira de Alvim, daughter of the Constable of Portugal, Nuno Alvares Pereira, brought great wealth to the House of Braganza, for the Constable's domain, the county of Barcelos, was the wealthiest in the kingdom. The Duke's second marriage was to Constance de Noronha, by whom he had no offspring.

Alfonso was succeeded by his son Ferdinand I, second Duke of Braganza, who was born in 1403 and died in Vila Viçosa on 1 April 1478. His grandfather, Constable Nuno Alvares Pereira, had granted him the title of Count of Arraiolos. He was appointed Governor of Tangier in 1445, whence he returned to Portugal in 1448 to assist his uncle, the Infante Peter, who had fallen foul of the first Duke of Braganza's unbounded hatred and envy. Unfortunately he did not arrive in time to prevent the battle of Alfarrobeira in 1449, in which the illustrious Prince was slain. His seriousness and integrity, so unlike his father's character, and his well-balanced personality, led King

The castle and city of Vila Viçosa, residence of the Kings of Portugal, in a seventeenth-century watercolour. The present castle of Vila Viçosa was built for James I (1479–1532), fourth Duke of Braganza.

La Ville.

le chasteau.

Alfonso v to entrust him with the Regency for the duration of the Arzila campaign.

He was succeeded by his eldest son, Ferdinand II, third Duke of Braganza, whose character and fate were to be so very different from his father's. He was born in 1430 and was executed in Evora in 1483 for betraying his country and plotting against the King's life.

His second son James I, fourth Duke of Braganza, was born in 1479 and died on 20 September 1532. He was taken to Castile at the age of four, immediately after his father's death on the scaffold at Evora, and spent his childhood there. After the death of King John II and the accession of Manuel I, James was granted permission to return to Portugal, and his father's confiscated property and title were restored to him. He was seventeen at the time and already showing signs of mental disorder. In 1500, negotiations were begun for his marriage to Eleanor de Mendoza, daughter of the third Duke of Medina Sidonia, which took place in 1502. But, ten years later, when he was already the father of two children, he was overtaken by morbid and groundless jealousy and, under the influence of the

intrigues of one of his manservants, the Duke ordered the killing of a page of whom he was suspicious and murdered the innocent Duchess by his own hand. The Duke then decided to organize an expedition to capture Azemmour in North Africa. The King entrusted him with the command of a fleet and an army 15,000 strong, to which he added a force of 4,000 infantry and 500 horsemen armed at his own expense. He landed near the fortified city of Mazagan and, thanks to the timidity of the people of Azemmour, took the city which he found undefended and virtually uninhabited.

When he died in 1532, he was succeeded by Teodosio I, the fifth Duke of Braganza. He was an educated man, a disciple of the illustrious humanist Diego de Sigeu, and devoted himself to the patronage of fine painting and sculpture. His younger half-brother Constantine, when still very young, was appointed ambassador to the Court of King Henry II of France. Later, in 1558, he was made Governor and Viceroy of India and filled his post with remarkable success.

Teodosio I died in 1563, and his eldest son, John I

John IV, eighth Duke of Braganza, entering Lisbon. Called to the Crown in 1640, when Portugal was liberated from subjection to Spain, he was the first King of this dynasty.

Alfonso VI, son of the first Braganza King, was called 'the Victorious' for his generals' victories over the Spaniards, but was incompetent and mentally ill and was forced to hand over the throne to his brother, Peter II.

became sixth Duke of Braganza. King Sebastian granted him the hereditary title of Duke of Barcelos before his marriage to his cousin Catherine, daughter of the Infante Edward, Duke of Guimarães. On the death of King Sebastian and of King Henry, the Duchess Catherine was one of the claimants to the Portuguese throne, but met with the unyielding opposition of Philip II of Spain, who resorted to force and had himself proclaimed King of Portugal. Philip sought to compensate the Duke of Braganza with a gift of 200,000 cruzados. He also conferred on the Duke the insignia of the Order of the Golden Fleece and showered him with honours.

John I's eldest son, Teodósio II, seventh Duke of Braganza, was a very cultured prince, well grounded in the subjects of mathematics, rhetoric and languages. When he was only eleven years old, his father sent him in his place to accompany King Sebastian on his African expedition. Teodosio took part in the battle of Alcazar-Qivir and was held captive after the defeat of the Portuguese army. He was eventually released, thanks to the King of Morocco's generous acquiescence to the requests of Philip II of Spain and of the Duke of Braganza.

Teodósio was a very austere and devout man, which was the cause of some measure of incompatibility with his elder son and heir, John II. His second son, Edward, was an interesting Prince. He was intelligent, very cultured and well-versed in the sciences and languages. Wishing to travel in Europe, he obtained the consent of his brother John II, by then Duke of Braganza after his father's death, and left for Germany in 1634 with a brilliant retinue of noblemen and servants. He

returned to Portugal in 1640, but not for long. At the Emperor's invitation, he left for Germany, where he joined the army. When his elder brother John was acclaimed King of Portugal in 1640, at the King of Spain's request, the Emperor had Prince Edward arrested lest he should place his experience at the service of the new Portuguese King. He was duly arrested in Regensburg on 4 February 1641, and was sent to Milan where he died in prison seven years later.

Teodosio II's elder son, John II, was born on 18 March 1604. On his father's death in 1630 he became eighth Duke of Braganza.

Great dissatisfaction was rife in Portugal, amongst the people and nobility alike, against the rule of Spain, and there were signs of rebellion. The most prominent of the country's noblemen organized a plot to overthrow Spain's oppressive rule and offered the Crown to the Duke of Braganza. At the outset, the Duke was somewhat reluctant, but finally decided to heed the advice of his wife, the Duchess Louisa. Thus, on 1 December 1640 a group of noblemen broke into the Royal Palace in Lisbon, killed Michael de Vasconcelos, Minister of Philip IV of Spain and III of Portugal, arrested the Vicereine, the Duchess of Mantua, and proclaimed the Duke of Braganza, King of Portugal, as John IV.

The consolidation of Portugal's independence was the cause of a war that went on for many years between the Portuguese and the Spaniards. The entire nation rose against Spain to free itself from the stifling oppression of sixty years. Despite her well-organized army Spain had little chance of throwing her full might against Portugal because she was tied down by the revolution in Catalonia. However, feelings of discontent began to emerge amongst the sections of the Portuguese upper classes whose interests were tied to the Spanish Crown. This seriously disturbed the internal life of the nation, then faced with the problem, of the appointment of a Prime Minister. The choice fell on Francis de Lucena, who soon proved himself a very wise ruler by passing legislation aimed at preventing the creation of a party supporting Castile.

However, this did not prevent many noblemen from fleeing to Spain, while the Archbishop of Braga, Sebastian de Matos de Noronha, started to recruit supporters for a conspiracy aimed at overthrowing the King and the monarchy, and with a view to handing over Portugal to the oppressor Philip IV. The Count of Vimioso had been approached to support the rebellion but, devoted to King and country, he immediately conferred with the Prime Minister, Francis de Lucena, and King John IV himself, and it was decided to act vigorously. The plotters were arrested, summarily tried and beheaded. This formidable example helped to consolidate the power of the King, who had enjoyed the support of the people and of the 'New Christians' (Jews who had adopted the Christian faith to avoid persecution) in the suppression of the conspiracy.

A very judicious man, John IV acted as wisely in choosing the most capable administrators as he did in choosing diplomats to represent him in the Courts of Europe, in his search for political support from France and England. He secured strong support from France, because Richelieu was sympathetic towards the Portuguese separatist movement. By intensifying his intervention in the war in Catalonia, he forced Philip IV to send more troops to that province, thus weakening his commitment on the Portuguese borders. In

addition France supplied Portugal with arms and ammunition which proved most valuable. The Portuguese General, Matias de Albuquerque, invaded Andalusia and managed to defeat the Spanish army. This military action was followed by ten years of truce. Overseas, the Portuguese succeeded in regaining their possessions which had been lost to the Spaniards. In Africa, Salvador Correia de Sá succeeded in re-conquering Angola; and in South America, all the territory the Dutch had occupied in Brazil was also regained.

John IV was a great musician and composer, whose works are still played by chamber and symphony orchestras. He was devoted to books and assembled an excellent library. It was on his initiative that the cult of Our Lady of the Immaculate Conception, whom he proclaimed Portugal's patron saint, took root in the country. As a mark of respect for the patron saint, he decided that the Portuguese monarchs would no longer wear the Crown, which was henceforth placed on a cushion at the King's side.

By his marriage to Louisa de Guzman, John IV had four sons and three daughters. His eldest son, Teodosio III, died of tuberculosis when he was only nineteen years of age. His third daughter, Catherine, became Queen of England by her marriage to Charles II in London on 21 May 1662. Her dowry included Tangier, Bombay and two million cruzados. Catherine had no children, only four miscarriages. The Queen remained in England for seven years after the death of her husband, but returned to Portugal in 1688

following the deposition of James II. She twice assumed the Regency of Portugal at the request of her brother Peter II.

King John died on 6 November 1656. Queen Louisa became Regent, as their eldest surving son Alfonso, of proven mental backwardness, was still under age.

Alfonso VI was born in Lisbon on 21 April 1643 and on the death of his brother Teodosio in 1653, he was made heir to the throne. Marked for life by a serious illness that afflicted him as a child, the Prince presented a pitiful picture of ill-health.

The emergence in Court of two opposing factions created great difficulties for the Regent. One of the factions was led by the Count of Cantanhede, later to become Marquis of Marialva, and the other by the Count of Odemira. Another group, headed by the Count of Castelo Melhor, was also active behind the scenes. Despite the Queen Mother's prudence and tact, the Count of Castelo Melhor and his supporters got the better of her. He gained a hold over the young King, persuading him to insist that the Queen should declare him of age and relinquish the Regency. Castelo Melhor was made Prime Minister on 29 June 1662 and governed wisely for the next five years.

But the Count of Castelo Melhor paved the way for his own downfall by underestimating the King's disability, and by making arrangements for his marriage to a Princess of France, Marie Françoise Isabelle of Savoy, daughter of Charles Emmanuel II of Savoy, Duke of Nemours. The impotent Alfonso VI

Joseph I, called 'the Reformer', not for his own character which was weak and indolent, but for the work of his Minister, Sebastian Joseph de Carvalho e Melo, Marquis of Pombal.

The royal palace at Lisbon. The city had become a patriarchal see at the time of John V, who had made large donations to the Pope from his gold mines in Brazil.

refused to fulfil his matrimonial duties, did not attend the marriage ceremonies and was indifferent to the beauty of the Princess. It was not long before Castelo Melhor had fallen out with the Queen and the King's younger brother, Prince Peter. The latter, at the head of the faction dissatisfied with such a state of affairs, ended up by imprisoning his brother, promoting the annulment of the marriage on the grounds of his proven impotence, assuming the Regency himself and finally marrying his sister-in-law. Ironically, Alfonso VI was called 'the Victorious', not through his own deeds on the battlefield, of which there was none, but because of the victories scored by his generals against the Spanish army, which put an end, once and for all, to Philip IV's designs on the Portuguese throne. Banished and imprisoned by his brother, Alfonso VI remained a captive until his death at Sintra on 12 September 1683.

Peter II, the youngest son of John IV, known as 'the Pacific', was born in Lisbon on 26 April 1648. His father instituted a house and estate on his behalf to ensure the creation of a new princely line concurrently with the royal one. He granted him the title of Duke of Beja and made him a gift not only of the city of the same name but also of all the property confiscated from the Marquis of Vila Real and his son, the Duke of Caminha. He also gave him the meadowland domains of Goleg, Borba, Mouchões and Silveira in the region of Santarém, and some towns in northern Portugal. With all these properties, a sumptuary estate was created under the designation of House of the Infantado. The Prince

took possession of it at the age of five, held its usufruct as Prince, Regent and even after his accession as King, and left it in legacy to one of his sons. Amongst the domains of the House of the Infantado was the Queluz estate which had been confiscated from Christopher de Moura, Marqius of Castelo Rodrigo. Later Peter II's grandson, the Infante Peter, built the magnificent palace that stands there today.

As has already been related, Peter II usurped the throne from his brother and ruled as Regent. On the death of Alfonso VI in 1683, he was acclaimed King. During his reign Portugal was forced to wage war on Spain, or, rather, on Philip V, in alliance with the English and the Dutch. The Portuguese army advanced as far as Madrid and returned victorious, but in fact it was an inglorious war, which failed in its purpose. Nevertheless, Portuguese independence was consolidated and until 1834 the Portuguese kings were to rule as absolute monarchs, even though in reality power lay with their ministers.

Peter II was succeeded by his son John V, called 'the Magnanimous', who was born in Lisbon on 22 October 1689 and died there on 31 July 1750.

Intelligent and vivacious, the Prince was fluent in French, Italian and Spanish, he devoted himself to the sciences and mathematics and, like his grandfather John IV, he was a great lover and enthusiastic patron of art and music. He introduced Italian opera to Portugal. Thanks to his wise choice of advisers, his administration contributed to the development of the country's industries. Overseas, too, national interests were safeguarded. Brazil, in particular, was greatly developed and emigration gradually turned it from a colony into a new kingdom.

One of his younger brothers was Francis (1691–1742). Despite his position as Grand Prior of the Religious Order of Crato, this Prince was devoid of scruples or dignity, he went as far as nurturing schemes to usurp the throne from his brother and paying court to the Queen Mara Antonia his sister-in-law.

Emmanuel (1697–1736) was the only prestigious figure amongst all the brothers of John V. As the King was not keen on allowing him to travel abroad to satisfy his spirit of adventure, the Prince fled secretly to the Netherlands and thence to Austria. He enlisted in the army commanded by Prince Eugene of Savoy and

215

The Lisbon earthquake of 1755, in a contemporary print. This tremendous catastrophe took place on 1 November, while the churches were crowded with the faithful celebrating the feast of All Saints.

soon emerged as a competent soldier, brave and heroic in battle. His deeds and prestige earned him the offer of the throne of Poland and, later, of a kingdom that it was intended should be created with the islands of Sardinia and Corsica.

John v was succeeded in 1750 by his son, Joseph I. At the outset of his reign he entrusted the tasks of government to three Secretaries of State, but soon one of them, Sebastian Joseph de Carvalho e Melo stood out as the most active, energetic and enterprising. Only five years after Joseph was acclaimed King, Portugal fell victim to a catastrophe which horrified the entire world, the 1755 Lisbon earthquake, which razed a large part of the city and caused great damage throughout the country. It was then that Carvalho e Melo emerged with the stature of a true statesman and the King entrusted to him all the decisions arising from such a grave situation. But the favouritism displayed by Joseph towards his Minister aroused the envy of a large section of the nobility which, led by the Duke of Aveiro, started to plot against the Minister and against the King himself. There was dissatisfaction amongst nobility and clergy alike, as both saw their privileges eroded, but only the Duke of Aveiro dared to encourage that dissatisfaction by plotting. On the night of 13 September 1758, as the King was returning from one of his amorous expeditions, his coach was shot at by men armed with blunderbusses. The King survived.

Carvalho e Melo took advantage of this attempt to consolidate his power. The inquiry he instituted laid the blame on many members of the nobility and of the Society of Jesus. As a result, death sentences were passed and many members of the nobility were imprisoned. The Society of Jesus was disbanded and its members expelled from the country. All the property of the Jesuits and of those sentenced to death was confiscated. Henceforth, the King trustingly granted full powers to his Minister, according him the title of Count of Oeiras, and later that of Marquis of Pombal.

All the major advances achieved, the balance attained in foreign policy, educational reforms, the development of trade, the rebuilding of Lisbon, and so on were the work of the Marquis of Pombal. The King endorsed all his measures, not unwittingly, as many believe, but because he trusted the intelligence and loyalty of his Minister. Because of these numerous measures contributing to the development of the nation, Joseph I became known as 'the Reformer'.

Joseph and Maria Anna, daughter of King Philip v of Spain, had four daughters, the youngest of whom, Maria Francisca Benedicta (1746–1829), married her nephew, Joseph, the heir to the throne. Unfortunately he died without coming to the throne, and for this reason, the right of succession was transferred to his brother, as will be related below.

Joseph I's eldest daughter, Maria I, was acclaimed Queen immediately after her father's death in 1777. She had been born in Lisbon on 17 December 1734 and died insane in Rio de Janeiro on 20 March 1816. The

day she was born, her grandfather John v created for her the title Princess of Beira, as that of Prince of Brazil was then held by her father, Joseph I. She was profoundly religious to the point of fanaticism, a fact for which she has been harshly criticized. Amongst the cultural and military institutions created during her reign were the Royal Academy of Sciences, the Royal Academy of Military Fortifications, and the Royal Observatory. In the sphere of education, at the suggestion of the Superintendent-General of Police, Pina Manique, she created the Lisbon 'Casa Pia' for the education of orphans and destitute children, whose drawing school produced many good artists. In Portuguese overseas territories, she promoted defensive measures against expansionist designs of the French, Dutch and Spaniards.

The Queen married her paternal uncle, Peter, who through this marriage became Prince of Brazil and later, as King Consort, Peter III. A rather unpopular figure, he is believed to have had little influence on the Queen's running of the country's affairs. The signs of the Queen's mental derangement, already present, became gradually more acute after her husband's death in 1786. In 1791 the balance of her mind suffered a further deterioration and in the following year worsened to such an extent that her son, Prince John, had to take her place in the daily affairs of government and subsequently was made Regent, a post that he occupied until his mother's death in 1816.

During the Regency period, Portugal's refusal to participate in the Continental blockade led Napoleon

to order his armies to invade the country. In November 1807, the royal family fled to Brazil and did not return to Portugal until 1821.

Queen Maria I and Peter III had six children. The eldest, Joseph, married his maternal aunt (Maria Francisca Benedicta). Endowed with a lucid mind, he received a thorough education from good masters oppointed by the Marquis of Pombal. It was Pombal's wish that he be groomed to replace his mother as successor to the throne, but this wish was thwarted by the death of his grandfather, Joseph I, in 1777. The Prince died of smallpox in 1788.

Maria's third child was John vi. As his elder brother, Joseph, had died without issue during their mother's lifetime, he became Regent as a result of Maria I's insanity. Only on his mother's death on 20 March 1816 was he acclaimed King as John vi. He was then in exile in Brazil with the rest of the royal family. He returned to Lisbon on 3 July 1821 to find the country in a state of political unrest that was very difficult to resolve. He had married Carlotta Joaquina, Infanta of Spain, daughter of King Charles iv. Her political ambition and thirst for power proved a great hindrance to her husband's tasks of government. She allied herself with

her youngest son, Michael, organizing conspiracies against the King.

When John VI was obliged to leave Brazil he left his eldest son Peter as Regent of Brazil, where a constituent assembly had been elected. Peter, however, decided to sever the ties with Portugal. On 15 September 1822 he proclaimed the independence of Brazil and a month later had himself acclaimed Emperor and Perpetual Defender of Brazil. Thus, John VI, having been King of Portugal and Brazil, died as King of Portugal only. His death in March 1826 led to a crisis of succession which brought about civil war.

Peter IV was the fourth of John VI's nine children. He was born in the palace of Queluz on 12 October 1798 and died there, in the very same room, on 24 September 1834. As already related, during his father's lifetime, he gave Brazil its independence by having himself acclaimed Emperor. On his father's death on 10 March 1826, the Regency Council which the King had entrusted with governing the country during his last illness, chaired by his daughter, the Infanta Isabel Maria, recognized Peter as successor to the throne. On 2 May of the same year Peter abdicated in favour of his daughter Maria da Gloria.

The issue of the right of succession soon brought about the formation of two opposing factions. One supported the Regency Council's decision on the legitimacy of Peter's claim, while the other held that he had forfeited it when he deposed his father from the Brazilian throne and lost his country that dominion on the American continent. The latter faction supported the youngest son of John VI, the Infante Michael, who was living in exile in Austria, as claimant to the throne.

Peter thought that he might resolve the dispute by giving his daughter Maria da Gloria in marriage to his brother Michael. The Princess was then seven years of age while Michael was twenty-four.

Michael arrived in Lisbon on 22 February 1828 to take up the post of Lieutenant of the Realm, to which he had been appointed by his brother on 3 July 1827. Unfortunately his inexperience, immaturity and poor upbringing led him to heed the advice of his mother, whose ambition knew no limits. Lulled by the persuasive incitements of the openly absolutist section of the nobility, Michael plunged the country into civil war by having himself acclaimed King by the Three Estates, Church, nobility and people, as was the tradition of the realm.

Meanwhile Peter IV was faced with internal problems in Brazil, where his popularity had diminished. After a series of mass demonstrations against him, and feeling that his rule had no support, he abdicated in favour of his son Peter on 7 April 1831.

Matters in Portugal grew worse. The liberals emigrated to England, Brazil and Terceira Island in the Azores Archipelago, where they organized the re-

sistance movement against the absolutist regime, under the command of the Count of Vila Flor. Peter IV left his son in Brazil to be acclaimed Emperor, entrusted Jose Bonifacio de Andrade e Silva with the care of his daughters Januaria, Paula and Francisca Carolina, and departed for Europe with the Empress and their two daughters, Maria da Gloria and Maria Amelia. Taking his title of Duke of Braganza, he became the leader of the liberal émigrés in France and England, chartered ships and joined the Count of Vila Flor in Terceira Island. An expedition was then organized comprising fifty ships and seven thousand, five hundred troops, which landed in Mindelo, near Oporto, on 8 July 1832. Entrenched in Oporto, Peter's forces withstood the attacks of his brother's troops and launched an offensive which ended with the defeat of Michael's army on 16 May 1834 and the signing of a peace agreement at Evora-Monte. Michael was expelled from Portugal and went into exile. On 19 September 1834 Princess Maria da Gloria was declared of age and acclaimed Queen Maria II. Peter IV died the following month.

Maria II was born in Rio de Janeiro on 4 April 1819 and died in Lisbon on 15 November 1853. She was declared of age and acclaimed Queen of Portugal in September 1834, but, in fact, by virtue of her father's abdication, she had been Queen since the age of seven. As a result of partisan strife in the aftermath of the civil war between the supporters of Michael and the liberals, Queen Maria II's reign was politically very

On Peter V's death, his brother, Louis I (below) succeeded to the throne. He married Maria Pia of Savoy, daughter of Victor Emmanuel II (below right in a photograph of the period).

on 11 November 1861. While he was under age his father ruled as Regent, and he was acclaimed King only on 16 September 1855. He was called 'the Hopeful'. Very cultured, learned and endowed with great political tact, he was much beloved by the people, but had to overcome countless political difficulties engendered by partisan strife. During his very short reign he was confronted by two major problems, anticlericalism and a cholera epidemic. His brother Louis succeeded him on the throne as Louis I. Louis also had to cope with much political strife and even seditious movements. He married the Princess Royal of Italy, Maria Pia of Savoy, the daughter of Victor Emmanuel II of Savoy, King of Italy. Maria Pia was to be among the Queens best loved by the Portuguese people.

Charles I was acclaimed King immediately after his father's death on 19 October 1889. Charles I was very cultured, in both the scientific and artistic fields. His reign was troubled by political problems at home and abroad. Apart from the British ultimatum of 1890, brought about by British imperialist expansion in Africa, there was partisan strife. Influenced by the freemasons and the *Carbonari*, a republican movement emerged, and revolution broke out on 31 January 1891. Charles's reign came to a tragic end when both the King and his eldest son, Prince Louis Philip, were assassinated in Lisbon on 1 February 1908.

Manuel II became King on the death of his father and brother. He had not been groomed for the tasks of kingship. The political ambition of the various parties made his short reign a turbulent one. The proclamation of the republic on 5 October 1910 brought

restless. As we have already seen, at the age of seven, on 5 November 1826, she was married by proxy in Vienna to her uncle, Michael. But Michael had failed to honour his word and repudiated the marriage, which was declared null and void by the Cardinal Patriarch of Lisbon on 1 December 1834. Mary's second husband was Prince Auguste de Beauharnais, the son of Prince Eugène de Beauharnais, Viceroy of Italy and Prince of Venice. The marriage ceremony was held by proxy in Munich on 5 November 1834, and in person on 28 January 1835 in Lisbon. Two months later, on 28 March, the Prince was suddenly taken ill and died. His death caused great unrest in Lisbon and the young Queen was obliged to suppress her grief and, though newly widowed, had to engage in negotiations for her marriage with Prince Ferdinand Auguste of Saxe-Coburg and Gotha. This third marriage took place by proxy on 1 January 1836, and in person on 9 April of the same year, in Lisbon. After the marriage the Prince was officially made Prince Consort and on 16 September 1837 was granted the title of 'His Most Faithful Majesty King Consort Ferdinand II of Portugal', and given the rank of Marshal-General in the Portuguese army. After the Queen's death in 1853 Ferdinand II became Regent while Prince Peter was under age. He was offered the throne of Greece in 1862 and that of Spain in 1868, but refused both. On 10 June 1869 he contracted a morganatic marriage with the singer Elisa Henzler.

Peter V succeeded his mother Maria II on the throne in 1853. He was born on 16 September 1837 and died

Charles I came to the throne in 1889 and was assassinated in 1908. His younger son, Manuel II, was the last King of Portugal and went into exile at the proclamation of the republic on 5 October 1910.

both his reign and the Portuguese monarchy to an end. In exile in England, the King's patriotism manifested itself on several occasions. He died on 2 July 1932, aged only forty-three, of a tracheal oedema, childless.

To relate the last part of the story of the House of Braganza, we must return to Michael I, the son of John VI, and for a short period, the husband of Maria II da Gloria. Influenced by the Absolutists, and by his mother, Michael disloyally broke his word and, having convened the *Cortes* in keeping with the tradition of consulting the Three Estates, had himself acclaimed King. He repudiated his marriage and declared that his previous decisions and oath had been made under coercion. The ensuing civil war came to an end only in 1834, with the complete defeat of his army, and Michael left for exile, after being made to swear that he would never again involve himself in Portuguese affairs. However, as soon as he landed in Genoa he declared the statement he had signed null and void and again asserted his claim to the throne.

Michael's marriage to his niece Maria II was declared null and void by the Cardinal Patriarch of Lisbon on 1 December 1834. He contracted a second marriage on 24 September 1851, in Kleinheubach, with Adelaide Sophie of Lowenstein-Wertheim-Rosenberg. During his life in exile, Michael used the title of Duke of Braganza. The Absolutists regarded him as King and his children as infantes, and asserted the legitimacy of his claim to the throne.

When Michael I died in 1866, his eldest son Michael was acknowledged as Duke of Braganza by the Portuguese Legitimists. Michael II followed a military career as lieutenant in the Austrian dragoons and took part in the occupation of Bosnia in 1876. He reached the rank of lieutenant-colonel, but resigned in 1916 when Portugal declared war on Germany and Austria, in order not to take up arms against his countrymen. He sought to achieve a reconciliation with Manuel II, and although the latter agreed to this, the move was opposed by politicians on both sides. On 31 July 1920, Michael II abdicated his rights in favour of his son, Edward. Through a pact signed in Paris on 17 April 1922, Edward was recognized by King Manuel II and by the Portuguese Monarchists as successor in the claim to the throne of Portugal. He married his cousin, Marie Françoise of Orléans and Braganza, and had three sons, Edward Pio, Michael and Henry, born between 1945 and 1949.

We must now look at Peter II, who was acclaimed Emperor of Brazil at the age of six on the abdication of his father, who ruled Brazil as Emperor Peter I and Portugal as King Peter IV. Peter II was born on 2 December 1825. His reign was upset by a series of revolutions, until the great military leader, General Lima e Silva, Duke of Caxias, finally imposed order in 1849. The 1865–70 war with Paraguay, from which

Brazil emerged victorious, was yet another focus of unrest. On 13 May 1888 the Emperor passed a law abolishing slavery, causing discontent amongst the sugar cane farmers and sugar producers. Finally, a military republican rebellion deposed the Emperor, who left for exile with his family on board the steamer *Alagoas* and arrived in Lisbon on 7 December 1889.

Peter's daughter, Isabel, Crown Princess of Brazil, succeeded her father as head of the Imperial House of Brazil. She was called 'the Redeemer' because she was a great advocate of the abolition of slavery. She was born on 29 June 1846 and died on 14 November 1921 in the Château of Eu in France. She married Gaston of Orléans, Count of Eu, and had three sons, who adopted their mother's surname as if inherited from the male line, because she was successor to the Imperial throne of Brazil and the legitimate representative of the Brazilian Braganzas. Her eldest son, Peter III, re-nounced, for himself and his descendants, the right of succession to the Imperial throne of Brazil in order to marry Countess Marie Elisabeth Dobrzensky von Dobrzenicz (their third child, Marie Françoise, as we have seen, married her cousin, Edward of Braganza). Isabel's second son, Louis of Orléans and Braganza, Crown Prince of Brazil, when he left for exile, served first in the Austrian army and later in the British army during the 1914–18 war. He died on 26 March 1920. His son, Peter IV, Henry of Orléans and Braganza, is the present Head of the Brazilian Imperial Family. He married Maria Elisabeth of Bavaria, and they have eight children.

Philip V, grandson of the Sun King, in an equestrian portrait by Jean Ranc. His naming as heir to the throne by the last Spanish Hapsburg, Charles II, led to the long War of the Spanish Succession.

The Bourbons of Spain

Rulers of Spain for two centuries, the Bourbons
had ascended to the throne at the will of
the Hapsburgs, their traditional enemies

The House of Bourbon came from France, where it
had occupied the throne since 1589. It succeeded to the
throne of Spain as a result of the will of the last
Hapsburg, Charles II, who died without issue in 1700.
As a result of various matrimonial alliances with
Austria and France – notably that of Maria Teresa,
daughter of Philip IV of Spain, with Louis XIV in 1659 –
two different parties had closely related claims to the
Spanish throne. These were the Archduke Charles of
Austria, great-grandson of Philip III, and the Duke of
Anjou, grandson of Louis XIV.

After the war with France, the gains obtained by
Spain from the Treaty of Ryswick in 1697 affected the
problem of succession. Louis XIV took advantage of
these concessions to force Charles II to decide in favour
of his grandson, actively supported by the pro-French
faction in the *Corte* at Madrid.

In 1699 came the death of Joseph Ferdinand of
Bavaria, who had been regarded as providing an
alternative solution to the succession claims of the
Austrians and the French, both of whom were stirring
up hostile forces in Europe, above all amongst the
English. Charles II, himself now near death, decided in
favour of the Duke of Anjou, who would reign as
Philip V.

The new dynasty arrived in Spain at the end of a
century of profound decadence and depression. The
population was diminished, the economy ruined, the
army battered and the navy practically non-existent
because of the numerous wars which a century of
hegemony by the Hapsburgs had caused throughout
Europe. Spain, who still held the world's most
widespread Empire, was aged, tired, and, above all, in
need of peace.

The Bourbon dynasty established in Spain a form of
absolute monarchy which was alien to the country's
native tradition and which was to a large extent an
adaptation of the French pattern of government which
found its clearest expression in the rule of Louis XIV.

The eighteenth century in Spain witnessed a regime
of 'benevolent despotism', a kind of revolution from
above which was both authoritarian and paternalistic.
Philip V, Ferdinand VI, and most especially, Charles III,
were models of this enlightened despotism.

Philip V was born in Versailles on 19 December
1683, the second son of the Great Dauphin and Maria
Victoria of Bavaria. He was proclaimed King of Spain
on 24 November 1700, and on 18 February of the
following year, he made his entrance into Madrid. The
pro-French faction, which had supported his rights in
the hope of preserving the unity and independence of
the Spanish monarchy, proved to have been completely mistaken in their hopes. Neither the fragmentation of the Spanish Empire, nor the impact of foreign
intervention could be avoided.

Louis XIV's desire to enlist the collaboration of the
House of Savoy in his plans led to the negotiation of
the marriage of Philip V with Maria Louisa, daughter
of Victor Amadeus II. Four children were born from
this union, among them two Kings of Spain, Louis I
and Ferdinand VI. Louis XIV kept himself informed of,
and actively guided, Spanish policies during this initial
period of the reign.

It was soon clear that war could not be avoided. The
struggle with Austria, who was supported by England,
was to be the price – subsequently made greater by the
Treaty of Utrecht – that Philip V had to pay for his
Crown. The battle of Luzzara in 1702 provided a
momentary success in an Italian campaign recommended by Louis XIV to slow down the Austrian

Philip V's family, in a painting by Van Loo. The King was married twice, first to Marie-Louise Gabrielle of Savoy, and then to Elizabeth Farnese, who schemed successfully to gain a throne for her sons, Charles and Philip.

advance. This victory won the King the soubriquet of 'the Courageous', a quality which, if ever possessed by Philip, he unfortunately lost very quickly. Later victories in Spain, at Almanza in 1707 and Villaviciosa in 1710, brought him closer to final victory, which was hastened by the accession of his opponent, the Archduke Charles, to the Austrian throne as the Emperor Charles VI.

At home, while the kingdom of Castile had recognized Philip as its legitimate sovereign, the pro-Austrian sympathies of Catalonia, afraid that its freedom would be circumscribed by centralism, spread to the remaining parts of the kingdom of Aragon, and only ended with the siege and taking of Barcelona in 1714.

The Treaty of Utrecht was to affect the whole country. Europe recognized Philip V but, at the same time, Spain lost her Italian possessions, which passed together with the Netherlands into the sovereignty of the Austrian Empire. Gibraltar and Minorca remained in the possession of England, whose collaboration with Austria made her the major beneficiary of the Treaty, both in territorial acquisitions and in substantial economic advantages obtained on the continent of America.

His first wife having died, Philip V contracted a marriage with Elizabeth Farnese, daughter of the Prince of Parma. Thus, from 1714 there began a period of Italian influence, which tended to correct the worst effects of the Treaty of Utrecht and aimed at

recovering the Italian territories for the benefit of the children of this second union. The interests of Spain were thus sacrificed to dynastic ambitions, and her foreign policy, linked to that of France through various treaties of collaboration – the 'Family Compacts' – was influenced by the alternation of war and peace in Europe. Undoubtedly, this foreign policy direction achieved its desired results. Charles, Elizabeth Farnese's eldest son by Philip v, was to occupy the throne of Naples and Sicily in 1735. The dukedoms of Parma, Piacenza and Tuscany were held by the Infante Charles for a number of years. Subsequently, under the terms of the Treaty of Aix-la-Chapelle in 1748, the first two plus Guastalla passed to the Infante Philip, the second son of Philip v and Elizabeth Farnese.

An obsessive attention to foreign problems, of which the gains in Italy form a part, is also revealed in Philip v's constantly nurtured desire to succeed to the throne of France. This became all the more acute when the problems of the French succession were increased by the death in 1723 of the Duke of Orléans, Regent of the young Louis xv, who was himself very ill. This hypothetical claim of Philip v to the French throne might explain his unexpected decision – ostensibly the result of nervous depression – to abdicate the Crown of Spain in favour of his eldest son, Louis I, whose reign represents scarcely more than a parenthesis in that of his father.

Louis I – the first Bourbon born in Madrid – mounted the throne on 15 January 1724, being at that time not yet seventeen years old. He married Louise-Isabelle of Orléans, daughter of the French Regent, but her flighty behaviour soon brought disaster to the marriage. Meanwhile the retirement of Louis' parents to the palace of La Granja did not prevent them from interfering frequently in matters of government. A fatal attack of smallpox brought the young King's short reign to an end on 19 August of the same year.

Philip v returned to the throne, and a second era began, in which the advantages gained in Italy were consolidated and Spain's involvement in European affairs increased in step with that of France. Meanwhile, Philip, increasingly overwhelmed by the strong personality of the Queen and slipping gradually into a neurotic state of isolation and melancholy, retired more and more from participation in the affairs of State. His life ended on 9 July 1746.

Within Spain, the reign of Philip v had brought with it the establishement of a form of centralism. Moreover, the right of succession to the Spanish throne was abolished by the importation of the Salic Law from France, which excluded women from the succession. This was to be the cause of serious dynastic conflicts in the future.

While the society and culture of Baroque Spain were drawing to a close, reforms in administration, economics and cultural life were endeavouring to give new life to the country. A renaissance of sea-power, of fundamental importance to the transatlantic route, the creation of cultural institutions and the construction of splendid royal residences, culminating in the Royal Palace in Madrid, were without a doubt positive results of the reign of the first Bourbon.

The reign of Ferdinand vi stood in distinct contrast to that of his father. While Philip's reign had witnessed a whole series of wars, peace was to be the dominant climate of Ferdinand's rule. Born in Madrid on 23 September 1713, Ferdinand had married Maria Barbara of Braganza, daughter of John vi of Portugal, thus returning to the Castilian tradition of Portuguese marriages.

With the death of his father, and the withdrawal of Elizabeth Farnese to the palace of La Granja, from which she keenly followed political affairs, Ferdinand continued the reformist policies of the previous reign until the Treaty of Aix-la-Chapelle, signed in 1748, which ratified the position of Ferdinand's brothers on their Italian thrones. As a result the reign steered a pacific middle course, between the continental power of France and the maritime power of England.

With this peace came stability, enabling the country to achieve a degree of mastery over its economic situation which was still precarious. The years of peace allowed the population to grow by some fifteen per cent annually between the years 1748 and 1768. This growth was further increased by attempts at re-populating semi-desert areas, the struggle against the immobility of entailed property in the search for a much-needed dynamism of wealth, the redemption of Crown revenues from the hands of creditors, and a plan for a new fiscal system based on a single tax which would lead to a more effective and socially just division of contributions.

The economic policy of his ministers, involving tax relief for industry, technical interchange with other European countries, the creation of new lines of

inherited the dukedoms of Parma and Piacenza in 1731, and was King of Naples and Sicily from 1735. One cannot hope to understand the reign of Charles III without taking into account this long period of apprenticeship and experience, and without remembering that he enjoyed the counsel of men such as Tanucci, who continued to advise him by letter during the first few years of his Spanish reign.

In 1738 Charles had married Maria Amalia of Saxony, who left him a widower in 1760 shortly after his arrival in Spain. The personality of this monarch is respectable rather than attractive. Although he exercised to the utmost his role as absolute ruler the simplicity and humanity of his personality, his calmness and serenity, his marked paternalism and religious sincerity all reveal him as an honourable, well-intentioned man, well acquainted with the problems surrounding him. In addition, he possessed the rare virtue: skill in choosing his advisers.

His foreign policy followed two main themes. First, in America, he came into conflict with British interests; second, in Italy, which aroused the fears and suspicions of the Court in Vienna. From the very beginning of his reign, the Austrian ambassadors judged that Spanish foreign policy would tend towards the necessary strengthening of the Spanish position in America, and the creation of a power base in Europe to facilitate the control of Italy. It was with these aims in mind that the 'Second Family Compact' was drawn up in 1761. This formed the basis of all Spanish activity abroad until the crisis of the reign of Charles IV, a consequence of the impact of the French Revolution. One important success of Charles III's foreign policy was the recovery of the island of Minorca. While Spain played an invaluable part in the independence of the United States of America.

On the home front, Charles III gave impetus both directly and through his excellent ministers to a programme of reform rooted in the spirit of the Enlightenment. He carried out a revolution in the commercial field by breaking the monopoly which the ports of Seville and Cadiz had exercised over trade with America, and by authorizing a process of regional trade with twenty American ports. This resulted in regional development which was especially noticeable in Catalonia, and which also caused considerable movements of population within the country. At the same time he laid emphasis on plans for repopulation.

The King also ensured that reforms were made in agriculture, which were beset with problems.

University life, hitherto a sad and lethargic shadow of what it had been in the sixteenth century also underwent great change, despite conservative reaction from broad sectors of society and the distrust of the still-active Inquisition.

This confrontation between Charles III, who, though

internal communication and decisive support for naval construction in order to restore Spain's naval power, was another aspect of reform from above, which was carried out despite the nation's general inertia.

But neither the personality of the King nor the achievements of his reign were brilliant, much less spectacular. Perhaps the reign's most positive achievements were a realization of their limitations, and the creation of a climate of peace.

The reign of Ferdinand VI was a short one, and his lack of a son prevented the Spanish monarchy from becoming better established in a national sense. Mentally unbalanced, he died on 10 August 1759.

His successor on the throne of Spain was not a young Prince inexperienced in the tasks of government. Ferdinand's brother, Charles, was a man of forty-four who had already ruled as a king for twenty-four years. Born in Madrid on 20 January 1716, he had

Charles III dining in the presence of the Court, in a painting by L. Paret y Alcazar. The personality of the enlightened and reforming absolute monarch was more worthy of respect than attractive.

open to the ideological currents of European thought, was a sincerely religious man, and the immobility of the clergy found its most surprising expression in the decree of 1767, expelling the Society of Jesus from all the territories of the Spanish Crown. By this decree, royal intervention in ecclesiastical matters, already evident in previous reigns, reached its culmination and its point of maximum tension with the Holy See.

Charles III made many changes to his capital city, Madrid. The old Villa de los Austrias was transformed into a modern, well-laid-out city with magnificent fountains, splendid public buildings, museums, gardens and broad avenues.

This very exciting era closed with the death of the King on 14 Decemeber 1788. Charles IV did not inherit his father's abilities as a ruler.

Charles IV was born in Portici in the kingdom of Naples on 11 November 1748. He came to the throne at the age of forty. He was interested only in leading a quiet life, of unchangeable habits. It is difficult to see in this the image of a king, or even of a man of State. He had too many bourgeois characteristics and plebeian tastes for the former, and he lacked sagacity and political cunning for the second. The comparison with his contemporary, Louis XVI of France, is inevitable.

In 1765 Charles had married his cousin Louisa Maria of Bourbon, daughter of Philip of Parma. Both their married life and the affairs of State were dominated by the mean personality of the Queen. It is now clear that Louisa Maria had a love affair with Manuel Godoy, a former bodyguard raised to the rank of Duke of Alcudia, Generalissimo and Prince of Peace. But neither the Queen's passion nor the affection which Charles IV himself had for Godoy, justify his dizzy ascent to the position of virtual dictator, which he exercised with the benevolent

approval of the King. Godoy must be seen not only as the royal lover and an intimate friend of the King, but also as the new man on the political scene, young and active, offering a fresh alternative to the old political advisers of Charles III.

The Spain of Charles IV could not escape the effects of the French Revolution. At first the events in France did not inspire grave misgivings and gave rise only to extra vigilance by the police and the Inquisition, the guardian of religious and political orthodoxy. However, after Louis XVI was guillotined and the French Republic was proclaimed, Spain sided with legitimist Europe. The war against the French National Convention ended with the Treaty of Basel, signed in 1795, when the conservative bias of France after the fall of Robespierre seemed to offer a better prospect to the alarmed European monarchies. A year later, the Treaty of San Ildefonso restored Spain's normal alliance with France, and Godoy's government was to be a pawn in Napoleon's European game. This explains Spanish participation in the campaign of 1805, in which the Franco-Spanish fleet was defeated by the English at Trafalgar. The Treaty of Fontainebleau, signed in 1807, granted permission for the Napoleonic army to cross Spain and attack Portugal, who was England's ally.

The Napoleonic intervention, resulting in the invasion of 1807, although apparently peaceful and the result of a treaty, coincided with a serious internal crisis. Opposition to Godoy increased as the serious situation abroad worsened the country's internal economic difficulties. Public opinion laid all the responsibility on Godoy for the crisis. The heir to the throne, Prince Ferdinand, became the centre of opposition to the favourite's government and in him reposed all the hopes of Spain.

A first plot against Godoy, hatched in the Prince's own quarters, was discovered and failed, but a second attempt – the uprising of Aranjuez of March 1807 – was entirely successful. The weak Charles IV agreed to deprive Godoy of his power and simultaneously abdicated his throne in favour of his son Ferdinand. The new King, Ferdinand VII, entered Madrid on 24 March 1807. It is significant that Napoleon's representative, his brother-in-law Joachim Murat, had established himself in the capital a day earlier. The presence of the French soldiers, whom the people looked upon, quite correctly, more as invaders than as allies, created a tense atmosphere close to popular revolt.

The history of modern Spain opens with the date, 2 May 1807. A patriotic and popular revolt, originating in Madrid and spreading throughout the country, was to turn into a civil war which served as a model for other European countries resisting the troops of Napoleon. The crisis of the Bourbon dynasty reached its height. Emperor Napoleon enticed Charles IV, Ferdinand VII and all the other members of the family onto French territory, and there they agreed to hand over the Crown of Spain. But the Spanish people did not accept the abdications of Bayonne, and in the absence of their legitimate monarchs, set themselves up in authority. For seven years there was a double government in Spain, that of the interloper Joseph Bonaparte, and that of the patriotic and revolutionary one of the Juntas – revolutionary in that its authority had risen from below – which governed in the name of the missing Ferdinand VII. The War of Independence was at the same time a genuine national revolution, producing the first Spanish constitution of 1812, which proclaimed the principle of national sovereignty and limited the powers of the monarchy.

Ferdinand VII was to prove a disappointment. Born in the Escorial on 14 October 1784, he was overshadowed in his childhood by the hated figure of Godoy. This instilled into him a mistrust of his parents, and above all a resentment towards his mother, of whose relations with Godoy he must have been aware. He developed an ignoble and egotistic personality. His humble attitude towards Napoleon, when he congratulated him in 1809 on his victories in Spain and offered himself as his 'most humble and obedient servant' typifies the level of his character.

When Napoleon was defeated and Ferdinand's throne was restored to him, the King refused to recognize the work of the *Cortes*, and abolished the constitution by the decree of Valencia in 1814. Absolutism was restored, while the constitutionalists, many of them heroes of the Independence, were imprisoned or went into exile. From this period until 1833 the government of the country took on a pendulum-like movement, swinging from a period of absolutism lasting six years to a brief liberal interval of three, then back again to a long decade of personal government. Altogether there were sixteen years of absolutism, during which uncompromising reaction was the order of the day.

Apart from the short three years of liberalism from 1820 to 1823 in which, coerced by a military coup or *pronunciamiento*, Ferdinand endured rather than accepted the limitations of the constitution, the King chose governments which were largely composed of mediocre men. With no concerted programme, they administered rather than governed the country and, if in economic matters they followed the reforming traditions of eighteenth-century Enlightenment, in cultural and political matters they proved ultra-conservative. There were colourless, static governments which enabled the King to be the unchallenged arbiter in everything. The existence of a parallel government, the *camarilla*, formed by friends and confidants of the King, shows his mistrust of his own

Sketch by Goya for an equestrian portrait of Ferdinand VII. The 'desired' King disappointed the hopes of Spaniards, who were loyal to him during the Napoleonic domination and the War of Independence.

ministers and his taste for petty Court intrigue.

A problem of succession now impinged on the ideological confrontation within the country. None of the King's first three marriages – with Maria Antonia of Naples, Isabel of Braganza and Maria Josepha Amalia of Saxony – had left him with an heir. The fourth, with his niece, Maria Cristina of Naples, produced two daughters. The Salic Law was still in force, so Ferdinand VII abolished it by a pragmatic sanction of 29 March 1830, restoring the traditional form of Spanish succession. But at the same time a party was forming around his brother Carlos Maria Isidro, the centre of an ultra-conservative sector which upheld the ideal of a monarchy of a theocratic tinge. This marked the beginning of the Carlist movement, which, with varying fortunes, lasted into the twentieth century and is still alive today. To counteract this, the liberal sectors organized themselves around Ferdinand's daughter Isabella, whose claim to the throne was thus mortgaged in advance to liberalism. On 29 September 1833, Ferdinand VII died, leaving the throne to a three-year-old child, with her mother, Maria Cristina, as Regent; an atmosphere of impending civil war threatened the country.

In opting for the liberal tendency, which had already suffered a schism between a conservative or 'moderate' liberalism and a radical or 'progressive' form, Maria Cristina ensured the survival of her Regency, which was faced with armed uprisings in several Spanish regions. These regions saw in the brother of Ferdinand VII not only their legitimate King but also a champion of their privileges, their religious faith and their political and social convictions. This was the first Carlist war.

Isabella II was born in Madrid on 10 October 1830, and was declared of age in 1843, when she was thirteen. Her reign is a difficult one to understand, supported as it was in its initial years by many who had been her father's political enemies. During the course of her reign nearly sixty governments succeeded one another, and two constitutions were enforced – the liberal constitution of 1837 and the moderate one of 1845, while a third, progressive constitution was on the point of being adopted in 1856. This was an era in which Spain, after seven years of civil war and the sterile political vacillations of the reign of Ferdinand VII, began to re-emerge into Europe and to take cautiously and rather belatedly to the industrial revolution.

In order to analyze this complex period, in which three forces acted on the government – the Crown, the army and the political parties – it is necessary to understand the personality of the Queen, the key piece in the game. The personality of Isabella II was elemental and contradictory. Profoundly Spanish, with a sympathetic openness, a good sense of humour and an undoubted generosity both material and spiritual, she nevertheless lacked the intelligence and the prudence required for her mission as a constitutional Queen.

The political vices, accumulated in the time of her father, remained entrenched in the *Corte*, and even grew in strength. Never, whether on the throne or later in exile, could Isabella dispense with the *camarilla*, with her confidants and the courtly intrigues. She also lacked the emotional and political companionship of a man who would carry out the role of prince consort with tact and energy. The choice of a husband fell on her cousin Francisco de Asiz of Bourbon who used his position to open the way to sectarian intrigue favouring an absolutist and theocratic power, in no way different from that espoused by Carlism, and which would eliminate every trace of liberalism from the government.

'The restored monarchy of Ferdinand VII,' portrayed
here by Luis la Cruz y Rios, 'accepted nothing, would
understand nothing, and could be grateful for nothing.'
This was one judgement of this ambiguous monarch.

Isabella II, painted by Franz Winterhalter. Her father, Ferdinand VII, who had no male heirs, abolished the Salic Law so that she could reign; this gave rise to 'Carlism'.

The reign of Isabella II has been called the regime of the generals, since the intervention of the army in the political scene, one of the constant features of the nineteenth century, made the insurrection or *pronunciamiento* the standard way of changing governments. Isabella II was to be the victim of this situation, which she herself had helped to create. In September 1868 a military uprising, combined with a revolutionary movement, removed her from the throne. Between 1868 and 9 April 1904, when she died in her residence in Paris, Isabella II endured a long period of exile during which she never lost hope of one day returning to the throne, and encouraged any plans for this which were proposed to her.

Isabella's son Alfonso XII differed from his predecessors in one important respect – he received a wide education both as a man and as a king. He was the first King of modern Spain whose education went beyond the limits of courtly adulation. It was completed in various European countries. Above all, he followed passionately the tragedy of Spain in its inability to find a viable regime. Between 1868 and 1874 a whole succession of governments were formed. During those years, the threads of a Bourbon restoration were being drawn together. The man who directed the movement of restoration was one of the most brilliant politicians of the nineteeenth century, Antonio Canovas del Castillo. His aim was to produce a monarchy which was at the same time old and new, which would combine the Spanish monarchic tradition with the liberal contributions of the bourgeois revolution.

In Alfonso, Canovas had a willing disciple, conscious of the mistakes of his mother's regime, with a modern spirit, open to reality, and conscious, too, of his responsibility to Spain and to Europe, ready to be the conciliatory King which Canovas' programme required. On 29 December 1874 a large sector of the army proclaimed him King. Canovas, who had hoped that he would accede to power through a call from the country via the *Cortes* and not by a military *pronunciamiento*, bowed to reality and took advantage of the favourable reaction in Spain.

The ten years of Alfonso's reign show him to be a King who was capable of pleasing broad sectors of European opinion – he did not hide his sympathies towards the German and Austro-Hungarian Empires – but who at the same time fulfilled Spanish hopes of what a king should be. He was sympathetic, close to the people, and with an open and unprejudiced nature. He married his cousin, Maria de las Mercedes of Orléans against the wishes of her mother, Isabella II, and a romantic aura was added to this already attractive figure. The death of Queen Mercedes after only six months of marriage, and the tuberculosis which gradually undermined his youth, both added to the King's picturesque image which, after his death,

was to remain alive in popular romantic songs.

Too much emphasis has been laid on the military leanings of Alfonso XII. Although brought up to admire the glories of European militarism typified by the Prussian model, Alfonso was certainly not himself a militarist. But he felt attracted to a certain heroic ideal and fulfilled with great dignity the role of soldier-king which Canovas had assigned to him. He was the head of an army in the service of the Crown and the nation, removed from factions and from political interest. Military success ended the third Carlist war, and won Alfonso XII the title of 'the Peacemaker'.

Alfonso married as his second wife, Maria Cristina of Hapsburg, the niece of the Emperor Francis Joseph, on 29 November 1879. When Alfonso died in the palace of El Pardo on 25 November 1885, his widow was expecting a child. The political leaders, Canovas and Sagasta, decided to uphold the Regency of Maria Cristina to preserve political continuity. Protected by the prudent and flexible constitution of 1876, and with the two governing parties, the conservative party of Canovas and the liberals under Sagasta, working together, the system of the restoration was maintained. Even the opposition – from the Carlists to the republicans – offered a truce to the régime represented 'by a widow and an orphan'. When Alfonso XIII was born he was already a king, a case unique in Spanish history and almost without precedent in European history. On 17 May 1886, Spain celebrated his birth with joyous demonstrations.

The childhood of Alfonso XIII under the tutelage of Maria Cristina, who proved a model of dignity and prudence as a Regent, was affected by three particular circumstances: the King's awareness of his exalted position from his earliest years; a strict military education which, following the model of the soldier-king, was to tie him closely to the army; and a religious education in which his own mother played an important part, being widely known for her austere and pious way of life. To these three factors must be added the effect of a tragic incident, which is one of the keys to an understanding of twentieth-century Spain. This was the crisis of 1898 – the Spanish-American War in which Spain lost Cuba, Puerto Rico and the Philippines, and which had a deeply traumatic effect on the country. Alfonso XIII shared the ideals of the cultural, economic and political movement known as *regeneracionismo* which were spread throughout Spain.

It was with all these encumbrances that he arrived at his majority in 1902.

Four years later, on 31 May 1906, he married one of the most beautiful princesses in Europe, Victoria Eugenia (Ena) of Battenberg, the grand-daughter of Queen Victoria of England. Their marriage day was marred by an anarchist attack on the couple in the Calle

Mayor in Madrid. This was to be neither the first nor the last attack which the King suffered during the course of his life. Three of his prime ministers – Canovas in 1897, Canalejas in 1912 and Dato in 1921 – were all assassinated by anarchists.

The reign of Alfonso XIII must be analysed in two different ways; from the international viewpoint, in the context of a Europe shaken by workers' movements and shattered by the First World War; and from the internal viewpoint which saw the decay of the political system forged by Canovas. This decay was accompanied by a rapid fragmentation of the great parties alternating in power, while the country was transformed demographically and socially.

With Europe at war in 1914, Alfonso XIII remained faithful to the neutrality chosen by his government. Those who were politically conscious in Spain were divided into two opposing camps, the Germanophiles and the supporters of the Allies. It was a conflict that the King experienced personally within his family, for he had an English wife and an Austrian mother. Although the government was neutral his sympathy for the Allies was evident.

Within Spain, he strove to carry out his role as a constitutional monarch, but the political climates that surrounded him made it impossible for him to resist the temptation to rule. His active and impulsive nature and above all his manifest interest in serving his country prompted him to intervene in the political process, more than once abandoning his role as arbiter and mediator. Although he intervened in politics, he was never a party man.

He was reproached by all for his encouragement of the army on the eve of the ill-fated military operation in Morocco which ended with the disaster of Anual in 1921. He was also widely blamed for accepting the military coup of General Primo de Rivera which suspended the constitution and opened the way to a dictatorship in 1923, even though this brought seven years of prosperity and reconstruction for the country. But nobody recalled the numerous occasions on which Alfonso XIII tried to preserve constitutional legality.

Gradually he was becoming isolated. Despite his proverbial geniality, with a common touch which was the characteristic of all his family, he was a solitary man. He finally found himself entirely alone in 1931 when, after the fall of the dictatorship, municipal elections were held in a vain attempt to return to constitutional normality. The results of these elections merely served to demonstrate the popularity of the republican regimes in the big Spanish cities. The king retired into exile with dignity.

There followed ten years spent in various parts of Europe – France, Switzerland, Italy – while he followed at a distance the ups and downs of the unstable Spanish republic and the tragic events of the civil war. In addition he had to endure the pain of seeing the diminution of his own family: in 1934 his youngest son, Gonzalo, died in an accident; and his first-born, Alfonso, died in Miami in 1938. His second son, Jaime, being a deaf-mute, in January 1941 Alfonso XIII renounced the Crown in favour of his third son, Juan. A month later, on 28 February, he died in the Grand Hotel in Rome. His last words, a testimony to his essential Spanishness and his Christian faith, were. 'Spain! My God!'

Nearly forty years of personal government by General Franco made distant and problematic the possibility of a return of the monarchy. Don Juan of Bourbon maintained the historical rights of the dynasty in exile, together with the notion of a European democratic style of monarchy. At the same time to cover all possibilities, he agreed to entrust the education of his first-born to Franco's control.

The last legitimate representative of the Carlists, Don Alfonso Carlos, died without issue in 1936, leaving his rights to Alfonso XIII's branch of the family. While many traditional Carlists accepted the double legitimacy of Don Juan of Bourbon, others followed Don Javier of Parma and then his son Carlos Hugo, who married Princess Irene of Holland. Carlos Hugo now seems to be marching under the paradoxical banner of Carlist-socialism. Carlism remains as a memory of a romantic and unrealizable ideal, and its real possibilities in present-day Spain scarcely go beyond the realms of folklore.

Prince Juan Carlos of Bourbon, the grandson of Alfonso XIII, was born in Rome on 5 January 1938, and educated in Spain, in the military academies and University of Madrid. He ascended the Spanish throne on 22 November 1975, two days after the death of Franco and in accordance with the latter's provisions for his succession. The monarchy, defined in the law of succession as 'Catholic, social and representative', aims to be related more to the historical tradition of Spain than to the monarchic type of constitutional liberalism. Embodied by a young monarch conscious of his duty, to Spain and to Europe, it appears as the one possible solution, supported by a majority of national opinion, and since 6 December 1978 by a constitution which has opened up new roads towards democracy.

Alfonso XIII, already King at birth. In 1931 he chose
exile saying: 'Let not a single drop of Spanish blood be
shed because of me.' The Spanish monarchy was
restored in 1975 with his grandson:

The Hohenzollerns

Electors of Brandenburg, they transformed
peripheral Prussia into the prime mover in
the unification of Germany

Frederick III, Elector of Brandenburg and Duke of Prussia, the German Prince who crowned himself 'King in Prussia', was delicate by nature. He had a crooked back, and used to wear an immensely long wig to hide his curvature. It is said that a wet-nurse dropped him as an infant so that the child was disabled, suffering from an injury to his spine from which he only gradually recovered.

Frederick III, son of Frederick William, the 'Great Elector' and Louisa Henrietta of Orange, one of the family of the Dutch Stadtholder General, was born on 11 July 1657 in the East Prussian capital of Königsberg. He was the eleventh Elector since the Holy Roman Emperor Sigismund had, in 1415, entrusted the barren Brandenburg Marches to the Hohenzollern Burgrave Frederick VI of Nuremberg with the title of Elector. The family came originally from Swabia, and the first recorded reference to a Count of Zollern is as early as 1061. About 1200, the Hohenzollerns (the name is presumably derived from some right to collect tolls or *Zoll*) had won the position of Imperial Burgrave of Nuremberg. In 1363 they attained the rank of Princes of the Holy Roman Empire. Frederick VI who, as Elector of Brandenburg, became known as Frederick I, also had estates in Ansbach and Bayreuth in Franconia. Frederick I was married to the beautiful Elsa of Bavaria, a member of the Wittelsbach family.

In 1525, the last Grand Master of the Teutonic Order, Albert of Hohenzollern, of the Franconian

Charlottenburg in Berlin, painted by M. Roch. Built for Frederick III, Elector of Brandenburg, it was the summer residence of his wife, Sophia Charlotte.

branch of the family, converted his State in Prussia into a secular duchy and, on Luther's advice, went over to the Protestant persuasion. Thereupon, the former Prussian territories of the Order passed under Hohenzollern rule, albeit on condition that the King of Poland retained his suzerainty – a link worth more on paper than in practice. The ducal line of Prussia died out as early as 1618, when the second of the line died insane. Prussia and Brandenburg were then united under a single ruler.

The Hohenzollerns in Berlin in the 1600s seem to have been fairly ordinary. Then suddenly a genius, alike in military skill and in statecraft, cropped up in the person of Frederick William, whom even his contemporaries simply called the 'Great Elector'. In 1640, at the age of twenty, Frederick William took over the government of a decayed petty German State, still suffering severely from the effects of the Thirty Years War. His marriage with the Orange Princess, a member of a gifted family, brought new blood into the Hohenzollerns. When the Great Elector died in 1688, Brandenburg-Prussia with its fine army had become one of the central powers of Europe, whose influence extended far over the Holy Roman Empire of German nations. The last links with Poland had already been ended in 1657 and 1660 by the Treaties of Wenlau and Oliva near Danzig.

Frederick William's successor, Frederick III, was not in the least like him. His injured back had made his childhood sad and difficult. Indeed, until 1674, he was not destined for the throne; the heir to the Electorate was his elder brother, Karl Emil, a hot-headed soldier for whom his delicate younger brother entertained a tremendous admiration. Then suddenly, in the war against France, Karl Emil died of a high fever combined with dysentery.

When Frederick came to power in 1688 it became clear that nature had compensated for his weakly body by equipping him with a lively, fantastically wide-ranging, mind – though also, of course, with the love of pomp and circumstance characteristic of so many of the Hohenzollerns. He soon showed that he was clever enough to hold his own inheritance together, with its widely scattered territories from western Germany to Prussia, by the way he dealt with a somewhat ominous question arising from his father's will. In two late instructions of 1680 and 1688, the 'Great Elector' had conceived a fairly extensive partition of his territories to provide for any members of his family who might yet be born. The executor of his will was the Emperor Leopold I, Frederick I's godfather. While still the heir, Frederick was able to get him to agree that the will should be annulled on his enthronement.

The Great Elector had received from the Emperor the district of Schwiebus, part of his Austrian-Silesian territories, at the same time renouncing old Hohenzollern hereditary claims dating from 1537 to the duchies of Liegnitz, Brigge and Wohlau. Frederick secretly promised the Emperor that, in recognition of his dubious role as executor, he would return the district of Schwiebus, but with the corollary that all declarations of renunciation of the Silesian hereditary rights were 'obsolete'. All this was to take on a new and fatal significance under Frederick's grandson, Frederick the Great.

Before his succession, Frederick had married his first love, Henrietta of Hesse-Cassel, still only a young girl. She died of smallpox, aged twenty-two in 1683. His second marriage, with Sophia Charlotte of Brunswick-Lüneburg, a woman far superior to him in will-power and imagination, was made more in accordance with courtly convention than from any personal attraction. But Sophia Charlotte, who on 14 August 1688 presented him with an heir, Frederick William, encouraged her husband in his intention to give a new face to the capital and royal city. The model for all German Courts in those days was the residence of Louis XIV at Versailles, even though Brandenburg-Prussia, in alliance with the Holy Roman Emperor, the Netherlands and England, had just resumed the war against France over the Spanish succession.

Frederick did not only want to be known as a powerful prince; he wanted also to be recognized as a patron of the arts and sciences. In 1694, he established a new university in Halle, making three with the colleges in Königsberg and Frankfurt on the Oder. In 1696 an Academy of Arts was set up in Berlin, in 1700 the Elector founded the 'Society of Scientists', the nucleus of the Academy of Sciences. The polymath Leibniz was brought to Berlin, as was the great architect Andreas Schlüter.

But what captured the Elector Frederick's imagination most of all was the idea of expanding the royal title. He saw how Hanover had become an Electorate, how in 1688 the Stadtholder of the Netherlands, a relative of his, had become King William III of England. In 1697 the Elector of Saxony, Augustus the Strong, got himself elected King of Poland on his promise to embrace the Catholic faith. It was impossible then for a German ruler to take the title of king, since the Holy Roman Emperor was also King of Germany. But Prussia had never formed part of the Imperial federation, so it was there, in his capital city of Königsberg, that Frederick arranged to crown

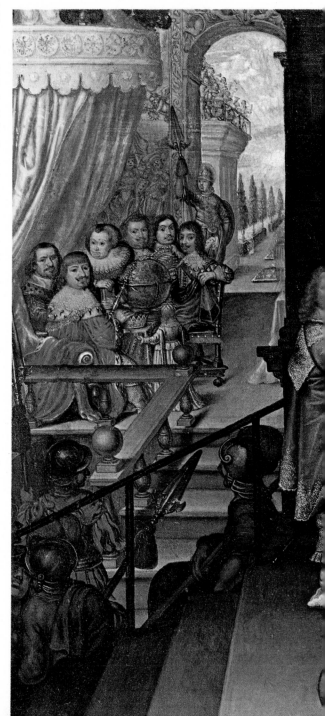

himself king. For that, however, he needed the agreement of the Emperor Leopold I. But Leopold in his turn needed Prussian help, since the life of the last, sick Hapsburg King of Spain, Charles II, was drawing to a close, and in the absence of any offspring in Madrid the Emperor and Louis XIV, both grandsons of Philip III of Spain and both sons-in-law of Philip IV, were putting forward claims to the giant Empire, which included the Spanish Netherlands, Milan, Naples, Sicily, Central and South America and the Philippine Islands in southern Asia. In return for an alliance between Brandenburg-Prussia and Austria to support his claim to succeed the Hapsburgs in Spain,

and for the raising of a force to take part in the campaign, Leopold consented to his godson assuming the title of 'King in Prussia'. On 1 November of that year Charles II of Spain died. On 16 November 1700, Vienna and Berlin finally came to terms about the dispatch of a force of eight thousand men for a payment of 150,000 guilders. On 24 November 1700 it was known in Berlin that all was settled.

The way was now open for the Elector Frederick III to become King Frederick I 'in Prussia'. Before Christmas, despite the unfavourable time of year, the King set out on the journey from Berlin to Königsberg with a huge train of three hundred carriages and

The first Hohenzollern King, in a painting by F. W. Weidemann. Frederick I, formerly Frederick III of Brandenburg, had himself crowned 'King in Prussia' on 18 January 1701.

coaches and wagons for baggage and provisions. At midday he would give a Court banquet, every evening there would be some form of celebration; it was the kind of existence in which he revelled. On Saturday, 18 January 1701, preceded by splendid proclamations accompanied by the thunder of cannon, fanfares of trumpets and heralds in ancient Roman dress, the coronation took place in the former Grand Master's castle – significantly, in a civil building.

The coronation, celebrated by a public holiday, the illumination of the city and a ceremonial drive by the royal pair, was matched only once in the history of the Hohenzollerns, when, one hundred and sixty years later, William I wished to demonstrate his unshakeable loyalty to tradition in the face of his disagreement with Parliament over the royal establishment. Since the ministers, and even more Parliament, were opposed to such quasi-medieval mysticism, he had to pay for the ceremonies out of his own pocket. The last two Prussian Kings, Frederick III and William II, could never have undertaken such ceremonies. Frederick was already mortally ill when he came to the throne. William II had a withered arm.

By the end of 1701 Europe was the richer by a new

kingdom, but it was valid only in one of its ruler's territories. Frederick was proud of the endless variety of festivals, concerts and ballets at his Court, and his Prime Minister, Johann Kasimir von Kolbe, Count of Wartenberg, encouraged his master's taste for such entertainments. Even more influential behind the scenes than this clever, obsequious courtier was the wanton Countess Wartenberg, the daughter of a seaman and a servant from the Lower Rhine, pretty as a picture, who had risen in the world first as the wife of a valet, then as Kolbe's mistress, and then, when the valet died, the minister married her.

This extravagant life was played out against a background of war – the War of the Spanish Succession, in which Prussian regiments fought with great distinction against France, and the Northern War, the attempt by the Swedish King Charles XII to crush Russia. The two most important government bodies of Prussia, the secret Cabinet Council and the secret War Council, were already attended assiduously by the young heir, Crown Prince Frederick William – an uncouth young man, sturdy, broad-shouldered, thick-set, regarded by Court society as a sort of super-sergeant, who nevertheless followed the despatch of business with a burning interest and hardly ever missed a session.

Frederick I had made an early marriage for his son, this rough Crown Prince Frederick William, again to a Guelph, Sophia Dorothea, daughter of the Elector George of Hanover, the future King of England. Their first two children died in infancy, but on 24 January 1712 there came into the world the longed-for heir, Frederick, whom his contemporaries were to christen 'the Great' – the greatest genius and at the same time the greatest enigma of this dynasty. King Frederick I died a year later, on 25 February 1713.

Many of the qualities seen in the first Hohenzollern to wear the Crown reappeared in his successors, notably in the ninth and last King of Prussia, the German Emperor William II: the passion for the arts and sciences, the ridiculous pomp, the love of the theatrical in his public appearance. All the Hohenzollerns had one fatal flaw – tactlessness; it was to show itself first in Frederick I's grandson Frederick II, 'the Great', and to be characteristic of the last King-Emperor to an exaggerated degree.

Frederick I had truly believed that the kingdom he had won for himself, which was never quite looked on as an equal by the wearers of the time-honoured Crowns of Europe, the Bourbons and the Hapsburgs, had only been made possible through the grace of God. Frederick William I, brought up initially in the dreary doctrine of predestination as a member of the Calvinist Reformed Church – the family had professed that branch of the evangelical faith since the beginning of the seventeenth century – was made aware, by contact

Frederick William I, on the right, with Augustus of Saxony, King of Poland, painted by de Silvestre. The 'Sergeant King' spent much money and effort on his army.

241

with the Halle theologian and teacher August Hermann Francke, of a new side to the evangelical faith, pietism, an intensified Christianity that stressed the direct relationship between man and God. In this way he came to see himself less as a beneficiary than as the first servant of the State, as God's representative upon earth.

His father had never been able to solve the problem of how to combine an expensive royal household with the maintenance of a strong army. Frederick William I stuck to the simple rule that expenditure must never exceed income. The first aim of the State which he wished to serve was the maintenance of an army as powerful as possible, no longer from foreign subsidies but from his own resources. With a ruthless hand he cleared out his father's household.

To earn money for the army, which he eventually built up to 78,000 men, the economy had to be stimulated and the administration reorganized. At the head of the whole administration, the King created the directorate-general of high finance, war and estates, under his personal control. This hard taskmaster performed the remarkable trick of creating an efficient national machinery both for the economy and for war, from which commerce and industry of all types profited. As a political economist he was unsurpassable, hard and crude as his methods may have been.

Prussia thus became the embodiment of thrift, order, diligence and dutifulness. The Hohenzollern monarchy was made up from territories of the most varied kinds, from Cleves, the Marches and Ravensberg in the far west, to Courland, Pomerania and East Prussia, which was separated from the centre of power in the Brandenburg Marches by the Polish King's territories in West Prussia.

The State's supreme concern was the army; the King himself wore general's uniform, and those around him always preferred uniform to civilian dress. For his life guard he picked out especially tall, strong young men, the famous 'Long Fellows'. The hunt for reinforcements of the right type became a hobby with him, in which he did not shrink from the most dubious methods. For the army in general, following a suggestion by General von Derfflinger, he introduced the so-called canton system, by which each regiment was given a certain area of recruitment which had to supply its own military contingent – a new idea in Europe in those days. The age of the absolute princes had known only mercenary levies.

Was life easy under Frederick William I? Definitely not. The life of his eldest son, Prince Frederick, was sheer hell under this father who despised the fine arts and spent his evenings smoking his pipe and drinking strong beer with his cronies – his *Tabakscollegium*. Even as a youth, Frederick had begun to display many-sided talents; to his father's infinite fury, he took after his grandfather. He did not seem to care for the military life at all. What he was really interested in was literature, drama, music. He was far more gifted than his grandfather, who had been distinguished only as a patron of the arts. When he was eighteen, Frederick tried a different solution. On a journey through southern Germany with the King, he and his close friend, Hans Hermann von Katte, tried to escape to England, where his Hanoverian uncle George had become King. The plot was discovered; the royal father, mad with rage, determined to do away with the Crown Prince and ordered both men to be executed. The Emperor persuaded him against it, and instead the Crown Prince was imprisoned in the fortress of Küstrin and, on his father's orders, was made to witness the beheading of his friend Katte.

At Katte's execution he fainted away. But, after the end of his imprisonment and a formal reconciliation with his father, his talents developed in two different directions – on the one hand, the poet and flute-player, the philosopher and historian, on the other, the outstanding officer and skilful administrator. From then on he seemed to develop two personalities. But he had no time at all for love and passion. Even the marriage with Princess Elizabeth Christina of Brunswick, arranged by his father, changed nothing in this puzzling attitude. The marriage was clearly never consummated; the Princess passed the fifty-five years of her married life in solitude. Her husband showed her every honour and respect – but he never showed her affection.

His father made no objection to his setting up his own Court at the castle of Rheinsberg, an idyll of intellectual conversation, and of academic and artistic activities with friends. The Crown Prince himself gave concerts and composed music. Here, too, he wrote his *Anti-Macchiavelli*, a mirror for the princes of his time.

The idyll was brought to an end by its own creator. On 31 May 1740 his father died of what was then called dropsy – in modern terms, a serious disorder of the circulation. He had never spared himself on his country's behalf, he had been a tireless worker, his only relaxation hunting and the evenings with his *Tabakscollegium*.

Frederick II said of himself that he was a philospher by inclination, a statesman by compulsion. But now this twenty-eight-year-old man was spurred on by the desire to see his name in the 'gazettes' and, in due course, in history. He had a well-ordered State at his disposal, a full treasury, an army to which hard training had given an unequalled rate of rapid fire. As Crown Prince, at the tragic time of Küstrin, he had already been considering how Prussia could be extended, wondering how those yellowing Silesian treaties could be activated. Silesia, one of Austria's richest provinces, must be made Prussian; then his

Frederick II playing the flute at a concert given for his sister Wilhelmina's visit. The King liked to be thought the most genial and enlightened monarch of his time.

kingdom would be numbered among the great powers of Europe.

When the German Emperor Charles VI died unexpectedly at the end of October 1740, Frederick II struck, and occupied Silesia. He put forward no hereditary claim; he did not negotiate; he simply anticipated the doubtful outcome of negotiations. The rest could be sorted out by jurists and diplomats. The European Courts were shocked. By twentieth-century standards, this was a war of aggression, a predatory war *par excellence.*

The age of absolutism had held different ideas about the ways in which a ruler might pursue the acquisition of territory. But now Frederick had sound arguments to make his use of force look retrospectively plausible in the eyes of the other Courts. The Emperor Charles VI, having no male heir, had by the Pragmatic Sanctions, which even Frederick William I had recognized, secured the succession of his daughter Maria Theresa to the Hapsburg hereditary territories of Austria, Bohemia and Silesia, Hungary and Croatia. Her husband, Duke Francis of Lorraine was to become German Emperor. All this was overturned when the Prussian King seized Silesia. He defended his new territory, in temporary alliance with Bavaria and France, in the two Silesian Wars of 1740–2 and 1744–5.

The philosopher-poet, had now become a warlord and statesman of the first order, a truly exceptional universal genius. He planned to celebrate his victories with poetry and philosophy at the newly-built palace of Sans-Souci, near Potsdam, without letting that interfere with affairs of State, the rebuilding of Silesia, the grand policy. Frederick's guests at Sans-Souci, who included the most cultured thinkers, especially from France, were quite remarkable for the Europe of those days. The King enjoyed being looked on as the most intellectual and enlightened Prince of his time. He became the most complete of atheists; but at the same time he allowed his subjects complete liberty of worship. Since, as head of the justiciary, the King had an objective jurisdiction applied even to himself, his subjects got the reassuring feeling that, amid all the harsh differences of rank and class, there was always a compensating fairness to be found in the person of His Majesty.

The years in Sans-Souci, from 1745 to 1756, have been called Prussia's 'Augustan age'. Once more the period of peace was brought to an end by its own creator. In 1756 it looked to the King as if an alliance was being forged between Austria and Russia. The Russian Empress Elizabeth, a daughter of Peter the Great, hated the upstart of Potsdam – while Frederick, tactless as usual, responded with barbed jokes about the Empress's love-life. France, whose alliance with him dating from the time of the Silesian War, expired in 1756, did not seem inclined to renew the link. The

Napoleon receiving Queen Louisa of Prussia, wife of Frederick William III, at Tilsit in 1807. The Queen pleaded in vain for the mitigation of the harsh peace conditions.

Electorate of Saxony and Poland followed the Viennese line. Before all the new alliances had been signed – that between Austria and Russia was already firm – Frederick II decided to strike as he had in 1740, to march into Saxony in July 1756 as a base for an advance into the Central European *glacis*, Hapsburg Bohemia.

The result was a world war. Frederick II, not yet known as 'the Great', had to cope with the disadvantage of a preventive war, in which he was not at first successful. Maria Theresa of Austria, Elizabeth of Russia, Louis XIV of France, and Frederick's own sister, Luisa Ulrica, Queen of Sweden, who hated her brother and wanted to see Swedish power re-established round the Baltic, all joined forces against the 'Marquis de Brandenburg', as they called Frederick II at the Court of Versailles. Frederick's only remaining ally was King George II of England, who was also Elector of Hanover, and he was himself engaged in a war against France in North America, the West Indies and India.

The war lasted for seven years. Brandenburg-Prussia was exposed by its fatal central position in Europe, with enemies on all sides. Frederick's victories, in 1757 at Rossbach over the French and the Imperial army, which the old Holy Roman Empire had mobilized against him, and in the winter battle of Leuthen, near Breslau, against the Austrians, showed the sovereign's skill as a commander in the field. The Russians, whom he defeated in 1758 at Zorndorf, overran East Prussia and finally appeared in Berlin. At this critical time Prussia was holding out only in the King's camp with the Prussian army.

In January 1762 the Empress Elizabeth died. Her successor, Czar Peter III of the House of Schleswig-Holstein-Gottorp, a grandson of the Romanov Czar Peter the Great on his mother's side, was an admirer of Frederick. He abandoned the anti-Prussian alliance and signed a treaty with the Prussian King. The Peace of Hubertsburg in 1763 put an end to the war, with Prussia retaining all its territory.

Frederick II, whom his people were soon to name

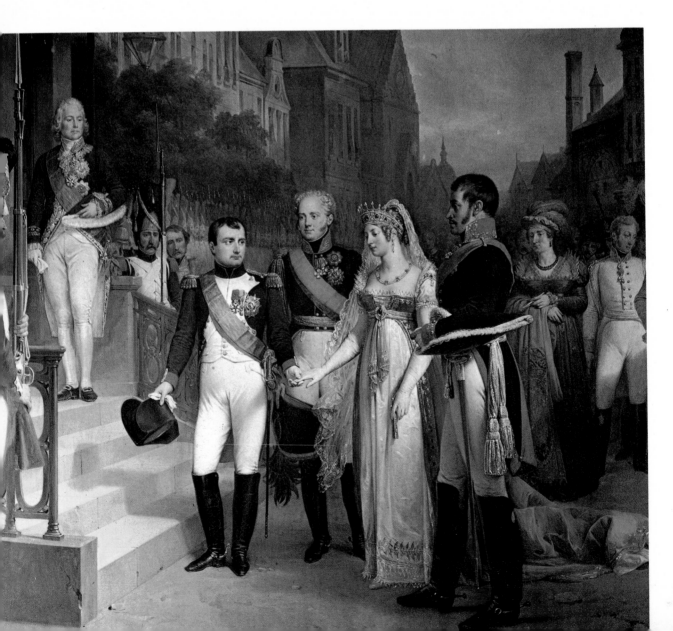

'the Great', was fifty-one years old. He joked about himself that he was losing a tooth every day and growing more and more grey. And yet, for the next twenty-three years, in spartan performance of his duty, he maintained his administrative and military machine. Under him, by a settlement with the princely House of Cirksena, Prussia gained distant East Friesland. Under him, through the partition of the collapsing Polish-Lithuanian kingdom, carried out in agreement with the Czarina Catherine of Russia, Prussia succeeded in gaining West Prussia and – with the reluctant consent of his old enemy Maria Theresa – the German bishopric of Ermland, far off towards East Prussia, thus linking East Prussia with his other territories.

But Prussia did not hold its breath when, on 17 August 1786, Frederick, whom they were now calling 'the Great', closed his eyes as a result of 'dropsy of the chest'. Instead, Prussia breathed a sigh of relief, for life had become hard under the old, capricious genius.

His successor stood ready, the 'Don Juan' of the Hohenzollern dynasty, Frederick William II, whom the Berliners called their 'fat lecher'. He was the son of Frederick the Great's brother Augustus William and of Louisa Amalia of Brunswick-Bevern, a sister of the unfortunate Prussian Queen. Prince Augustus William had been counted the handsomest man in the kingdom; his brother disowned him because he was alleged to have refused to serve as a general at the start of the Seven Years War. He died, of grief, in 1758.

Frederick William II was forty-four years old when he ascended the throne. The great King had trained him scrupulously as future heir to the throne, and despite his own lack of faith, had had him thoroughly instructed in religious matters. The Prince, a Herculean figure, running badly to fat in his later years, was far from stupid. He was interested in music and had a gift for it, played the cello excellently and was a patron of Mozart. Besides his passion for music and the theatre, however, he had another great passion, for beautiful women.

In 1765 the great King arranged a marriage for him with his cousin, Elizabeth of Brunswick-Bevern, whose mother was a sister of the Queen. The marriage remained without issue and was dissolved after four years, allegedly because the Princess repaid the constant unfaithfulness of her husband by having an affair with an officer. The woman who dominated Frederick William was Wilhelmine Encke, born in 1756, the daughter of a horn-player in the band of the Prince of Anhalt-Dessau, whom he first met when she was a strikingly pretty girl of fifteen. He had her educated in the manners of the French Court and swore to her on his 'princely word of honour', writing on a piece of paper in his own blood, that he would never desert her. Wilhelmine, on Frederick the Great's

order, went through a form of marriage with a valet called Rietz; later she was ennobled as Countess von Lichtenau, and she remained at the King's side until he died. Three of the five children of this liaison died young, but the surviving son and daughter were raised by Frederick the Great, shortly before his death, to the rank of Count and Countess of the Marches.

In spite of 'Madame Rietz', as the favourite was called at Court, the Prince was married again in 1769 to someone of his own rank, the Princess Louisa, daughter of the Landgrave Louis IX of Hesse-Darmstadt who was probably insane. Like her father, the new Crown Princess saw ghosts and spirits, preferred to sleep during the day and stayed awake all night. She became old and bent long before her time. This odd marriage produced six children, including the future King Frederick William III, born on 3 August 1770.

Neither 'Madame Rietz' nor his crazy legitimate wife stopped Frederick William II from entering into new liaisons, the next being with the beautiful lady-in-waiting Julie von Voss, a niece of the Countess Voss, Mistress of the Royal Household. Julie von Voss became Countess von Ingenheim. Her aunt, a very puritanical person, insisted that the relationship, from which a son was born, should be blessed by the Church, and the King made a morganatic marriage. The clergy in Berlin gave it their blessing on the grounds that Martin Luther had already approved

such a marriage for the Landgrave Philip of Hesse. Julie von Voss died very soon, of consumption, and the King contracted a second morganatic marriage with the Countess Sophia Dönhoff, a very designing lady.

These activities lent the Court a long unknown air of frivolity. But it happened that the King's chief adviser, General von Bischoffswerder, and his former pastor, Johann Christoph Woellner, were fellow-members of the Rosicrucian Order, and they persuaded the King to join them. The declared objects of the Order were the spiritualization and purification of men, against the Enlightenment and in opposition to the established Church. In Berlin the Rosicrucians held séances,

attended by the monarch, at which they raised the spirits of Alexander the Great and Julius Caesar and also of the King's lately deceased son, Alexander von der Mark, to give their counsel to His Majesty. Sensuousness and mysticism heralded the approach of the Prussian Rococo.

The sinister background to all this was provided by the French Revolution of 1789, which Frederick William II, in league with the Emperor Francis II, tried vainly to oppose from 1792 to 1795, and the final partition of the Polish-Lithuanian Empire amongst Prussia, Russia and Austria in 1793 and 1795. This gave Prussia substantial parts of western and northern

Poland, including Warsaw, the former capital. Such a great expansion of territory proved too much for the powers of the administrative machinery that Frederick the Great had set up for a more limited area. The State declined; corruption crept into the public offices. Oddly enough, however, this post-Frederick nation, which was indeed to become, as the late King had wished, an empire in which everyone was treated on the principle: 'To each his own (*suum cuique*), his duties and his rights', brought into being the great achievement of the 'general provincial law for the Prussian State'. The general provincial law was submitted in 1794, codifying the existing order in case of the overthrow of the feudal absolutist system that had prevailed in France, but still laying down some statutory rules for the entire kingdom.

The life of the 'Well Beloved', as people called Frederick William II, came to an end at nine in the morning on 16 November 1797, when he was fifty-three. The first thing the new ruler, Frederick William III, did was to order the arrest of the hated 'Madame Rietz', whom he had encountered the previous night still beside his father's sickbed. Her fortune was confiscated on the grounds that it had been amassed by 'extortion', and the Berlin clergy revenged themselves on the 'sinful' Rosicrucian by refusing their blessing at the funeral ceremony in the cathedral. The son burned the letters his father had written to the 'Countess' with his own hands.

Frederick the Great had prophesied grimly that under his nephew 'the women' would govern. That did not quite happen, for Frederick William II had always taken care that his mistresses should not interfere in politics, which was his own exclusive business. When the Countess Dönhoff had dared to try to interfere, he had her exiled to Switzerland. It was Frederick William III who was dominated by a woman. During the difficult times of the Prussian defeat by Napoleon and the great administrative and social reforms of Stein and Hardenberg, he stood in the shadow of Queen Louisa, born on 10 March 1776, the daughter of the Duke Charles I of Mecklenburg-Strelitz and of a Princess of Hesse-Darmstadt. First her mother and then her stepmother died early, and Louisa was brought up in the style of the French Court by her grandmother, the old Landgravine of Hesse-Darmstadt. Louisa was a very beautiful woman, but had had little basic education; no one could really have called her clever.

The young pair built themselves a modest country seat at Gut Paretz, near Potsdam. In seventeen years of married life, she presented her husband with nine children, among them the future King Frederick William IV and, in 1797, King William I, who in 1871 became Emperor of Germany.

Frederick William IV, a fine, virile figure of a man,

was emotional, odd and, inhibited. His great-uncle Frederick the Great had ensured that he had a strict religious upbringing, and in consequence he cherished the conviction that God, before whom, as he said, all men were equal in church, had only given him more power than other people so that he could use it to do them good. And since, as he himself declared, he was 'of limited understanding', he was anxious to find himself the best advisers.

A predilection for the military art had become traditional among the Hohenzollerns, but the King much preferred exercises in peacetime conditions to the real test of training in war. His chief adviser, the Foreign Minister von Haugwitz, surrounded by a Europe submerged under the war of Austria, Russia and Britain against the Corsican Emperor Napoleon, followed the policy of neutrality that Frederick William II, in his amorous idleness, had favoured since the Peace of Basel in 1795. The final, catastrophic result, in 1806, was a Prussia in isolation fighting a war against Napoleon. First the collapse of the Frederick's State, and then the immensely severe Peace of Tilsit in 1807 which cost Prussia half her territories and limited the monarchy to the province of Saxony, the Electorate of Brandenburg, Pomerania, Silesia and East Prussia, awoke the Queen's hidden power. In 1806 she accompanied her husband into the field, she shared the flight of the royal family as far as Memel in farthest East Prussia, in July 1807 she risked a pilgrimage to Napoleon to try, in vain, to negotiate a mitigation of the peace terms. The self-appointed Emperor, an uninhibited hedonist, admired her beauty but made no concessions.

Louisa backed up her remarkably irresolute husband in carrying out the reforms that had been set in motion by Baron von Stein, the King's chief minister since the defeat. Stein's reforms included the concept of a responsible ministry, the abolition of serfdom on the land, freedom of trade and commerce and communal autonomy. The King had always thought such reforms necessary but had never got round to implementing them. The Queen personally disliked the blustering Baron, while he thought the Queen stupid, arrogant and superficial. But that did not alter the fact that Louisa was the hope of all right-minded people, that she was convinced that Prussia had sunk so low because it had failed to keep pace with world events.

One pregnancy after another, combined with worries over the King and the nation, were more than the Queen's heart could stand. The royal couple returned to Berlin in December 1809, and soon after, on the morning of 19 July 1810, she died in her beloved Paretz.

Frederick William III survived her until 1840. Napoleon had demanded the dismissal of Baron von Stein, and the man who succeeded him as the King's adviser was the future national Chancellor, Carl August von Hardenberg, whom Louisa had esteemed much more highly than the prickly reformer. Hardenberg, whom the King raised to the rank of prince, led Prussia to a renaissance through the two wars of liberation of 1813–4 and 1815. Frederick William III had the royal wisdom to let him take the lead. Since he was a man who could not get on without the love of a woman, the King, like his father before him, went through a form of morganatic marriage, with the Church's blessing, with the Countess Augusta von Harrach, daughter of a high Prussian official, and made her Princess von Liegnitz.

On Whit Sunday, 7 June 1840, Frederick William III passed away after a short illness. As long before as 1817 he had brought about the union of the Lutheran Protestant Church and the Reformed Church in the Old Prussian Union, with Lineey as the chief bishop. Throne and altar drew nearer to one another in that age of burning liberalism. But Frederick William III was never really to recognize the two decisive problems of the period, the establishment of a 'Prussian Diet', a Parliament, which Stein had already called for, and the movement for the unification of Germany.

His successor, Queen Louisa's favourite son Frederick William IV, was quickly overtaken by these problems. As a child he had been sensitive, with a marked talent for drawing, but incapable of concentrating on serious studies for any length of time, and he entered on his reign with an extraordinary conception of the divine right of kings. He seriously imagined that as King he had been endowed by God with superhuman mental and spiritual powers far exceeding those of other mortals. He used to make public speeches, described by Friedrich von Gagern, one of the liberal leaders, as 'sermons', which scarcely marked him out as a man of action. His predecessors had given orders, but he gave lectures. Never, he swore, should a piece of paper – a constitution, that is – come between him and his people. In 1847 he tried to dodge the constitutional issue by calling a 'United Diet' from the provincial diets. But the opposition was now talking openly of the rights of the 'people of Prussia', an idea culled from the new vocabulary of German national liberalism. When, in February and March 1848, the blast of the citizens' democratic revolution swept from Paris through Germany and Austria, the nerves of this highly strung visionary, prince and theologian, broke down. Though the troops finally regained control in the serious street fighting in Berlin on 18 and 19 March 1848, Frederick William IV gave in to the rioters, granted them the constitution he had already promised on 18 March, and even appeared in public with his head uncovered in homage to the martyrs of the revolution.

When, in 1849, the democratically elected German national assembly offered him the Crown of a new German Empire, the reply was again that he, the King, could never accept the Imperial Crown from the hands of the people. His Foreign Minister, Joseph Maria von Radowitz, tried in 1849–50 to bring about a German alliance under Prussian leadership. When Austria, the other leading power with Prussia in the German confederation, sent an ultimatum in protest, Frederick William IV retreated again in the Treaty of Olmutz, signed in 1850.

The result of all the revolutionary uproar was a new reaction in Prussia, which at least now had an elected Parliament possessing the important constitutional right of approval of the budget. In 1857 Frederick William IV suffered a stroke followed by renewed apoplexy, which impaired his powers of speech and other essential brain functions. Since his marriage with Princess Elizabeth of Bavaria had been childless, he was succeeded by his brother, Prince William, first as Regent and then, after his death on 2 January 1861 at the palace of Sans-Souci, as King. In 1848 the people of Berlin had abused William as the 'grape-shot Prince' and had wanted to storm his palace in Unter den Linden, because they thought – quite mistakenly – that the Prince had commanded the troops in the fighting at the barricades. Frederick William IV had asked him to take refuge in England for a time.

William I was sixty-four when he came to the throne and already looked like a patriarch. He was, in fact, the last father-figure on the Prussian throne. A true soldier, he had his share of hard trials. In 1826, under pressure from his father, Frederick William III, he had been obliged to give up his marriage with Princess Elisa Radziwill, the sweetheart of his youth. Genealogical experts had worked out that Elisa, daughter of the Polish grandee and Prussian Governor of Poland,

The triumph of Prussia and the Hohenzollerns in 1871. After Napoleon III's defeat, William I was acclaimed as Emperor by the German princes at Versailles.

Prince Anton Radziwill, was of inferior rank, although the Radziwills, one of the most powerful families of the old Polish-Lithuanian Empire, had already married with the Hohenzollerns once, in the seventeenth century. It was also suggested that there was a danger that this 'Polish marriage' could damage the friendship between Prussia and Russia, which had become traditional. The Prince obeyed like a good soldier.

The marriage he contracted instead in 1829, with Princess Augusta of Saxe-Weimar-Eisenach, granddaughter of Goethe's patron Karl August, was not a happy one. The Princess was far better educated than her husband, and suffered from an awkward feeling that she had left civilized Weimar for a land of barracks that was a cultural desert.

Although opposed by his ministers and by Parliament, with its progressive majority, William I went ahead with his self-coronation at Königsberg at

his own expense, arranging it for the anniversary of the battle of Leipzig, 18 October 1861. He had an extraordinary sense of royal dignity and the royal touch.

William I's public life was overshadowed by Otto von Bismarck, the greatest statesman that Prussia, and indeed Germany, ever knew. From 1862 onwards Bismarck, the Brandenburg-Pomeranian landowner, had shaped the destinies first of Prussia and, from 1871 of the new German Empire, first as Prime Minister of Prussia, then as Federal Chancellor of the North German Federation, and finally as Imperial Chancellor. 'It is hard,' said old William I with a sigh, 'to be Emperor under Bismarck.'

But is it not also possible that Bismarck's career would have been quite inconceivable without this dignified, sometimes obstinate and morose, but in the last analysis, consistently sensible sovereign? William I

251

A grand dinner at the Court of William II in 1900. On dismissing Bismarck, the Emperor said: 'Same course as before, full steam ahead.'

possessed the inner sovereignty that allowed him to give a free hand to this remarkable man, who in 1862 delivered him from the parliamentary battle over the reform of the army, who gave him the victories over Austria in 1866 and over France in 1870–1 – and also to the brilliant Chief of Staff, Helmuth von Moltke.

When the King of Prussia saw how, in 1866, after the defeat of Austria and the old German confederation, Bismarck got rid of the hereditary dynasties in Hanover, Hesse-Cassel and Nassau with a stroke of the pen to round off the greater State of Prussia, it gave him much to think about. In this triumph of power politics, what had happened to the divine right? At first, Bismarck's skilfully and scrupulously worked-out plan to get the princes of the confederation and the burgomasters of the free cities in the headquarters at Versailles to elect the King of Prussia hereditary 'German Emperor' seemed quite incomprehensible. It had always been in the mind of the soldier-King William I that Prussia would have to unite Germany by the sword. He wanted the title of 'Emperor of Germany', which was quite unacceptable to the princes of the confederation. Anything else would just be *Charaktermajor*, honorary major, the rank granted to an ordinary captain when he retired. With some difficulty, Bismarck won him over to his plan. On 18 January 1871, the anniversary of the coronation of the first 'King in Prussia', William I's son-in-law, the Grand Duke of Baden, led the first cheers for the 'Emperor' in the throne-room of the palace of Versailles. He was careful at that moment not to use the proposed description of 'German Emperor'. King William I thus became *primus inter pares* among the twenty-one princes of the confederation and the heads of the three Hanseatic cities of Hamburg, Bremen and Lübeck.

His new role called for tact and sensitivity, both of which the old Emperor possessed in good measure. The policies of this new power in Central Europe in its relations with the other great powers, Britain, Russia and Austria-Hungary, also needed political flair, and that Bismarck could provide.

Two attempts to assassinate the eighty-one-year-old Emperor in Berlin, in May and June 1878, showed how there were still social questions that demanded solution. These attempts were the work of cranks – the social democratic opposition to the old order had nothing to do with them, but Bismarck did try to counter them, first by his 'laws against socialists', and second by the creation of the first comprehensive social insurance system in the world.

The great hope of all progressives at that time was the doughty Prince Frederick William, who was supported in his preference for a constitutional regime and in his dislike of Bismarck by his English wife Victoria, the oldest daughter of Queen Victoria.

During the Parliamentary conflict of 1861–2, the Crown Prince had openly opposed his father, to the King's extreme annoyance. But with all his apparent liberalism, Frederick William also had a very highly developed conviction of the importance of his own princedom. No one can really say how this dream-Emperor of all the liberals would have reigned, because in 1887 he was taken ill with cancer of the larynx. The old Emperor died just before his ninety-first birthday, on 9 March 1888. His successor, who as Emperor took the name of Frederick III in memory of Frederick the Great, succumbed to his fatal illness after a reign of only ninety-nine days, on 15 June 1888.

The new reign began with a *coup de main*. As soon as his father died, Crown Prince William had the New Palace at Potsdam surrounded by a regiment of life guards, which had been kept in readiness under cover for days, to prevent his hated English mother from sending important papers to England. The new ruler, born on 27 January 1859 and now twenty-nine years

old, revealed himself as energetic, rash and – a result of his inner uncertainty – apparently thoughtless. The serious complexes that resulted from his congenital defect, a crippled left arm, and from his hard upbringing by Georg Hinzpeter, a tutor still considered controversial, bore their fruit. Hinzpeter made the heir everything that Prussians expected a Prince to be, a good rider and a conscientious officer. His relationship with his father, with whom he shared a need for adulation, was outwardly cordial, but he grew to hate his mother because she made him feel that she saw through his weaknesses.

Nonetheless the world, and especially the Germans, at first admired the young Emperor. He seemed to be so completely different from all other men; richly talented, interested in a thousand things, from art (as he understood it) to science, and at the same time endowed with the Hohenzollerns' love of pompous, theatrical display. He believed that he ought to appear progressive even on labour questions, and dismissed

Bismarck when they came into conflict over these. So the statesman who had created Prussia-Germany disappeared from the stage.

William II had been married since 1881 to Princess Augusta Victoria of Schleswig-Holstein, a simple and basically very noble wife. Six sons and a daughter were born of the marriage. Augusta Victoria understood nothing of politics and did not wish to understand anything; all she wanted was to be a good wife. But the presence at her side of her husband, with his nervous restlessness, his love of travel, his capriciousness, and his taste for third-rate, tactless witticisms, must have been far from easy for her.

But the Emperor was above all just what rapidly expanding German industry wanted, with his ideas of German world prestige and especially his plans for the building of a fleet. The latter took shape in 1897 under the Secretary of State for the Imperial Navy, Grand Admiral von Tirpitz, an outstandingly skilful organizer. Indeed, he influenced an entire period before the

William II, by L. Noster. The last of the Hohenzollern rulers, he abdicated at the end of the First World War and survived until 1941, the 'fabulous monster of our times'.

First World War, the era of 'Wilhelminism', a strange compound of megalomania, superficial splendour, Byzantine flattery at Court and an emphasis on the new Empire's 'shining armour'. This no longer meant much to the Prussians, but William II was an emotional orator who got carried away by an inherent pathos and the desire to please. He made some terrible *faux pas*. At the embarkation of the expeditionary force sent to China as a result of the Boxer Rising, he gave them the watchword: the Germans were to 'wreak havoc like the Huns' – a stupidity that the enemy was to exploit to the full in their propaganda in the First World War.

This post-Prussian Wilhelminian Empire would really have needed another series of Stein-Hardenberg reforms to reconcile the increasingly active labour movement with the prevailing order, and to familiarize the German social democrats, the strongest party in the German Parliament in 1912, with the conception of loyal opposition. The Emperor did not see this, or realized it too late. As a result of a foreign policy that no longer contrived, as Bismarck had contrived, to maintain a carefully balanced relationship with the other great powers, Britain and Russia, everything led inexorably to the catastrophe of the First World War.

The Emperor never wanted the war, but he did not know how to stop it. Possibly His Majesty's pride had suffered a severe shock when, in 1908, the British *Daily Telegraph* published a private interview in which the Emperor had told an acquaintance that he was a great Anglophile, but that this view was not shared by the majority of Germans. Publication had been authorized by the negligence or carelessness of the Imperial Chancellor, Prince von Bülow. A wave of indignation swept through Germany, and the Emperor completely broke down. He had believed himself the idol of the Germans. But then nothing happened – no abdication in favour of his son, Crown Prince William, who was not much better anyway, and no critical resolution by Parliament, still not used to open opposition.

In the 1914–18 War of mass mobilization, the Emperor, like his forefathers before him, went to war with a monstrously inflated headquarters but did not actually take command. Once so highly honoured, he now became a mere shadow. He lost contact with the army, for the men at the front, his place was taken by the supreme commander, Field-Marshal von Hindenburg, a father-figure who became a sort of substitute Emperor. When the line was about to break in 1918 and the Allies announced that they would not negotiate with the Emperor either for an armistice or

even for a peace, and when his beloved navy mutinied, there was no other possibility open to the Emperor but a prompt, voluntary abdication in favour of one of his younger sons – the Crown Prince had also by now been branded a 'war criminal'. But the Emperor was unwilling to abdicate. The end came on 9 November 1918, when revolution broke out in Berlin and the last Imperial Chancellor, Prince Max von Baden, announced William II's abdication over his head, while the Emperor stayed in his army headquarters at the watering-place of Spa in the Belgian Ardennes. Then, when a republic was proclaimed in Berlin, William abdicated as German Emperor, but still not as King of Prussia.

However, this shadow-King now let himself be persuaded by his companions, who were afraid that mutinous sailors might suddenly appear in Spa, to abandon his army and his kingdom. Early in the morning of 10 November 1918, he took refuge in the neighbouring neutral country of Holland – a step that looked like a despairing flight. It was still not until 28 November 1918 that he finally renounced all rights as King of Prussia.

William II lived in exile in Holland for twenty-three years. When Augusta Victoria died in 1921, of a severe heart attack, he made a second marriage in that same year with Princess Hermine zu Reuss, the widowed Princess of Schönaich-Carolath. For most of the time he lived at Castle Doorn. For a man so fond of travel, so restless, this limitation on his movements was irksome, and he compensated for it by hard physical work and scientific study. Curiously enough, to the rest of the world he was still 'the Kaiser' – 'a fabulous monster of our times', a British writer called him. When he died at Doorn Castle on 4 June 1941, German soldiers mounted guard, not now under the command of a Hohenzollern but of the 'Führer' Adolf Hitler, who had conquered and occupied Holland. There was a time in 1933–4 when the ambitious 'Empress' Hermine had believed she could persuade Hitler to bring the Emperor back to Germany. There were still big estates belonging to the family, especially in their former Prussian territories. In 1945 they were confiscated by the Red Army. The last 'Empress' died of starvation in 1947 at Frankfurt on the Oder. The only Hohenzollerns who now claimed the throne were the descendants of Prince Charles of Hohenzollern-Sigmaringen, from the old Swabian line, who in 1866 had become Prince, and later King of Rumania. In 1947, under Soviet pressure, King Michael I of Rumania was forced to abdicate.

The House of Savoy

Descendant from a feudal vassal from
Burgundy, bestowed lands bestriding the western alps,
this oldest reigning family in Europe provided unified
Italy with a monarchy

Up to the Second World War the history taught in Italian schools was arranged according to reigning dynasties. Otherwise very little would have been heard of the House of Savoy before the time of Amadeus VIII, who was granted the title of Duke by the Emperor Sigismund in 1416. The new Duke succeeded in uniting into one state all the scattered domains of the various branches of his family, and investing it with its first settled laws, the 'general statutes'.

The medieval rulers of the dynasty were of no great importance, prudent but hardly striking characters. A number of earnest hagiographers have worked on their history, inventively interpreting Sabaudia – the early name for Savoy, first used in the fourth-century Roman history of Ammianus Marcellinus – as being derived from *salva via* and indicating that the mission of the princes of that House was the salvation of their subjects' souls. They also recounted that the first Count was Humbert, a feudal vassal from Burgundy, who arrived in Italy in the eleventh century and, because his hands were as white as lilies, was known as 'the White-handed'. The countship was bestowed by Emperor Conrad II, surnamed the Salic. Humbert's lands, bestriding the western Alps, gave him command of the mountain passes, a key position during the Imperial invasions of Italy, enabling the holder to juggle with two expansionist policies: a Burgundian one towards France, and a second in the direction of the Po valley and Italy.

The Counts of Savoy lost no chance of aggrandize-

The Daniel Gallery, with a ceiling painted by Daniel Seyter in 1690, in the royal palace at Turin, the residence of the Kings of Sardinia and of the first King of Italy until 1865.

ment, making alliances on the principle of not participating in war, because they were too weak, but of profiting from the wars of others, taking care never to commit themselves irrevocably to either side. They pursued the same policies in the internal struggles between the chief and cadet branches of the family, and between the dynasty and its vassals.

At first the French-speaking transalpine territories were predominant (on the Piedmont side, the powerful marquisates of Monferrato and Saluzzo, and the county of Asti, belonging to the Orléans family, stood in the way of Savoyard expansion) and the dukedom was, in fact, a vassal of France, though with varying periods of comparative independence when the neighbouring power was afflicted with internal crises or engaged in war. The duchy, being mountainous, was economically poor.

Among the rulers of Savoy who advanced that dynasty's expansionist policy were Odo, son of Humbert, whose wife, the Marchesa Adelaide di Susa, brought him the countship of Turin as part of her dowry; Amadeus VI, the crusader (called the Green Count from the colour of the surcoat he wore at tournaments), who first formed an alliance with the Viscontis of Milan to chase the Angevins out of Piedmont, then himself seized some of the Visconti cities (the first manifestation of that policy of non-alignment towards the Po valley), and was later nominated as mediator – a sign of considerable prestige – at the Treaty of Turin between Genoa and Venice in 1381; and Amadeus VII, the Red Count, who by his marriage to the Countess of Nice obtained an outlet to the sea.

In 1434 Amadeus VIII abdicated to become a hermit and subsequently the anti-Pope, under the name of

Amadeus VI, Count of Savoy, known as the Green Count. By taking some cities from the Visconti in the fourteenth century, he initiated the eastward expansion of the Alpine State.

Felix V. With the abdication of Amadeus, the dukedom was plunged into a prolonged crisis, caught in a vice between two powerful States. For years her immediate neighbours, France and the kingdom of Milan, which became a Spanish dominion, exerted a double pressure – or sometimes attraction – on the little duchy, determining the uncertainty and oscillations of her policy.

Amadeus VIII was succeeded by Ludovic I, unsuited to his position and under the thumb of his wife Anna, daughter of the King of Cyprus, Jerusalem and Armenia, a beautiful, ambitious, scheming woman and a sower of discord. It was Anna, the mother of sixteen sons, who brought with her the Holy Shroud, the sheet in which, according to tradition, Christ was wrapped after His deposition from the cross: the possession of this relic was the source of great prestige for Savoy.

As soon as the Hundred Years War was over, France occupied Savoy, the Alpine passes and the chief towns of the duchy. The Duke at that time was the feeble Charles III the Good, whose greatest wish was to reign in peace. He imagined that, being a brother-in-law of the Emperor Charles V and uncle of Francis I of France, he could reconcile those two implacable rivals. As things turned out, he was ground between the upper and nether millstones and subjected to every sort of humiliation.

It fell to his son, Emmanuel Philibert (1553–80), nicknamed Ironhead because of his obstinacy, to restore the fortunes of a State in which all strong points lay in the hands of the French and Spanish, and where the land, devastated by invasions and plague, was almost deserted. Two years after he had led a Spanish army to victory over the French at San Quintino, the Treaty of Cateau-Cambrésis of 1559 gave him back his dukedom, mutilated though it was, and shorn of the territories of Geneva and Vaud. France retained Saluzzo and, together with Spain, kept a few garrisons in the land. The only circumstance in Savoy's favour was the temporary state of equilibrium and peace between her two powerful neighbours. Shrewd and tough, little given to learning but expert in the martial arts, the Duke rolled up his sleeves and set to work, creating an army by conscription, a police force and a small fleet, which had the honour in 1571 of taking part in the battle of Lepanto. He succeeded in getting rid of the foreign garrisons, then transferred his capital from Chambéry in Savoy to Turin, thus giving new impetus to what the Savoyard historians call 'the Italian destiny' – in reality a self-interested move with an eye to possible expansion. An authoritarian despot, he persecuted the Jews and the Waldensian sect. His exchequer was replenished by higher taxation. Although this strengthening of the State suppressed all political liberty, for the peasants it meant a defence against the excessive power of the landlords.

Everything Emmanuel Philibert had been at such pains to achieve was dissipated by his son, Charles Emmanuel I, who succeeded in 1580 and remained in power for half a century, plunging without hesitation into the French religious wars, the two wars of succession in Montferrat and the first stage of the Thirty Years War. Enormously ambitious and utterly reckless, he defied Henry IV of France and won back Saluzzo, but paid for it with transalpine possessions of far greater value. At his death the duchy was once more in dire straits, invaded first by one and then by the other power, its army disbanded, the treasury bled white.

As early as 1631 Charles's son, Victor Amadeus I, was forced to restore the fortress of Pinerolo to France. The decline of the dukedom continued for another fifty years, accelerated by the civil war between the *madamisti*, that is to say the francophiles who supported Victor Amadeus' widow, Marie Christine of France, known as Madame Royale, and the *principisti*, the hispanophiles who favoured the deceased Duke's brothers, Cardinal Maurice and Thomas, Prince of Carignano. However, to cast a brief look forward into the history of the House of Savoy, it must be said that, in general, wars advanced the fortunes of that dynasty of soldiers. From the three wars of succession that embroiled Europe in the first half of the eighteenth century, they emerged with a royal Crown. The Napoleonic Wars left them admirably placed to make their great leap forward towards the Crown of all Italy, which finally became theirs through the wars of independence. Conversely, in times of peace, Piedmont languished.

The first Prince of Savoy to achieve royal status was Victor Amadeus II. Having succeeded in 1675 while still a minor, he had to submit to the Regency of his mother, the French Princess Marie Jeanne de Nemours, and obey Versailles in all things. Irascible, energetic, astute, unscrupulous and a clever tactician, he brought his State bureaucracy up to date and reorganized the army. This achieved, he threw himself into foreign politics, dominated at the turn of the century by the figure of Louis XIV. It was at the French King's behest after the Revocation of the Edict of Nantes that he allowed the French to enter Piedmont and return to their persecution of the Waldensian sect, whom his father, Charles Emmanuel II, had already massacred with zeal. Nevertheless, he defied Louis by joining the League of Augsburg against France in 1690. It was a bold gesture, for he had only eight thousand fighting men, and the French, who held Casale and Pinerolo, had defeated his troops more than once. In the end, however, it turned out well for him, because the Sun King, wearied by the length of the conflict, and solely to win Victor Amadeus away from the League, ceded him the two fortresses.

It was during the wars of succession that the Savoys achieved their diplomatic masterstroke. In the War of the Spanish Succession, Victor Amadeus II reached the height of shameless opportunism: he began the war as an ally of France and finished it on the other side. When Turin was besieged in 1706 as a reprisal, he was saved by the arrival of his distant cousin of the Carignano branch of the family, Prince Eugene of Savoy, the terror of the Turks, and a military commander who had already refused a regiment in the army of Louis XIV to enter the service of the Austrian Emperor. Once again, having made the expedient decision at the right moment, Victor Amadeus sailed before the wind: the Treaty of Utrecht (1713) awarded him Montferrat and other territories, and the more ambivalent gift of a royal Crown. At first it was the Crown of Sicily, but after only seven years, in order to settle some international difficulties that had arisen, he was forced to relinquish the kingdom of Sicily in exchange for that of impoverished Sardinia.

The first Savoyard King finished his days as a prisoner in the castle of Moncalieri. In 1730 he had abdicated in favour of his son, Charles Emmanuel III; when later he changed his mind, the new King had his father arrested. Although he took part in the Wars of the Polish and Austrian Succession, Charles Emmanuel did not reach Milan, as he had hoped, but he did extend his boundaries as far as the River Ticino by the Treaty of Aix-la-Chapelle in 1748.

Unlike Milan, Florence, Naples and the other Italian towns which shared in the fervour of new enterprise blown into the peninsula on the reforming winds of the Enlightenment, the State of Savoy passed apathetically through the long peace between the Treaty of Aix-la-Chapelle and the Napoleonic invasion. Giovanni Battista Bogoni, the minister who had reformed the laws of Sardinia, was dismissed; the schools and society of Piedmont were dominated by the Jesuits, creating a climate in which the rising middle class felt no attachment to dynasty or Court. The livelier intellectuals preferred to live abroad. Turin's reaction when the French Revolution broke out was to become one of the chief centres of Italian Jacobinism. Against its exponents Victor Amadeus III (1773–96) took extreme measures. To help the French royalists, the sovereign allied himself with Austria, but mistrust was mutual. The Austrian Emperor was apprehensive of Savoyard fickleness, while the King of Sardinia suspected that his ally planned to recapture the territories lost during the wars of succession. Napoleon invaded and defeated them both. At the Armistice of Cherasco in 1796, Victor Amadeus III was forced to surrender Nice and Savoy and to allow Napoleon to occupy several fortresses as bases against Austria. Soon Piedmont, too, was annexed to France and her rulers took refuge in Sardinia to await events.

The Congress of Vienna treated the House of Savoy with generosity, restoring to it Piedmont with Savoy and Nice, in addition to all the territories of the vanished Republic of Genoa, not only from hatred of all that was republican but also to form strong buffer States along the borders of a still unsettled France. It is clear that Savoy's dominion was not, in fact, strengthened by these annexations, for Liguria was always to remain a centre of unrest, the land of Mazzini, Garibaldi and so many other enemies of the dynasty. It was, in any case, the only potential ally of the 'revolutionaries' (in other words, nationalists and liberals), who were well aware that to reach their objectives they would have to fight their Austrian overlords in the Italian peninsula.

Encouraged, however, by these decisions in his favour, Victor Emmanuel I (1802–21) returned from his island of exile on 20 May 1814, to a warm welcome from the war-weary population. He arrived in the Piazza Castello at Turin with his general staff. That night there were grand illuminations and the King drove through the streets till one o'clock in the morning. The King took the restoration at its face value. The courtiers' clocks had stopped when the French arrived. Now the royal entourage reopened the Court calendar where it had left off in 1798 and each returned to his former post – to see so many of them waxing fat in well-paid sinecures was not an edifying spectacle.

Everything introduced by Napoleon was destroyed: there was even a question of demolishing the new bridge over the Po until the Queen discovered that it shortened her way to church. Because it was Napoleonic, the civil code that France had extended to Piedmont was repealed and the old laws brought back, including the feudal trappings, the majorat (right of primogeniture), private tribunals, discriminatory laws against the Jews and the Waldensian sect, and privilege of clergy. Education became once more a Jesuit monopoly. The old punishments, too, the lash and strappado, were reinstated. There remained, to sustain a vague hope of future action, Savoy's ill-concealed antipathy to Austria (not unconnected with designs on Lombardy), which went hand-in-hand, however, with a stubborn aversion to all liberal ideas. When in 1821 the liberals rose in revolt and the army mutinied, Victor Emmanuel I, unwilling either to make concessions or to spill blood in repressing a movement in which so many patrician names were involved (those of the nobles who had come to terms with Napoleonic rule and had been appalled at the reactionary turnabout of 1814), left Turin, abdicating in favour of his brother Charles Felix. Since the latter was at Modena, he appointed as Regent his cousin of the Carignano branch, Charles Albert, who was in touch with the liberals at that time, and immediately granted their request for a constitution. All this occurred within a week, from 6 to 14 March.

Even before he reached Turin, however, Charles Felix repudiated the Regent's promise and, to help restore order, called in the Austrians, who stayed in Piedmont till 1823. In that same year Charles Albert went to Spain to extinguish by force of arms the last

sparks of revolt, making himself an object of hatred as the betrayer of Italian liberalism, but regaining the confidence of the King, who might have chosen another successor. Eight years later, on his cousin's death, he duly came to the throne.

The contrast between Charles Felix and Charles Albert is more apparent than real. The former, a true reactionary, was convinced that the world would soon be swept clean of all those – in his view – wicked and sacrilegious innovations introduced by the French Revolution and diffused throughout Europe by that adventurer Napoleon – the rascal, as he called him. Charles Albert's philosophy was also based on throne and altar, the divine right and absolute power of kings, care of his subjects being the ruler's Christian duty, but not the right of the people. His character, however, was considerably more complex. He belonged to a branch of the family which, separated from the main trunk for nearly two hundred years, regarded the dynasty with a critical eye. He, too, was critical, but only on behalf of the more modern brands of absolutism he had seen in action under later Napoleonic rule. His long years in opposition had taught him to hide his true convictions.

Born in 1798, he spent his youth in Paris and Geneva, far removed from the mouldering Court of Savoy. He had been an officer in the Imperial dragoons and Napoleon had honoured him with the title of count. The romantic atmosphere surrounding his early years left him with an irrepressible longing for glory, to satisfy which only one path seemed open to him: to wrest the land from Austrian domination and to form a kingdom of Northern Italy. Inspired by these projects he let his praises be sung as 'the sword of Italy'.

'Defy the challenge of the foreign horde,
Spring to the saddle and unsheathe your sword!'

But, in view of the disparity between his forces and those of Austria, he had no choice but to ally himself with the enemies of the Hapsburgs – and in Italy that meant the abhorred liberals, if not the republicans. Hence his eternal indecision and political contradictions. Yet another kind of torment wracked his soul. At nineteen years of age he had married the sixteen-year-old Austrian Archduchess Maria Theresa of Hapsburg-Lorraine, but after three months he was already tired of her and sought consolation elsewhere. Seized by scruples of conscience, he would repent, only to start his infidelities once more. He kept his love letters in his prayer-book.

Although he did not understand the necessity of including the rising middle classes in his government, Charles Albert carried out some useful reforms along the lines of eighteenth-century enlightened despotism. But when, in 1848, he was forced into the agonizing decision of granting his country a constitution in order

Emmanuel Philibert, Duke of Savoy (1553–80), known as Ironhead. He restored the Savoyard State and moved its capital from Chambéry in Savoy across the Alps to Turin.

to secure liberal support against Austria, he had to seek advice from his confessor in order to overcome his last scruples, since he feared that to abrogate the principle of divine right might be a mortal sin.

Matters did not go well. He succeeded in forestalling and curbing the republican and independence movements in Italy, but at the price of a fatal lull in operations, a brake on the advance of democracy, political intrigues, and a pressure for annexation that infuriated the people of Lombardy and Venetia and contributed to the ultimate victory of Austria. Following the disastrous defeat at Novara on 23 March 1849, the King declared his regret at not having 'found death on the field of battle', left his throne to his son Victor Emmanuel II, and died soon afterwards in exile at Oporto.

The new King, the last of Sardinia and the first of all Italy, was at his most successful in the areas of his four dominating passions: women and the hunt, war and politics. This last was a somewhat rare gift in rulers, especially of the dynasty in question, whose motto was 'one Savoyard rules at a time', and who considered the hereditary principle no concern of the people. He was given to chasing girls – especially peasant girls – from his early youth (and, indeed, he never gave up the chase). It was one way of escaping from his father's dismal and boring Court, run on the lines of a barracks, with its official balls as merry as funerals. Of his education by a regiment of clerics he declared, 'I never learnt anything that mattered' and his class reports confirm that impression, especially in comparison to those of his brother Ferdinand, Duke of Genoa. He was good at physical exercises but was tone-deaf: it was said that the only music he enjoyed was the rumble of cannons. In spite of these defects, Victor – in the final analysis – was the only one of the four Savoyard Kings of Italy who had true majesty, even if a touch of barbarism made him appear more like an ancient Lombard chief than a European monarch.

On occasion the King could be violent. When, after his death, an inventory was taken of his bedroom furniture, a fragmented walking-stick was found bearing a label in his handwriting that said: 'This stick was broken on the back of don Margotti to thank him for what he wrote about Rosina.' Don Margotti, editor of *L'Armonia*, was found one night beaten and bleeding on his own doorstep; Rosina Vercellana, the daughter of an army drum-major, was the King's mistress in 1847. Sometimes brusque in his manner, at other times jolly and good-natured, he cared little for etiquette and was at ease with his people, yet never forgot he was King and far above them. Victor was rather corpulent, with something of the air of a D'Artagnan. When he visited London in 1855, Queen Victoria was struck by his rolling eye and quantities of hair. 'His moustache and side-whiskers grow together in the most *peculiar* way,' she wrote in her diary: she would have been surprised to learn that Cavour and d'Azeglio had persuaded him to shorten his handlebar moustache by several centimetres so as not to alarm her. Later in life he took to dyeing his hair to conceal the advancing grey.

He was King of Sardinia from 1849 to 1861, and of Italy from 1861 to 1878, and it was in his reign that the *Risorgimento* drew to its conclusion. He survived a difficult beginning, the change in the constitution, the Genoa revolt and the bitter pill of a peace treaty that allowed Austrian troops into Alessandria. Being of an authoritarian cast of mind, he had no sooner mounted the throne than he dismissed the governor in charge and appointed as Prime Minister de Launay, a reactionary general with Austrian leanings. It was not long, however, before he realized how much the maintenance of the constitution would lessen the influence of Mazzini by attracting the nationalists and liberals of other Italian States away from him and towards the policy of Piedmont. The myth of the 'upright King, the creator of unified Italy', was born. He made it possible for d'Azeglio's government, and still more for that of Cavour, to develop the new institutions necessary for putting the new constitution into full effect. There were considerable psychological difficulties to be overcome, as when the proposed laws on the religious orders gave rise to a series of family quarrels. The clerics (with the support of the Queen and Queen Mother, whom the liberals contemptuously referred to as the 'Austrians') worked on his superstitious mind to convince him that these quarrels were signs of the wrath of God. Later, when Rome was removed from the Pope's jurisdiction, he found himself in sad conflict with his deeply religious daughter, Clothilde, his 'Chichina', the apple of his eye; he was excommunicated.

The King's reputation was enhanced by the Two-year War of 1859–61, the 'heroic age' which helped to establish his reign. Everything was at stake. Either he would be reduced to plain 'Mr Savoy' or become King of all Italy. Through the Crimean expedition and the Congress of Paris – to say nothing of the bartering away of Nice and Savoy, and the sacrifice of Chichina, married so young to Prince Joseph Charles Bonaparte, an irreligious playboy known as Plon-Plon – he succeeded in forming an alliance with Napoleon III. Nevertheless, in none of his confrontations did he adopt a servile attitude. Thus, in the second War of Independence, Custozza and Novara were finally reconquered. The King was not a great military commander but he had no fear of danger. On the battlefield of Palestro the admiring Zouaves called him their corporal, and for twenty years after that day his name was included in the evening roll-call as 'Corporal Victor Emmanuel of Savoy', to which the sergeant-major would reply 'absent on duty as King of Italy'. On 8 June 1859 the dynasty's ancient dream came true at last, and he rode into Milan as a conqueror at the side of the Emperor of France.

Two years later, on 17 March, the unification of the peninsula was proclaimed and Victor assumed the title of King of Italy, but refused to change his numerical attribute II into I. Thus the first King of Italy was a 'second': so as not to offend his ancestors, he said. In reality it was the victory of the monarchic-annexationist policy over popular revolution. The unity of Italy was achieved by bringing to perfection the Savoyard artichoke-eating method. This involved consuming one leaf after the other, that is to say, by a

series of more or less forcible annexations (irrespective of whether or not the dethroned sovereigns were relations of Victor Emmanuel), so that far from being the amalgamation of constituent parts that Mazzini had foreseen, it was simply an extension of the kingdom of Sardinia. The sole concession made by Victor Emmanuel to the ideology of the 'revolution' was to accept the idea of being King not only 'by the grace of God', but also 'by the will of the people', which did not hinder the remorseless process of

Emmanuel Philibert led the Spanish army to victory over the French and so earned the restoration of the duchy, although diminished, at the peace of Cateau-Cambrésis in 1559.

'Piedmontization' of the new nation that followed.

His co-operation with Cavour, which he saw as a compromise with the traditional forces of moderation, ran a stormy course. He looked with a jaundiced eye on the transformation of the new regime from 'constitutional' – in which he wanted to follow the Prussian model – to 'parliamentary'. 'Ministers come and go. The King remains,' was one of his maxims. The constitution – which it remained for him, since he had not rescinded it – clearly allowed the supremacy of the

head of State over Parliament. He had no intention of renouncing any fraction of prerogative. Victor Emmanuel pursued his own policies which, in view of the royal power he enjoyed, do not always appear to have been well considered or wise. He also tended to conduct affairs behind the backs of his ministers, especially when he plotted rebellion in Galicia, the Balkans and Transylvania (using his own ambassadors and his own spies, some of whom were ex-lovers of his, and also by liaising with Mazzini), in order to

find thrones for his children, until Amadeus settled himself on the Spanish, and Maria Pia on the Portuguese one. He recongnized the expediency of a truce with Garibaldi before even Cavour, and, once the latter was dead, managed to advance his personal policies still further, often in conflict with the president of the council. Nevertheless, he was always able to find devoted ministers: Ricasoli, Rattazzi, Minghetti, Lamarmora, Lanza, Sella, Depretis and Visconti-Venosta were all loyal servants in spite of their King's disdain for correct constitutional procedures.

He was utterly prosaic ('Scipio's helmet,' he used to say, 'is handy for making pasta'), and felt homesick away from his beloved Turin. When the capital was moved to Florence, he declared passionately to Minghetti that he, the King, was the only person being made to pay for the operation.'I am the one who has always lived here with all my childhood memories, my habits and my loves.' In 1870, against all political good-sense, he wanted to rush to the aid of Napoleon III, who had given him such valuable support in 1859, and was only restrained with difficulty by Lanza, who threatened to resign, and Sella. However, he did not show the same gratitude towards Garibaldi, who nevertheless remained under the King's spell and went on believing that he had no part in the events that led the Italian government to order attacks on the guerilla chief and his arrest. The fact was that the King despised the 'common rabble' (by which he meant the 'brigands' from the south, the workers and peasants oppressed by taxation, or the Irredentists who upset his relations with Vienna), of which he considered Garibaldi to be the representative.

He disliked staying in Rome and seldom went there, maintaining that it stank of cooked cabbage. In reality he did not feel cut out for life in the new capital. He did

not get on well with the Roman aristocracy, the 'black' (the clerical or Papal) section of which had fiercely opposed the advent of the Savoyards. He had no presentable wife, for after his Queen, Maria Adelaide of Austria, had died, he had married the beautiful Rosina Vercellana, whom he created Countess of Mirafiori and Fontanafredda. He left his son Umberto as commandant at Rome, accompanied by his daughter-in-law, Margherita. He himself lived at Mandria in Piedmont with Rosina and the Mirafiori children, intervening in the political sphere with ever more sudden, yet effective, decisions, confined almost entirely to foreign affairs and the army. He thought Italy should be militarily formidable to enable her to pursue a strong foreign policy, and that when a leftist government came to power, his direct involvement in those two sectors would reassure foreign powers that chaos did not reign in Italy. Besides, what could these middle-class governments of the Left ever understand of foreign and military affairs? (Nevertheless, he concerned himself with the so-called 'parliamentary revolution' which in 1876 secured the ultimate defeat of the historic Right, and brought in the leftist ministry of Depretis. He was even among those that encouraged this turning point, for to increase military expenditure and enlarge the civil list was just what he wanted – Victor Emmanuel was notoriously spendthrift – and he hoped that the Left would not place too many obstacles in his way.)

In his last years he was tired, irritable and idle. He dreamed of 'crowning his days with a victory' (according to Crispi, who was paying him a visit), and considered conducting a war in the Balkans, over the Eastern Question. With the end of the Second Empire in France and of the Papal States, with the rise of Prussia and the fall of the historic Right, his old world had fallen to pieces. A gypsy had told him that he would die in the Quirinale Palace, which for that reason he avoided: the prophecy came true on 9 January 1878. He seemed to have contracted an ordinary chill and no one expected the end. He was only fifty-seven years old.

> 'Let us bow down on the frozen tomb
> That holds the body of King Manuel
> Who first wed Italy to liberty'

sang one of the many poets inspired by the departure of the Father of his Country. But where should that tomb be? The death of a King of Italy was no simple matter. Turin claimed the mortal remains of its former sovereign to inter them at Superga with his ancestors, but Crispi proposed the Pantheon for his last resting place, and got his way. The new King, Umberto, softened the blow to Turin's pride by presenting the town with 'the dear and glorious mementoes', that is to say, his father's medals, the sword dented with the

blows it had warded off, and the plumed helmet surmounted by a golden eagle. This was only one of the controversies that ushered in the new reign, others being the debate over the burial place, the clash with the Vatican, which refused to countenance the obsequies of the excommunicated King in any of the four great churches of Rome, the impressive funeral procession followed by a week's lying-in-State in the mortuary chapel of the Quirinale. The dead King's cheek was marked with a large stain: a clumsy embalmer had spilt on it some of the dye intended for the beard.

The funeral was the first move in the deliberate construction of the 'Great King legend', designed to mean as much to Italy as Pius IX did to the Catholics, or Garibaldi to the democrats. Certainly Victor Emmanuel II was far more praised and popularized after death than in life, with a secular canonization culminating in the huge and ugly Victor Emmanuel monument in Rome. He had known how to play the

Charles Albert, of the Carignano branch, which
originated in the seventeenth century. He became King
of Sardinia in 1831 through the extinction of the direct
line at the death of Charles Felix.

part expected of him and he had probably guessed that
his life would be mythologized, and therefore wanted
some of his letters returned to him. Years later, when a
member of the fascist quadrumvirate, de Vecchi di Val
Cismon, became Director of the Institute of
Risorgimento History, he represented the old King as
a precursor of Mussolini because he distrusted
Parliaments, was a militarist, a champion of Italian
aggrandizement and against the 'little Italy' policy.
This picture of him as a proto-fascist is as false as the
one representing him as a liberal and a fervent
supporter of the constitution.

Unlike his father, Umberto decided to be I rather
than IV, as he was in the order of Savoy princes bearing
his name; assuming implicitly the continuation of his
sovereignty, he felt no need to dissolve the Chamber of
Deputies. There were only two intervals of democracy:
even Victor Emmanuel II had introduced his reign in
1849 with a show of democracy (more show than
reality, for his opposition to Radetsky was merely to
promote the legend, when, during the negotiations
leading up to the Armistice of Vignale, the latter called
for the abrogation of the Constitution); while the
beginning of Victor Emmanuel III's reign was to seem
very democratic in comparison with the last years of
Umberto. To start on the Left and finish on the Right
became the recurring pattern of the kings of Italy.

The Crown passed from Victor Emmanuel II to

Umberto I at a critical moment. The son did not enjoy
the same prestige as his father who – turning even his
defeats to good account – had lost Lombardy and then
Venetia to the Austrians, the south to the Bourbons
and Rome to the Pope. Neighbouring France was now
a Republic, and there were some at Court who feared
that Italy was coming to the same conclusion. This
situation suited the Pope, who saw it as the prelude to a
general collapse that would lead to the return of
temporal power to the papacy: Pius IX had reacted to
Umberto's accession with a diplomatic note renewing
his protests against the 'iniquitous despoliation' of the
Church. There were other signs of unrest in the
country: governments were unstable; at Florence a
bomb was thrown at the procession returning from the
Great King's funeral, the attack, though anonymous,
being clearly a protest from the submerged Italy that
ate black bread and had no vote; the aged Garibaldi
sent a message deploring the cost of military fortifications, royal palaces and Crown possessions. The
nation was isolated and Austria replied to Irredentist
demonstrations by organizing army manoeuvres in the
Tyrol. The sailors of Trieste cried, 'Death to Umberto!'

'King of Italy – the very idea ages one,' declared
Umberto. He was neither cut out nor prepared for such
problems. With little learning, and no experience, he

nevertheless had other interests: horses and women were his passions, too.

His married life was not happy Margherita had married the position rather than the man. She was Umberto's first cousin, being the daughter of Ferdinand, Duke of Genoa, and had inherited German blood through her mother, a Princess of Saxony. Margherita possessed a very strong sense of royalty and, once on the throne, made it her mission to keep the King's prestige as high as possible. She loved culture and, although she, too, was somewhat lacking in education she spoke French and German, read Dante, studied art and music, wrote novels and verses. An intellectual was indeed a novelty in the House of Savoy and in striking contrast to her husband.

In spite of the absence of conjugal love between them, Margherita had a great influence on the King, helping him to overcome his aristocratic indolence and be easier in his dealings with those around him. Margherita would have been the ideal consort for a pre-French Revolution King, absolute, paternal, solicitous of his people and especially of his soldiers. Her lack of sympathy with the liberal-democratic system that was evolving with so much difficulty during those years was total, even though she was fairly adept at concealing her true sentiments.

Married in 1868, Umberto and Margherita had a son, Victor Emmanuel – their only child – born in the following year. They arranged for him to be born in Naples to secure the allegiance of the South, especially of the Neapolitan nobles who still hankered after their kings. When the municipality of Naples presented the royal parents with a cradle made of tortoiseshell, mother-of-pearl and coral, in appalling taste but costing a great sum raised by subscriptions from schoolchildren, Umberto was assailed by angry Italian critics.

Given the new royal couple's high standards regarding the practical details and outward appearance of the royal office, it is easy to imagine what thought and care they bestowed on the official tour of the peninsula in the late summer of 1878. Already, ten years previously, Umberto and his wife had shown themselves on the occasion of their marriage, halting at the old capitals of central Italy, Piacenza, Parma, Modena, Bologna and then Florence, where the mayor, the Marquis Ginori, had offered the seventeen-year-old bride a marguerite wrought in diamonds, the beginning of the 'margaretization' of Italy. A second stage in the journey brought them to Genoa and Venice, a third to Naples, Messina and Palermo. Everywhere they went there were endless processions,

Victor Emmanuel II at a sitting of Parliament in Turin, painted by Tetar van Elvan. Politically gifted, Victor Emmanuel associated himself with the unification of Italy, in which he played an important part.

rains of flowers, fairy-tale tournaments. Now that they were King and Queen the magnificence was even greater, the travelling still more intensive.

Everywhere the royal couple were greeted with enthusiasm due mostly to the Queen's popularity. And she did her best to become inconspicuous and take second place, hoping that some of her popularity would be passed on to the King.

At Naples, the last stop of the tour, an unforeseen event disturbed the festivities. The anarchist Giovanni Passanante, an unemployed cook, sprang out of the crowd and flung himself at the door of the royal carriage. The moment passed in a flash. The Queen threw the mass of flowers that lay in her lap at the assailant's face crying, 'Cairoli, save the King!' The

Prime Minister seized Passanante by the hair and gave him an ugly cut on the leg. Umberto escaped with a graze on the arm, and continued his royal progress as if nothing had happened. In fact a great deal had happened: the Queen, a considerable inventor of slogans, announced shortly afterwards that 'the spell of the royal House was broken', while the King, back in his palace, as matter-of-fact as his father, remarked with some wit, 'Let us go to table; we'd better not keep the cooks waiting now we know what they're capable of!' He was a soldier and behaved as well here as he had on the field of Villafranca during the 1860 war. Nevertheless, the encounter with Passanante had left him with those wide-open eyes that Olimpia Savio described as 'scared'. Later he took to wearing a

Victor Emmanuel II, King of Italy, receiving Garibaldi at the Quirinale Palace. It is to his credit that he saw the value of an agreement with Garibaldi, earlier and more fully than Cavour, at a crucial moment of the Risorgimento.

corselet of chain mail against the day when the assassin would exchange his romantic dagger for the more functional revolver. The immediate political consequence of the attempt was the fall of the Prime Minister, Cairoli-Zanardelli, who had tried to replace rule from above by the correct application of liberal principles: he fell because Parliament accused him of allowing republican associations to survive and attack the king and the establishment.

Under Queen Margherita – who soon won over most of the 'black' nobility that had opposed the Savoy entry into Rome – the Quirinale became the most brilliant court in Europe. Even members of the leftist party, the 'barbarians' who did not know how to dance, came to its receptions as a matter of course. The Queen also had her 'salon', frequented by the nobility, officers, and, above all, men of culture and members of the right-wing party, extreme opponents of the official policies. The King was bored by the conversation of these earnest men and seldom attended his wife's receptions.

There was another area in which the prestige of the Crown was high – that of national calamity. Umberto's reign was stricken with disasters such as earthquakes and cholera epidemics. The King always hastened to the scene. Unlike the treacherous and complex field of politics, here he knew what he had to do and did it without hesitation. Endowed with a certain fatalism, he ignored advice to avoid risk of contagion. The country admired him, the Queen was proud of him; he was a generous giver and earned the title of 'the good King.' His ambition, however, like his father's, was centred on foreign policy. He aspired to pursue the policy of a great nation, to abandon the renunciatory formula of 'emerging with clean hands'. In 1882, Italy entered into the Triple Alliance with Germany and Austria. The pact was a reaction to French imperialism (France's occupation of Tunisia) and brought the country out of its isolation. But for Umberto and Margherita, who had long urged the government in that direction, it was simply a pact between crowned heads, which would secure the four objectives they had most at heart: the building of a monarchical barrier across Europe, a sort of international league against the 'great beast' (the anarchists and republicans, not forgetting that 'sly fox', the Vatican, lying in wait); a justification for increasing military expenditure (which in 1882 amounted to 172 million lire and in 1895 rose to 326 million) and strengthening the army; providing a means of ensuring internal order in the face of the 'subversive elements'; and the promotion of an expansionist policy. Umberto lavished every care on his army, never missing a review or manoeuvre, fighting with unexpected energy against any proposal for its reduction, himself choosing the ministers for the various armed forces. To bring the Triple Alliance safely into harbour he travelled to Vienna in 1881 (a visit never returned) and did not hesitate, having been appointed colonel-in-chief of the Von Benedek 28th Infantry Regiment – a regiment that had fought against the Italians at Novara and Custozza – to wear its uniform at gala dinners and Court concerts. It was an insult to the memory of the *Risorgimento*. From that moment Irredentism became a problem, the republican Oberdan writing on the walls of his house, 'Down with the Austrian colonel!' In these circumstances, making it impossible for the House of Savoy to follow the popular anti-Hapsburg policy, where could he turn for glory? The answer was Africa. Umberto encouraged Crispi's imperial dreams by having the coinage stamped with a portrait of himself as Emperor of Abyssinia. But on 1 March 1896 came the disaster of Adowa. It was a mortal blow to the King's prestige, one that he sought in vain to soften by the marriage ceremonies of the hereditary Prince in October of that year: 'No festivities,' wrote Carducci, 'as long as the shame and damage last.' There was no more respect for Umberto in conversations after that. His closest colleagues mistrusted him because he was inconstant and a 'sieve'; the republican news-sheets discussed his civil list, one of the largest in Europe, with irreverence. On 22 April 1897 a blacksmith, Pietro Acciarito, attempted to emulate Passanante, hurling himself on the King, who was on his way to the royal Derby at Capanelle.

269

Victor Emmanuel II entering Venice after the city's annexation, painted by Induno. In his last years, before his death in 1878, he would have liked 'to crown his days with a victory'.

Umberto seemed oppressed and aging; he fell asleep during audiences; Farini, the President of the Senate, had to follow him out hunting if he wanted to discuss public affairs. The frequent absences of the King provided food for gossip, because now, in addition to his first love, Eugenia, he was frequenting the 'fatal Countess', Vincenza di Santafiora. Another breath of scandal scorched him when the Bank of Rome failed and it was discovered that one of its more foolhardy operations had been the rescue of the Banca Tiberina in which Eugenia had invested her money. In 1898 he conferred, on his own initiative, the cross of the Grand Military Order of Savoy on General Bava Beccaris, who had regarded himself as upholding the honour of the army when he gave the order to fire on the unarmed people of Milan protesting against the price of bread.

Umberto now began to entertain the idea of a *coup d'état*, challenging the legality of the existing constitution, but that plan was scotched by elections. On 29 July 1900, at Monza, Gaetano Bresci, an anarchist from America, avenged the dead of Adowa and Milan by shooting the King in the back. Umberto had not worn his chain-mail corselet that day because the weather was so hot.

Victor Emmanuel III succeeded to the throne. His mother had tried to bring him up to be very different from his father: serious, firm in his decisions, a Savoyard, at last, who was cultured, regal in his bearing. She would have liked him to be handsome and dashing too, like a Renaissance nobleman, but in that she was thwarted by his awkward appearance. He was a tiny man, with such short legs that the minimum height for an officer had to be lowered to one metre fifty, so that he should not be disqualified from entering the army of which he was commander-in-chief. His parents entrusted his education to the severe Colonel Osio, who had been military attaché in Berlin and admired the Prussian model. The finished product was a young Prince who could speak foreign languages, understand dynasties and heraldry, had studied history, especially the military kind, and knew the army regulations. But he lacked imagination. Insecure but obstinate, he was endowed with a strong sense of duty, adhered strictly to timetables, and was indeed something of a fusspot. His hobbies were coin-collecting, shooting, fishing and sailing about in his yacht. Unlike his mother, he was bored with music other than military, did not care for the arts, disliked Crispi with his African dreams, feared yet despised the Germans, and ignored all religious problems. He shared, however, her urge to defend the credit and interests of the Crown and her mistrust of democratic ways. His education had done little to help him understand the society he had been called upon to rule. It had not rid him of his Piedmontese disregard of the South, his anti-feminism or his feeling against Jews.

Unwillingly, he accepted the office of sovereign which his birth as only son had so peremptorily thrust on him. He took refuge instead in the privacy of family life with the Montenegrin Princess Elena Petrovic, sturdy and above normal height, whom he married in 1896. She, too, lacked a regal appearance, but she was affectionate, a good mother and adhered confidently to her simple principles.

Crispi was delighted with a marriage which seemed full of promise for Italian expansion in the Balkans,

270

even though the kingdom of Montenegro was recent, small and unimportant. The more ambitious supporters of dynastic policy, however, spoke of the 'marriage to the dried figs'; Kaiser William II called Elena 'the daughter of that rascally swine of Montenegro', while Princess Helen of Aosta referred to 'my cousin, the shepherdess', hurting the Hereditary Prince's feelings so that he withdrew still further into himself. His wife's relations were considered even more insupportable.

In his speech from the throne on his accession after the assassination at Monza, he expressed his intention of placing his trust in Parliament and the constitution. This plain and simple declaration brought new hope after the crises and reactionary moves of the previous years. On the death of Saracco, he appointed Zanardelli as Prime Minister, and in 1903, Giolitti – the two bugbears of Umberto's Court. People began to speak of a 'liberal monarchy' and then of 'socialism', referring to the carrying out of Giolitti's programme of

reform. It was undoubtedly the best period of Victor Emmanuel's reign, the King was on cordial terms with his Prime Minister, and they conversed together in the Piedmontese dialect and were agreed on entirely divesting the Triple Alliance of its extremist character. Giolitti left him practically no problems to solve, and he lived contentedly dividing his days between the Quirinale, where much of the once celebrated pomp had been stripped from the public ceremonies, and where he worked in his office like a bureaucrat, and the Villa Ada in the Via Salaria, separated from the outside world by a high wall.

There was little life at Court, few contacts with the aristocracy, which was passing through an economic and social crisis, but a great deal of home life. Children had been born to the royal couple at last, sadly disappointing the hopes of the hateful Aosta cousins, who were the heirs presumptive to the throne. Then, in 1904, came a son, Umberto. The children were brought up very freely, spending as much time as possible in the open air of the park, when dynastic needs did not supervene. Their grandmother, Margherita, used to lament that Elena taught her daughters to knit and make cushions and cakes, but not to 'be princesses', so she was very pleased when the schooling of her favourite grandchild, Umberto, was put into the hands of Admiral Bonaldi, a tutor with barrack-room ideas of education, reminiscent of Colonel Osio.

The accord between King and Prime Minister ended with the outbreak of the First World War. Giolitti was a neutralist, but the King was eager for intervention on the side of Britain and France, ignoring the advice of his mother who, with her clear reactionary vision, foresaw with dread that war might bring with it the collapse of central authority and the advance of democratic ideas. Victor Emmanuel was for intervention because he wanted the completion of Italy's unity, but also because he could not bear the two Emperors to whom he had been bound by the Triple Alliance. To inveigle the country into war, he allied himself with the

section of the populace that was inflamed with the ideas of d'Annunzio and Mussolini, working events in such a way that Parliament, in which the majority was neutralist, voted for war. In this breakaway from constitutional orthodoxy, many historians see Italy's first step on the road to fascism. During the war, having made his uncle, the Duke of Genoa, Regent, he amused himself among his troops, taking hundreds of photographs. The newspapers called him the 'soldier King'. It was he who, after the rout of Caporetto in 1917, impressed his new allies by taking up his defensive position on the River Piave rather than the Po.

Italy in the time of Giolitti was no bed of roses: the electoral methods used by the government, the awakening of the proletariat, the growing misery of southern Italy, and the despairing crowds of emigrants were all symptoms of a desperate situation, the echoes of which penetrated even the muffled drawing-rooms of the Court. Three events shook the King: the revolver shots fired at the royal carriage by the young anarchist mason, Antonio d'Alba, on 14 March 1912; the 'red week' two years later, when the cities of Emilia and the Campagna hoisted the republican flag; and the collapse of so many thrones after the war. Lastly, he had become accustomed to the suspension of constitutional freedoms during the war, and this tipped the balance. With the workers roused by the saga of the Russian Revolution (the Red Peril), the returning soldiers demanding the fulfilment of the promises made, and the treasury emptied by the Libyan enterprise and the Great War, the King began to think that 'government by the sword', so dear to his father, was not such a bad idea after all. He was ready for fascism. Then, on the night of 27 October 1922, having hamstrung the head of government by declaring a stage of siege, he went back on his own signed undertaking, deliberately turned against the government in office, and opened the way to the march on Rome by a minority party. He himself stayed at San Rossore, ostensibly on holiday but, in fact, keeping an eye not so much on his mother, who made no attempt to conceal her sympathy for the blackshirts, as on his Aosta cousin, who, if Victor put a foot wrong, might well seize the Crown.

In no time the fascist government had become a dictatorship. After the Matteotti affair, during which the King remained deaf to all appeals from the opposition, he took Mussolini with him to recuperate at San Rossore. He was convinced that the old ruling class, now swept aside, was worthless and would never get back on its feet. During the next twenty years, the King and the President of the Council met regularly twice a week to discuss government business.

The King, for his part, had an inferiority complex before the glaring eye, jutting chin and political fantasies of this pugnacious peasant from the Romagna, and accepted everything with apathy: the despoiling of the constitution by the abolition of the parliamentary system, the suppression of parties and the freedom of the Press, the establishment of the militia and the Grand Fascist Council, the alliance with the Germans whom he loathed and, finally, the war. It is difficult to understand the reasons for so much renunciation. Even the Crowns that fascism added to his own (the Crowns of Ethiopia and Albania, as well as the kingdom of Croatia for one of his Savoy relations, Aimone of Spoleto) hardly account for such total passivity, especially as they did not come till later. Clearly the regime suited him: the trains ran to time, the people were kept in order, the country gained in prestige.

Suppressing his former anarchistic feelings and confining himself to the private invective so deligently recorded in the 'diary' of Galeazzo Ciano, Mussolini was respectful to the King, but kept him out of the limelight which Victor Emmanuel, in any case, preferred to avoid. Their relationship ran into difficulties only in matters that affected prerogatives of the Crown, principally on four occasions: when the Grand Council regulated the succession to the throne; at the institution of the marshalcy of the Empire, which placed King and Duce on the same level; when it was observed that the coat-of-arms displayed on the flag of conquered Albania was not that of the House of Savoy; and when, in 1940, the Duce claimed the supreme command of the armed forces, a post which the constitution had assigned to the monarch. There was talk of a diarchy, and in external appearances that was true enough, since the 'Royal March' was balanced by *Giovinezza*, the army by the fascist militia, the arms of Savoy by the lictorian fasces, the cuirassiers by the musketeers, the royally-appointed Senate by the fascist Chamber of Deputies, the Quirinale by the Palazzo Venezia, and whereas King saluted with hand to hat, the Duce did so with outstretched arm. In reality, the more the King gave way to him, the greater grew Mussolini's sphere of influence. Victor Emmanuel's prestige fell ever lower.

Visiting Calabria and Sicily towards the end of 1941, the King suddenly realized that Italy was standing on the edge of the abyss. He heard the rumbling of anarchy, saw with his own eyes the indiscipline and lack of resources; to his intimates he painted the blackest picture of the situation. He wanted the Italian troops recalled from Russia to defend their own frontiers, and advised Mussolini, when he left for a meeting with Hitler at Salzburg, not to insist on his claims to Nice, Savoy and Corsica. He was gradually becoming aware of the necessity of disengagement. Pietro Acquarone, minister to the royal family, was already working in that direction. He was deep in a conspiracy with Ciano and Grandi, and with some members of the aristocracy and the old anti-fascists, even though the King still despised these and called them phantoms and ghosts. The most difficult task facing Acquarone was to persuade the King to act.

In the late afternoon of 25 July 1943, Mussolini went to Villa Ada for the last time to bring the King the report of the Grand Council session. The King had finally decided: he considered that the dictator had been dismissed. On the way out Mussolini found the *carabinieri* waiting for him with a motor ambulance, 'for protective purposes', the King assured him. But the Queen disapproved: Savoyard hospitality, she said, must never be associated with setting a trap for arrest. What to do with Mussolini now? There was temptation in the highest quarters to rid themselves of their problem by giving him a discreet push into the sea during the voyage to the island of Ponza. Even the King rejected that idea, saying that Mussolini might still prove useful. For him the best solution seemed to be to retain fascism, but without its former leader. During the ensuing Badoglian era, he was completely opposed to the restoration of party government or any serious cleaning-up of the country's affairs, realizing that a genuine enquiry into the regime could only bring trouble and new responsibilities. On 8 September he slipped away with his family, Badoglio, and a group of generals along the Via Tiburtina to embark on his corvette *Baionetta* and sail away to Brindisi.

'The King's Italy', over which he and his government exercized authority with the consent of the Allies, numbered no more than two million inhabitants. Even so, Victor Emmanuel was unable to grasp that the situation had radically changed. He was still concerned with questions of protocol and prestige. The fascist journals depicted him in vulgar caricature; the parties and papers of anti-fascism attacked him with merciless severity, would not collaborate with him, and held him responsible for fascism and the war, a point carried to its conclusion by Togliatti who said, 'First let us root out the nazi-fascists, then we can deal with institutional questions.' Even monarchists such as Croce, de Nicola and Badoglio advised the King to abdicate. 'I shall not do that till the war is over,' he replied. In the end the Allies, convinced that he was nothing but an encumbrance, did whatever they wanted without consulting his wishes. He wanted to surrender his position to his son in Rome, but instead had to do so before the liberation of that city, which he was not allowed to enter; he had to leave the villa at Posillipo, which was his retreat, when George VI of England arrived in Naples. Sorrows were added to humiliation, for his daughter Mafalda died in Buchenwald and the Queen was losing her sight. On 9 May 1946 he abdicated in favour of his son, and that same evening left for Egypt, where King Farouk and Queen Fawzia

were awaiting him. He died on 28 December 1947 in the villa he had bought in Alexandria and rechristened Yela, the Montenegrin name of his wife.

Within eighteen months of Victor Emmanuel III's departure, Italy became a republic. Her last King, Umberto II, tried, during the flight to Ortona, to insist on returning to Rome to do his duty as a soldier. 'My God,' he cried, 'what a sorry figure I cut!' But his father would not allow it.

He became King by stages. On 5 June 1944 he was made Lieutenant General of the kingdom; he became King in the full sense of the word on 9 May 1946, less than a month before the referendum on the monarchy. In the current fervour of controversy, his father's abdication was interpreted as one last throw to change the way the game was going, to show the electorate a face less compromised by the past. And, indeed, Umberto had never been fascist or pro-German in his sentiments (nor did he appeal to the Germans, who thought him a fop. Himmler said of him: 'A year in the Hitler Youth Army might do him some good.'), but unfortunately his severely formal education had accustomed him to conform, and he had always given the impression of accepting the fascists. During the war he was Inspector of the Armed Forces, first on the Western and then on the Central-Southern front.

A tall, handsome, pleasant-mannered man, he recalled his ancestor, Charles Albert, in his mixture of the religious and the amorous. He was always 'between the sanctuary and the alcove', as Domenico Bartoli put it. During the very short time that fate allowed him to occupy the throne, the 'May King' displayed patience, good will and dignity, belying the reputation for foolishness his earlier years had left behind.

On the 2 June 1946 the referendum ended the reign of the House of Savoy. Thirteen million voted for a republic, less than two million for the monarchy. Torn between the government of De Gasperi, which considered the matter closed, and his advisers, who quibbled as to the meaning of the expression 'voting electorate' (on the grounds that, if blank and spoiled voting papers were counted, the republic did not have a majority), King Umberto did not propose to relinquish his rights. He wanted to wait for the verdict of the court of appeal, entered into arguments with the government and altogether made a poor exit, leaving behind a proclamation in which he spoke of 'an affront to the laws'. It must be said, however, that he rejected the extremists' advice to revoke the Cabinet's mandate, transfer its powers to the minister to the royal family and retire to Naples (the South had voted in favour of the monarchy) to control the situation from there. 'I do not want a throne stained with blood,' he replied. At four o'clock in the afternoon of 13 June he boarded an aeroplane and joined his family in Portugal. He is at present living in Cascais.

Victor Emmanuel III with the minister Salandra among the troops at the front in 1915, by Beltrame. He came to the throne in 1900 and when he died in exile, Italy had been a republic for a year and a half.

Third Interlude

THE ROLE OF THE QUEENS

Few queens ruled in their own right rather than as queen consorts; there were only sixteen among the dynasties included in this book, seven queens of England, four in the Romanov dynasty and only five in all the other dynasties together. Three of the English queens followed each other on the throne without a break. In 1553 the dying Tudor King, Edward VI, named Jane Grey as his heir, but after only thirteen days she was overthrown by Mary Tudor, known as Bloody Mary, who reigned until 1558. She was succeeded by her younger half-sister Elizabeth I, the only unmarried queen in the history of Europe, who reigned for forty-five years until 1603. Elizabeth's contemporary, Mary Stuart, was Queen of the Scots from 1542 to 1568, so that within the space of half a century Britain contained at least three female sovereigns. After Elizabeth I there were two Stuart queens on the English throne: Mary, the elder daughter of James II, who, with her husband William of Orange, came to the throne in 1689, and her younger sister Anne (1702–14). More than a hundred years passed before another woman ruled Britain; Victoria came to the throne in 1837 and ruled until 1901, sixty-four years. The seventh English queen is Elizabeth II, crowned in 1953 and still reigning.

The four czarinas of the Romanov dynasty all ruled in the eighteenth century but have little else in common. Catherine I (1725–7), a peasant of Polish origin from Lithuania whose original name was Martha Skavronska, had been the servant and mistress of Menshikov, the friend of Peter the Great. She succeeded in making the Czar fall in love with her and marry her in 1712, and when Peter died in 1725, she assumed power despite the opposition of the clergy and the boyars. Within a few years she was succeeded by Anna Ivanovna (1730–40), Elizabeth (1740–61) and Catherine II (1762–96), who was very different from her namesake. Catherine II was in fact a cultured German Princess who had been educated in France and was the friend of Voltaire,

Diderot and d'Alembert. This, however, did not prevent her from conspiring against her husband Peter III and probably arranging his death.

The other great 'enlightened' monarch, Catherine's contemporary, Maria Theresa of Hapsburg (1740–80), by succeeding to the throne, brought about a European war which lasted eight years, but from which she emerged victorious. Three Iberian sovereigns complete the picture: two queens of Portugal, Mary I (1777–1816) and Mary II (1826–53), and the Spanish Isabel II (1833–68), whose reign began with a civil war against the Carlists, supporters of her uncle Don Carlos, and ended in 1868 when a successful uprising forced her to flee to France and abdicate.

THE FATE OF THE DYNASTIES

The twentieth century has seen a great destruction of ruling houses; in little over half a century, between 1910 and 1975, eleven of the seventeen dynasties that used to govern Europe have been overthrown. Those that fell were the rulers of Portugal (1910), of Russia (1917), of the German and Austro-Hungarian Empires (1918), of Spain (1931), Albania (1939), Rumania (1940), Yugoslavia (1945), Bulgaria (1946), Italy (1946) and Greece (1975). Only the northern monarchies survived, those of Great Britain, Denmark, Sweden, Norway, Belgium and Holland, to which can be added the restored Spanish monarchy.

As many as eight of these eleven dynasties were overthrown in the upheavals of the two world wars. In the first, fell the ancient monarchies of the Romanovs, the Hohenzollerns and the Austrian Hapsburgs; in the second, the Italian and the Balkan monarchies. On 7 April 1939, Italian troops occupied Albania, forcing the King, Ahmed Zogu, to flee to Britain; in 1940, Carol II of Rumania was overthrown by a fascist coup d'état led by Antonescu; and in 1945 and 1946, with the setting up of popular governments, the Yugoslav and Bulgarian monarchies also fell.

Five of the 'great' dynasties have disappeared in this century (the Braganzas, Romanovs, Hohenzollerns, the Austrian Hapsburgs and the House of Savoy) and another four in the last (the French Bourbons, the Bonapartes, the Neapolitan Bourbons and the Brazilian Braganzas), and almost all were dramatically overturned. In previous centuries, however, several of the dynasties that disappeared did so through the natural extinction of the family line.

Four dynasties died out in this way, the Capetians with Charles IV in 1328, the Valois with Henry II in 1589, the Tudors with Elizabeth I in 1603, and the Spanish Hapsburgs with Charles II in 1700. In 1328 the succession to the French throne took place peacefully, the Capetians being followed by a younger branch, the Valois. 261 years later, when the last of the Valois,

Henry III, was stabbed to death by Jacques Clément, the accession of the Bourbon Henry IV was less peaceful; France was racked by terrible religious wars and the aspiring King, a Calvinist, could only win the Crown by converting to Catholicism. The succession of the Stuarts after the Tudors, whose line ended with the Virgin Queen Elizabeth, did not create immediate problems. On the other hand, the death of the last Spanish Hapsburg, Charles II, sparked off a war that involved all the great powers and lasted more than ten years.

Two dynasties were unwillingly compelled to stand down from the throne: the Stuarts in 1688, and the French Bourbons in 1830. The Stuart James II was forced to flee hastily to the Court of Louis XIV of France when his son-in-law, William of Orange, landed in England. On 27 July 1830 the people of Paris rose against the Bourbon Charles X, who had organized a coup d'état; forty-eight hours later, the King was forced to withdraw his oppressive measures and abdicate in favour of his grandson, the young Henry, Duke of Bordeaux. But it was too late; the chamber of deputies and that of peers, under pressure from the barricades, had already proclaimed the fall of the House of Bourbon and named Louis-Philippe, Duke of Orléans, to take charge of the realm.

Three times during the nineteenth century the fate of a monarch was decided by a war – in 1815, 1860 and 1870. The Bonapartes twice lost their throne by a terrible defeat, Waterloo in 1815 and Sedan in 1870. Ten years earlier, in 1860, it had been the turn of the Neapolitan Bourbons to pay the price of a ruinous military campaign with the loss of their throne, when their army was defeated by Garibaldi's irregulars.

Three dynasties were overturned by the three great revolutions of modern European history: the Stuarts in 1649 by the Puritans led by Oliver Cromwell, the Bourbons in 1792 by the French Revolution and the Romanovs in 1917 by the Russian Revolution. The Stuarts and the Bourbons lost power only temporarily, but both Charles I and Louis XVI were beheaded. After abdicating in his own name and that of the Czaravitch Alexis on 15 March 1917, Nicholas II, last of the Czars, was transferred to Siberia and executed with his whole family at Ekaterinburg on 16 July 1918.

In the first half of the twentieth century, five dynasties fell and were replaced by republics. Within the space of a few years the Braganzas lost the Crowns of Brazil and of Portugal; in 1889 Peter II, Emperor of Brazil, was overthrown by a revolt, and in 1910 Manuel II was ousted by republican and anti-clerical forces. In 1918 military defeat led to the collapse of the Austrian Hapsburgs and the Hohenzollerns. After the last allied offensive in October 1918, the Austro-Hungarian Empire disintegrated and the young Emperor Charles I on 18 October attempted in vain to transform his dominions into a federal Empire. Hapsburg power ceased to exist when, from 29 to 31 October, Yugoslavia, Czechoslovakia, Austria and Hungary established themselves as independent States. Three days later, Kaiser William fell: on 28 October the German navy mutinied at Kiel; on the night of 7 and 8 November in Munich the socialist Kurt Eisner proclaimed the Bavarian Socialist Republic; on 9 November the revolution spread to Berlin and on 10 November, after vainly attempting to hold on at least to the Prussian throne, William II fled to Holland. The Spanish Bourbons lost their throne in 1931 in a peaceful transfer of power to the republican government, following the victory of the republican parties in the municipal elections in April. Eight years later, at the end of the bloody civil war, Francisco Franco formally restored the monarchy, but it was only after his death in 1975 that Juan Carlos, grandson of Alfonso XIII, ascended the throne. For the House of Savoy the end came on 2 June 1946, when the people in a referendum voted for a republic.

ROYALTY IN FIGURES

The Hapsburgs are not only the 'longest' of the European dynasties, they can also boast of the most crowned heads: twenty-six (twenty-two Emperors and four sovereigns from the Spanish branch). Next come the Romanovs with eighteen Czars, followed by the Braganzas and the Capets with fifteen monarchs each, the Plantagenets fourteen, the Valois thirteen, the House of Savoy twelve, the House of Hanover-Windsor eleven, the Stuarts and the Bourbons of Spain ten, the Hohenzollerns nine, the Bourbons of France seven, the Tudors six, the Bonapartes five, and finally, the Bourbons of Naples and the Hohenstaufens four each.

Calculating the average length of reign from the duration of each dynasty and the number of its monarchs, shows the most 'durable' to have been those of the Bourbons of France: an average reign of thirty-one years per monarch. Next come the Stuarts, thirty years six months, closely followed by the Hapsburgs, twenty-six years and seven months. Then come the House of Hanover-Windsor twenty-three years and ten months, the Plantagenets twenty-three years and seven months, the Bourbons of Spain, the Bourbons of Naples and the Hofenstaufens twenty-three years, the Capets twenty-two years and eight months, the Braganzas twenty-two years and three months, the House of Savoy nineteen years and six months, and the Tudors nineteen years. Bringing up the rear are the Romanovs sixteen years and ten months, the Hohenzollerns thirteen years, and finally the Bonapartes with an average reign of eleven years for each of their five representatives.

The House of Hanover-Windsor

An act of Parliament, intended to exclude the Stuarts
from the British throne, settles the Crown upon a
German electoral house, related however to the Stuarts

A less prepossessing-looking man than King George I of Great Britain (reigned 1714–27) would be difficult to imagine. Fifty-three at the time of his accession to the throne, he was short, stocky, pale-skinned, bulbous-eyed and heavy-jowled. Nor was his manner any more attractive. Shy and awkward, the King gave the impression of being a coarse, aggressive and unimaginative man. He certainly had none of the 'style' of his Stuart precedessors.

Yet it was through his relationship to the Stuarts that George I inherited the British throne. His mother – Sophia, wife of the Elector of Hanover – was the granddaughter of King James I and VI. Thus, when Parliament, in its determination to keep a Roman Catholic off the British throne, passed an Act of Settlement in 1701, it was to the Protestant Princess Sophia and her descendants that the succession passed. In 1714 the Electress Sophia died, shortly followed by Queen Anne, the last Stuart monarch, who left no heirs. Sophia's son, George, found himself King of Great Britain, and he arrived to claim his inheritance, on 18 September.

He brought, besides his unfortunate appearance, a host of other liabilities. One was the widely-known fact of his inhuman treatment of his pretty and feather-brained wife, Sophia Dorothea of Celle. Having got rid of her lover, by murder, it was rumoured, George divorced her, forbade her to see her children and shut her up in the castle of Ahlden for the next thirty years.

The Blue Room at Buckingham Palace. The present residence in London of the British royal family was acquired by George III in 1762, and rebuilt in a neo-classical style by John Nash.

He made good this lack of a consort by bringing with him not one, but two German mistresses. Both were hideous. Ehrengard von Schulenberg was as thin as a rake; Charlotte Kielmansegge as fat as a pig. The former he transformed into the Duchess of Kendal and the latter into the Countess of Darlington. To his unimpressed subjects, however, these rapacious ladies remained 'The Maypole' and 'The Elephant and Castle'.

The rest of the King's circle was hardly more acceptable. Like his ageing mistresses, they were chiefly concerned with lining their pockets. 'Bah!' the King is said to have advised a Hanoverian servant, who complained of the thievery at the British Court, 'It is only English money – steal like the rest!' This money-grubbing, combined with the King's distaste for the grandeurs of his position, ensured that the British Court become one of the dreariest and least cultivated in Europe. The King's stormy relationship with his son and heir, the Prince of Wales, merely added to its generally undistinguished tone. For long periods, father and son refused to speak to each other. In this, they set the pattern for almost all future Hanoverian relationships between monarch and heir.

That the King preferred his native Hanover, of which he remained Elector, to his adopted kingdom, there is no question. He returned to Hanover as often as possible, and although he could speak some English, German remained his first and favourite language.

On the face of it, a less promising candidate as the founder of a dynasty would have been difficult to find. But found a dynasty he did. The fact that this dynasty has proved to be one of the most stable and durable in Europe was in no small measure due to the King's generally underrated talents.

George I of Great Britain. Elector of Hanover and son of a grand-daughter of the Stuart James I, he came to the English throne in 1714 through the Settlement Act of 1701 which excluded Catholics from the succession.

George II, like his father, preferred Hanover and, conscious of his own inadequacy, let himself be guided by the Queen, Caroline of Ansbach, and by his ministers, including the famous Walpole.

George Augustus had come into his own.

Yet his own turned out to be not so very different from his father's. George II was equally unattractive to look at – fleshy, pop-eyed, big-nosed – and his manner was hardly more polished. He, too, could be stubborn, irascible and uncouth, a man of limited intelligence and narrow outlook. The King became increasingly obsessed with the less important aspects of his illustrious position: with punctuality, genealogy, uniforms, decorations and Court etiquette. In time, his Court was hardly less dull than his father's. Although his English was better, he shared George I's love of Hanover and would return to it almost as often.

In the matter of a consort, however, the situation was very different. George II's Queen, Caroline of Ansbach, was a voluptuous, vivacious and intelligent woman, keenly interested in affairs of State. Ignoring her husband's many infidelities (for he had the usual Hanoverian sexual appetite), Queen Caroline tried to influence him politically. In this she was successful. It was due, for instance, to her promptings that the King retained the services of his late father's Prime Minister, Sir Robert Walpole. George II was fond of his lively

For George I was no fool. He might have been devoted to Hanover but he took a keen interest in British politics. He might have been uncouth, but he was an accomplished diplomat. He might have been uncultivated but he was an excellent judge of music. Shrewd, diligent and well-versed in foreign affairs, George I concerned himself actively in the business of the monarchy. During his reign, the delicate balance between the authority of the Crown and the rights of Parliament was established. The very fact that George I had gained his throne by an Act of Parliament ensured the acceptability, if not of himself, then at least of the monarchy. And, by using one minister as chief or 'prime' minister (in his case, Sir Robert Walpole) as a link between the Crown and the House of Commons, the King, albeit unconsciously, laid the foundations of a successful system of constitutional monarchy.

He died, quite suddenly, of a cerebral haemorrhage on 2 June 1727, while on a journey to his beloved Hanover. So little did his British subjects regret his passing that they allowed him to be buried at Osnabrück, where he had been born, sixty-seven years before. His body lies in Hanover, but his descendants still reign in Britain.

'Dat', exclaimed the new King, George II (reigned 1727–60), on being told of the death of his father, 'is one big lie!' He could not, in other words, believe his luck. At one stroke he had got rid of a parent whom he hated and become the King of Great Britain. The years of friction between his father's boring Court at St James's and his own, more lively, household at Leicester House were over; at the age of forty-four,

Queen and when she died in 1737 he claimed that he had never come across anyone fit 'to buckle her shoe'.

Where George II most strikingly resembled George I was in his relationship with his elder son, Frederick Louis, Prince of Wales. He loathed him. Indeed, the quarrels between George II and his father had been as nothing compared with the quarrels between George II and his son. The virulence of the King's, and the Queen's, remarks about the Prince of Wales was equalled only by the virulence of his remarks about

them. 'Look, there he goes,' the Queen once cried, on catching sight of her elder son. 'That wretch! that villain! I wish the ground would open this moment and sink the monster to the lowest hole in Hell!' And it appears that the Prince of Wales's only interest in his mother's last illness was to know if she were yet dead. However, George II had the satisfaction of outliving his hated son. When the Prince of Wales died in 1751, his father still had nine years to live.

For all his shortcomings, King George II was not an

Queen Charlotte of Mecklenburg-Strelitz, wife of George III, with two of her sons. Unlike his father and grandfather the third Hanoverian King was a faithful husband whose wife gave him fifteen children.

entirely unsuccessful monarch. He was, for one thing, very cool in the face of physical danger. At the battle of Dettingen, in 1743, during the war of the Austrian Succession, he led an allied army to victory over the French. Two years later, when his Stuart rival, the romantic Young Pretender, invaded Britain, the King remained remarkably composed.

His interest in both foreign and domestic affairs was lively. But in the final analysis, it was George II's very weaknesses that proved to have been his strengths. Conscious of his own inadequacies, he had the good sense to allow himself to be guided by those two capable politicians, the Queen and Walpole. And even when both these influences had disappeared – the Queen through death, Walpole through politics – the King preferred his ministers to take final responsibility.

In this way, perhaps unwittingly and grudgingly, George II upheld that balance between Crown and Commons. His thirty-three-year reign ended on notes of both triumph and farce. On 25 October 1760, at a time of great British military successes abroad, King George II died of a heart attack, in the lavatory.

With the accession of George III (reigned 1760–1820), Britain gained its first – and last – thoroughly respectable Hanoverian King. It also gained its first thoroughly British Hanoverian King. Unlike his great-grandfather, George I, or his grandfather, George II, George III did not stand with one foot in Hanover. In fact, he never even visited it. With him the Hanoverian dynasty became rooted in Britain.

Yet George III looked no less German than his predecessors. Twenty-two years old at the time of his accession in 1760, he was fair and florid, with his family's prominent blue eyes. But here the resemblance ceased. Unlike the two earlier Georges, George III was a virtuous, honest, cultivated, good-hearted and

deeply religious man. He was a keen and progressive farmer; his nickname, 'Farmer George', was as much a compliment as a nation's endearment. He might not have been particularly intelligent or far-seeing, and he could be stubborn, but he was well-intentioned.

He was also very much of a family man. Only twelve when his father – George II's abhorred son Frederick – died, George had become deeply attached to his mother, Princess Augusta of Saxe-Gotha. In the year after his accession, in a spirit of duty, he married Princess Charlotte of Mecklenburg-Strelitz. In this small, plain but resolute Princess, George III found the perfect partner. The marriage, which lasted for well over half a century, was extremely successful. George III was a faithful husband and Queen Charlotte bore him no less than fifteen children.

But even in this happy marriage, the old pattern of antagonism between King and heir reasserted itself. Before long, the Prince of Wales, the future George IV, had infuriated his father by his political opposition and his social indiscretions.

To these domestic disappointments were added political vicissitudes. The King's sixty-year reign, during which Britain began to change from a predominantly rural into an industrial country, saw serious religious controversies, the loss of the American colonies, the beginnings of an Empire, the long struggle against Revolutionary and then Napoleonic France, and the emergence of a more rigid party political system. Often, these problems were simply too immense for the honest-to-goodness monarch to handle, yet he never shirked them. All in all, George III greatly enhanced the prestige of the Crown.

In 1788, at the age of fifty, the King began to act strangely. He was even reported to have been seen talking to a tree in the belief that it was the King of Prussia. Not unnaturally, it was generally assumed that he had gone mad. For some six months the King was put away and subjected to the most barbaric treatment. By the spring of the following year he had recovered. In the years that followed he had several relapses and by 1810 he was regarded as being completely insane. His eldest son was proclaimed Regent. During the last ten years of his life – blind, bearded and apparently deranged – George III roamed aimlessly around a special apartment at Windsor Castle. Twentieth-century medical research has claimed that he was suffering from a disease known as porphyria: a poisoning of the nervous system by an excess of red pigment in the blood. He died, aged eighty-one, on 29 January 1820.

George III is generally remembered as the 'Mad King' who lost the American colonies for Britain, but in his lifetime he was greatly loved for being a bluff, well-meaning and honest man.

If George III had been the best Hanoverian King, his son George VI (reigned 1820–30) was undoubtedly the worst. By the time that he was proclaimed Prince Regent, at the age of forty-eight in 1811, he was already the gross, vulgar, self-indulgent creature that he was to remain for the rest of his life. A youthful admission that he was 'rather too fond of women and wine' had been amply borne out. Not only wine, but most alcohol, plus gargantuan meals, soon spoiled his good looks and splendid figure. His love life was equally indiscriminate. Two affairs, one with Perdita Robinson and the other with Lady Melbourne, were followed by a form of secret marriage to a twice-widowed Roman Catholic, Maria Fitzherbert. The marriage was invalid, for the Royal Marriages Act of 1772 prohibited members of the royal family, under the age of twenty-five, from marrying without the sovereign's permission. But valid or not, the marriage did not stop the Prince from embarking on yet another liaison, this time with Lady Jersey. Nor did it prevent him from agreeing – so that Parliament could pay his debts – to marry his cousin, Princess Caroline of Brunswick, in April 1795.

The marriage was a disaster. For coarseness and profligacy, there was not much to choose between the Prince and Princess of Wales. Soon after the birth of their daughter, Princess Charlotte, in 1796, the couple separated. George continued his dissolute, debt-ridden way of life and, after some years in England, Caroline went roaming the Continent in the company of a handsome chamberlain.

On becoming Regent (and few spread rumours of George III's insanity with more zest than his son), the Prince broke with his life-long political associates, the Whigs led by Charles James Fox, and retained his father's Tory ministers. This underlined the general belief that 'Prinny' was irresolute and vacillating, a man not to be trusted. And although this Hanoverian generation was spared the customary antagonism between father and son, the Prince Regent's relationship with his only child, Princess Charlotte, was hardly serene. In 1816 she married Prince Leopold of Saxe-Coburg (whom her father was to hate as heartily as he would have hated a son of his own) but she died, in childbirth, the following year.

George IV's accession, in 1820, gave him the opportunity to indulge his taste for ceremonial, for there was no denying that he was a great showman and that he had excellent taste. His encouragement of the architect John Nash, his restoration of the royal palaces, his building of the bizarre Brighton Pavilion, indeed all the elegance of the Regency period, bears witness to his undoubted sense of style. Yet even his gorgeously staged coronation was marred by the arrival of his wife, who had to be turned away from the doors of Westminister Abbey: George IV was determined that she should not be crowned Queen. A Parliamentary attempt to dissolve the marriage and deprive Caroline of the title of Queen was abandoned, but her death in 1821 saved her husband from any further embarrassment.

George IV's ten-year reign, from 1820 to 1830, did nothing to redeem his reputation as a slothful and faithless debauchee. Bewigged, rouged, corseted, surrounded by his favourites and neglectful of his duties, he lived an increasingly withdrawn life. When he died at the age of sixty-seven on 26 June 1830, few of his subjects regretted his passing.

'Who is Silly Billy now?' asked the triumphant William IV (reigned 1830–37) of his Privy Councillors as they knelt for the first time in homage before him. The answer is that he was as he had always been, and that his behaviour on his accession to the throne was even sillier than usual. For the sixty-four-year-old King William IV was so delighted to have lived long enough to succeed his brother, George IV, that during the first days of his reign he made no attempt to hide his child-like excitement.

A bluff, uncomplicated, florid-faced man who had spent his youth in the navy, William IV was very different from his late brother. Of his predecessor's flamboyance he had none. Only in the irregularity of his early love life had William, then Duke of Clarence, resembled him. A long spell with Mrs Dorothea Jordan, the actress, who bore him ten children (they were given the surname of Fitzclarence), was followed by several proposals of marriage to an assortment of rich but reluctant young ladies.

So matters might have continued had not Princess Charlotte, only child of the future George IV and thus heir to the throne, died so suddenly in 1817. To ensure the continuance of the dynasty, her pack of profligate uncles turned their backs on the delights of bachelorhood and rushed a variety of foreign princesses to the

altar. Clarence's choice was Princess Adelaide of Saxe-Meiningen. Alas, the marriage failed in its most important purpose: no child born to Princess Adelaide lived beyond babyhood. By the time William ascended the throne in 1830, it was apparent that his Crown would pass to the little daughter of his younger brother Edward, Duke of Kent – Princess Victoria.

Once on the throne, Silly Billy, although intellectually limited, proved to be a better King than his predecessor. He was certainly more conscientious. 'I have done more business with him in ten minutes than with the other in as many days,' claimed the Duke of Wellington. During the passage of the most important measure of his reign – the Reform Bill of 1832 – the King had the good sense not to oppose it. But he was surprised to discover to what extent this Parliamentary reform had curtailed his powers: for with the Reform Bill the power to nominate the government passed out of the hands of the sovereign into that of the electorate. It was a very important step towards the limiting (and ultimately the saving) of the British monarchy.

Domestically, William and his Queen recreated something of the atmosphere of George III's day – simple, unpretentious, informal. There were times when it seemed as though William IV resembled his father in more sinister ways as well: his bluster and excitability led many to believe that he, too, would one day go mad. Certainly the loathing of the King for Princess Victoria's mother, the widowed Duchess of Kent, seemed hardly rational. His dearest wish, the King declared, was to stay alive until his niece turned eighteen; this way he would prevent her mother from becoming Regent. His wish came true – by a month.

With the majority of his subjects, the honest-to-goodness William IV was very popular. There could not be much wrong, surely, with a King among whose

first acts on ascending the throne had been to replace his French chefs with English ones. Nor with one among whose last requests was for his doctor to 'see if you cannot tinker me up', to last out the anniversary of the battle of Waterloo. He did last, and William IV died, two days later, on 20 June 1837.

There had not been many years – during the previous century and earlier – that the British throne had not been occupied by some gross or eccentric old man. Now, at dawn on the morning of 20 June 1837, a small, eighteen-year-old girl in a dressing gown and slippers was told that she was the Queen of England. With the accession of Victoria, it was almost as if the House of Hanover had changed its image. And indeed, as the sovereignty of Hanover could not pass to a woman, Victoria's uncle, the Duke of Cumberland, became King of Hanover, while she became the first Hanoverian monarch to wear the Crown of Great Britain only. She was also the country's last Hanoverian sovereign, for her heir, Edward VII, was to take his father's name: Saxe-Coburg and Gotha.

Queen Victoria (reigned 1837–1901) at the start of her reign was an engaging person: lively, emotional, conscientious and honest. Her common-sense was one of her most outstanding characteristics. Yet despite the fact that she would always have a mind of her own, Queen Victoria was to be subject to the influence of the various men with whom she was associated. Indeed, the story of her life is very much the story of these masculine influences.

Her father, George III's fourth son, Edward, Duke of Kent, had died when she was a few months old, and Victoria was raised by her mother. But it was to her mother's brother, Prince Leopold of Saxe-Coburg (husband of the late Princess Charlotte and afterwards King of the Belgians) that she turned for guidance. This, her 'Dearest Uncle' was only too ready to give, and became the first of her mentors.

The second was Lord Melbourne, Victoria's first Prime Minister. With this attractive and urbane elder statesman, the highly emotional Victoria all but fell in love. Melbourne may have been a shade too lackadaisical in his approach to public affairs, but he gave his young sovereign a very good grounding in the workings of constitutional monarchy.

He was superseded by the great love and strongest influence on Queen Victoria's life: her handsome cousin and husband, Prince Albert of Saxe-Coburg and Gotha.

In the course of their twenty-two-year marriage, Albert moulded, or at least guided, Victoria's character. She was forever trying to live up to his example. Largely due to the somewhat strait-laced Albert, Victoria's Court set a high moral standard; the home life of the British royal family (nine children were born of the marriage) became a byword for domesticity and respectability. Politically Albert was a considerable force: his level-headedness invariably overrode his wife's more emotional reactions to public affairs. But perhaps his greatest contribution was the defining of

287

Royal visits in the Victorian era: the British sovereigns
as guests of the French in 1845, in a painting by
Winterhalter showing Louis-Philippe and some of his
ten children with Victoria and Albert.

the role of a constitutional monarch: the lifting of the Crown high above the hurly-burly of political life.

Prince Albert's death in 1861 left the forty-two-year-old Victoria desolate. For the following dozen or so years she all but withdrew from public life. She became the 'Widow of Windsor' – a dour, dowdy, neurotically withdrawn figure, obsessed with her grief and her health. Only after the most persistent and tactful cajoling would she carry out any public duty. This excessive and prolonged seclusion brought a slump in her popularity. Her subjects were not to know that their Queen was carrying out the private business of the monarchy as always. To many she seemed merely a parsimonious recluse.

The Queen was gradually coaxed out of her mourning by two men. One was a Scottish ghillie, John Brown; the other was a Jewish-born politician, Benjamin Disraeli. In a way these two very different men represented – or rather, appealed to – two sides of Queen Victoria's complex nature. John Brown was a handsome, bluff, no-nonsense Highlander; Benjamin Disraeli was an astute, romantic, silver-tongued statesman. But both men treated her as a woman first and a queen second; this was the secret of their success with her. To Brown, Victoria was 'Wumman'; to Disraeli she was the 'Faerie Queene'. And if Brown, by his protective and honest-to-goodness ways, re-awakened her interest in life, Disraeli, by his tact, his flattery and his brilliance, re-awakened her interest in her calling. Under his skilful guidance, Victoria developed into a great Queen.

The last twenty-five years of her reign saw Queen Victoria at her most impressive. The dignity of the short, plump, black-clad figure in the white widow's cap was immense. Her imperiousness, her experience, her forthrightness and her shrewdness gave her an air of great authority. The doyenne of Europe's sovereigns, she reigned over the greatest and most powerful Empire that the world had ever known. With her children and grandchildren married into most Continental Courts (her direct descendants would sit on no less than ten European thrones), she was known as the Grandmama of Europe. Her Diamond Jubilee in 1897 was a triumphant affair: in the person of this little Queen under the lace parasol was symbolized all the might of the British Empire.

Queen Victoria died on 22 January 1901 at the age of eighty-one, after a reign of over sixty-three years – the longest in British history. The Hanoverian dynasty could not have climaxed, or ended, more magnificently.

During Queen Victoria's long reign, discord between monarch and heir had again manifested itself. Both Victoria and Albert had high hopes of their eldest son Bertie – Albert Edward, Prince of Wales. They were determined that he was to be a model Prince: diligent, intelligent, unsullied. To this end they subjected the youngster to a rigorous course of training. It had all been to no purpose. Bertie might have been amiable and affectionate but he was also slow, lazy and stupid. Of his father's serious-minded Coburg characteristics he showed no trace; he seemed to be all Hanoverian. There appeared to be very little doubt that Bertie was about to go the way of Queen Victoria's wicked uncles.

Each passing year seemed to confirm this apprehension. Bertie even looked Hanoverian. His eyes were pale blue, bulbous and heavy-lidded; his figure was becoming increasingly corpulent. More and more, he seemed to be living, as his disapproving mother only too frequently pointed out, purely for pleasure. She even blamed the death of the Prince Consort in 1861 to the fact that her husband's spirit had been broken by the news of Bertie's sexual misconduct.

The Prince of Wales's marriage in 1863 to the beautiful but scatter-brained Princess Alexandra of Denmark did nothing to temper his frivolity. Gregarious, well-mannered and warm-hearted, the Prince of Wales spent the greater part of his time racing, gambling, shooting, travelling, dressing up, eating out and making love. He was forever involved in some scandal, including appearing as witness in a divorce suit, or embarked on yet another liaison. Nor was he as amiable and resolute a personality as was generally supposed. To those who knew him well, the

Three of Queen Victoria's grand-daughters, daughters of the Prince of Wales, later Edward VII; Victoria, Maud and Louise, in a portrait of 1883. Maud became Queen of Norway.

Prince of Wales was moody, restless, easily depressed. He lacked application, he could never bear to be alone, and he was easily affronted.

The main problem was that he did not have enough to do. This was Queen Victoria's fault. For one thing, she had a very poor opinion of his abilities (she considered him irresponsible, immature and indiscreet); for another, she was determined that no one should play the political role that her late husband had once done. Any suggestion that the Prince of Wales be more closely involved with the workings of the monarchy was always rejected by the Queen. He could carry out the social and ceremonial duties of the monarchy; but no more. And so, until his sixtieth year, the Prince of Wales frittered away such talents as he possessed. Not until 1901, on his mother's death, did he ascend the throne. His reign lasted for only nine years but they were of exceptional brilliance. Although not a particularly clever man, Edward VII (reigned 1901–10) had a great sense of style and considerable diplomatic gifts. His reign was a succession of great State occasions, of magnificent State visits, of glittering balls and banquets and receptions. With the decorative and perennially youthful Queen Alexandra by his side, King Edward VII restored to the British monarchy a lustre unknown since the days of the Stuarts.

Because of his many State visits, King Edward VII earned the somewhat exaggerated reputation as a supreme royal diplomat: the 'Peacemaker' of Europe. With over half the thrones of Europe occupied by his relations, he seemed eminently well-equipped for the role. Only by his German nephew, Kaiser William II – the son of his sister Vicky – were his efforts seen in a different light: as a Machiavellian attempt to encircle Germany with enemies. And indeed, a mere four years after the 'Peacemaker's' death on 6 May 1910, Europe was at war.

Edward VII had been the first monarch of the Saxe-Coburg and Gotha dynasty. His son, George V (reigned 1910–36), was the last. For in 1917, in the flood of anti-German feeling that swept through Britain during the First World War, the British Royal House changed its name to Windsor.

George V was a very different man from his exuberant father. Forty-four at the time of his accession in 1910, he had none of Edward VII's panache. Slender, blue-eyed, neatly bearded and moustached, George V was a not unimpressive-looking man but he had very little taste, or talent, for the showier aspects of his task. His youth had been spent in the navy (not until the sudden death of his elder brother, Albert Victor, the Duke of Clarence, in 1892, had George become heir to the throne) and all his life George V retained something of the bluff, uncomplicated, methodical manner of his navy days. He might not have been a clever man, but he was a consistent and conscientious one filled with a sense of responsibility and respect for the constitution.

Sharing George V's strong sense of duty was his wife, Queen Mary. As Princess May of Teck, she had once been engaged to her husband's brother, the Duke of Clarence; on his death, George had inherited both his brother's rights of accession and his fiancée. The couple were married in July 1893. Despite the fact that both were somewhat undemonstrative and inarticulate, the marriage was extremely successful. Six children were born during their first twelve years together. Extremely shy by nature, Queen Mary was a woman of great dignity and considerable presence; where the King was content to lead the life of an English country gentleman, she had wider interests. Their Court, after the glitter of the Edwardian era, was decorous, domestic, sedate.

Through all the upheavals of his twenty-six-year reign, George V remained essentially unchanged. Political crises, troubles in Ireland, State visits (including the magnificent Delhi Durbar in 1911), the First World War, the first Labour Government, the General Strike, the great slump – all these affected the dutiful King deeply but they did not much alter his attitudes. He remained what he had always been, a simple, serious-minded, conservative country squire. This was why, on the occasion of his Silver Jubilee in 1935, he was so astonished at the enthusiasm of the London crowds. He had never courted popularity, but here was gratifying proof that his subjects had come to appreciate his far from spectacular qualities: his steadfastness, his common sense, his impeccable constitutional behaviour. He died, this well-loved 'Sailor King', at his beloved country home, Sandringham, on 20 January 1936.

Never had an heir to the British throne been more popular than George V's eldest son Edward (or David, as he was known to the family). If his father had been a

Edward VII, painted by Luke Fildes in 1901. Queen Victoria's son came to the throne at the age of sixty and was considered an able diplomat in a Europe in which half the kings were his relatives.

George V with Queen Mary, their son Edward, who
abdicated before his coronation, and their daughter
Mary, painted by Sir John Lavery in 1913. In 1917 the
King changed his German surname to Windsor.

somewhat withdrawn figure, Edward was anything but
remote. In fact, he was only too accessible. For some
fifteen years, from the end of the First World War until
his accession in 1936, the Prince of Wales was the
darling of the British Empire. Slim, slight, good-
looking, with an enduring boyishness that belied his
years, he was a prototype Prince Charming. From the
days that he had been the first English prince to address
the Welsh in their own tongue at his Investiture in
Caernarvon Castle, he had caught the public imagination. No international personality was as well-
known, no country boasted a better roving ambassador, no bachelor in the world was more eligible.
Heir to the most firmly established throne in the world,
the Prince of Wales nonetheless seemed to epitomize
his times: he appeared casual, unconventional,
impatient of protocol, and determined to enjoy every
minute of every day.

Yet to those who knew him well, the Prince was not
quite the golden boy that he appeared to be. He had
some serious defects of character. He lacked serious-
mindedness. He seldom read, he was not really
interested in politics, he avoided anyone who was too

scholarly or informed. He was impulsive, restless,
unreliable. Lacking inner resources, he gave himself
over to the pursuit of pleasure. He loved parties,
practical jokes, fancy dress. But at the same time he
had a strong streak of melancholia; during his ever
more frequent black moods he could be petulant and
inconsiderate. The Prince was not even as democratic
or progressive as he was imagined to be; his apparent
enlightenment was merely a reaction to the stuffiness of
his father's Court. He recoiled, he once claimed, 'from
anything that set me up as a person requiring homage';
it was this diffidence in public that led many to believe
that he was less concerned with his position than was
actually the case.

For women, of course, the Prince of Wales had an
irresistible attraction. He, on the other hand, was
generally attracted to married women, particularly if
they were of a motherly, somewhat domineering type.
So it is not surprising that when, in 1931, he met a
twice-married, sophisticated and independent-minded
American, Wallis Simpson; he fell in love with her.

By the time of his accession in 1936, Edward VIII, the
first bachelor king in one hundred and seventy-six

years, was determined to make Mrs Simpson his wife. But it soon became apparent that there was no way by which he could marry this, by now, twice-divorced woman without giving up his throne. After a period of agonizing indecision he decided to abdicate. On 10 December 1936, after a reign of less than eleven months, Edward VIII, the first British monarch to do so voluntarily, abdicated in favour of his younger brother, the apprehensive Duke of York. A few months later, in France, he married Mrs Simpson.

For most of the remaining thirty-six years of his life, as the Duke of Windsor, he lived an aimless life of exile. He died, a somewhat tarnished figure, but supported always by the woman for whom he had given up his Crown, in 1972.

'I will do my best to clear up the inevitable mess,' wrote the new sovereign, George VI (reigned 1936–52), 'if the whole fabric does not crumble under the shock and strain of it all.' For indeed, the abdication crisis had severely shaken the institution of the monarchy in Britain. What was now needed, to shore up the prestige of the throne, was a very special sort of King. On the face of it, the new sovereign did not seem to be the right man. Forty years old at the time of his sudden accession, George VI was a somewhat unimpressive figure – slightly built, highly strung, diffident. He suffered both from gastric trouble and an acute stammer. His scholastic record had been abysmal; his naval career unspectacular; his public duties merely adequately performed. Nor had he been trained for his new position. Of those qualities of calmness, strength and self-confidence considered necessary at this particular time, the new King seemed to have none.

But George VI had other less obvious – and, in the end, more valuable – advantages. For one thing, he had an unshakeable sense of duty; for another, a brand of quiet courage. Temperamentally unsuited for his task, he had the determination to do it as well as he possibly could. His air, after the somewhat devil-may-care attitude of his elder brother, was earnest, respectable, orderly. Unlike his father George V (whom he resembled in many other ways), George VI had the capacity to learn and change and develop.

He had the advantage, too, of the support of two exceptional women. One was his mother, the redoubtable Queen Mary, and the other was his wife, Queen Elizabeth. Indeed, on his marriage to Lady Elizabeth Bowes-Lyon in 1923, the then Duke of York gained a life partner of inestimable value. Not only was she a loving, serene and sympathetic wife who, together with their two daughters, Princess Elizabeth and Princess Margaret, ensured that he enjoyed a happy home life, but she proved to be an accomplished Queen Consort. Where he was hesitant, she was assured; where he was awkward, she was graceful; where he invariably looked preoccupied, she was always smiling. That

George VI made such a success of his reign was in no small measure due to his radiant and charming Queen.

The reign was crowded with incident. At the time of George VI's Coronation on 12 May 1937, the aggressive intentions of Nazi Germany were already becoming clear. Two royal tours – to France in 1938 and to Canada and the United States in 1939 – were destined to underline Britain's special relationship with these countries. Throughout the desperate years of the Second World War, the King and Queen set a splendid example by their courage and their concern. 'I'm glad we've been bombed,' declared the Queen when Buckingham Palace was hit, 'it makes me feel I can look the East End in the face.'

Peace brought a Labour Government into power. A natural conservative, the King nevertheless adjusted both to the sweeping social revolution and the changing relationship between the Commonwealth and the Crown. It was during his reign, for instance, that the British sovereign ceased to be Emperor of India. In 1947 the royal family carried out a strenuous tour of southern Africa, but plans to tour Australia and New Zealand the following year had to be scrapped because of the King's illness. From that time on, he was never really well. In 1951 he was operated on for cancer of the lung and on 6 February 1952 he died suddenly and peacefully from a coronary thrombosis. He was only fifty-six years of age.

'For Valour' were the words that Winston Churchill inscribed on his wreath for George VI, and nothing could better epitomize the successful struggle of this dedicated man to master his shortcomings and prove himself a worthy King.

In a radio broadcast to mark her twenty-first birthday on 21 April 1947, Princess Elizabeth, heir to the British throne, made what she called a 'solemn act of dedication'. 'I should like,' she said in that still girlish voice, 'to make that dedication now. It is very simple. I declare before you all that my whole life, whether it be long or short, shall be devoted to your service and to the serve of our great Imperial Commonwealth to which we all beong ...'. This earnest young Princess was not granted much time before she was called upon to carry out, in full, her vow of dedication. Within less than five years her father, George VI, had died and she had become Queen.

At twenty-five Elizabeth II seemed far too young, immature and reserved for her overwhelming task. Like the late King, she had a somewhat withdrawn quality. Despite her good looks – her blue eyes, her glowing complexion, her radiant smile – she appeared to lack the poise, authority and ease of manner of a successful public figure. On the other hand, she was blessed with a natural dignity, an obvious sincerity and her full share of the family sense of duty. She was also blessed with a husband who could provide the very extrovert qualities that she lacked. For her marriage in

1947 to the former Prince Philip of Greece had introduced into the royal family a young man of strong views and wide-ranging interests. Between 1948 and 1964, the couple had four children – three boys and a girl – who together set an example of harmonious and closely-knit family life.

With the years, Queen Elizabeth II has gained in stature. That 'solemn act of dedication' proved to be no idle phrase-making. Through all the vicissitudes of her calling – the long arduous and sometimes dangerous tours, the nerve-wracking State occasions, the often boring official duties, the speechmaking, the decision-making, the television appearances, the inevitable criticism – she has given herself unstintingly. She would, on her own admission, have been far happier as 'a lady living in the country, with lots of horses and dogs', but this has never tempted her to put her own interests first. Her private life is as much like that of an English country lady as it is possible to be, but the dedication with which she carries out her public duties cannot be faulted.

In a world where monarchy can so easily become an anachronism, both the Queen and Prince Philip have done their utmost to make it a vital and meaningful thing. It is no easy task. Always, the Queen must steer a middle course. Somehow the mystique of monarchy must be maintained without the monarch becoming too remote or stuffy or divorced from everyday life. The pomp of a State occasion remains just as important as the informal royal 'walkabout'. She is expected to appear as a quasi-mythical figure in full evening dress and tiara in the blazing sunshine of some African country, yet be able to talk, as woman to woman, to someone at a point-to-point.

It would be difficult to imagine any sovereign fulfilling this dual role more successfully than Elizabeth II. Her natural gravity gives her the necessary dignity for State occasions and with the years has come an increasing relaxation of her former tense manner. The small, beautifully groomed figure with the wide smile has revealed herself as a woman of charm and warmth and wit. Already extremely popular, one may be sure that her popularity will increase with the length of her reign.

Of the personal political power once held by Queen Elizabeth II's ancestor – the founder of her dynasty, George I – hardly a vestige now remains. And that has been the saving of the dynasty. By a gradual yielding up of their prerogatives, the sovereigns of the Houses of Hanover and Windsor have kept their thrones. Elizabeth II's position, both as the Queen of England and as the head of the great multi-racial Commonwealth of Nations, is a purely symbolic one. That she happens also to be a decorative woman, a loving mother and a conscientious and unpretentious person, can only add to the lustre of this position.

Queen Elizabeth II. She came to the throne
at the age of twenty-five (her ancestor Victoria
became Queen at eighteen) and has ruled for
twenty-seven years (1979).

The Bourbons of Naples

With the rebirth of an independent sovereignty, the Kingdom
of the Two Sicilies saw a period of progress and
the laying of the first foundations of a national state

The Bourbon dynasty of Naples began with Charles (reigned 1735–59), the elder son of Philip v of Spain and Elizabeth Farnese. In February 1734, during the War of the Polish Succession, the Infante led his father's troops towards the kingdom of Naples. Apart for the resistance of the Austrian Imperial forces at Bitonto, the Spanish–Bourbon reconquest of southern Italy and Sicily turned out to be little more than a route march. On 10 May of the same year, preceded by a proclamation in which the conquest was hailed as a liberation from the 'tyranny of the Austrian Government', Charles of Bourbon – to whom Philip v had ceded, along with the royal title, his own rights to Naples, Sicily and the Tuscan seaports known as the Presidi – entered the capital in triumph, welcomed with demonstrations of joy by the populace.

The rebirth of independent sovereignty, both in itself and through the psychological boost it gave the Neapolitans, started a period of progress in the country's history and brought the southerners a sense not only of recovery, but of great advances lying ahead of them. And, indeed, despite Spain's resistance to any loosening of the bonds of dependence, the new sovereign, though neither able nor desirous at first to assume complete freedom of action, nevertheless laid the first foundations of a 'national' State. Crowned in Palermo in 1735 as King of Sicily, but making Naples his permanent headquarters, Charles of Bourbon

A parade a Piedigrotta in the time of Charles VII, in an anonymous eighteenth-century painting. The great-grandson of the Sun King was the first Bourbon to rule in Naples, and later became Charles III of Spain.

married in 1738 Maria Amalia of Saxony, daughter of Augustus III, King of Poland.

During the early years of his reign, the Bourbon Prince struck foreign observers as a shy young man without any effective authority, bigoted, obsessed with hunting, given to pomp and display and inclined, through his complete lack of personality, to delegate the responsibilities of State to his ministers. Slowly and gradually, however, King Charles grew up. No sooner had he rid himself of the heavy hand of Spain, than he declared his wish to be concerned henceforth with the intricacies of government, freely choosing his own counsellors. These included Fogliano of Piacenza and the Marquis Squillace, but it was Bernardo Tanucci who proved outstanding. Charles cared sincerely for the well-being of his subjects, and the political line which he himself pursued with conviction was one opposed to 'privilege'. Within limits set by the country's 'educated class', he sought to improve the pitiable living conditions of the South and based his own actions on a cautious policy of reform.

Now that the centuries-long exploitation of the land by foreign powers had come to an end, local resources could be used for the benefit of the nation. Public works were undertaken, needs arising from its new independence provided for, including, above all, a navy and an efficient army. In the economic field the Bourbon government was concerned with encouraging trade and increasing local manufacture in general. In the year 1738, for instance, a great tapestry workshop was set up at San Carlo alle Mortelle, while in 1743 the porcelain factory at Capodimonte was founded, enterprises which placed Naples on a level with the most progressive towns of Europe.

Efforts to reorganize the country's judiciary; the blows inflicted, at least during the early years, on the economic, legal and political aspects of the feudal system; the new order imposed on the nation's economy by a land register; and the reform of public financial administration and tax collection; the firmness with which the government pursued the policy, begun in the previous era, of freeing the kingdom from subjection to the Roman Curia: all these advances were achieved during the first Bourbon period.

The reign of Charles also witnessed a notable revival of learning and the arts. Excavations were started at Herculaneum in 1738 and Pompeii in 1748, leading to the foundation of the *Accademia Ercolanese*; opera was encouraged by the building of the splendid San Carlo opera house in 1737; royal patronage was bestowed on artists such as Vanvitelli, Solimena and De Mura. The flowering of that characteristic expression of eighteenth-century Neapolitan artistry, the *presepe*, or glorified Christmas crib, is yet another example of the widely ranging creative activity in Naples at that time. Of the vast architectural works begun in this reign, though not completed till the next, the royal palaces at Capodimonte and Caserta, the *Foro Carolino* and the *Reale Albergo dei Poveri*, an enormous hospice for the poor, still remain to bear witness to the artistic enterprise of King Charles.

No summing up of the reign of the first Bourbon monarch would be complete without the verdict of Benedetto Croce: Taken as a whole, these were years of 'resolute progress', foreshadowing the subsequent movement of reform that arose not as a contrasting reaction, but as a 'continuation and intensification' of the preceding era.

When Charles of Bourbon, summoned to succeed his brother Ferdinand VI on the throne of Spain, left for Madrid on 6 October 1759, there began in Naples the long reign of his heir, Ferdinand IV (reigned 1759–1825).

Ferdinand remained coarse and uncultivated all his life. This may have been due to the inadequate education imparted by his tutor, the Prince of San Nicandro, or to his domination by the Regent Tanucci during his minority. When he came of age, he married Maria Carolina of Hapsburg, daughter of the Empress Maria Theresa and thus sister to Joseph II, Leopold, Duke of Tuscany, and Marie Antoinette of France. Impulsive, intelligent, voluble, full of enthusiasm, the young Queen longed to leave her mark on the country's destiny. Once she had given birth to an heir, she was admitted to the Council of State and set out to break the bonds, personified by Tanucci, that still tied Naples to the Spain of Charles III. Maria Carolina's influence over the mind of the King grew daily stronger, helped, no doubt, by his natural propensity

to devote himself entirely to his favourite pastimes. Nevertheless, his gift for passive resistance, added to a certain native shrewdness, enabled him on several occasions to mitigate the Queen's hysterical impulses and sudden decisions.

In two particular instances, Ferdinand was able to cast aside his disinclination for positive action: in his passion for the Capodimonte porcelain factory; and in his enthusiastic patronage of an enlightened scheme – which indeed came to fruition – for a Utopian communal society at the silk mills of San Leucio. In effect, the King, though presenting an easy target to

sarcasm in his way of life and choice of companions, did not entirely fail to fulfil his royal duties. During the 1770s and 1780s, he supported the reforming zeal of his government with his personal feeling for the national dignity and that, although extremely religious, he did not let himself be bullied by the Roman Curia. But it was Maria Carolina, protector of the freemasons and darling of the progressive opposition, who set the internal and, still more, the foreign policies of the Neapolitan State on a new course. It was due to the Queen that the naval fleet, under the direction of Sir John Acton, who was made Secretary of State in 1779,

grew in strength and efficiency. Efforts to revive the economy of southern Italy by strengthening relations with the East seemed destined for success; equally clear were signs of a new vitality at home. At about the same time the hard struggle against the Church culminated in the expulsion of the Jesuits and the confiscation of all their goods. In the political field, the open repudiation of the feudal overlordship, claimed for centuries by the Holy See, was underlined after 1780 by the refusal to send to Rome the symbol of Naples' traditional homage in the form of a white palfrey accompanied by 7000 gold *scudi*.

*Ferdinand, known as 'Big Nose', painted by
Camuccini; he was Ferdinand IV of Naples and III
Sicily until 1816 and then, after the Congress of
Vienna, Ferdinand I of the Two Sicilies.*

In the climate of optimism that now inspired Neapolitan life it seemed as if Naples, that privileged, parasitic city, indifferent to the miseries of the provinces, was being transformed into the capital of a modern State, a focal point drawing together the overall interests of the 'nation'. Above all, the younger generation of intellectuals made a considerable leap forward. Modelling themselves on the teachings of Antonio Genovesi, they widened the scope of their philosophical enquiry and subjected every aspect of social life to careful investigation. Naples became one of the capitals of European Enlightenment and, as Franco Venturi pointed out, the liveliest and most liberated city of late eighteenth-century Italy. During those two eventful decades the monarchy also lent its support to those intellectuals and scientists who, up to 1792, were intensely active in their efforts to solve the country's problems. Reforms and attempts at reform were applied particularly to the land and agricultural labourers. Though all too often their immediate effect failed, yet they are of special interest not only because they help to explain the social conditions which later influenced the revolution of 1799, but also because they paved the way for the innovations of the period of French rule and the final abolition of feudalism.

More bitter and, in the outcome, fruitless was the struggle waged by the Neapolitan government and intelligentsia in those same years against the predominant feudal powers in Sicily.

The agreement between the political aristocracy and the absolute monarchy, already profitable and full of promise for the future, was broken by the sudden and violent course of events in France. Maria Carolina, encouraged by the Court's condemnation of the actions of the regicides in Paris, and, against the advice of the country's wisest ministers and diplomats, induced the King to sign the treaty of 1792 allying the Neapolitan navy to the interests of Great Britain. This dragged Naples into a hazardous war with France, twice exposing the country to the dangers of invasion in 1799 and 1806. The plan for an economic revival in southern Italy had to be abandoned. The horrors of the revolution and the consequent ferocious reaction of the Bourbons opened up a breach between monarchy and nation that was never completely healed, and led in just over fifty years to the ultimate fall of the royal House.

In the face of the French advance the King and Court fled to Palermo, leaving Naples to the mercy of the enemy army. The experiment of an enlightened democratic republic, subject to the will of the French generals, limited in effect to the city boundaries and accompanied by outbreaks of anarchic violence in the surrounding countryside, was doomed to failure. Movements for reform had remained the exclusive concern of an intellectual minority, while the urban proletariat and the peasants on the land still clung to the old order. However, after 1799 and the reconquest of Naples by Cardinal Ruffo's army of the masses, the personal responsibility of the sovereigns for the fierce repression that followed has cast a shadow on them which cannot easily be dispersed. The breakdown of the Peace of Amiens and the occupation of Puglia by the French led to renewed passive acquiescence towards England and new, irremediable, conflict between Napoleon and the Bourbons. Finally, on 27 December 1805, the victor of Austerlitz proclaimed to his army at Schönbrunn that the dynasty of Naples had ceased to reign. On 9 February of the following year, Ferdinand IV, abandoned by his Anglo–Russian allies, was once more the first to fly. By the 14th of the

Alas, no sooner was the restoration established than all measures of reform were shelved. As a result, the *Carbonari*, who had been in favour of the King's return, were sufficiently disillusioned to become a centre of attraction for all the discontented who still hoped against hope that they might secure, if only gradually, a constitutional charter. They knew nothing of the ties the monarchy had formed with Austria through the secret treaty of 12 June 1815, nor of the consequent difficulties placed in their path. These lost illusions sparked off the uprising of 1820. During the nine months of constitutional rule, every proposal of reform put forward by those in power came up against the immovable conservatism of the peasant masses, a brake to progress that rendered their efforts fruitless. The situation was further complicated by events in Sicily, where the administrative policy pursued by the Minister de Medici during the five years from 1815 to 1820, combined with the economic crisis, gave rise to an explosion of popular discontent. Independence from Naples and the constitution of 1812 were the watchwords of the Sicilian movement. Ferdinand I's attitude towards these revolutionary events was very understandable and in line with his previous convictions. At the Congress of Laibach he threw off his mask and repudiated not only the ideas of the revolution but also the attitude of his son, the Hereditary Prince Francis, appointed Vicar-General during the constitutional period.

The blind reaction that followed the uprisings of 1820 condemned not only the leaders of the revolt but also those who, in perfect good faith, believed they were serving the joint interests of dynasty and country. That error was fatal to the Bourbons: it turned into enemies a great many men who would have willingly continued to serve the State. Once again the Bourbon government showed its inherent incapacity to solve the problems of its own existence. In 1824, essentially rescinding the promises contained in the decree of 16 May 1821 imposed by European diplomacy, the Bourbons abandoned or, at best, distorted the projected measures.

In 1825 Ferdinand I died. There followed the brief reign of his son, Francis I (reigned 1825–30), married first to the Archduchess Maria Clementina of Austria and then to Maria Isabella of Spain. For the Kingdom of the Two Sicilies this was a period of transition and readjustment that seemed to carry to excess the typical faults of Bourbon misgovernment, such as bigotry, corruption and an over-powerful police. But, on the other hand, the financial policy of de Medici's second ministry laid the foundation of that economic revival of the South that came to fruition in the following period.

On the death of Francis I in 1830, Ferdinand II (reigned 1830–59) succeeded to the throne and a new

month the French were in his capital and on 19 March the little Neapolitan army was defeated at Campotenese.

This was the beginning of the 'French decade', a period of radical reform in the whole social, economic and political life of southern Italy. But the new ruling class brought with them new aspirations to national independence, destined to make themselves felt as soon as the interests of the South conflicted with those of the tottering Napoleonic Empire. It was then not too difficult for Anglo–Bourbon propaganda to set the nascent *Carbonari* against Murat. This secret society was making its first trial insurrections in Calabria and the Abruzzi. From there it passed to Sicily where, on the orders of Lord William Bentinck, Ferdinand of Bourbon was forced to assume the guise of a constitutional monarch. So great was the desire for peace that the return of the old King to Naples in 1815 was greeted with some emotion, even relief. There, under his new title of Ferdinand I, he prepared to reign over the restored monarchy. Maria Carolina had died in exile in Vienna, and Ferdinand was planning to marry his mistress, the Duchess of Floridia, and to project a new image of himself. Sovereign and subjects seemed to have forgiven each other for what had passed.

In this allegorical painting by N. De Laurentiis, the twelve provinces of southern Italy pay homage to Francis I. His five-year reign is considered a period of transition.

experiment in understanding between southern Italy and the Bourbons began to take shape. The new King's policy of expanding the country's economic life and injecting fresh vigour into the administration of the kingdom did, in fact, succeed in producing renewed enthusiasm for the Bourbon monarchy. The recall of the exiles, symbolic of the spirit of reconciliation enamating from the King, brought to Naples a breath of modern European culture and raised hopes that the political structure of the Neapolitan State would be reformed. Many adherents of Murat were thus converted to the idea of a Bourbon monarchy run on the lines of belated eighteenth-century reformism.

Thus the new reign started off in an atmosphere of almost idyllic confidence in the young ruler who removed old abuses, drove out the Court clique of his father's time, made his desire for civil progress felt in every branch of the administration, turned his attention to the army, concerned himself with the economic prosperity of the country, encouraged trade by a moderate protectionist policy and, in short, convinced casual observers and even the suspicious

Ferdinand II, the fourth and penultimate Bourbon to occupy the Neapolitan throne. He reigned in the crucial period of the Italian Risorgimento, *and saw the shattering of the idyllic confidence that marked the beginning of his reign.*

chancelleries of Europe that the Bourbon monarchy was developing into an almost liberal State. They did not perceive that Ferdinand's sole purpose was to perfect, in order to consolidate and preserve, the administrative structure of the realm bequeathed to him by his predecessors, and that the suggested changes in the role of the sovereign were a political move to graft on to the trunk of the old monarchy, conceived at the Congress of Vienna, the administrative ideals of the Napoleonic Empire, reminiscent of Naples under Murat.

Quick perception and a particularly keen memory, strong nerves and confidence in his own good sense were characteristics and qualities which, combined with a full awareness of the wide gaps in his education, bred in Ferdinand a feeling of irritation and distrust when faced with the educated or governing classes, whom he finally relegated to purely executive functions. The end result was fatal: in the Neapolitan concept of kingship, all responsibilities fell ultimately on the shoulders of the monarch, whose principal mistake lay in his failure to understand that there could be no progress or economic improvement without accompanying ethical and political problems. What is more, Ferdinand's basically materialistic ideas soon began to appear the very antithesis of the new southern civilization with its revised outlook on life – generous, heroic, in a word, romantic – so fervently embraced in

Naples during the years between 1830 and 1848. The tradition of liberty, kept alive by the continued underground work of the secret societies, as well as memories of the past, was reinforced by the economic and intellectual development of the provincial bourgeoisie who were growing in number during those years. The series of unsuccessful revolts that broke out in Salerno and Sicily as well as the Abruzzi and Calabria were unmistakeable signs of the fire lurking beneath the cinders, and served to link in men's minds the revolution of 1820 with that of 1848.

Ferdinand II, convinced that in its legal and administrative system Naples already rejoiced in everything the other States of Italy were crying out for, had no idea of the gulf that was opening up between him and the country. The revolution of 1848 took him completely by surprise; its very unexpectedness turned his tremendous confidence in himself and his own strength to utter discouragement. Having felt himself equal to any situation, he had never foreseen that there might come a time when he would have need of people capable of serving him with intelligence or at least devotion. Only in the hour of need did he realize that he stood quite alone.

The man to whom the King entrusted the task of drawing up the new constitution was Francesco Paolo Bozzelli, a returned exile considered as one of the leaders of the moderate liberal movement. However, the 'constitution', signed by the government on 10 February 1848 and put into force on the following day, was more conservative than moderate in its principal clauses. Nor surprisingly, then, the charter was soon overtaken and rendered valueless by the course of events in Europe, above all by the downfall of Louis-Philippe, on whose constitution it had been modelled.

Meanwhile the Sicilian revolution had broken out. After the first few months, Ferdinand recovered his spirits and became aware that neither constitutional government nor British intervention could pacify the island and that the new form of rule did not allow him full freedom of action in his attempts to solve the thorny question that became his obsession. He therefore welcomed the idea of a league between the Italian States or even participation in the war, although that was against his innermost convictions, in order to gain a guarantee, and at least moral support, from the other sovereigns of the peninsula in his duel with Sicily. But in this he was doomed to bitter disappointment. As a result, mistrust filled Ferdinand II's thoughts once more, and instilled into his mind the suspicion that the Neapolitan radicals wished to hasten the army's departure to Upper Italy not only in the national interest, but in order to reduce the military forces inside the country so that they could more easily overthrow the social and institutional order. Ferdinand's suspicions were confirmed by the insur-

Maria Cristina of Savoy, by C. De Falco. She was the daughter of the King of Sardinia, Victor Emmanuel I, and the first wife of Ferdinand II; after her death, he married Maria Theresa of Hapsburg-Lorraine.

rection of 15 May. The conflict between King and Parliament concerning the oath of allegiance was merely the superficial symptom of a deep internal crisis.

The grave tactical error of the liberals, and one of the chief causes of the constitutional experiment's failure in Naples in 1848, was not to have agreed on the timing of the reforms, which should have been achieved gradually, one by one. It was shrewd of the King to have seen immediately that the one possibility of victory for absolutism lay in widening the differences between the various shades of liberal opinion. He showed considerable cunning in turning to his own advantage the divisions, doubts and mistakes of his adversaries.

A return to order – or anarchy? That was the alternative that Ferdinand II set before the people of southern Italy, and the answer was easy to guess. In fact the country had no choice but those two painful alternatives: the liberals themselves had to admit that they lacked the strength to fight on two fronts at once. The King's *coup d'état*, if it can be so called, and the gradual return to absolutism were aided by the unshakeable constitutionalism of the moderate Neapolitan liberal, the poor fighting spirit of the 'democrats' and – it must be added – the support of those citizens who, though originally in favour of the constitution, now saw the possible triumph of the Italian revolution as the end of southern Italy's existence as an independent State. After three months of confusion, the events of 15 May fully restored the King's former self-confidence. He lost no time in profiting from the situation by recalling the army from Upper Italy to maintain internal order and to reconquer Sicily.

It was purely blind reaction. Proud of being the first European monarch to rebel against the 'radical faction' that threatened to overthrow the social order, Ferdinand followed his chosen path unswervingly. The revolution of 1848 signalled the end of hope in regional States, the supporters of federalism were destroyed and a new era came into being. From then onwards, as Benedetto Croce pointed out, the old kingdom of Naples 'as an idea' was finished. The reactionary fervour of Ferdinand could find no support in the political and administrative institutions of the State: he had no choice but to come to terms with the opposition. Isolated, prematurely aged, turning almost exclusively to his family, to which he was greatly attached, and the practice of his religion, Ferdinand – who, after the death of his first wife, Maria Cristina of Savoy, had married a Hapsburg Princess, the devoted Maria Theresa – spent his last years trying to cope with the situation.

The bureaucratic absolutism of the sovereign was imbued for one of his disposition by a growing mistrust of his ministers, and suspicions as to the honesty of the entire ruling class, that became truly pathological. After 1851, foreign diplomats accredited to the Court of Naples were stressing the grossly abnormal state of affairs brought about by the concentration of all power in the hands of the King and prophesying that, if Ferdinand should suddenly die, the whole framework of the State would immediately fall to pieces. The Neapolitan State was virtually doomed. After the public attacks on Naples during the Congress of Paris the situation between Britain and France on the one hand and Naples on the other became so tense that in October 1856, diplomatic relations with the Two Sicilies were severed. In the following year, Carlo Pisacane's attempted uprising removed the danger of a Murat-style solution to the Southern Question and brought the old revolutionary tactics of Mazzini into disrepute. But its failure did not show, as the Bourbon Press tried to suggest the day after the rebels' landing at Sapri, the solidity of the kingdom or the devotion of the people to Ferdinand II. It was only the calm before the storm, and with the death of Ferdinand II the gravity of the situation became clear.

The war of 1859 had already begun. The young King, Francis II, who had come to the throne in June of that year, had no wish to break with the court circles that kept so stubbornly to the obsolete ways of the previous reign. He missed the opportunity of an agreement with France based on the acceptance of a constitution of the Napoleonic type, and – yet more serious for the fate of the kingdom – ignored the hand held out by Piedmont, offering an alliance, if only for tactical reasons. Thus the Two Sicilies persisted in the traditional isolationist position and an anachronistic faith in Russian support. Basically direct, not overly intelligent, limited in education, Francis II was a rather timid, very religious young man, the son of Ferdinand II's first wife, Maria Cristina of Savoy. He was well aware of the difficulties in which he floundered, and sought to fulfil his painful duties as King with Christian resignation and patient conscientiousness. Unfortunately his character was weak and indecisive,: and he let himself be dominated and swayed by events. Even in the King's immediate environment the royal family was anything but closely knit, ranging in opinion from the old-fashioned liberalism of his uncle, the Count of Syracuse, a patron of artists and craftsmen, married to a Princess of Savoy, to the ambitious activism of the Count of Aquila, who was plotting with the French representative Brenier. There were, moreover, widespread suspicions of the Queen Mother, Maria Theresa of Austria, of whom it was said – quite unjustly – that she designed to surplant her stepson on the throne with her own son, Louis, Count of Trani. It was in this atmosphere that news arrived at the Neapolitan Court of the victorious march of

An anonymous painting in the tradition of paternal and humanitarian absolutism: Ferdinand II of the Two Sicilies with his suite of officers visiting the people of Melfi, victims of an earthquake.

Garibaldi on Palermo in May 1860, and of its shameful surrender (twenty thousand men, fully equipped for battle and protected by an efficient naval squadron, had given in to a few thousand Sicilian insurgents and followers of Garibaldi). From that moment whispers of treason, so easily circulated in such an atmosphere, combined with the legend of the invincible leader, produced their effects: they echoed through the panic-stricken Court of Naples, sapping the will to resist and disappointing friendly diplomats, who began to believe the kingdom must be crumbling.

With the surrender of Palermo, collapse was imminent. Those same courtiers who until then had seemed the most reactionary now urged the King to concede the constitution. But to open windows to the winds of change, to recall the exiles, to restore the freedom of the Press while Sicily was in flames was only to hasten disaster. The constitutional Romano–Spinelli government in power at the time could not, with the best of intentions, do otherwise than concede without too much fuss southern Italy to Garibaldi – and thereby all the rest of the peninsula. In effect, the constitution broke up the old regime without putting

anything new or efficient in its place, so that the provincial officials took refuge behind the overturning of the governmental structure, caused by the royal decree of June, to excuse their own incompetence. By July and August opinion had it that the end was drawing near. Even the most favoured of the old courtiers began to think of the future, and the royal family itself soon followed their example.

On the 6 September 1860, Francis II left the capital to save it from the danger of civil war, and tried desperately to reorganize his troops to oppose Garibaldi. The Bourbon army, which had shown such unexpected fighting power at Caiazzo, Triflisco, Santa Agata and the battle of Volturno, facilitated, without meaning to, the plans of Cavour and the single task entrusted to the army of Victor Emmanuel II of Savoy. On 26 October, when the meeting took place between Victor Emmanuel and Garibaldi at Teano, the Bourbon forces withdrew behind the River Garigliano. The following day, Francis II issued a proud proclamation to his soldiers, urging them to fight on. Three days later a large scale reconnaissance attempted against the advance posts on the Garigliano

307

resulted in the defeat of the Sardinian troops. It was the
last victory of the Bourbon army.

Then came the final moment of glory for the
Bourbons of Naples: the defeat of Gaeta. It was here
that the King's young wife, Maria Sophia of Bavaria,
revealed her heroic spirit. 'Her Majesty the Queen,'
wrote Francis to Napoleon III, 'desires to share my
fortunes to the end, dedicating herself to organising the
care of the sick and wounded in our hospitals.' Advised
to surrender by the French Emperor, who could not
leave his ships off Gaeta indefinitely, on 13 January
1861, the King replied with some dignity and, at the
same time, issued a cleverly-worded manifesto in
which, referring to the wave of discontent caused, very
naturally, by the transition from the old to the new
regime, he sought to compare national patriotism with
'Neapolitan' patriotism. Even the radical Silvio
Spaventa admitted that the proclamation made a deep
impression. Meanwhile, on the 19th, the French
squadron sailed away and Francis II was left to his own
resources. By 13 February, it was clear that resistance
was no longer possible; perforce the young King
agreed to surrender. On the following day, amid
touching marks of affection from his soldiers, he
embarked with his Queen for exile in Rome. The defeat
of Gaeta – where Queen Maria Sophia had scorned
every danger to share the hardships of the siege with
the soldiers – drew the attention of all Europe to the
bearing of the royal pair and showed clearly the part

played by the Bourbon army in its desperate attempt to
save the independence of the old kingdom.

After fierce resistance, Messina and Civitella del
Tronto also fell in early March. Thus the dynasty of the
Bourbons of Naples disappeared for ever.

Exiles in Rome, the deposed King and Queen with
their Court stayed at first in the Quirinale as guests of
the Pope, then moved to the Farnese Palace, which was
still their property and only later sold to France. In the
early days, Rome housed a large population of emigrés
from the South, who caused much disturbance and,
through their contacts with legitimists from all parts of
Europe, as well as with other political 'brigands', fed
the illusory hope of a speedy restoration. These
aspirations died away with the passing of the years and
the weakening of links with the people of southern
Italy, even though pro-Bourbon groups and a legitimist Press persisted wearily and were not entirely
extinguished until 1914.

In 1867 – after the peace between Italy and Austria –
Francis II, while retaining for a few more years a
President of the Council in the person of Pietro Ulloa,
officially dismissed the rest of his ministers and the
network of diplomats he had maintained at those
foreign Courts that had not yet recognized the
kingdom of Italy. In 1870, even before 20 September,
Francis was given the opportunity to leave Italy and,
after a short stay in Paris, moved to Bavaria, where he
more or less settled down, renouncing all claims to
kingship. He died, aged fifty-nine, at Arco in the
Trentino. Maria Sophia survived him by many years,
dying at last in 1925.

On the death of Francis II in 1894 the Neapolitan
legitimists proclaimed as 'King' his brother Alfonso,
Count of Caserta, born in 1841, who distinguished
himself in the papal army at Mentana and especially in
Spain as leader of the northern troops during the
Carlist campaign. He assumed the title 'Pretender to
the throne of Naples'. Only in the last years of his life,
after the reconciliation of State and Church in Italy,
did he re-establish relations with the Italian royal
family. It was natural, then, that after he died in May
1934, his eldest son and successor, Ferdinand Pio,
Duke of Calabria, dropped his claim to be the
Pretender, but called himself 'Head of the House of
Bourbon of the Two Sicilies' (and in that capacity reformed the Constantinian Order of St George, of
which the king of Naples was traditionally Grand
Master'. In 1938 his daughter, Princess Lucia, married
Eugene of Savoy, Duke of Ancona. Thus the old
Prince, born in exile in Rome and held at his baptism
by Pope Pius IX, was able to visit Naples and southern
Italy several times, renewing ties with the ancient
patrician families of the South and arranging during
the second post-war period, for the archives of his
House to be transferred to the State Archives of

Naples, where they now remain.

Charles, Ferdinand's younger brother, renounced all claims on the Neapolitan branch and became a naturalized Infante of Spain when he married the Princess of the Asturias. Thus when Ferdinand died the title of head of the family passed to the third-born, Renier, Duke of Castro. The succession was not accepted without protest by Alfonso, son of Prince Charles, supported in his claim by Don Juan, pretender to the throne of Spain. He held that his father's renunciation of the title Prince of Naples was invalidated by the fall of the Spanish monarchy, even though it had been solemnly renounced before the *Cortes* of Madrid. With regard to the Constantinian

Order of St George, the Italian judges upheld the claim of Prince Renier who, when he died in 1973, was succeeded as Head of the House and Grand Master of the Order by his son Ferdinand, also Duke of Castro, born in 1896 and father of another Charles, upon whom, in recognition of the traditional title of the heirs to the throne of the former kingdom, the appellation Duke of Calabria has been bestowed. Meanwhile, the National Italian Association of the 'Knights of the Holy Military Constantinian Order of St George', which now devotes itself mainly to good works, has been granted legal status as a charitable institution by a decree of the President of the Italian Republic of 30 March 1973.

The Bonapartes

An ancient and noble house of Italian origin which
reached its zenith with the military genius of
Napoleon, Emperor of the French

The Bonapartes come from ancient and noble stock.
They originally came from Italy and settled in Corsica
at the beginning of the seventeenth century. The
armorial bearings of the Bonapartes of Treviso and
Florence are virtually identical to those of the Corsican
branch of the family. Jacopo Bonaparte, who lived in
San Miniato, recounted the story of the Sack of Rome,
in which he took part, and Bonaparte visited his last
direct descendant, Canon Philip, during the great
Italian campaign in 1796. For centuries in Italy the
Bonapartes led a furious life of intrigue, war, victory
and defeat.

At the beginning of the seventeenth century,
François Bonaparte left Sarzane for Corsica, and his
eldest son, Jerome the Magnificent, was elected Leader
of the Council of Elders, deputy to the Senate of
Genoa. François II ruled the city in 1626. In 1757,
Joseph II, a member of the Council of Elders, was
granted the grand duchy of Tuscany in recognition of
his privileges and as confirmation of his noble title. In
1769, Charles-Marie was granted the title of
Archbishop of Pisa and in 1771 the Superior Council
of Corsica decreed that his nobility had been proven
for at least two hundred years. The family settled in
Ajaccio and became influential, forming alliances with
the Colonna, Costa, Bozzi and Ornano families.

In 1741, Joseph, an elder of the town, married
Marie-Severina Pallavicino. Their daughter married
Nicolò Pallavicino and their son, Charles-Marie,

*General Bonaparte at the Arcole bridge, in the
celebrated painting by Lejeune. The future Emperor,
son of the Revolution, belonged, in fact, to an ancient
noble family.*

studied law at Rome and Pisa. On 2 June 1764, at the
age of eighteen, this dashing, well-bred, handsome
cavalier married Letizia Ramolini, the daughter of a
Corsican general inspector of highways and bridges.
When her father died, her mother married François
Fesch, a Genoese captain of the Marines, and they had
a son Joseph, a future Cardinal and uncle of Napoleon.

Letizia was a great beauty. She was also a very
serious girl and a good housekeeper, deeply religious,
poorly educated and passionately attached to her
husband. The young married couple, who normally
lived in Corte, had a son in 1765 and a daughter in
1767, both of whom died at an early age. Charles-
Marie was quite well off, for he owned some lands
which brought in a modest income. He was one of
Paoli's secretaries and a member of the National
Assembly.

On 7 January 1768, Letizia gave birth to a son
named Joseph, at the very moment of the outbreak of
war with France. Charles Bonaparte personally
composed the proclamation of war for the youth of
Corsica and he actively participated in the campaign
and the ensuing Corsican victory at Borgo on 7
October 1768. But the French brought in reinforcements and defeated the Corsicans at Ponte-Novo. On
13 June 1769, Paoli escaped on two English ships and
Letizia, who was pregnant with Napoleon at the time,
went into hiding on the Mont-Rotonde with the
remnants of the Corsican army. The Corsican deputies, including Charles, handed in their resignations
to the Count of Veaux. The refugees were given
permission to return to their homes and the
Bonapartes came back to Ajaccio.

From that time, Charles Bonaparte accepted union

with France and, while law and order were being established in Corsica under the harsh rule of de Marbeuf, he returned to his studies at the University of Pisa where, on 30 November 1769, he was awarded his doctorate. In 1771 he was appointed assessor to the judge of the Civil and Criminal Court in Ajaccio.

Napoleon was born, as Letizia had wished, on Assumption Day, 15 August 1769. He was brought up by his mother and a nurse, Camilla Carbone, who was greatly attached to him. Letizia was very strict and at an early age he was sent to college in Ajaccio where he learnt to read. The child soon developed a domineering and aggressive nature.

The Bonaparte family rapidly increased in number:

Lucien, born 1775; Maria-Anna, known as Elise, in 1777; Louis in 1778; Marie-Paulette, known as Pauline, in 1780; Marie-Annonciade, known as Caroline, in 1782; and finally, Jerome, in 1784. Letizia exercised a strict and frugal rule over her little world.

Charles Bonaparte was entitled to certain rights as a result of his noble status and he prevailed on de

Marbeuf to assist him in placing Joseph and Napoleon in a college at Autun. He was hoping for an ecclesiastical appointment for Joseph and a scholarship to the Royal Military School for Napoleon. After leaving Autun, Napoleon gained a place at Brienne where he studied classics, but he was always an outsider and felt lonely and homesick for Corsica.

On leaving Brienne, Napoleon entered Military School in Paris, where he received an excellent, all-round education, but he still led a very solitary existence. On 24 February 1785, Charles Bonaparte died in Montpellier, in the arms of his eldest son, Joseph. The children were made wards of court under the protection of Dominique Forcioli, lawyer to the Superior Council of Corsica.

At the age of sixteen years and fifteen days, Napoleon was made a lieutenant in the artillery and joined the Fère regiment, garrisoned at Auxonne. This regiment was an ideally composed unit, within which he completed his military education, applying himself unremittingly to his work. He adopted the habit of summarizing every book he read and this was to prove the secret of his outstanding ability. He made frequent trips to Corsica to visit his family, to support and advise Letizia, and he gradually became the acting head of the family. He took Louis back to France with him and set him to work, behaving like a father to the boy, sharing his modest income with his young brother to enable them both to lead a somewhat spartan existence. When Napoleon was transferred to Valence, he was quickly swept up into the social set there.

He still often returned to Corsica where he was naturally on the side of the French and managed to get himself appointed lieutenant colonel of a Corsican battalion. During this time, Joseph and Lucien were dabbling in politics, which brought them into conflict with Paoli, who regarded any 'sons of Charles' with suspicion. Following the riots in Ajaccio and Bastia and the unsuccessful expedition to the island of La Maddalena, the safety of the Bonaparte family was placed in jeopardy as a result of Lucien's impudent attack on Paoli in a club in Toulon, and on 11 June 1793, they were obliged to escape by boat to France.

The Bonaparte family, by now almost destitute, disembarked at Toulon and settled in the village of La Valette, where Napoleon's sisters led a rural existence which they found very agreeable; Napoleon himself joined General Carteaux's army, took part in the capture of Avignon, wrote *Souper de Beaucaire* and finally joined an artillery regiment which led the siege of Toulon against the English. There he showed remarkable ability and courage; he conceived the plan of attack on the town, personally directed the entire operation and was largely responsible for overcoming English resistance and taking Toulon. It now appeared that his career was assured and, in fact, he was

nominated to take command of the Alpine Artillery, but was unfortunately compromised by his friendship with Robespierre's brother. He was denounced, arrested and had the greatest difficulty in justifying his conduct. Hastening to Paris to defend himself, he proposed such a remarkable plan of attack on Italian territories that he was readmitted to the army, but was transferred to the west where his one wish, above all others, was to rejoin the army of Italy.

During this time, Joseph was living in Marseille, where he married Julie Clary, the daughter of an influential tradesman. Napoleon had a brief romance with Julie's sister, Désirée. They became engaged, but once Napoleon entered the elegant and frivolous world of the Directory, he soon forgot Désirée and became

engaged to Joséphine, the widow of Viscount de Beauharnais. The Bonapartes, however, were strongly opposed to the entry into their midst of a Creole girl, however charming she might be, and this was a lady of doubtful morals who had achieved public notoriety as the mistress of Paul Barras. Furthermore, she already had two children by her previous marriage, Eugène and Hortense, and the Bonapartes feared that Napoleon's favours would misguidedly be bestowed on the undeserving heads of his step-children, to the detriment of his own nephews and nieces. The marriage between Napoleon and Joséphine took place on 19 Ventôse, year IV (9 March 1796), at a civil ceremony which upset Letizia. Napoleon was put in charge of the army of Italy by Paul Barras, and a few

days later he left Paris in the company of Junot and Marmont.

Napoleon Bonaparte left Nice along the Corniche on 13 Germinal, year IV (2nd April 1796). He was leading an army of four divisions, totalling 37,705 men, poorly armed and badly dressed. With these soldiers Napoleon won the victories of Millesimo, Dego, Mondovi and Montenotte, when he successfully split the Sardinian army from the Austrians, forcing the King of Sardinia to make peace and defeating the immaculately dressed, well-armed Austrians in a series of battles in the Po valley, culminating in Lodi on 10 May 1796. He entered Milan, cheered by the local inhabitants, and was welcomed at a series of parties to celebrate his triumph.

However, the great captain, hero and conqueror of Italy was not happy. He was burning with love for Joséphine who, in Paris, was already forgetting her husband in the arms of Lieutenant Charles and only rarely did she reply to the impassioned letters written to her by Bonaparte. In spite of all the worries that beset him and his precarious state of health, Napoleon proved to be as good a diplomatist as he was a great military leader. He liberated the Italians and led the army against the Austrians at Arcola, Rivoli, La Favorita, Mantua and Castiglione. He took Venice and planned to go on to Vienna to dictate his terms of peace. The Directory grew alarmed at the glorious rise of a man who conducted his own foreign affairs. But how could they oppose him when the much-needed gold, silver, works of art and other spoils flowed in from Italy?

Joséphine put in occasional appearances, escorted by the inevitable Charles, and succeeded in calming the impatience of her ever more besotted husband. She held Court at Mombello and showed as much dedication as her husband in entertaining ambassadors from the old established Courts of Europe. Bonaparte was concerned by the lack of action on the part of the Rhine army, which was far larger than the army of Italy. Suddenly, on the eve of his offensive, instead of marching on Vienna as planned, he opened negotiations in Udine, signed the Treaty of Campo–Formio on 17 October 1796, swept like a flash of lightning through the Congress of Rastatt and finally arrived in Paris, covered in glory.

This was a dangerous situation for the Directory, and although they feared him, they appointed him Chief of the army of the Orient. Bonaparte realized that it would be impossible to invade the British Isles and, instead, conceived the bold plan of an expedition to Egypt to attack the route to India. He had to pass through the English shipping line on his way to Egypt. On 19 May 1798, Bonaparte embarked at Toulon and was luckily able to escape the attention of Nelson, seized the island of Malta and finally landed at Alexandria in July 1798.

He had left his family behind in France and he was worried, not without good reason, about Joséphine's behaviour. He had prevented an absurd marriage between Pauline and Fréron, who was living with an actress, and had married her instead to Leclerc, an officer on his general staff. He was so preoccupied with the matters in hand that he quite forgot his family worries and marched on Cairo. He fought and won the battle of the Pyramids, rapidly reorganized the administration of the country and founded the *Institut d'Egypte* with the help of the splendid group of intellectuals who had followed him there from France. But the French fleet was destroyed by Nelson at Aboukir on 25 July 1799: there was no hope of reinforcements and it was now impossible to return to France. Anyone else would have despaired at this turn of events, but not Bonaparte. He conquered and transformed the whole of Egypt, took an expedition into Syria with the intention of attacking the route to India and recruited several allies on the way. But he ran into trouble at St John of Acre and had to return to Cairo where, much to his dismay, he learnt of the continuing unfaithfulness of his wife, Joséphine.

No doubt he tried to forget her in the company of Madame Fourès, and he also became engrossed in the impressive work being carried out by the *Institut d'Egypte*, home of Egyptology. His enemies were waiting to attack him, and he won a land victory at Aboukir. In spite of this success, he decided to return to France. At daybreak, on 7 Fructidor, year VII (24 August 1799), he weighed anchor and sailed to the Gulf of Juan, narrowly escaping the British fleet near the coast of France.

During his absence, the Directory had demonstrated its own imcompetence. Bonaparte hurried to Paris, contemplated the situation and decided to seize power himself. On his return, he wanted to be rid of Joséphine. But, with her two children, Eugène and Hortense, she entreated him with bitter tears not to send her away and finally succeeded in persuading her enraged husband to let her stay with him. They were reconciled.

With the help of Joséphine, Lucien, Joseph and Leclerc, Bonaparte prepared to take his bid for power during the course of numerous meetings with Siéyès, Cambacérès and Fouché. Bernadotte, who had married Désirée Clary and had thus become Joseph's brother-in-law, did not take part. Envious and jealous, he was already an adversary, but Bonaparte forgave him everything in memory of his former fiancée, and all his life regretted breaking off his engagement to her.

On 18 Brumaire, year VIII (18 November 1799), in the early morning mist, Parisians would have seen the dazzling procession of Bonaparte and his general staff as they went along the boulevards on their way to the Council chambers. Everything went smoothly, in spite of the fact that Bonaparte had never before shown any great talent for public speaking. But the situation became dangerous the following day when Bonaparte visited St-Cloud to win over the Assembly of Five Hundred. Here he met with strong opposition and was already wavering when Lucien, President of the Assembly, came to his aid and called on Caroline's husband, Murat. Murat brought in his grenadiers, bayonets at the ready, and they chased the deputies out into the park. By that evening, Bonaparte had successfully taken over.

The Consular Court was quickly established, with a similar atmosphere to Mombello, near Milan, where the conqueror of Italy had been in residence. It was a young Court and the starring role was played by the First Consul's family. Antagonism between the Bonapartes and the Beauharnais family was growing: luckily Joséphine was a charming hostess at her beautiful estate of Malmaison, and it was here that Napoleon came to work and relax.

But France was once again threatened by war: the Austrians had 140,000 men in Italy under Melas, and 18,000 British and 20,000 Neapolitans were being drafted in as reinforcements; Vienna had 120,000 men in Germany and the Russians were getting ready to support them. Bonaparte organized a reserve army and led it across the Great St Bernard Pass. He entered Milan and subsequently won the brilliant victories of Mombello and of Marengo.

Bonaparte returned to Paris the conquering hero. His victory had put a stop to all the conspiracies that were being hatched up against him. More powerful than ever, he hastened to reorganize his armies, to reconstruct the administration of France with the help of Lucien and his foreign affairs with the help of Talleyrand, to perfect the legal apparatus by means of the Civil Code and the judiciary and financial machine through the Bank of France.

Bonaparte directed the affairs of his family and arranged marriages for his entourage to protect his own interests. Joséphine, who wanted to draw the Bonaparte and Beauharnais families closer together, used her influence to this end by marrying Hortense to Louis, but it was not a happy match.

The First Consul, meanwhile, was busy pursuing the pacification of western France. The Jacobin conspiracies of Cerrachi and Aréna were but a shadow on a beautiful landscape; Joseph, now promoted to the post of diplomat, was organizing the Congress of Lunéville and Moreau was engaged in a campaign at the head of the Rhine army. He used a cunning strategy which brought about the great victory of Hohenlinden on 3 December 1800, but he believed himself to be Bonaparte's rival and his success went to his head, contributing to his future downfall. The Armistice of Steyer put an end to the hostilities and Joseph was able to continue negotiations with Cobenzl at Lunéville. But a tremor of fear ran through the family when an attempt by an infernal machine in the Rue St-Nicaise nearly put an end to the brilliant career of Bonaparte. He escaped this conspiracy and was able to continue his unremitting work of the reorganization of France. Letizia accused him of working too hard.

The First Consul wanted to bring prosperity and peace to France and to erase the more painful traces of the Revolution. His entourage had no wish to draw closer to Rome, but Bonaparte wanted religious peace. He had a meeting with Cardinal Martiniana in Milan, much to the delight of the Bourbon claimant to the French throne, Louis XVIII, who supported Cardinal Maury in the Concordat negotiations. When he returned to Paris, Bonaparte received Monseigneur Spina and he instructed Abbé Bernier to negotiate with him, as he wished to deal quickly with the Pope. The negotiations progressed and after a further conference with Joseph at Consalvi, the Concordat was signed on 21 September 1801. The majority of the population was sincerely pleased with this agreement, which brought about religious peace, in spite of opposition from the Right and extreme Left.

The First Consul also wished for peace abroad. Joseph was given the task of negotiating peace with Britain and a preliminary agreement was signed in London on 1 October 1801, much to the delight of both countries. The peace treaty was signed at Amiens on 4 Germinal, year IX (27 March 1802). Both Bonaparte and the government of Great Britain were aware of the fragility of this peace.

The attempt on his life by the infernal machine had shown the need definitively to consolidate Bonaparte's government. He was offered the consulate for life. Madame Bonaparte and Fouché did not advise it, but his family desired it, and it was proposed by Cambacérès, voted by the Senate and ratified by a plebiscite which revealed only eight thousand dissenters. Shortly afterwards, Santo Domingo was conquered by Leclerc, accompanied by his wife, Pauline, who returned sorrowfully to France after his death. During this period, the First Consul was encountering serious problems with his family: he got little pleasure from Joseph or Lucien; while Louis and Hortense were not happy together, in spite of the birth of their son.

During the course of 1803, under the influence of William Pitt, England broke the Treaty of Amiens, and Bonaparte was forced to organize the military camps at Boulogne, St Omer and Montreuil. At home he was faced with the same indomitable adversaries as before and Georges Cadoudal's conspiracy showed him the extent of the dangers that threatened him. He felt himself surrounded by treason and in reprisal arranged to have the Duke of Enghien, a Bourbon prince of the Condé branch, kidnapped from Baden. The Duke's execution at Vincennes on 20 March upset Joséphine and outraged the rest of Europe.

In France there was a desire for a hereditary ruler to ensure a continuity of leadership and to put a stop to English intrigues. Approaches from provincial authorities and from the army increased day by day; Joseph and Lucien worked on the Assemblies and the advent of the Empire was decided on by the Senate. A public plebiscite to test national opinion gave 3,572,329 votes of approval out of a total of 3,574,898 votes cast. The Senate therefore unanimously conferred the hereditary title of Emperor, in direct line of succession, on Napoleon, Joseph, and Louis Bonaparte.

Napoleon wanted to be crowned by the Pope, and succeeded in winning over the Supreme Pontiff. Cardinal Fesch presided at a religious wedding ceremony between the Emperor and the Empress Joséphine in Notre-Dame on 10 Frimaire (30 November 1804).

One of the first things the Emperor did was to write to the English King, proposing peace, but the British government delayed in replying. Napoleon therefore encouraged the King of Spain to join battle, and he also decided to settle the Italian Question. He proposed that Joseph should become King of Italy, but the latter declined for fear of jeopardizing his succession to the Empire, nor would Louis allow his son to become adoptive King of Italy to succeed Napoleon. For this reason, Eugène was granted the

honour of becoming Chancellor of State and the Emperor decided to take the Crown of Italy himself and to nominate Eugène as Viceroy. Napoleon was crowned in Milan on 26 May 1805.

But on 11 April 1805, the Third Coalition against France had been formed and the Emperor, anticipating the onset of war, hurriedly annexed Genoa for the French, gave Lucca to Elise, and nominated Louis Governor of the Cisalpine States. Jerome arrived in Europe with his wife and was made captain of a frigate. The Emperor refused to see Lucien's wife, but despite his undisciplined nature, Louis was made Governor of Paris. At the military camp in Boulogne, Napoleon grew impatient at the delays and inaction of his admirals. He railed at Decrès and accused Villeneuve of cowardice and treason. But he finally abandoned the proposed invasion of England, returned to Paris and proceeded with his preparations for the Danube campaign.

The Emperor left Paris on 24 September 1805; he manoeuvred the Grande Armée across Württemberg and surrounded General Mack at Ulm. After Ney's victory at Elchingen, the Austrians abandoned the town and surrendered. Napoleon had taken forty

thousand prisoners and forty Austrian flags. Unfortunately, at the same time Admiral Villeneuve and the combined fleets of France and Spain had suffered a devastating defeat at Trafalgar, which provided incontestable evidence of England's supremacy at sea: a fact which made an invasion of the British Isles impossible to contemplate.

There was a financial crisis in Paris and Russia's somewhat ambiguous attitude towards France placed the flank of the Grande Armée in considerable danger; but in spite of this, the Emperor pursued his original plan, continued down the Danube, scattering the enemy before him, arrived in Vienna and marched on to the plains of Moravia to confront the Russians, who had belatedly come to help the Austrians. On 2 December, before the Russians had had time to intervene, Napoleon won a magnificent victory against the Russians and Austrians at Austerlitz. Murat's part in this battle was also much praised.

After the battle of Austerlitz, Napoleon returned to Munich to attend the wedding of Eugène de Beauharnais and Princess Augusta of Bavaria. He found her very pretty and soon allayed any fears Joséphine may still have had about the marriage. It

320

was the first of the great alliances linking the Bonapartes with the ruling families of Europe. Napoleon was very attentive to the Queen of Bavaria and her Court, and when Eugène arrived, Napoleon made him shave off his military moustache to make him more attractive to Princess Augusta. He sent a message to the Senate and to the three Colleges of Italy, announcing his adoption of Eugène. The nuptial blessing took place on 14 January 1806, in the royal chapel. Through this marriage, Napoleon found himself allied with the House of Wittelsbach and consequently most of the ruling houses of Europe.

Europe had been surprised and alarmed by the treaties of Pressburg and Schönbrunn which had followed the victory of Austerlitz, and Metternich rapidly formulated plans for a new coalition. During the course of 1806, Napoleon proceeded with the organization of his Empire, at the same time sending Joseph to Naples to supervize the surrender of Italy.

The Emperor wished to create feudal benefices to bestow on his loyal supporters. He founded the grand duchy of Berg, which was given to Murat, and he placed Louis on the throne of Holland. Napoleon adopted Stéphanie de Beauharnais and then arranged her marriage to the Prince of Baden. Joseph was appointed King of Naples and Sicily.

Desiring peace, the Emperor made advances to England, but his foreign policy ran into trouble with Austria, Russia and Prussia who were unhappy about the creation of the Rhine Confederation. Berlin burned with a feverish desire for war. On 25 September 1806, Napoleon left Paris to lead the Grande Armée, which was already stationed in Germany. The speed of his manoeuvres disorientated Prussia, and on 14 October he won two victories at Jena and Auerstädt, followed by a homeric pursuit of the Prussian army which culminated in its destruction and Napoleon's triumphal entry into Berlin.

The military situation was excellent, but England still remained undefeated. In the Decree of Berlin, dated 21 November 1806, Napoleon laid down the conditions for the Continental Blockade which was to have serious consequences for him. The Emperor marched on the Russians who were busy assembling large contingents. The Grande Armée crossed the Narew, but after the battles of Pultusk and Golymin and the seizure of Soldau, Bonaparte decided to set up his winter quarters. He went to Warsaw in January 1807, and there he met the beautiful Maria Walewska. She became his 'Polish woman', in the hope of obtaining independence for Poland. It was a gracious but short-lived romance, as the Russians resumed the offensive in February 1807 and Napoleon had to return to war. He won the difficult victory of Eylau from the Russians in the middle of a violent snowstorm. After the battle of Osterode he settled in

Finkenstein, where he was joined by Maria Walewska. Joséphine was jealous and wanted to visit him, but Napoleon would not allow her to come.

On 26 May, Danzig surrendered after a memorable siege and Marshal Lefèbvre gained a duchy for himself. Thanks to this prize, Napoleon's position was excellent, but the Russians attacked Ney. After the battle of Heilsberg, Napoleon resumed hostilities and defeated Bennigsen at Friedland on 14 June 1807. The Russian army was pursued as far as Tilsit where Emperor Alexander, who wished for peace, called a halt to the fighting. Two armistices were negotiated with Russia and Prussia and the Peace Treaty was signed at Tilsit on 7 and 9 July, with the two powers, on a raft built on Napoleon's instructions, in the middle of the River Niemen, in the presence of Queen Louisa of Prussia.

Once again, Napoleon dominated Europe. He returned to Paris, gave new impetus to the great work of building his Empire, and presided over the wedding between Jerome and Catherine of Württemberg. From the Alps to the Pyrenees, from the North Sea to the Gulf of Taranto, from the mouth of the Elbe to the source of the Inn, France was surrounded by peoples she had once conquered. Through the wisdom of the Emperor, they had now been given back their independence and peace.

Until the end of 1807, the Emperor had enjoyed a remarkable success without making any serious mistakes. From this time on, driven by the need to maintain the Continental Blockade, and by a dynastic desire to establish his relatives on the thrones of Europe, he was to commit major errors of judgement which would compromise the very existence of his great Empire.

During the course of 1808, life at Court was glamorous and extravagant. Napoleon went to northern Italy and visited Lucien, but they no longer understood one another. He ordered Junot to take an expedition to Portugal but himself returned to Paris, uncertain of what action he should take with regard to Spain. He finally sent a large contingent to the Peninsula, ignoring the wishes of the King of Spain's son, Prince Ferdinand, who wanted to marry one of his nieces. He also circulated a rumour that he was planning to marry the Grand Duchess Catherine of Russia, which greatly alarmed Metternich.

Charles IV of Spain wrote to Napoleon, demanding to know his intentions and the Emperor sent him a very curt reply. Murat was appointed Lieutenant General of Spain and Napoleon pressed forward with the invasion of the Peninsula. He subsequently left for Bayonne in the company of Joséphine, and contemplated offering the Spanish throne to Joseph. Charles IV came to see him, accompanied by the Queen and Godoy, 'the Prince of Peace'. The King soon gave

way to Napoleon's demands and, after signing the
Treaty of Bayonne, he went to Valençay to visit
Talleyrand. Joseph was appointed King of Spain, an
appointment which resulted in a revolt by the Spanish
people. The Grande Armée had to confront the entire
population and suffered vast, irreplaceable losses
during the course of this struggle. General Dupont was
surrounded and had to surrender at Baylen and Joseph
was forced to evacuate Madrid. The Emperor sent
substantial reinforcements, but the arrival of the
English in Portugal forced Junot to evacuate his
troops. Bonaparte went to Erfurt to meet Czar
Alexander I and Francis I, the Emperor of Austria,
before an audience of kings.

Meanwhile, in Spain, the Grande Armée continued
to suffer heavy losses and Joseph called incessantly for
reinforcements to quell the guerilla war. The Emperor
felt that he himself should be present and following a
brief visit to Paris, he said a reluctant farewell to
Joséphine and travelled in haste to Bayonne, where he
gave a vigorous boost to the military operation. Soult
took Burgos, the French army seized Santander,
Lannes won a victory at Tudela and Napoleon was
triumphant at Somo-Sierra. He marched on Madrid,
which he also captured. Joseph wanted to renounce the
Spanish throne but the Emperor forced him to stay on
and took the Grande Armée over the Sierra
Guadarrama in pursuit of the English. But during this

time, Austria was rearming and forming a new coalition and, in addition, Talleyrand and Fouché were busy plotting treason in Paris. Napoleon hastily returned to Paris, dwelling with regret on the recent events in Spain which he now realized had been an irreversible error on his part.

In April 1809, observing the difficulties France was experiencing in Spain, Austria plunged once more into war. Napoleon left Paris with Joséphine, and like a flash of lightning won a string of victories at Abensberg, Landshut, Eckmühl, Regensburg, where he was wounded. He once again captured Vienna and Essling, and finally won the Battle of Wagram on 5–6 July, which put an end to the war. But while this brilliant campaign was being conducted on the Danube, fighting continued in Spain with little sense of direction, since Napoleon was not there himself to co-ordinate the military operation. The English landed on the Island of Walcheren, threatening Antwerp. The peace conference opened at Altenburg and the Treaty of Schönbrunn was signed on 14 October 1809, much to the satisfaction of Napoleon and the regret of the Emperor Francis I.

Napoleon returned to Fontainebleau, contemplating divorce, because he felt that the birth of a son would guarantee the preservation of the throne for his dynasty. He discussed with Cambacérès the possible choice of a wife from the Hapsburg or Romanov families. In spite of her great distress, Napoleon informed Joséphine that he wanted a divorce and Napoleon's separation from Joséphine by mutual consent was settled. The Empress retired to Malmaison and the Senatus–Consultum ratified the divorce. At the same time, the Emperor demanded Louis' abdication from the throne of Holland, as he was opposing Napoleon's policies.

Napoleon sounded out the Czar and the Emperor of Austria to find out what they thought of his proposed remarriage. The former was reticent, whereas the Vienna Cabinet was greatly in favour. An Austrian marriage between Napoleon and Marie-Louise, daughter of Francis I was therefore decided on and the contract was signed by Champagny and Schwarzenberg. Marshal Berthier went to Vienna to conduct the marriage by proxy, as was the custom, and the new Empress travelled to France. Napoleon came to meet his new bride at Compiègne, where they spent their wedding night. The civil marriage was conducted at St-Cloud by Cambacérès and the religious ceremony took place in the Salon Carré at the Louvre. From thenceforth, Metternich made efforts to bring France and Austria closer together, but Napoleon wanted to deal with Russia. A short while later, the Austrian Emperor was informed of Marie-Louise's pregnancy. It was a great joy for Bonaparte.

Shortly afterwards, Bernadotte's election by the Swedish Diet went unopposed by the Emperor. This election was to cause complications with Russia, but Napoleon had always favoured Désirée Clary's husband in memory of the past. However, Bernadotte lost no time in showing himself to be an enemy of France.

As the birth of his child drew near, Napoleon took great care of the Empress. He watched over the birth with the greatest concern. On 19 March 1811, the Duchess of Montebello came out of the Empress's room wearing her day dress and everyone understood that the moment was approaching. The night was long and finally, the child was born and after seven anxious minutes the young King of Rome uttered his first wail.

A signal was given from the middle of the Tuileries. Everyone counted the gunshots coming from Les Invalides and at the twenty-second and twenty-third, they jumped for joy, raising a greaty cry of 'Long Live the Emperor'. The Emperor wanted to show the child to his people and the army. He was radiant with pleasure and everyone tried to catch a glimpse of him as he passed by.

The Emperor took up his work once more and planned the construction of a vast palace for the little King of Rome. At this time, Joseph returned to Spain but in Naples, Murat was showing signs of excessive independence. Napoleon ordered the dissolution of the army of Naples and Murat gave way to his wishes.

Russia was assembling her armies along the western frontier and Napoleon withdrew his troops, by now inured to the hardships of war, from Spain and replaced them with divisions of conscripts. The winter season in Paris was in full swing, there were numerous balls and the Emperor went to live in the Elysée Palace as it was closer to the Bois de Boulogne than the Tuileries, and consequently offered better hunting facilities. It was not a comfortable palace, and he caught a cold while he was there. At the end of March 1812, Napoleon went to live at St-Cloud: the life there was gay and social. Nobody wanted to dwell on the

Louis Bonaparte with his son Napoleon Louis.
Napoleon made his brother marry Hortense, daughter
of Joséphine Beauharnais, and created him King of
Holland in 1806. He was forced to abdicate in 1810.

prospect of the approaching war.

Early in the morning of 9 May, Napoleon and Marie-Louise left St-Cloud to go to Dresden, where Napoleon was to meet the Austrian Emperor and the German princes. But he was still sending his troops towards Russia and he himself went to Niemen to join his formidable army of 678,080 men, from France and elsewhere in the Empire.

On 24 June 1812, Napoleon crossed the river with the Grande Armée, hoping to surround and destroy Czar Alexander's army. But they retreated before him, and the Emperor had to pursue them into Russia until they called a halt to defend Moscow, the sacred city. The victory of Borodino in September was a costly one and brought with it the dubious prize of the city of Moscow, which had been burned to the ground to prevent the conqueror from enjoying his victory.

Napoleon was hesitant about the next step to take, and finally resigned himself to retreat. But the order was given too late, as the Russian winter was already drawing in. The sufferings of the Grande Armée were beyond endurance and the death toll, especially during the crossing of the Beresina, was appalling. The Emperor brought only sixty thousand disheartened men straggling back to Germany, but General Malet's uprising forced him to return in haste to Paris to restore law and order to the capital city. Large cracks were now appearing in the fabric of the Empire: Eugène was attempting to reorganize the Army of Germany from the surviving wreckage, but Murat refused to take on this thankless task and returned to Naples; the family was worried and disheartened.

The Emperor alone remained undaunted. Court life resumed and Napoleon signed the Concordat with the Pope at Fontainebleau. Events were occurring at an alarming pace: Prussia was rearming; Spain was gradually being evacuated; the Russians entered Warsaw; and Prussia declared war. Russia and Austria were drawing closer together, and, in spite of Caroline's moderating influence, Murat could not decide what step to take next.

Before leaving Paris to join his army, Napoleon appointed the Empress as Regent and settled a sum of money on her for her requirements during his absence. Marie-Louise was broken-hearted when her husband departed, full of confidence and eager to rejoin his troops as he always was on the eve of battle. The Armée had by now been reinforced by young conscripts who were to become the 'Marie-Louise' soldiers and would later distinguish themselves in heroic French military tradition. However, the army was not of the same calibre as at Austerlitz, Jena or Friedland, and it was vastly outnumbered by the coalition armies. After the victories of Weissenfels and Lützen, and the occupation of Leipzig, Napoleon wrote to Marie-Louise, ordering her to ask her father

to make peace. She was unsuccessful, but after the victory of Bautzen, on 20 May 1813, the enemy agreed to attend a congress and an armistice was concluded. This was only a device to gain time, as the allies had already jointly signed the Treaty of Reichenbach, designed to bring about Napoleon's downfall.

After the defeat at Vittoria in Spain, Joseph was removed from the throne and Soult appointed Lieutenant General. The Congress of Prague came to nothing, Austria once again declared war and Napoleon concentrated his troops round Dresden where he won another battle. But the effects of this victory were outweighed by Vandamme's defeat at Kulm and Ney's defeat at Dennewitz. The allies strengthened their coalition with the Treaty of Teplitz on 9 September and continued their advance on Germany. Jerome fled from Cassel and retired to Coblenz, thus bringing about the end of the kingdom of Westphalia.

The allies decided on a joint march on Leipzig, where Napoleon was stationed with his entire force. 'The Battle of the Nations' took place on 16–19 October and Napoleon suffered a resounding defeat, due largely to his betrayal on the battlefield by the Saxons. The Grande Armée was forced to retreat towards France and, on the way, ran into the Bavarians who were attempting to prevent Napoleon's progress to Strasbourg. The ensuing battle of Hanau resulted in the defeat of the Bavarians. From that moment invasion was imminent.

Napoleon had taken up the defensive position all over Europe: in Holland; in Italy where Eugène defended the plain of Veneto against the Austrians, and in Spain, where the French Army was retreating from Wellington's advance, which was soon to threaten the southern frontier of France.

Schwarzenberg crossed the Rhine at Basel and Alsace was invaded in January 1814. Murat joined forces with the allies. Napoleon once again entrusted the Regency to Marie-Louise and opened what was to be one of his most brilliant campaigns, on the plains of eastern France. With only a small number of troops, who were nevertheless fired with ardent patriotism, he successfully attacked the invading armies, won victories at St-Dizier, La Rothière, and continued towards Troyes. In Paris, however, anxiety was growing and Talleyrand was busy conspiring with the royalists.

A Congress was held at Châtillon-sur-Seine from 5 February to 19 March 1814. Although the Emperor had given the Marquis de Caulaincourt a free rein, he hesitated and Czar Alexander broke off the negotiations. Courageous and clear-sighted, and supported by the heroic 'Marie-Louise' troops, Napoleon won battles at Champaubert, Montmirail, Château-Thierry and Vauchamps. He once again attacked

The end: Napoleon on board the British ship HMS Bellerophon *after the defeat at Waterloo. He had said that he wanted to live freely in England, supervised and protected by the law, but he was taken to St Helena.*

Schwarzenberg and won victories at Montereau, Méry, Rheims and Craonne, which helped to revive the morale of the Parisians. This was vital, for Cambacérès had ordered prayers to be said, much to the Emperor's irritation. Joseph did nothing, in the hope of disconcerting the Regent.

At Rheims and St-Dizier, Napoleon was hesitant as to his next move. He thought of retreating to Lorraine, but the allies decided to march on the capital. The Emperor was afraid of losing control of the war and so decided to return to Fontainebleau.

On 27 March, evening at the Tuileries was spent in the usual manner. Queen Hortense played a round of whist with the Empress, Talleyrand and Molé, but the Regent's Council decided that Marie-Louise and the King of Rome should leave Paris. They were already on their way to Chartres when the coalition troops arrived at the gates of Paris. Fighting broke out at Charenton, and at the Trone and Clichy gates, but the defence was badly organized and on 30 March 1814, Paris surrendered.

At Fontainebleau, Napoleon wanted to attack the coalition army in Paris, where they were being welcomed by the royalists. The Emperor was inspecting the guard at Essones when the Senate voted to depose him, a vote in which both the Legislative Corps and the Highest Court participated. Urged on by his field-marshals, Napoleon declared on 4 April that he was ready to renounce the throne. The field-marshals went as ambassadors to Paris, but Marmont ordered his troops to go behind the enemy lines and thus destroyed the Emperor's last chance of a reasonable settlement. He was forced to sign the act of Abdication. The field-marshals returned to Paris and, during the night of 10/11 April, a treaty was signed giving the island of Elba to Napoleon, and the duchy of Parma, Piacenza and Guastalla to Marie-Louise, together with various other endowments to members of the Bonaparte family, generals and other servants of the Emperor. Downhearted, Napoleon tried unsuccessfully to commit suicide.

The family was split up; the Austrian Emperor ordered Marie-Louise and the King of Rome to Rome, while Napoleon said farewell to his troops in the courtyard of the Cheval Blanc at Fontainebleau and departed for Elba on 20 April 1814. He was in great danger throughout his journey. On 29 April, he set sail from St Raphael in an English frigate, and on 30 April

The Empress Eugénie, wife of Napoleon III, painted
with her ladies by Franz Winterhalter in 1855. The
Empire was restored by the great Napoleon's nephew,
the son of Louis and of Hortense Beauharnais.

he left the French shores.

At ten o'clock in the evening of 3 May 1814, the Emperor landed at Portoferraio, the main port of the island of Elba. It was a tiny kingdom for the leader of a great empire, but fortunately he was accompanied by a battalion of his former guard. He longed for Marie-Louise and his son, but only Princess Pauline arrived to keep him company and the Emperor's hopes were never fulfilled. A Congress was held at Vienna and the rulers of Europe agreed that they did not wish to lose such valuable hostages. Maria Walewska, accompanied by her son by Napoleon, came to visit him on Elba and this brought him some consolation. In any case, Marie-Louise, however, was engaged in a liaison with Neipperg and had already lost interest in Napoleon.

Joseph feared that he too could be forced to live on the island of Elba and was afraid of the effect that the climate might have on Julie and his children. He had bought himself a castle at Prangins on the shores of Lake Geneva and there he welcomed Jerome, Catherine, and even Marie-Louise, who was on her way to Aix-les-Bains. Lucien remained in Rome, where he had been well received by the Pope, and he led the life of a Roman aristocrat, calling himself Prince of Canino. Louis was in Switzerland, where he refused to see Hortense. Jerome retired to Austria, buying large estates near Trieste, and adopting the title of Count von Hartz. Elise returned to Italy, where she gave birth to a son at the castle of Passariano. Hortense went to Plombières then on to Baden, where she joined Eugène, and finally returned to the castle of St-Leu. Letizia made a short visit to Napoleon on the island of Elba, but she did not stay. Thus the Bonaparte family was scattered over the length and breadth of Europe.

Napoleon was surrounded by spies, but he was quite resigned to the events taking place in France. Besides, Fleury de Chaboulon had told him in detail of the discontent of the army and of a large section of the population. Short of money, fearing abduction and even an attempt on his life, the Emperor decided to return to France. The prudent General Drouot, fearing the consequences of this mad enterprise, tried to dissuade him, but on 26 February 1815, Napoleon disembarked at Portoferraio, slipped past the English fleet and landed at the Gulf Juan.

Now began the astounding adventure of the Flight of the Eagle. Without having to strike a single blow, Napoleon entered the Tuileries where his faithful followers were waiting for him. He found Hortense there in mourning for Joséphine who had just died, following a visit from Czar Alexander. Princess Julie, also in mourning, and Madame Clary were present as well. The Emperor was carried through the rooms of the Tuileries with his eyes closed and a smile on his face, like a sleepwalker.

The next day, Napoleon formed his ministry and with customary speed, he began to regroup his troops. He sincerely hoped for peace and, later, on St Helena, he deplored the blindness of the European rulers who had joined together to crush him. The Treaty of the Quadruple Alliance was signed at Vienna on 25 March and Louis XVIII soon joined the allies.

Napoleon wrote to Marie-Louise to call her to his side, but she became ever more distant, stating that she had never really loved him, but had only admired his greatness. She now declared herself so shocked by him that she had vowed to go on foot on the famous Maria Zell pilgrimage, if he was captured. She was, in fact, at this time completely besotted with Neipperg.

La Vendée was incited to rebellion but this was suppressed immediately, and the Marquis of La Rochejaquelein was killed near Croix de Vie. This insurrection was to deprive Napoleon of a total of thirty-five thousand men at Waterloo. In Naples, Murat was defeated and he fled to France. Later he was to return to Italy to be shot down by his subjects.

These events saddened the Emperor, but on 12 June 1815, he regained his spirits on leaving Paris for Belgium at the head of his reconstituted Armée. He began by winning two victories at Quatre-Bras and Ligny, but at Waterloo he came up against the vast English army with its Belgian and Dutch reinforcements. The battle proved indecisive and Napoleon impatiently awaited the arrival of Grouchy who was on the right flank with his troops. But it was the Prussian General, Blücher, who arrived instead, and in spite of the prodigious efforts of the Guard, the Grande Armée was defeated and Napoleon was involved in a tragic retreat. He himself returned to Paris while his army was being pursued by the victorious allies, and the English and Spanish forces occupied the southern provinces.

Once again, the coalition armies arrived at the gates of Paris and the capital had to surrender at the beginning of July 1815. The Grande Armée, which, in spite of everything, had not lost its appetite for war, was disgruntled at the surrender of Paris and this gave rise to numerous intrigues led by Fouché, the Chief of Police.

Napoleon, who had abdicated in favour of his son, went to Malmaison, where he offered to resume leadership of the army. His proposal was not accepted and he left for Rochefort with the intention of seeking refuge in America. The British Prime Minister, Lord Liverpool, and Metternich wanted to be rid of him. Napoleon arrived at the island of Aix but delayed in boarding a ship for America. The English fleet tightened its surveillance and he was left with no alternative but to go on board the HMS *Bellerophon*, declaring that he wanted only to live the life of a free man in England under the protection of her laws. He was taken to the shores of England, but he was then transferred to the HMS *Northumberland* and deported to the island of St Helena.

During this time, Hortense, who had greeted Napoleon with affection at Malmaison, went to Geneva where she met Letizia and Cardinal Fesch on their way to Italy. Napoleon's mother had retained her forceful spirit declaring she was proud to be Napoleon's mother.

The island of St Helena lies in the middle of the South Atlantic Ocean, an ugly rock buffeted by the winds and the sea. The British Government ensured that the Emperor remained under close surveillance. He was accompanied by only a handful of his faithful entourage, and no members of his family. The Emperor set to work, dictating his account of his campaigns and reign, showing an admirable and surprising objectivity and judgement. Letizia and Hortense wanted to join him on St Helena, but he would not permit it, as he did not want them to witness the humiliating circumstances in which he found himself.

One of the subjects which he liked above all to dwell on was the Empress Joséphine. He said that with her he had enjoyed an ordinary, bourgeois marriage, in other words, a very tender and close relationship, sharing the same bedroom and the same bed.

Hortense and Stephanie were not happy with their husbands and Joséphine had often scolded them for their capricious and independent behaviour. But immediately after Joséphine's divorce, Stephanie returned to her husband and thereafter they had a very happy marriage.

Pauline had been too extravagant and impulsive, while, on the other hand, Letizia was too parsimonious – an excess of caution on her part, for she feared above all that one day she would find herself with nothing.

Napoleon thought of Joséphine as 'a very good sort', and of Julie as 'the best of creatures'. Jerome was a squanderer whose excesses had been shocking, and his wife had behaved admirably when he wanted her to divorce him. Thus, the Emperor judged his family, with indulgence and calmness, forgetting the wrongs they had done him. He hoped that some day his son would rule France, if the nation rebelled. He remained passionately attached to the boy.

Elise died on 7 August 1820 at Villa Vicentina, near Aquileia. Her death made the Emperor fear his was not far away.

The Emperor's health, shaken by his long and cruel captivity, was weakening. The climate had also been a contributory factor. When dictating his memoirs to Montholon, his first thought was for his son and he left the boy some advice: 'My son,' he said, 'must not think of avenging my death; he should learn from it. He should always remember what I have done; he should

always remain, as I have, firmly French, right to his fingertips. All his efforts should be directed at achieving peace. If he were to continue my wars, not out of necessity, but in imitation of my career, he would be merely an ape. To imitate my work would be to suppose that I had achieved nothing. The achievement would be to show the strength of the foundation, to explain the entire plan of the construction which had only just begun. The same thing is not done in a century. I was forced to subdue the people of Europe with arms; today, they must be persuaded. I saved the Revolution which was foundering; I cleansed it of its crimes. I showed it to the world, splendid and glorious. I sowed the seeds of new ideas in France and Europe; they cannot go backwards. Let my son reap all that I have sown. May he develop all the elements of prosperity contained in the soil of France. At this price, he may still be a great ruler.'

'Let my son often read and reflect on history,' the Emperor wrote. 'Therein lies the true philosophy. He should read and reflect on the wars of the great generals, it is the only way to learn about war. ... But all that you tell him and all that he learns will only be of

use if in his heart he has the sacred flame, that love of good which alone achieves great things. ... But I hope that he will be worthy of his destiny.'

The Emperor suddenly felt unable to continue; his voice faded and Montholon, alarmed at his appearance, begged him to stop dictating. The essential points had been said. After a painful effort, Montholon heard the words, '*France, armée, Tête l'armée, Joséphine*' ('France, army, head of the army, Joséphine).

At 5.45 pm on 5 May 1821 Napoleon Bonaparte gave up his soul to God.

The death of the Emperor deprived the Bonaparte family of their titles and thrones. What was to become of its various members who were scattered throughout Europe? The fate of his wife and son had constantly preoccupied Napoleon during his exile on St Helena. Marie-Louise had made no effort to join him and she soon forgot him in the arms of an Austrian General, Neipperg, whom she married after the death of the Emperor. In 1815, she had been given the lifelong sovereignty of Parma, Piacenza and Guastalla, and she preferred the comforts of life at Court to the rigours of a tragic exile on St Helena. She failed even to carry out her duties properly with regard to the King of Rome. She very quickly parted from the poor child, who had not wanted to leave Paris or France. He was reduced to the rank of an Austrian archduke and throughout his brief life he remained devoted to his father, homesick for France and longing to know the whole truth, which was kept from him. In his gilded cage at Schönbrunn, the King of Rome became first the King of Parma, then, in 1818, the Duke of Reichstadt, and finally, on the death of the Emperor, Napoleon II. He wasted away at Schönbrunn until, in 1832, he finally died. In 1940, his ashes were brought back to Paris by Hitler and were placed next to his father in the vault at Les Invalides. It was only fitting that this should be his last resting place.

Letizia, Napoleon's mother, had retired to Rome. After the Emperor's death, she led a dignified, retired life in the Eternal City. The other members of the family led a nomadic existence: Joseph, who had become Count of Survilliers, lived in the United States, in England and then in Florence; one of his daughters married a son of Lucien, and the other married a son of Louis, who became a member of the *Institut de France* and died in Paris in 1857. Lucien lived in Rome until his unexpected death at Viterbo in 1840. Elise, who had tried in vain to keep her estates in Tuscany, had retired to Trieste, where she had died in 1820. First in Rome and then in Florence, Louis led the life of a great Roman nobleman, right up till his death in Leghorn in 1846. Pauline also lived in Rome and died there in 1825. Jerome, the ex-King of Westphalia, had taken refuge in Trieste, Rome and then Florence and he returned to Paris in 1848. After the death of her husband Murat, King of Naples, Caroline had gone to Trieste and then on to Frosdorf, where she lived under the name of the Countess of Lipona, an anagram of 'Napoli'.

The destiny of Hortense, daughter of Empress Joséphine, was different. Exiled by the Second Restoration, ex-Queen of Holland, and separated from Louis Bonaparte, she lived in the small castle of Arenenberg, on the shores of Lake Constance. Of her three sons, Napoleon Charles, Napoleon Louis and Charles Louis Napoleon, only the last survived. He had a brilliant destiny, he was to become Emperor of the French.

Charles Louis Napoleon had inherited the family taste for government, and in particular, a love of intrigue. He became associated with the Italian *Carbonari* and in 1831 he participated in an uprising in central Italy. He saw himself as destined to continue in the illustrious Bonaparte tradition. Neither the dangers nor the difficulties could deter him from his perilous course. In 1836 his attempt to incite the garrison at Strasbourg to insurrection forced him into exile in America. He hurried back to the bedside of

Hortense, who died the following year, and he then went into exile in London. In 1840, he attempted an unexpected attack on Boulogne, but he was captured and condemned to life imprisonment in the fortress of Ham. He escaped in 1846 and returned to England.

The revolution of 1848 enabled him to return to France and, sustained by the Napoleonic legend, he secured the presidency of the Republic. It was a title which did not satisfy him, he quarrelled with the Assembly, and, confident of popular support, he carried out a daring *coup d'état* on 2 December 1851. This was endorsed by a plebiscite which paved the way for a consular regime, extending his presidency for a period of ten years.

In November 1852, Prince Napoleon held a further plebiscite and following this, on 2 December 1852, he assumed the title of Emperor of the French. And so began the period of authoritarian Empire which lasted from 1852 to 1859. During this time France was engaged in a series of wars: the Crimean War in 1854; the Italian War in 1859, when the French army revisited the battlefields of its glorious 1796 campaign, and won for France the territories of Nice and Savoy; and in the war in Algeria, in which the Emperor showed himself to be a true liberal at heart.

In 1853 Prince Napoleon had married a beautiful Spanish girl of noble birth, named Eugénie Montijo. In 1856 she bore him a son, Eugène Louis Napoleon, whose destiny was to be a tragic one.

Napoleon III was deprived of his traditional support from the Catholics, who disapproved of his policies with regard to the Holy See, and from the industrialists, who opposed the policy of free trade practised by the government. Nevertheless, he hoped to gain the respect of the working man through his liberal ideas. The period of the Liberal Empire opened under favourable auspices, for public opinion desired peace both in internal and foreign affairs. This hope was not to be fulfilled, since the concessions made by the Emperor only served to reinforce revolutionary opposition and strikes were numerous.

In foreign affairs, the expedition to Mexico in 1862 achieved nothing, the interview in Biarritz, followed by the defeat of Austria at Sadowa was another failure, the Roman question was a third, and the disasters resulting from foreign policy culminated in the irreparable defeat of 1870. The surrender of Sedan on 2 September was followed by the Emperor's dethronement, proclaimed in Paris two days later. He was taken into captivity at the Castle of Wilhemshohe, near Cassel, but once the peace treaty was signed, he retreated to Chislehurst in England where, weakened by sorrow and poor health, he died in 1873.

The hopes of the French Bonapartists now rested on the Prince Imperial, who was immersed in his military studies at Woolwich with the English artillery. He left in 1875 and, bored by being in exile, he went to South Africa in 1879, where he was killed after being wounded seventeen times while fighting the Zulus. After this tragic death, the Bonapartist party turned its attention to Prince Victor, born in Meudon in 1862, the son of Prince Jerome (Plon-Plon), who was himself the son of Jerome Bonaparte. Exiled from France under the law which banished all pretenders to the throne, he settled in Brussels in 1886. In 1910 he was married in Italy to Princess Clementine, the daughter of King Leopold II of the Belgians, and had two children, Princess Clotilde born in 1912, and Prince Louis Napoleon, born in 1914. Prince Victor had applied in vain to the French government for permission to join the ranks of the French army.

His son was luckier. At the beginning of 1939 he asked President Daladier if he could carry out his military service in France, but he received no reply because of the exile law. In September 1939, a second, and then a third demand, were not met because the exile law was invoked. The Prince then offered his services to the British Royal Navy, but his offer was declined. On 19 March 1940, a certain individual named Blanchard joined the Foreign Legion at Ain: it was Prince Louis Napoleon. He was sent to Sidi Bel Abbès, where he stayed until the armistice, never having entered the fight. He returned to his castle at Prangins on the shores of Lake Geneva, but resolved to join the French army. He was arrested during a dramatic crossing of the Pyrenees and spent four and a half months in Fresnes and at Neuilly, where he was released by the Gestapo. He joined the French Resistance and then signed up under the name of Monnier in the 17th Light Infantry Batallion, at Chateauroux. He fought in the Brenne in the 'Charles Martel' brigade where he was wounded twice. He was subsequently admitted by General de Gaulle into the French Forces of the Interior under the name of Monfort, after being cited by General Koenig. On 14 February 1946, the Prince was awarded the Croix de Chevalier of the Légion d'Honneur, which he received from General Béthouart.

On 16 August 1949, the Prince married Alia de Foresta, daughter of a legitimist family of Italian origin which had settled in Provence some four centuries previously. This marriage produced twins on 19 October 1950, Charles and Catherine, a daughter, Laure, in 1952 and a second son, Jerome, in 1957. It is this family that today upholds the glorious name of Napoleon Bonaparte.

The Capets

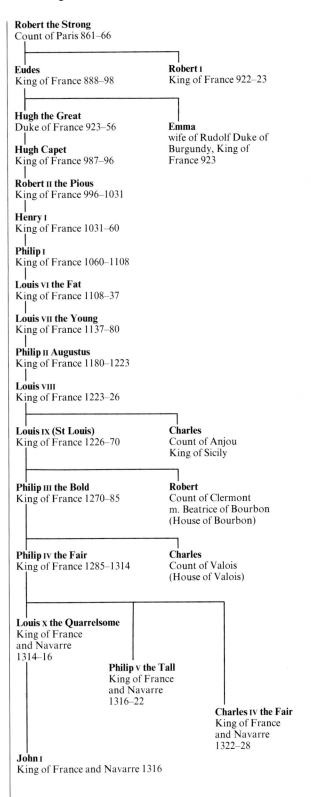

Robert the Strong
Count of Paris 861–66

Eudes
King of France 888–98

Robert I
King of France 922–23

Hugh the Great
Duke of France 923–56

Emma
wife of Rudolf Duke of
Burgundy, King of
France 923

Hugh Capet
King of France 987–96

Robert II the Pious
King of France 996–1031

Henry I
King of France 1031–60

Philip I
King of France 1060–1108

Louis VI the Fat
King of France 1108–37

Louis VII the Young
King of France 1137–80

Philip II Augustus
King of France 1180–1223

Louis VIII
King of France 1223–26

Louis IX (St Louis)
King of France 1226–70

Charles
Count of Anjou
King of Sicily

Philip III the Bold
King of France 1270–85

Robert
Count of Clermont
m. Beatrice of Bourbon
(House of Bourbon)

Philip IV the Fair
King of France 1285–1314

Charles
Count of Valois
(House of Valois)

Louis X the Quarrelsome
King of France
and Navarre
1314–16

Philip V the Tall
King of France
and Navarre
1316–22

Charles IV the Fair
King of France
and Navarre
1322–28

John I
King of France and Navarre 1316

Hohenstaufens

Frederick of Büren
d. before 1094

Frederick of Hohenstaufen
Duke of Swabia 1079–1105

Frederick
Duke of Swabia 1105–47

Conrad III
Duke of Franconia 1115
King of Italy 1128
King of Germany and Emperor
1138–52

Frederick I Barbarossa
Duke of Swabia 1147
King of Germany 1152
Emperor 1152–90

Henry VI
King of the Romans 1169
King of Germany 1190
Emperor 1190
King of Sicily 1194–97

Philip
Duke of Swabia 1196
King of Germany 1198–1208

Frederick II
King of the Romans 1196
King of Sicily 1198
King of Germany 1212
Emperor 1215–50

Beatrice
m. Otto of Brunswick
King of Germany 1198
Emperor 1209–15

Conrad IV
Duke of Swabia 1235
King of Germany 1237
d. 1254

Enzio
King of Sardinia
d. 1272

Manfred
King of Sicily 1258
d. 1266

Conradin
Duke of Swabia d. 1268

Plantagenets

Geoffrey IV
Count of Anjou d. 1151
m. Matilda, daughter of Henry I
King of England

Henry II
King of England 1154–89

Richard I Coeur de Lion
King of England 1189–99

John Lackland
King of England 1199–1216

Henry III
King of England 1216–72

Edward I
King of England 1272–1307

Edward II
King of England 1307–27

Edward III
King of England 1327–77

Edward
the Black Prince d. 1376

John of Gaunt
(House of Lancaster)

Edmund of Langley
(House of York)

Richard II
King of England 1377–99
d. 1400

House of Lancaster

John of Gaunt
Duke of Lancaster d. 1399

Henry IV
King of England 1399–1413

Henry V
King of England 1413–22

Henry VI
King of England 1422–61 and
1470–1

Edward
Prince of Wales d. 1471

House of York

Edmund of Langley
Duke of York d. 1402

Richard of Coningsburgh
Earl of Cambridge d. 1415

Richard
Duke of York d. 1460

Edward IV
King of England
1461–70 and 1471–83

Richard III
King of England 1483–5

Elizabeth
m. Henry VII Tudor
King of England

Edward V
King of England d. 1483

Hapsburgs

Werner II
Count of Hapsburg d. 1096

Otto II
Count of Hapsburg d. 1111

Werner III
Count of Hapsburg d. 1167

Albert III the Rich
Count of Hapsburg d. 1199

Rudolf II
Count of Hapsburg d. 1232

Albert IV the Wise
Count of Hapsburg d. 1239–40

Rudolf I
Count of Hapsburg 1239–73
Duke of Carinthia 1276–86
King of Germany 1273–91

Albert I
Duke of Austria and Styria
1282
King of Germany 1298–1308

Albert II the Lame
Duke of Austria d. 1358

Albert III
Duke of Austria d. 1395

Albert IV the Patient
Duke of Austria d. 1404

Albert V (II)
Duke of Austria 1404
King of Germany 1438–9

Ladislas Posthumus
King of Hungary 1445
King of Bohemia 1452–57

Leopold III
Duke of Styria d. 1386

Ernest the Iron Duke
Duke of Styria d. 1424

Frederick III
Duke of Styria 1424
Emperor 1440–93

Maximilian I
Emperor 1493–1519

Philip the Fair
Duke of Brabant
Count of Flanders 1482
King of Castile 1504–06

Margaret
Governor
of the Low Countries d. 1530

Charles I (v)
Emperor
(Spanish Hapsburgs)

Ferdinand I
Emperor
(Austrian Hapsburgs)

Spanish Hapsburgs

Charles I (v)
King of Spain 1516
Emperor 1519–56 d. 1558

Philip II
King of Spain 1556–98

Don Carlos
Prince of the Asturias d. 1568

Philip III
King of Spain 1598–1621

Philip IV
King of Spain 1621–65

Charles II
King of Spain 1665–1700

Austrian Hapsburgs

Ferdinand I
King of Bohemia 1526
and of Hungary 1527
Emperor 1558–64

Maximilian II
Emperor 1564–76

Anna = **Albert III**
of Bavaria
Charles
Duke of Styria d 1590

Rudolf II
Emperor 1576–1612
Emperor 1576–1612

Mathias
Emperor 1612–19

Ferdinand II
Emperor 1619–37

Ferdinand III
Emperor 1637–57

Leopold I
Emperor 1658–1705

Joseph I
Emperor 1705–11

Charles VI
Emperor 1711–40

Maria Amalia
m. Charles Albert of Bavaria
(Emperor Charles VII 1742–45)

Maria Theresa
Queen of Bohemia and of
Hungary 1740
m. Francis Stephen
Duke of Lorraine
(House of Hapsburg-Lorraine)

335

Valois

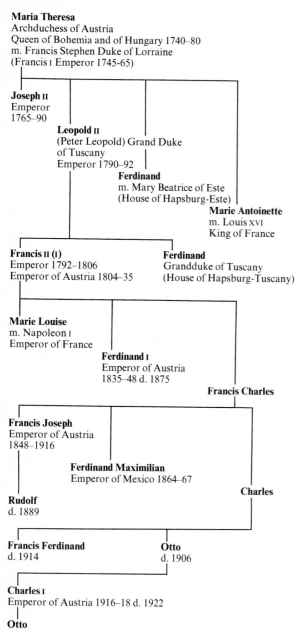

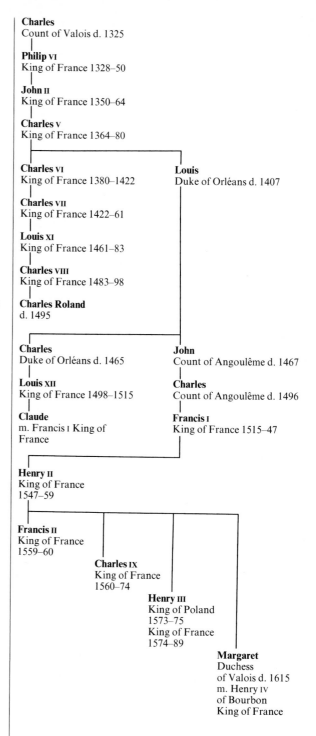

Hapsburg-Lorraine

Maria Theresa
Archduchess of Austria
Queen of Bohemia and of Hungary 1740–80
m. Francis Stephen Duke of Lorraine
(Francis I Emperor 1745-65)

Joseph II
Emperor
1765–90

Leopold II
(Peter Leopold) Grand Duke
of Tuscany
Emperor 1790–92

Ferdinand
m. Mary Beatrice of Este
(House of Hapsburg-Este)

Marie Antoinette
m. Louis XVI
King of France

Francis II (I)
Emperor 1792–1806
Emperor of Austria 1804–35

Ferdinand
Grandduke of Tuscany
(House of Hapsburg-Tuscany)

Marie Louise
m. Napoleon I
Emperor of France

Ferdinand I
Emperor of Austria
1835–48 d. 1875

Francis Charles

Francis Joseph
Emperor of Austria
1848–1916

Ferdinand Maximilian
Emperor of Mexico 1864–67

Charles

Rudolf
d. 1889

Francis Ferdinand
d. 1914

Otto
d. 1906

Charles I
Emperor of Austria 1916–18 d. 1922

Otto

Charles
Count of Valois d. 1325

Philip VI
King of France 1328–50

John II
King of France 1350–64

Charles V
King of France 1364–80

Charles VI
King of France 1380–1422

Louis
Duke of Orléans d. 1407

Charles VII
King of France 1422–61

Louis XI
King of France 1461–83

Charles VIII
King of France 1483–98

Charles Roland
d. 1495

Charles
Duke of Orléans d. 1465

John
Count of Angoulême d. 1467

Louis XII
King of France 1498–1515

Charles
Count of Angoulême d. 1496

Claude
m. Francis I King of
France

Francis I
King of France 1515–47

Henry II
King of France
1547–59

Francis II
King of France
1559–60

Charles IX
King of France
1560–74

Henry III
King of Poland
1573–75
King of France
1574–89

Margaret
Duchess
of Valois d. 1615
m. Henry IV
of Bourbon
King of France

Stuarts

Walter
sixth High Steward
m. Marjorie, daughter of
Robert Bruce
King of Scotland
|
Robert II
King of Scotland 1371–90
|
Robert III
King of Scotland 1390–1406
|
James I
King of Scotland 1406–37
|
James II
King of Scotland 1437–60
|
James III
King of Scotland 1460–88
|
James IV
King of Scotland 1488–1513
m. Margaret Tudor
daughter of Henry VII King of
England
|
James V
King of Scotland 1513–42
|
Mary
Queen of Scotland 1542–67
d. 1587
|
James VI (I)
King of Scotland 1567–1625
King of England 1603–25

Elizabeth
m. Frederick V
Elector Palatine
|
Sophia m. Ernest Augustus
Elector of Hanover
House of Hanover

Charles I
King of England 1625–49

Charles II
King of England 1660–85

James II
King of England 1685–88
d. 1701

Mary II
Queen of England 1689–94
m. William III of Orange,
King of England 1689–1702

Anne
Queen of
England
1702–14

James Edward
the Old Pretender d. 1766

Charles Edward
the Young Pretender d. 1788

Henry
Cardinal of York d. 1807

Tudors

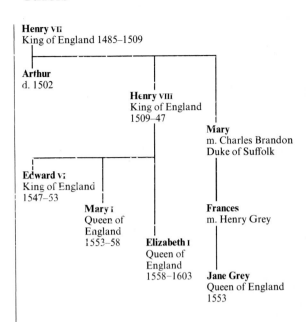

Henry VII
King of England 1485–1509

Arthur
d. 1502

Henry VIII
King of England
1509–47

Mary
m. Charles Brandon
Duke of Suffolk

Edward VI
King of England
1547–53

Mary I
Queen of
England
1553–58

Frances
m. Henry Grey

Elizabeth I
Queen of
England
1558–1603

Jane Grey
Queen of England
1553

Bourbons of France

Henry IV
(descendant in the ninth
generation
of Robert of Clermont
son of St Louis)
King of Navarre 1562
King of France 1589–1610

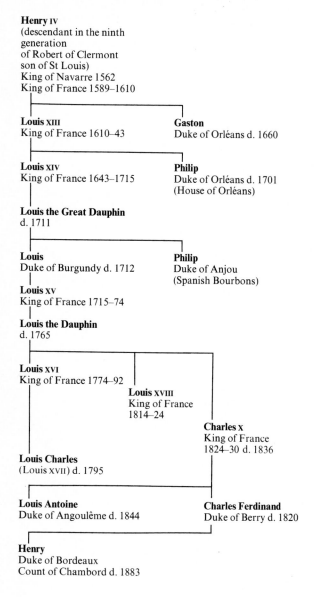

Louis XIII
King of France 1610–43

Gaston
Duke of Orléans d. 1660

Louis XIV
King of France 1643–1715

Philip
Duke of Orléans d. 1701
(House of Orléans)

Louis the Great Dauphin
d. 1711

Louis
Duke of Burgundy d. 1712

Philip
Duke of Anjou
(Spanish Bourbons)

Louis XV
King of France 1715–74

Louis the Dauphin
d. 1765

Louis XVI
King of France 1774–92

Louis XVIII
King of France
1814–24

Charles X
King of France
1824–30 d. 1836

Louis Charles
(Louis XVII) d. 1795

Louis Antoine
Duke of Angoulême d. 1844

Charles Ferdinand
Duke of Berry d. 1820

Henry
Duke of Bordeaux
Count of Chambord d. 1883

Romanovs

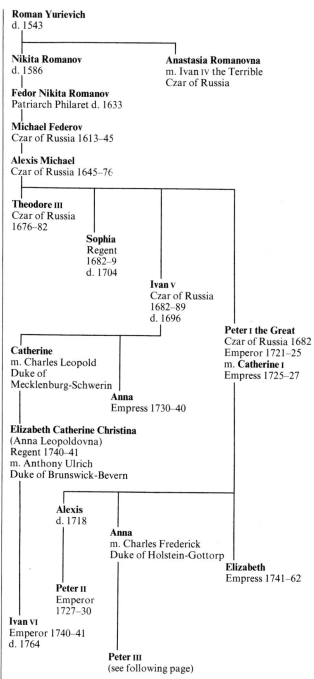

Roman Yurievich
d. 1543

Nikita Romanov
d. 1586

Anastasia Romanovna
m. Ivan IV the Terrible
Czar of Russia

Fedor Nikita Romanov
Patriarch Philaret d. 1633

Michael Federov
Czar of Russia 1613–45

Alexis Michael
Czar of Russia 1645–76

Theodore III
Czar of Russia
1676–82

Sophia
Regent
1682–9
d. 1704

Ivan V
Czar of Russia
1682–89
d. 1696

Peter I the Great
Czar of Russia 1682
Emperor 1721–25
m. **Catherine I**
Empress 1725–27

Catherine
m. Charles Leopold
Duke of
Mecklenburg-Schwerin

Anna
Empress 1730–40

Elizabeth Catherine Christina
(Anna Leopoldovna)
Regent 1740–41
m. Anthony Ulrich
Duke of Brunswick-Bevern

Alexis
d. 1718

Anna
m. Charles Frederick
Duke of Holstein-Gottorp

Elizabeth
Empress 1741–62

Peter II
Emperor
1727–30

Ivan VI
Emperor 1740–41
d. 1764

Peter III
(see following page)

Peter III
of Holstein-Gottorp
m. Sophia Frederica Augusta
of Anhalt-Zerbst
Catherine II
Empress 1762–96

Paul I
Emperor 1796–1801

Alexander I
Emperor 1801–25
Grand Duke of Finland 1809
King of Poland 1815

Nicholas I
Emperor 1825–55
King of Poland 1832

Alexander II
Emperor 1855–81
King of Poland 1855–67

Alexander III
Emperor 1881–94

Nicholas II
Emperor 1894–1917 d. 1918

Braganzas

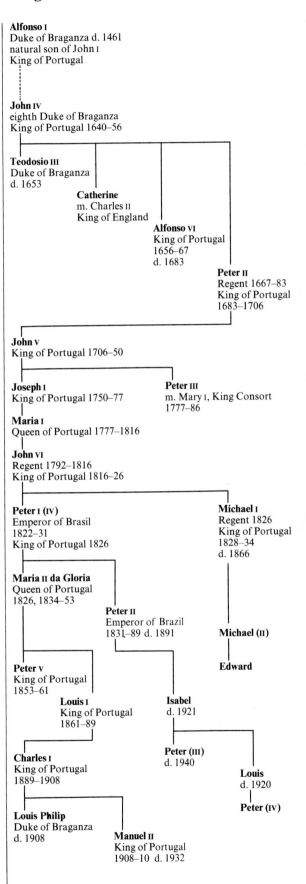

Alfonso I
Duke of Braganza d. 1461
natural son of John I
King of Portugal

John IV
eighth Duke of Braganza
King of Portugal 1640–56

Teodosio III
Duke of Braganza
d. 1653

Catherine
m. Charles II
King of England

Alfonso VI
King of Portugal
1656–67
d. 1683

Peter II
Regent 1667–83
King of Portugal
1683–1706

John V
King of Portugal 1706–50

Joseph I
King of Portugal 1750–77

Peter III
m. Mary I, King Consort
1777–86

Maria I
Queen of Portugal 1777–1816

John VI
Regent 1792–1816
King of Portugal 1816–26

Peter I (IV)
Emperor of Brasil
1822–31
King of Portugal 1826

Michael I
Regent 1826
King of Portugal
1828–34
d. 1866

Maria II da Gloria
Queen of Portugal
1826, 1834–53

Peter II
Emperor of Brazil
1831–89 d. 1891

Michael (II)

Peter V
King of Portugal
1853–61

Louis I
King of Portugal
1861–89

Isabel
d. 1921

Edward

Charles I
King of Portugal
1889–1908

Peter (III)
d. 1940

Louis
d. 1920

Louis Philip
Duke of Braganza
d. 1908

Manuel II
King of Portugal
1908–10 d. 1932

Peter (IV)

Bourbons of Spain

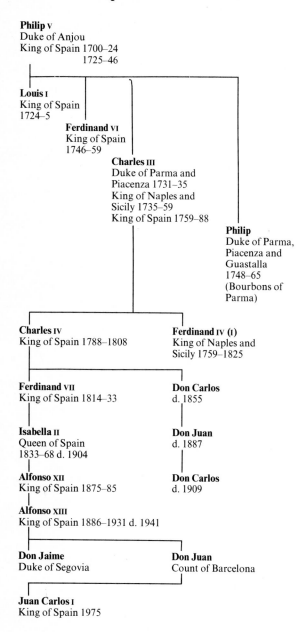

Philip v
Duke of Anjou
King of Spain 1700–24
        1725–46

Louis I
King of Spain
1724–5

Ferdinand VI
King of Spain
1746–59

Charles III
Duke of Parma and
Piacenza 1731–35
King of Naples and
Sicily 1735–59
King of Spain 1759–88

Philip
Duke of Parma,
Piacenza and
Guastalla
1748–65
(Bourbons of
Parma)

Charles IV
King of Spain 1788–1808

Ferdinand IV (I)
King of Naples and
Sicily 1759–1825

Ferdinand VII
King of Spain 1814–33

Don Carlos
d. 1855

Isabella II
Queen of Spain
1833–68 d. 1904

Don Juan
d. 1887

Alfonso XII
King of Spain 1875–85

Don Carlos
d. 1909

Alfonso XIII
King of Spain 1886–1931 d. 1941

Don Jaime
Duke of Segovia

Don Juan
Count of Barcelona

Juan Carlos I
King of Spain 1975

Hohenzollerns

Frederick I
Elector of Brandenburg 1415–40
descendant (sixth generation)
of Frecerick III Count of Zollern d. 1201

Frederick II
Elector of Brandenburg
1440–70

Albert Achilles
Elector of Brandenburg
1470–86

John Cicero
Elector of Brandenburg 1486–99

Joachim I Nestor
Elector of Brandenburg 1499–1535

Joachim II Hector
Elector of Brandenburg 1535–71

John George I
Elector of Brandenburg 1571–98

Joachim Frederick
Elector of Brandenburg 1598–1608

John Sigismund
Elector of Brandenburg 1608–19
Duke of Cleves 1609 and of Prussia 1618 d. 1620

George William
Elector of Brandenburg
Duke of Cleves and of Prussia 1619–40

Frederick William
the Great Elector 1640–68

Frederick III (I)
Elector of Brandenburg 1688
King in Prussia 1701–13

Frederick William I
King in Prussia 1713–40

Frederick II the Great
King in Prussia 1740
King of Prussia 1773–86

Augustus William
Prince of Prussia
d. 1758

Frederick William II
King of Prussia 1786–97

Frederick William III
King of Prussia 1797–1840

Frederick William IV
King of Prussia 1840–61

William I
Regent 1858
King of Prussia 1861
Emperor of Germany
1871–88

Frederick III
King of Prussia
Emperor of Germany
1888

William II
King of Prussia
Emperor of Germany
1888–1918 d. 1941

Frederick William
d. 1951

William Frederick
d. 1940

The House of Savoy

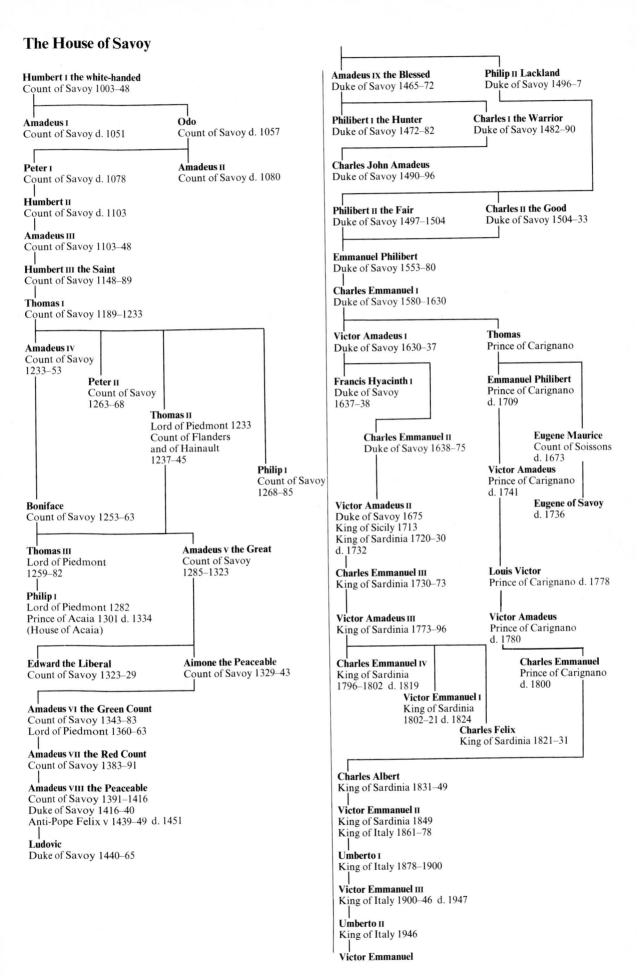

Humbert I the white-handed
Count of Savoy 1003–48

Amadeus I
Count of Savoy d. 1051

Odo
Count of Savoy d. 1057

Peter I
Count of Savoy d. 1078

Amadeus II
Count of Savoy d. 1080

Humbert II
Count of Savoy d. 1103

Amadeus III
Count of Savoy 1103–48

Humbert III the Saint
Count of Savoy 1148–89

Thomas I
Count of Savoy 1189–1233

Amadeus IV
Count of Savoy
1233–53

Peter II
Count of Savoy
1263–68

Thomas II
Lord of Piedmont 1233
Count of Flanders
and of Hainault
1237–45

Philip I
Count of Savoy
1268–85

Boniface
Count of Savoy 1253–63

Thomas III
Lord of Piedmont
1259–82

Amadeus V the Great
Count of Savoy
1285–1323

Philip I
Lord of Piedmont 1282
Prince of Acaia 1301 d. 1334
(House of Acaia)

Edward the Liberal
Count of Savoy 1323–29

Aimone the Peaceable
Count of Savoy 1329–43

Amadeus VI the Green Count
Count of Savoy 1343–83
Lord of Piedmont 1360–63

Amadeus VII the Red Count
Count of Savoy 1383–91

Amadeus VIII the Peaceable
Count of Savoy 1391–1416
Duke of Savoy 1416–40
Anti-Pope Felix v 1439–49 d. 1451

Ludovic
Duke of Savoy 1440–65

Amadeus IX the Blessed
Duke of Savoy 1465–72

Philip II Lackland
Duke of Savoy 1496–7

Philibert I the Hunter
Duke of Savoy 1472–82

Charles I the Warrior
Duke of Savoy 1482–90

Charles John Amadeus
Duke of Savoy 1490–96

Philibert II the Fair
Duke of Savoy 1497–1504

Charles II the Good
Duke of Savoy 1504–33

Emmanuel Philibert
Duke of Savoy 1553–80

Charles Emmanuel I
Duke of Savoy 1580–1630

Victor Amadeus I
Duke of Savoy 1630–37

Thomas
Prince of Carignano

Francis Hyacinth I
Duke of Savoy
1637–38

Emmanuel Philibert
Prince of Carignano
d. 1709

Charles Emmanuel II
Duke of Savoy 1638–75

Eugene Maurice
Count of Soissons
d. 1673

Victor Amadeus
Prince of Carignano
d. 1741

Victor Amadeus II
Duke of Savoy 1675
King of Sicily 1713
King of Sardinia 1720–30
d. 1732

Eugene of Savoy
d. 1736

Charles Emmanuel III
King of Sardinia 1730–73

Louis Victor
Prince of Carignano d. 1778

Victor Amadeus III
King of Sardinia 1773–96

Victor Amadeus
Prince of Carignano
d. 1780

Charles Emmanuel IV
King of Sardinia
1796–1802 d. 1819

Charles Emmanuel
Prince of Carignano
d. 1800

Victor Emmanuel I
King of Sardinia
1802–21 d. 1824

Charles Felix
King of Sardinia 1821–31

Charles Albert
King of Sardinia 1831–49

Victor Emmanuel II
King of Sardinia 1849
King of Italy 1861–78

Umberto I
King of Italy 1878–1900

Victor Emmanuel III
King of Italy 1900–46 d. 1947

Umberto II
King of Italy 1946

Victor Emmanuel

House of Hanover-Windsor

Ernest Augustus
Elector of Hanover
m. Sophia, granddaughter
of James I King of England

George I
Elector of Hanover
King of England 1714–27

George II
Elector of Hanover
King of England 1727–60

Frederick Louis
Prince of Wales d. 1751

George III
King of Hanover
King of England 1760–1820

George IV
Regent 1811–20
King of Hanover
King of England
1820–30

William IV
King of Hanover
King of England
1830–37

Edward Augustus
Duke of Kent

Victoria
Queen of England 1837–1901
m. Albert of Saxe-Coburg-Gotha

Edward VII
King of England 1901–10

George V
King of England 1910–36

Edward VIII
King of England 1936
Duke of Windsor d. 1972

George VI
King of England 1936–52

Elizabeth II
Queen of England 1952

Charles
Prince of Wales

Bourbons of Naples

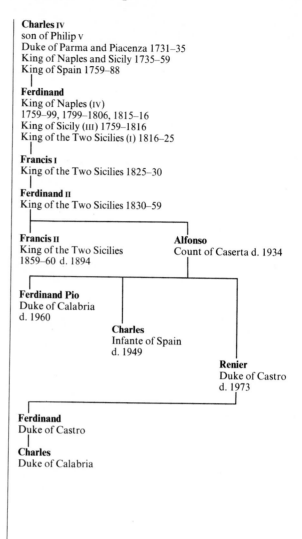

Charles IV
son of Philip V
Duke of Parma and Piacenza 1731–35
King of Naples and Sicily 1735–59
King of Spain 1759–88

Ferdinand
King of Naples (IV)
1759–99, 1799–1806, 1815–16
King of Sicily (III) 1759–1816
King of the Two Sicilies (I) 1816–25

Francis I
King of the Two Sicilies 1825–30

Ferdinand II
King of the Two Sicilies 1830–59

Francis II
King of the Two Sicilies
1859–60 d. 1894

Alfonso
Count of Caserta d. 1934

Ferdinand Pio
Duke of Calabria
d. 1960

Charles
Infante of Spain
d. 1949

Renier
Duke of Castro
d. 1973

Ferdinand
Duke of Castro

Charles
Duke of Calabria

Bonapartes

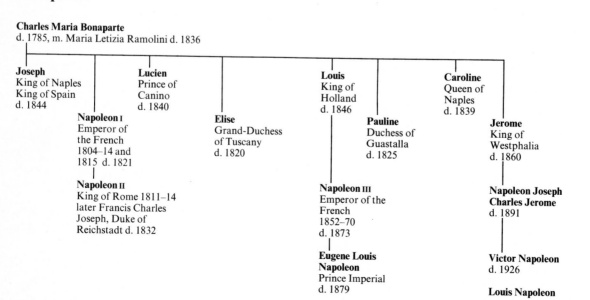

Charles Maria Bonaparte
d. 1785, m. Maria Letizia Ramolini d. 1836

Joseph
King of Naples
King of Spain
d. 1844

Lucien
Prince of
Canino
d. 1840

Louis
King of
Holland
d. 1846

Caroline
Queen of
Naples
d. 1839

Napoleon I
Emperor of
the French
1804–14 and
1815 d. 1821

Elise
Grand-Duchess
of Tuscany
d. 1820

Pauline
Duchess of
Guastalla
d. 1825

Jerome
King of
Westphalia
d. 1860

Napoleon II
King of Rome 1811–14
later Francis Charles
Joseph, Duke of
Reichstadt d. 1832

Napoleon III
Emperor of the
French
1852–70
d. 1873

**Napoleon Joseph
Charles Jerome**
d. 1891

**Eugene Louis
Napoleon**
Prince Imperial
d. 1879

Victor Napoleon
d. 1926

Louis Napoleon

PICTURE SOURCES

10: Vienna, Österreichische Nationalbibliothek, ms. fr. cod. 2549 fol. 164 r.
11: Mondadori Archives. 12/13: Paris, Archives Nationales. 16: Paris, Bibliothèque Nationale (Mondadori Archives). 17: Paris, Bibliothèque Nationale. 18: Paris, Bibliothèque Nationale. 19: Paris, Bibliothèque Nationale. 21: Paris, Bibliothèque Nationale, ms. fr. 6465 fol. 247 v. 23: Paris, Bibliothèque Nationale, ms. fr. 5716. 25: Champigny-sur-Veude, Ste. Chapelle (Paris, Lauros-Giraudon). 26: Paris, Bibliothèque Nationale, ms. fr. !3568. 28: Biblioteca Vaticana, cod. Chigi L. VIII 296. 29: Mondadori Archives. 31: Freising Cathedral (Rainer Lehmann). 33: Heidelberg, University Library. 34: Milan, Arborio Mella. 35: Brussels, Bibliothèque Royale Albert 1ᵉʳ. 37: Biblioteca Vaticana. 38: Aachen, Cathedral treasury (Bildarchiv Foto Marburg). 39: Palermo, Cathedral treasury (Publifoto). 40: Biblioteca Vaticana, ms. pal. L. 1071. 42: Ministry of Public Building & Works (Crown copyright). 43: Mondadori Archives. 44: London, British Museum, ms. Cotton Vitell. A. XIII f. 4 v. 45: Berne, Bürgerbibliothek. 46: London, British Museum, Cotton ms. Claudius D. II. 47: London, British Museum. 48: Oxford, Bodleian Library. 49: Canterbury, Cathedral (A. F. Kersting). 50: Oxford, Bodleian Library. 51: London, British Museum, Harl. 1319. 52: London, British Museum, Harl. 1319 fol. 50. 53: London, British Museum, Harl. 1319 fol. 53 v. 54: London, British Museum, Roy 20 and VI. 55: London, National Portrait Gallery. 58: Paris, Bibliothèque Nationale, ms. fr. 83 f. 205. 59: London, British Museum, Roy 18 d. II. 60: London, National Portrait Gallery. 62: Stowe (Buckinghamshire), by kind permission of Stowe School (Geoffrey Wheeler). 64: Mondadori Archives. 65: Frankfurt, Städelsches Kunstinstitut (Kurt Haase). 66: Vienna, Kunsthisorisches Museum (Erwin Meyer). 68: Paris, Musée du Louvre. 69: Brussels, Musées Royaux des Beaux-Arts de Belgique. 70/71: Madrid, Museo del Prado (Florence, Scala). 72/73: Amsterdam, Rijksmuseum. 75: By kind permission of His Grace the Duke of Bedford. 76/77: Greenwich, National Maritime Museum. 79: San Lorenzo de El Escorial, Real Monasterio (Patrimonio Nacional) (Barcelona, Edistudio). 80: Vienna, Kunsthistorisches Museum (E. Meyer). 81: Madrid, Museo del Prado (David Manso Martin). 82: Vienna, Kunsthistorisches Museum (E. Meyer). 83: Vienna, Kunsthistorisches Museum (E. Meyer). 84: Vienna, Kunsthistorisches Museum (E. Meyer). 85: Vienna, Kunsthistorisches Museum (E. Meyer). 86: Vienna, Österreichische Nationalbibliothek (Stepanek). 87: Innsbruck, Hofburg (E. Meyer). 89: Parma, Galleria Nazionale (Vaghi). 90/91: Vienna, Kunsthistorisches Museum (E. Meyer). 93: Aglié, ducal castle (Turin, Rampazzi). 94/95: Vienna, Hofburg (E. Meyer). 96/97: Trieste, Miramare Castle (Lucchetti). 98: Schönbrunn, ballroom (E. Meyer). 99: Vienna, Historisches Museum der Stadt Wien (E. Meyer). 100: Mondadori Archives. 101: Mondadori Archives. 104: Paris, Bibliothèque Sainte-Geneviève, ms. 814 fol. 125 r. (Paris, Giraudon). 105: Mondadori Archives. 106/107: Bibliothèque Nationale, ms. fr. 2645 fol. 321 v. 108: Mondadori Archives. 109: Mondadori Archives. 110 above: Paris, Musée du Louvre. 110 below: Dijon, Musée des Beaux-Arts (Paris, Lauros-Giraudon). 111: Paris, Private Collection (Paris, Giraudon). 112: Blois, château (Jean Feuillie). 113: Mondadori Archives. 114: Paris, Musée du Louvre. 115: Vienna, Kunsthistorisches Museum (E. Meyer). 117: Chambord, château (Jean Feuillie). 118: Chantilly, Musée Condé (Paris, Giraudon). 118/119: Anet, château (Milan, Nimatallah). 119: Chenonceau, château (Milan, Nimatallah). 120: Paris, Bibliothèque Nationale. 121: Chantilly, Musée Condé. 122: Paris, Musée du Louvre. 124: Siena, Cathedral(Grassi). 125: Mondadori Archives. 126/127: Edinburgh, Scottish National Gallery. 129: London, Society of Antiquaries. 131: Paris, Musée du Louvre (Paris, Bulloz). 132: Edinburgh, Scottish National Portrait Gallery. 133: London, J.Y. Sangster Collection (London, John Freeman). 134: Edinburgh, National Galleries of Scotland. 138: London, British Museum. 139: Mondadori Archives. 140: Castle Howard, Yorkshire (Precision St. Alban's). 141: London, Royal Academy of Arts. 142/143: London, College of Arms. 144: London, National Portrait Gallery. 145: Hampton Court Palace, Surrey (London. Picturepoint). 146: Musée de Versailles (Paris, Giraudon). 147: S.W. Digby Collection. 148: London, British Museum. 149: London, British Museum. 150: Greenwich, National Maritime Museum. 152: Mondadori Archives. 153: Paris, Bibliothèque Nationale ms. fr. 5091 f. 15 v. 154/155: Paris, Destombes Collection (Paris, Scarnati). 157: Paris, Musée du Louvre (Florence, Scala). 158/159: Musée de Rennes (Paris, Bulloz). 159: Paris, Musée du Louvre (Paris, Giraudon). 160: Musée de Versailles (Paris, Scarnati). 161: Paris, Musée Carnavalet (Paris, Scarnati). 163: Musée de Versailles (Paris, Scarnati). 164/165: Musée de Versailles. 166: Paris, Bibliothèque Nationale, Cabinet des Estampes. 167: London, Wallace Collection. 168/169: Musée de Versailles. 170: Musée de Versailles (London, Mary Evans Picture Library). 172/173: Göteborg, Konstmuseum. 173: Musée de Versailles (Paris, Giraudon). 175: Musée de Versailles (Paris, Bulloz). 176/177: Paris, Bibliothèque Nationale. 178: Paris, Musée Carnavalet (Paris, Giraudon). 179: Paris, Bibliothèque

Nationale. (Paris, Scarnati). 180: Musée de Versailles (Paris, Bulloz). 183: Chartres, Musée des Beaux-Arts (Paris, Giraudon). 185: Chambord, château (Paris, Roger-Viollet). 188: Moscow, Historical Museum (Novosti). 189: Mondadori Archives. 190/191: Clement Ingleby Collection. 192: Musée de Versailles (Paris, Scarnati). 193: Moscow, Kremlin State Museum. 194/195: Pushkin, Catherine's Palace (Novosti). 196: Stockholm, Nationalmuseum. 197: Mondadori Archives. 198: Luton Hoo, Luton, Wernher Collection. 199: Vienna, Heeresgeschichtliches Museum (E. Meyer). 200: Novosti. 202: Moscow, Historical Museum (Novosti). 203: London, Victor Kennet. 204 above: Moscow, Historical Museum (Novosti). 204 below: Mondadori Archives. 205: Mondadori Archives. 206: Rome, Biblioteca Russa Gogol (Savio). 207: Anne S.K. Brown Military Collection. 208: Lisbon, Agencia Dias da Silva. 209: Mondadori Archives. 210: Paris, Bibliothèque Nationale. 211 above: Lisbon, Agencia Dias da Silva. 211 below: Paris, Bibliothèque Nationale. 212: London, British Museum. 213 left: Lisbon, Agencia Dias da Silva. 213 right: Lisbon, Agencia Dias da Silva. 214 above: Lisbon, Agencia Dias da Silva. 214 below: Lisbon, Tourist Board. 215: Lisbon, Agencia Dias da Silva. 216: London, Mansell Collection. 217 above: Lisbon, Agencia Dias da Silva. 217 below: Lisbon, Agencia Dias da Silva. 218: Lisbon, Agencia Dias da Silva. 219: Lisbon, Agencia Dias da Silva. 220 above: Lisbon, Agencia Dias da Silva. 220 below: Mondadori Archives. 221: Lisbon, Agencia Dias da Silva. 222: Madrid, Museo del Prado (Barcelona, Edistudio). 223: Mondadori Archives. 224: Madrid, Museo del Prado (Barcelona, Edistudio). 225: Madrid, Museo del Prado. 226: Madrid, Museo del Prado (David Manso Martin). 227: Madrid, Museo del Prado (Barcelona, Edistudio). 228: Madrid, Museo del Prado (Florence, Scala). 230: Agen, Musée (Paris, Giraudon). 231: Madrid, Museo Romántico (Barcelona, Edistudio). 232: Madrid, Palacio Real (Barcelona, Edistudio). 235: Madrid, Museo del Ejército (Barcelona, Edistudio). 236: Charlottenburg, castle (Berlin, Steinkopf). 237: Mondadori Archives. 238/239: Berlin, Verwaltung der Staatlichen Schlösser und Gärten, Schloss Charlottenburg. 240: Verwaltung der Staatlichen Schlösser und Gärten, Schloss Charlottenburg. 241: Dresden, Gemäldegalerie (Deutsche Phototek). 243: Steinkopf, Berlin. 244/245 Dahlem, Nationalgalerie. 246: Musée de Versailles (Service de documentation de la Réunion des Musées Nationaux). 247: Berlin, Verwaltung der Staatlichen Schlösser und Gärten, Schloss Charlottenburg. 248: Berlin, Staatliche Museen Preussischer Kulturbesitz Nationalgalerie (Berlin, Walter Steinkopf). 249: Berlin, Staatsbibliothek. 251: Berlin, Schloss Friedrichsruh (Berlin, Staatsbibliothek). 252/253: Berlin, Archiv für Kunst und Geschichte. 254: Hechingen, Burg Hohenzollern (Berlin, Staatsbibliothek). 256: Turin, Palazzo Reale (Florence, Alinari). 257: Mondadori Archives. 258: Turin, State Archives. 261: Turin, Galleria Sabauda (Turin, Rampazzi). 262/263: Madrid, Escorial (Barcelona, Archivio Mas). 264: Palermo, cathedral. 265: Turin, Galleria Sabauda (Turin, Rampazzi). 266: Turin, Galleria Sabauda (Florence, Alinari). 266/267: Turin, Museo del Risorgimento (Turin, Rampazzi). 269: Bergamo, Museo del Risorgimento. 270/271: Milan, Museo del Risorgimento. 272: Milan, Domenica del Corriere. 275: Milan, Domenica del Corriere. 278: Buckingham Palace, by gracious permission of Her Majesty the Queen. 279: Mondadori Archives. 280 above: London, National Portrait Gallery. 280 below: London, National Portrait Gallery. 281: London, National Portrait Gallery. 282: Royal Collection, by gracious permission of Her Majesty the Queen. 283: Petworth (Sussex), Petworth House. 284/285: London, National Portrait Gallery. 286: Windsor Castle, by gracious permission of Her Majesty the Queen (Gordon Ltd). 287: Royal Collection, by gracious permission of Her Majesty the Queen. 288: Kensington Palace. 289: Windsor Castle, by gracious permission of Her Majesty the Queen (London, John Freeman). 290: London, National Portrait Gallery. 291: London, National Portrait Gallery. 292: London, National Portrait Gallery. 293: Mondadori Archives. 294: Mondadori Archives. 295: London, Camera Press. 296: Naples, Museo di S. Martino (Barcelona, Edistudio). 297: Mondadori Archives. 298/299: Naples, Museo di S. Martino (London, John Freeman). 300: Naples, Royal Palace (Naples, Parisio). 301: Naples, Villa Floridiana (Naples, Parisio). 302: Naples, Museo di S. Martino (Naples, Parisio). 303: Naples, Galleria Nazionale di Capodimonte (Naples, Parisio). 304: Naples, Galleria Nazionale di Capodimonte (Naples, Parisio). 305: Naples, Galleria Nazionale di Capodimonte (Naples, Parisio). 307: Naples, Museo di S. Martino (Naples, Parisio). 308: Milan, Civica Raccolta delle Stampe Bertarelli. 309: Naples, Museo di S. Martino (Naples, Parisio). 310: Paris, Musée du Louvre. 311: Mondadori Archives. 312/313: Musée de Malmaison. 314: Rome, Galleria Borghese (Florence, Scala). 315: Malmaison (Paris, Giraudon). 318/319: Paris, Musée du Louvre (Paris, Giraudon). 320: Musée de Versailles. 322, 323: Rome, Museo Napoleonico (Rome, Savio). 324: Musée de Versailles (Paris, Giraudon). 325: Rome, Museo Napoleonico (Rome, Savio). 327: Greenwich, National Maritime Museum. 328: Compiègne, château (Paris, Bulloz). 330: Versailles (Paris, Giraudon). 331: Mondadori Archives.